C000019405

EMPOWERING WOMEN

From Murder & Misogyny to High Court Victory

Dr Susie Allanson with Lizzie O'Shea
Foreword by Natasha Stott Despoja AO

Image gallery

Visit www.wilkinsonpublishing.com.au to view the image gallery for this book.

Authors' Note

We have tried to be true to the facts of this campaign and to the people involved, but inevitably we will have overemphasised some aspects and some people, while unfairly overlooking others. Our apologies to those who feel that our account is unfair to them or their experience. We have used the term 'women' throughout but wish to highlight that trans-men and gender diverse people also may experience pregnancy and abortion.

Acknowledgement of Country

We acknowledge the traditional custodians of the land on which this book was written. Our country is a land where awful wrongs were done, and continue to be done, to Aboriginal people. We pay our respects to the elders of this country, past, present and emerging.

First published 2021 by Wilkinson Publishing Pty Ltd
ACN 006 042 173
Wilkinson Publishing
PO Box 24135, Melbourne, VIC 3001, Australia
Ph: +61 3 9654 5446
enquiries@wilkinsonpublishing.com.au
www.wilkinsonpublishing.com.au

© Copyright Susie Allanson and Lizzie O'Shea 2021

All rights reserved. No part of this publication may be reproduced, stored in a retrieval system or transmitted in any form by any means without the prior permission of the copyright owner. Enquiries should be made to the publisher.

Every effort has been made to ensure that this book is free from error or omissions. However, the Publisher, the Authors, the Editor or their respective employees or agents, shall not accept responsibility for injury, loss or damage occasioned to any person acting or refraining from action as a result of material in this book whether or not such injury, loss or damage is in any way due to any negligent act or omission, breach of duty or default on the part of the Publisher, the Authors, the Editor, or their respective employees or agents.

Cover and book design by Tango Media.
Printed and bound in Australia by Griffin, a part of Ovato.

ISBN: 9781925927634
A catalogue record for this book is available from the National Library of Australia.

Contents

Foreword

'This book is about an act of terrorism against women that ended with the death of a man'. This was how I began my foreword to Dr Susie Allanson's 2006 book *Murder on His Mind*, her compelling story about the murder of her Clinic's security guard, Steve Rogers, by an anti-abortion extremist. In a riveting account of that atrocity, Susie uses her clinical psychology expertise to examine a true crime and analyse the psyche of a killer hell bent on murdering those with whom he disagreed.

Fifteen years later, this foreword describes a book, written by Susie with Lizzie O'Shea, that is about the murder of a man that ended with an historic victory for women. As Susie proclaims, *'We won! Women won! Safe Access Zones won! Human Rights won! A win for the fairness and compassion of our lawyers, law makers, our High Court Justices and our society. A win for doing the decent thing.'*

Susie has been doing the decent thing for women for decades. Her commitment to women's rights is unshakeable and her passion for change unstoppable. I had the privilege of meeting Susie twenty years ago when I visited the Fertility Control Clinic in the aftermath of that awful murder. I was shocked by what had happened and appalled by the chronic indignities and abuse women and staff suffered. Worse, our society seemed inured to how women were being targeted by the extreme and religious right with provocative and harmful rhetoric and actions. Abortion safe access zones, or 'bubble zones' as they were known then, seemed an obvious and simple solution. It was a debate my political party and I were keen to progress.

While the issue of gendered violence is a complex one, at its heart it is also simple: to change the story that ends in violence against women, we must begin with gender equality and respect for women. This notion underpins Susie's personal narration, the comments from key people interviewed for the book and the action by women and their allies behind closed doors, on the street, in workplaces, in parliaments and law courts, and in women's health clinics. These advocates, activists, lawyers and friends were empowered women, and their actions were aimed at empowering other women. A moral in this powerful story is that a group of determined and empowered women can do anything. Susie and Lizzie write that, 'every day, in large and small ways, women are heroes'. They should know. Their resilience and passion helped create change in the highest court in the land.

Susie's personal narration is compassionate, insightful and good humoured. In a conversational tone, she elucidates the frustrations and lessons, sadness and joys of this long but successful campaign *by* women to 'change the story' *for* women. Susie fetes generously the many women she found along the way who agreed with and supported her. This book shows how the actions of one woman, such as Susie Allanson or Fiona Patten, Lizzie O'Shea or Solicitor General Kris Walker, a High Court Chief Justice, indeed any of us, can tip the scales in favour of women. *Empowering Women* celebrates women who worked across jurisdictions and political parties, even across professions, to bring about much-needed change.

I have seen first-hand Susie's willingness to collaborate, her exemplification of sisterhood. Whether that was working on safe zones for clinics, or amendments to enable access to the abortifacient RU486 or when I tabled legislation to allow for transparency on pregnancy counselling advertisement.

As Susie and Lizzie write: *In a world where victories for progressive causes are often few and far between and campaigns for women, for their reproductive rights and to prevent violence against women, are even harder to win, ours is a precious triumph.* It is a triumph and deserves to be claimed and proclaimed loudly. But the fight for women's rights, especially sexual and reproductive rights, requires eternal vigilance.

Empowering Women speaks to the way good law-making and good law-yering can change lives for the better, but it is also a loud challenge to the gendered nature of our legal and parliamentary systems so rooted in patri-archy. In Australia, law, policy and cultural attitudes around abortion have not only limited women's access to their most basic and fundamental human rights, they have been an indicator of progress for gender equality across the board. As long as a woman's value is measured against her ability or willingness to reproduce, she will not enjoy equality before the law, she will not enjoy a life free from violence, her capacity and agency to make decisions will not be recognised.

With the rise of women demanding an end to violence against women in our Federal Parliament, our business, schools, institutions and our homes, *Empowering Women* is an inspiring story of its time that shows how it can be done.

Natasha Stott Despoja AO

Member of the UN Committee for the Elimination

of Violence Against Women

Author of *On Violence*

A Message From Hugh de Kretser, CEO Human Rights Law Centre

We must never take progressive social change for granted. Things which seem everyday now often took years and decades of advocacy, campaigning, strategy, suffering and sacrifice to achieve. It is vital to remember and reflect on how change was won; as a memory against injustice; to remain vigilant against the risk of regression; and to spur efforts for further progress.

Empowering Women is an important, compelling, accessible and entertaining account of the struggle to realise women's reproductive health rights in Victoria and Australia. The lessons laid out in the book will resonate with the broader women's rights and human rights movements.

Susie Allanson has dedicated her career to helping women, through her work as a psychologist and as a somewhat accidental, but supremely effective, changemaker. Susie could not stand by as women were harassed, abused, intimidated and exposed to risks of violence when trying to access abortion services.

While this is a story of ultimate victory, it is also a story of the failures of many male-dominated institutions to protect women's rights. It is a story of the vital importance of having women in positions of power, in the law, politics, health, the media and in civil society. It is a story of setbacks and disappointments in the long and often tedious process of litigation and law reform. It is a story of how you can lose the litigation and still win the broader cause.

But it is above all a story of tenacious, brave and smart advocacy over many years by many women. Women like Susie. It is Susie's personal story of what it takes to achieve change, with insights and lessons powerfully articulated by the brilliant Lizzie O'Shea.

We must recognise and celebrate the contributions of Susie and so many others who helped to make this change happen. Their work has protected the rights of millions of women in Australia. The victories achieving safe access zones in Victoria and Tasmania, and the successful defence of those victories in the High Court, provided momentum for advances across the country. Safe access zones laws now guarantee safe and private access to abortion services in every Australian jurisdiction except Western Australia, and that is set to change later this year (2021). There has been a wave of law reform decriminalising abortion in Queensland, New South Wales, the Northern Territory and South Australia. Again, only Western Australia remains, for now.

It was an honour to be asked to write this foreword. Susie is inspiring. Change happens because of people like her.

HUGH DE KRETSER
EXECUTIVE DIRECTOR, HUMAN RIGHTS LAW CENTRE

PROLOGUE

Celebration

Tuesday 30 April 2019

The coalescing of key and extraordinary people at particular points in time makes something possible. Sometimes you can create the ground for that. But you can't make up the people.

MARILYN BEAUMONT (2010)

We're clinking glasses at an elegant and casual after-work party at a hotel in Melbourne, Australia. The hosts are the Fertility Control Clinic Medical Director of 45 years standing, Dr Louis Rutman, and me, the clinic's Clinical Psychologist for 26 years. I retired two years earlier. Lou will never retire.

The guests include family, clinic staff, friends, advocates, lawyers and law makers: our team. Tonight we are celebrating the High Court of Australia's landmark judgement handed down on 10 April 2019. Seven Justices unanimously upheld women's right to see their doctor without facing intimidation and harassment. In Justice Nettle's words:

Women seeking an abortion and those involved in assisting or supporting them are entitled to do so safely, privately and with dignity, without haranguing or molestation.

Hooray!

In 2001, when the murder of our security guard by an anti-abortion fanatic catapulted us into advocating for safe abortion access, sweeping gendered change was yet to happen. Parliament and the Justice system were dominated by men and a male gaze. Safe abortion access would not have, and did not, receive a hearing in Parliament. Safe access would not have been legislated, and probably would not have survived a challenge in the High Court. Back then, it was hard to imagine the High Court giving this green light to abortion safe access zones rolling out across Australia.

Women choosing to terminate a pregnancy, and health workers involved in providing abortion, used to be routinely abused by religious extremists amidst a collective denial of women's lived experience and human rights. The word *abortion* was not spoken in polite society. As Gideon Haigh observed in his book, *The Racket* (p.11):

> *It was the second Vatican Council that classified abortion an 'unspeakable crime', and in public discourse so it has been—not just unutterable but invisible, the stuff of innuendo, euphemism and sordid anecdote. This has wrapped the procedure in mystery, sealing it off especially from men—a peculiar circumstance given that it has been mainly male conclaves whose decisions have determined its availability.*

But now, in our hallowed Parliament and the highest court in the land, powerbrokers and legal highfliers have spoken definitively in favour of a woman's right to abortion and right to be treated with respect. The High Court of Australia has enshrined protection of women's reproductive choice. Everyone here feels it in their bones: the world has tilted towards a fairer axis.

We breathe in the joy and share the stories. Nibble on hors d'oeuvres and sip from long-stemmed glasses. Tinkle of spoon on glass for hush, as the room hears from Kristen Walker QC, Solicitor General for Victoria, the government's most senior legal advocate and adviser, who appears for the Crown in important cases.

Six months earlier Kris held everyone in thrall in the High Court of Australia. Tonight, Kris does so again. Kris has an exquisite mind that eloquently cuts through to what is important. She also is a generous and humble human being. Whenever Kris speaks, she sets my mind wondering and reaching for more. Tonight is no exception. I catch my breath as I hear Kris say:

> *From a personal point of view, this is one of the cases of which I am most proud in my career as a barrister. My time on my feet in oral argument is probably my favourite four hours of work ever.*

I look around the room at attentive, happy faces: Human Rights Law Centre Legal Director Emily Howie, CEO Hugh de Kretser and colleagues;

Maurice Blackburn Lawyers solicitor Lizzie O'Shea and colleagues; Claire Harris QC; Kris Walker's team and Victorian Government Solicitors Office Anesti Petridis and colleagues; and Monash Castan Centre for Human Rights Tania Penovich and colleagues. All have expressed similar sentiments. I'm so grateful they feel so much love for this landmark case that delivered a new beginning for women's freedom from violence and humiliation. We fought the good fight and we won.

The love is also writ large on the faces of family members who lifted us up when we fell and cheered us on, never knowing if we would ever achieve this victory. The love is all over the faces of friends whose work progresses women's health rights: Lou Rutman, Janice Nugent, Susan Hopkins, Annarella Hardiman, Candy Broad, Rita Butera, Beth Wilson and Leslie Cannold. Absent friends like recently appointed Magistrate Therese McCarthy, Peter Hanks QC, and lawyer Rachel Ball, and politicians caught up in Parliament this evening, like Fiona Patten, Jill Hennessy, Colleen Hartland and Mary Wooldridge also experience this case as a special triumph. Women won and we feel proud. Celebration!

Ours was a successful campaign. In a world where victories for progressive causes are often few and far between, and campaigns for women, for their reproductive rights and to prevent violence against women, are even harder to win, ours is a precious triumph. We must jealously guard a victory like this. We need to claim it and shout it from the rooftops. We mustn't allow it to be lost to the black hole of history that has erased so much of women's work and women's contributions to humanity. This story needs to be told because too often women's work is belittled, or outright ignored. This is a story of women organising—with courage, without ego and on behalf of each other—to tip the scales of society in favour of women's autonomy.

This win was decades in the making and against the odds: hard work, collaboration, well-judged boldness and luck. We must wring every wisdom from the extraordinary people who made this campaign a success. We must learn every lesson, like: expect significant change to require a long term commitment; be principled but not so rigid that you miss opportunities; important allies may arrive unexpectedly so you better be prepared; struggling for change can be exhausting, even devastating at times, but it is also inspiring, gratifying, and a source of pride... But, perhaps the most important lesson is:

When we are designing a world that is meant to work for everyone, we need women in the room.

CRIADO PEREZ (2019, P. XIII)

Tonight I listen to Kris's words and wonder at the way the whole campaign showcased 'women in the room'. Women made this happen. Women in media, health, advocacy, law and politics. Women everywhere who spoke up, who inspired and challenged men to champion women.

I had been just one woman, getting nowhere fast. Until I found the right women. I found Emily Howie. Em found others. They found Lizzie. Few became many. I was bolstered by working with passionate and clever legal and health professionals, politicians and advocates, who made me feel optimistic about the future. Women and men were serendipitously and purposefully brought together by a Divine Feminine to create an enlightened age for women's abortion rights. With safe access to the means to control our fertility, women can access the world. Without it, women are held hostage to biology and violence. Without it, women are not fully emancipated nor treated as fully human. This High Court win says that women are complete persons entitled in their own right.

Still, as Kris speaks, I realise I cannot quite fathom how our case grew to be so special to such extraordinary people who routinely do exceptional work. They champion the cause of so many whose dignity and human rights are abused. Wins can be hard to come by, but maybe the deeper truths of this campaign passed me by. I have been too busy living it, and my feelings are still bittersweet. Delight and relief, but also disbelief and exhaustion at the thought of everything that has passed, shame at my helplessness, regret that it took so long, and anger that the cost was so high.

I was privileged to be consulted by women in crisis who trusted me with their inner-most thoughts and deeply personal matters, but outside the clinic they were abused for being women. I was enriched working with dedicated and decent clinic colleagues who are like family to me. But they were insulted, threatened and assaulted, and our security guard Steve Rogers was murdered.

We were unlike any other workplace. For too long, authorities—that could have and should have stopped the abuse—did nothing. At times, our campaign felt too hard to bear.

I had no idea what I was getting myself into, decades ago, when I first walked through the Fertility Control Clinic door, the first and largest freestanding private abortion clinic in Australia. Ignorance is bliss, until it's not.

PART ONE

MURDER & MISOGYNY

CHAPTER 1

In Your Face and Space

1991: The 1970s and beyond

If men could get pregnant, abortion would be a sacrament.

ANONYMOUS 'WOMAN TAXI DRIVER' TO FLORYNCE KENNEDY
(GLORIA STEINEM, 1983)

Remember 1991? Women wore wide trousers, broad shoulder pads and big hair, and donned technicolour lycra to work out at aerobics classes. No? Apologies, that's the best I could come up with. In early 1991 my third child was not yet six months old and I didn't have a clue what was going on in the actual world. Huge chunks of my memory banks are devoid of current affairs. Only one place on the planet existed: the mother-bub-children-family cocoon.

His-story 1991: Bob Hawke was the prime minister of Australia (to be replaced by Paul Keating in December 1991), humanitarian eye surgeon Fred Hollows was Australian of the Year, music entertainer Billy Joel toured Australia, *The Simpsons* premiered on TV, Hawthorn was reigning AFL premiers, George H W Bush sat in the US President's seat, the Cold War had ended and the Gulf War had begun, there was a Royal Commission into Aboriginal Deaths in Custody... History is full of lessons never learnt. Round and round the world goes.

Her-story 1991: Victoria had its first female premier, Joan Kirner (WA's Carmen Lawrence pipped Joan for the title of Australia's first female premier by a few months), Victorian non-aboriginal women had had the right to vote for 83 years and the right to stand for election for 67 years, while aboriginal women had had the right to vote for less than 30 years. During the twenty or so years leading up to 1991, Australian women had gained the right to equal pay (although this has still not arrived in the real world), paid maternity leave for Commonwealth employees and some others, single mother's pension, no fault divorce, government-funded women's refuges, the contraceptive pill, and 'lawful' abortion in Victoria and some other states.

But in 1991, if you were a woman in Victoria wanting a lawful abortion, it's likely you had no idea abortion still sat in the Crimes Act, or that backyard abortionists, and the deaths and damage they caused to women, had been banished only 22 years earlier. In 1991, the odds were now 100% in your favour that you would *not* die from an elective abortion, and around 90% that you'd get on with your life the very next day. If you were poor enough, and if there was room for you, you could access an abortion at the Royal Women's Hospital, the largest, if not the only, public abortion provider. If not, with a small Medicare rebate you would pay for your abortion in the private system, for example at the Fertility Control Clinic, the largest private abortion provider. In 1991, you had 0% chance of having the morning after pill, a medical abortion, or an iPhone to Google-Maps your way to an abortion provider. And in 1991, as you attended your appointment for your lawful abortion at a proper medical clinic, chances were that anti-abortion extremists would target and abuse you, turning your private health decision into a public nightmare. You were likely to feel the stigma of abortion acutely.

When did access to abortion fall off the feminist priority list? Did I have any idea what I was doing when I voluntarily stepped into the merry-go-round of abortion stigma and politics, and the dangerously unpredictable sideshow of cruel and creepy anti-choice villains?

In my white, well-educated, but pre-paid-maternity-leave world, my husband took the more traditional uninterrupted career path to provide a steady income for our family. My first professional role at the Royal Children's Hospital would be the only full-time salaried position I ever held. After having each of my children, I took on different sessional clinical roles, aiming for the flexibility to be both health professional and primary hands-on parent. I loved my family and I loved clinical psychology.

After my first child in 1981, a clinical psychologist friend embarking on maternity leave to have twins asked if I would step in for her at a private girl's school—just two sessions per week. Flexibility!

After my second child in 1984, I set up private practice working primarily with children and with stressed, seriously ill teachers (it was the era of harsh school closures and toxic mischief in its implementation). Two early-start days a week in the clinic room, plus home office paperwork and phone calls. Flexibility!

After my third and last child in 1990, clinical psychologist and friend Kath MacPherson was spreading her wings interstate and asked if I would take on her role at the Fertility Control Clinic—time commitment unknown, but hopefully, Flexibility!

Becoming a mum was worth at least ten years of professional development and bucket loads of empathy. When years later I argued for lessening the Australian Psychological Society mandatory professional development requirements while psychologists were parenting infants and small children, the APS brushed the idea aside. This from a society for professionals supposedly with deeper understandings of the importance and demands of the mother-baby and father-baby early relationship. What hope for the rest of society? The more we talk about 'work-life balance', the less there seems to be, not helped by the fact that the work of caring for your own children is usually only deemed worthy of payment when that carer is not you. I tip my hat to today's mum and dad pioneers realigning, sharing, swapping the gender-based roles of paid work and unpaid work.

In my small and old fashioned 1991 world, my initial meeting with Fertility Control Clinic Medical Director Dr Louis Rutman and Gynaecologist Mr Ian Roberts took place one afternoon in a beautiful heritage-listed two-storey Victorian terrace. 'Virginia' and an adjoining two-storey terrace comprised the Fertility Control Clinic. The property did not conjure a health clinic, nor an abortion clinic. Set in a lush old world garden behind a head-high brick fence on Wellington Parade in East Melbourne, the Heritage Council Victoria Register considered that 'Virginia is architecturally significant as a grand statement of 1860s inner suburban sophistication and pretension'. In

1991, the property had shed its sophistication and pretension, and its virginal name had acquired considerable irony.

Clinic Manager, Janice Nugent, would have made sure this first meeting took place in the afternoon rather than the morning, and initially she encouraged me to work in the afternoons rather than mornings. 'Let me stop you right there,' I can imagine her saying to Lou, 'We're not going to scare her off when she's only just got here.'

But I was a morning sort of person, to be back at home in the mid-afternoon suited my children and my version of mothering, and mornings were when the clinic action happened, in more ways than one.

Up a rather grand staircase, followed by a rabbit warren run to Lou and Ian's personal office at the rear of the clinic, I sank into a lounge chair so deep I thought I might be stuck there. Prophetic.

Like facing any job interview, I felt a little nervous about our meeting, but I had come armed with my personal and professional experience, a thirst for learning, and my ideas about what I thought I could bring to the job.

Personally, I brought the unique, lived experience of being a woman. Like every woman, I'd faced my own reproductive health challenges, and I knew about the heartbreak and joy faced by friends, family and clients. I hardly knew a woman who had been lucky enough to have had the same number of pregnancies as she had children. Fertility brought miscarriage and abortion, still birth and infertility, single and multiple births, motherhood and death. It brought loss and pain, joy and hope, triumph and responsibility, complexity and delight.

Professionally, I brought more than a decade of clinical experience that had already magnified my appreciation of both the mundane trials and vexed medical, relationship, financial and psychosocial complications involved in avoiding pregnancy, becoming pregnant and being pregnant. I recognised the life-changing impact of having children. I had no doubt about the crucial necessity of women having comprehensive reproductive healthcare and family planning options, including abortion. Based on my predecessor Kath's briefing, I also brought a fascination for the job, and the paradoxical understanding that my expertise was a drop in the ocean: I would face a steep learning curve to develop and refine my clinical skills to suit this unique setting.

There was no official job description, so I'd brought with me my own ideas for the position, including a typed proposal to leave with Lou and Ian at the conclusion of the interview. I wanted the job: clinical sessions for those women experiencing pregnancy/abortion ambivalence or more complex circumstances; in-house professional supervision and development for the pregnancy counselling team; simple data gathering and research to inform best practice, the wider knowledge base, and policy; and advancing women's health and FCC's reputation through appropriate networks.

The partners' role description for me seemed much simpler and bound up with the legality of abortion provision in Victoria. That legality relied on the 1969 trial of East Melbourne doctor Kenneth Davidson charged under s65 of the *Crimes Act 1958* with providing unlawful abortion. In the Supreme Court, Clifford Menhennitt ruled in R v Davidson [1969] VSC 667:

> *For the use of an instrument with intent to procure a miscarriage to be lawful the accused must have honestly believed on reasonable grounds that the act done by him was (a) necessary to preserve the woman from a serious danger to her life or her physical or mental health (not being merely the normal dangers of pregnancy and childbirth) which the continuance of the pregnancy would entail; and (b) in the circumstances not out of proportion to the danger to be averted.*

With the ruling of Menhennitt, 'it now was not merely socially unwelcome for a woman to be rational; it was legally inconvenient', Gideon Haigh observed wryly in his book *The Racket* (p.145). But like others, Haigh, an expert on Victoria's political, legal and social history of abortion, expressed considerable admiration for Menhennitt's approach to the case and his decision:

> *If there was such a category as unlawful abortion, did that mean that, under certain circumstances, abortion could be lawful? ...basically, Menhennitt took [1930s English case known as the Bourne standard] and applied it in an Australian context and came up with a ruling that's surprisingly elegant in the sense that it's explicit where it doesn't have to be, and it's vague*

where it sort of needs to be. And it suited everyone that a judge would take this out of the hands of the legislature and out of the hands of the police, who were finding it, at that stage, very difficult to deal with.

GIDEON HAIGH (2019)

In other words, Menhennitt's ruling encouraged everyone to look away. Retired Appeal Court Judge Marcia Neave further elucidated the 'doctrine of necessity' in Menhennitt's 'judge-made' abortion law:

Justice Menhennitt said, in this case if the doctor performed these abortions believing it was necessary to do so and a reasonable person would think it was necessary to do to save the life or the mental health of the [woman] then in those circumstances the crime of abortion was not committed.

MARCIA NEAVE (2019)

Former Health Services Commissioner of Victoria, Beth Wilson, also observed the significance of Menhennitt:

It was an extraordinary time. Women were beginning to have their voices heard. We were described as 'shrill' to try to shut us up but I think women had just had enough of being told by quite extreme people on religious and moral grounds that we had to be lesser citizens and stay in the kitchen, barefoot and pregnant. We wanted more from life, and Menhennitt was a really important part of saying to us, 'You are citizens. You have legal rights'…

The Menhennitt ruling kind of brought women out of the dark shadows of always having this threat of unwanted pregnancies hanging over them. It led the way towards greater reforms for women because it freed them up to be able to do things like I did, go and study law, get involved in public life. So, I think it's, for me personally, one of the most important pieces of judge-made law and an excellent example of the courts, in fact, being more progressive than the Parliament itself.

BETH WILSON (2019)

In some respects, Menhennitt's ruling is an even more dramatic departure than [USA] Roe v Wade, and it was a standard that was widely imitated and became the basis of the law going forward in other states as well…

Menhennitt was a clear and rigorous legal thinker, who knew how to fortify a judgement against external challenge... The remarkable thing I think about the Menhennitt ruling is that despite its extremely controversial nature, despite the political environment, despite feminist and anti-feminist ideology, it was never appealed in the duration where it was applied, which was for almost 40 years.

GIDEON HAIGH (2019)

Twenty years before I met Fertility Control Medical Director Dr Louis Rutman, the 1971 Levine ruling in NSW case, R v Wald [1971] DCR 25, extended the definition of danger to a woman's life or body to include consideration of economic, social or medical reasons. Sexist language aside (Menhennitt and Levine only referred to doctors using a male pronoun), Menhennitt and Levine provided women and abortion-providing doctors with a legal 'out' albeit: according 'the doctor a primacy in decisions relating to abortions' (Haigh, 2008); with criminal ambiguity still attached—in Victoria and other Australian states and territories, 'lawful' abortion remained in the *Crimes Act* rather than the *Health Act*; and ensuring abortion was the only medical procedure where 'the doctor-patient relationship is regularly overridden by uninvolved third parties' (de Crespigny and Savulescu, 2004, p 201).

In this criminally ambiguous world of abortion, Dr Louis Rutman's priority for me was that I provide an additional safety net to the clinic, staff and patients by attending to the needs of more complex patients. I intended to do that by ensuring that the clinic carried out all it could to facilitate a woman making what she felt was the right decision for her about whether to terminate or continue her pregnancy, plus the other bits and pieces I'd decided would be important in my role.

Kath had told me cheerfully, absurdly and somewhat ominously that Lou would be happy with me as long as I didn't have two heads. As Kath is clearly a highly perceptive clinical psychologist, and I do have only one head, Lou was happy to take me on as a sessional consultant. I had no idea then that I would stay at the Fertility Control Clinic for the next 26 years. My clinic role would be exactly as I had envisioned, and something completely different.

The *completely different* stemmed from the fact that the Fertility Control Clinic had the unenviable status of being unlike any other health clinic or workplace: the clinic was targeted mercilessly by religious anti-abortion and anti-contraception fanatics.

Occasional anti-abortion marches comprising hundreds of people, and organised by Pro Life, Right to Life and Save the Babies groups, ended up outside the clinic and spilling onto the road, and attracted a hefty police presence. Entering or exiting the clinic was nigh impossible. The odd anti-abortion extremist trespassed on FCC property (a vase knocked over in reception here, a back access gate to the clinic chained up there, a scuffle or rant inside the front gate). It could be tense.

A smaller religious group placed themselves and their anti-abortion displays on either side of the footpath along the clinic boundary during the busier time for patient arrivals from 7:30 am until 10 am, Monday to Friday, and for entire days during 40-day 'vigils'. To access the healthcare of their choice, women had to run a gauntlet. To attend work each day, staff were branded 'murderers' who worked at a 'slaughterhouse'. Police were regularly called to attend. It was a circus, with a fire-eater dancing around a powder keg.

When I stepped into the clinic in 1991, staff and patients had already suffered years of similar targeting. I had never worked anywhere where anything like this occurred. Well, how many people have? It impressed me as both ridiculous and appalling. I didn't know then that it would continue for another 25 years.

Like other staff, my concern lay with the distress this godly gauntlet caused our patients and their companions (partners, relatives, friends, children). Like other staff, I would huff and think or speak unkind thoughts, then take a deep breath and suppose that it was the price you paid to live in a democracy (really? I thought democracy meant being respectful of others); they were probably nice people really (but not nice to us); there was nothing we could do (nothing?); they had a right to hold strong views and to express them (but surely not like that, and not here). It was not right.

The footpath harassment and the stigma of unplanned pregnancy and abortion clung to our patients in uncomfortable knots of shame, fear, anger, and tears. Women presented to us for contraception, pap tests, pregnancy testing, sexually transmitted infections, abortion, and more. Our experienced counsellors and doctors provided a safe space to discuss deeply personal issues, reassured and bolstered with kindness and evidence-based information, and witnessed women's distress ease, mostly.

Despite abortion's seedy past and traduced present, nine out of ten pregnant women arrived clear about their decision to have an abortion. My colleagues identified the small proportion of women with more complex circumstances, distress, or unresolving decision ambivalence, and referred them on to me.

Women tended to be reluctant to see 'the psychologist'—another stigma of sorts, but by the end of a session they were usually relieved, grateful and wished they had seen me sooner. Women ultimately decided to continue or terminate their pregnancy. A very rare cohort experienced such unresolving ambivalence that their only alternative was to continue the pregnancy by default—still a legitimate way of making this unique decision.

The safety of the clinic space un-silenced a woman's concerns: conflictual/broken relationships/employment, addictions, violence, loss, trauma, poverty, indecisive/perfectionist/anxious personality styles born to survive unkind childhoods, vulnerabilities associated with current or previous pregnancies/births/children and serious mental or physical illnesses, fetal abnormalities and pregnancy medical risks, everyday responsibilities that had grown overwhelming, and all manner of other life goals, challenges and obligations irreconcilable with being pregnant.

Abortion turned out to be only one of myriad reproductive health issues women faced. I would hear up close and personal about Western medicine's brilliance, but also its deeply ingrained sexism. The latter included for example: decades where women with the painful and debilitating condition endometriosis were tagged neurotic or hysterical, and where diagnosis and treatment development was shunned; early IVF efforts, spawned from animal treatments, that treated women little better than cows. Amongst vastly more serious and not so 'casual' sexism—I had been told that I had a 'juicy cervix' myself, ah, nothing like being looked on as a lump of meat.

I was nothing if not an expert listener, and both my patients and my colleagues gave me an in-depth understanding of the normal and vital crises of being born a woman, and how these matters of supreme importance were societally silenced, trivialised and controlled. I would be touched by both women's vulnerability and strength: the mother of two presenting with a planned pregnancy after her husband suicided; the 46-year-old pregnant mother of adult children turned away by her GP with a menopause diagnosis and without a pregnancy test; the twenty-something pregnant woman determined not to have children and doom them to her own terminal genetic illness; the 40-year-old pregnant Aboriginal woman who as breadwinner and problem solver for her whole extended family did not want or need another family; the woman whose pregnancy crisis was the catalyst to planning an escape from her violent relationship; the pregnant and lonely international student desperate to avoid the shame and poverty of single motherhood...

While most women presented confident in their decision, some who found their way to me confided that if they had an abortion, 'I'm scared I'll go to Hell; God will punish me by taking away one of my children; I might die; I'll become infertile; I'll be a murderer; I'm being selfish...' Women, and our society, lacked a compassionate and positive woman-centred language and voice acknowledging the centrality of reproductive complexity in women's relationships and agency: abortion as a moral and sensible decision made by moral and sensible women.

The loudest abortion voice proclaimed glory to God and the exalted 'unborn'. It boomed from a male celibate pulpit and from those who said they were offering 'curb-side counselling', 'prayers' and 'help' to women on a public footpath. They were unashamed about telling others they should be ashamed. Well, except for the priest arriving at the clinic with his 'girlfriend' and demanding that she abort her pregnancy for his sake. And except for the woman who had harassed women in front of the clinic, but then presented asking for the very same thing for which she had vilified other women. And except... We humans are awfully prone to hypocrisy, especially where religion is concerned.

Clinical psychologists powerfully and subtly work with the thoughts, language, beliefs, emotions and behaviour of a person. But clinical psychologists also know how important the environment of a person is too. So we also work with parents and partners, teachers and carers, GPs and psychiatrists, lawyers, courts and workplaces, to create an environment supportive of clients' therapeutic progress and wellbeing.

In the clinic's case, the external environment was not supportive of a woman's wellbeing. A woman visiting the clinic was sabotaged before she walked in the door, and again when she walked out. Our good work and woman-centred care was book-ended by harassment and silencing. God-fearing, anti-abortion, woman-hating language and imagery dominated the streetscape outside the clinic. Women's well-intentioned and considered decisions were warped into sin and selfishness. Lies were presented as frightening medical fact. At a time already challenging enough, our patients were intimidated and harmed. They were denied the chance to apply their agency at a critical time. That had to change.

This chronic abuse of women by a religious anti-abortion group was a form of gaslighting. Gaslighting has intrinsically misogynistic connotations, and harks back to a 1938 British play, *Gas Light*, later adapted to a film. I still remember seeing the old black and white movie on the TV one night as a young teenager, a creepy tingling down my back. Written by Patrick Hamilton, *Gas Light* depicts a husband's psychological manipulation of his wife to the point where she goes mad. By denying his wife's perception of real events, that he in fact has re-arranged, and insisting it is all in her mind, she eventually no longer trusts her own perception of reality. The title and term gaslighting come from scenes involving the gas lights in their house where, for example, the husband negates his wife's accurate perception that the gas lights have been turned down or are flickering.

Gaslighting has almost exclusively been used to describe the insidious, chronic male abuse of women behind closed doors within intimate relationships (Stern, 2007). But who could forget the female Nurse Ratched gaslighting psychiatric patients in *One Flew Over the Cuckoo's Nest*? Or the Catholic Church's chronic gaslighting of the LGBTIQ community and victims of priests' sexual abuse. Or the ongoing gaslighting of Indigenous people and asylum-seekers. More recent attempts at gaslighting an entire population by prominent politicians, particularly by US President Trump, will perhaps ultimately provide more understanding of the institutionalised abuse of power that women have copped since poor old Eve bit into an apple.

Sadly, psychoanalyst Sigmund Freud showcased himself as a reluctant, but nonetheless expert, gaslighter. Back in the 1890s, Freud believed his female patients' reports of sexual abuse by male relatives and friends and developed his *Seduction Theory* linking such traumas to his patient's subsequent mental illness. But the community of almost exclusively male psychiatrists at the time did not believe their female patients at all: women had not been victims of sexual abuse but were fantasists and hysterical liars. To avoid his own social and professional exclusion, Freud retracted his theory and his belief in women's veracity (Masson, 1984/2003). To have opened the door to see and understand the invisible woman, only to slam the door shut…

A collective and public gaslighting of women has occurred down the eons: women's good intentions and experiences have been notoriously disbelieved, misrepresented and ignored. Anyone unsure of this should revisit the earlier era of witch hunts, or examine the discourse around Australia's first and only female prime minister, Julia Gillard, or witness a current sexual assault case where the defence is sure to call the female victim a liar, fantasist and a scorned woman out for revenge. Or look at the modern political culture of Canberra, in which allegations of sexual assault are scattered across generations of political powerbrokers, with accountability hard to come by. It's like these gaslighting techniques are now spelt out in a *Defence Against Sexual Assault Charges* playbook.

Today, powerful voices are demanding that women be believed, and that our justice system be re-imagined to deliver justice and protection to women. But back in the 1990s, there were no voices standing up for our patients and staff who were copping a public gaslighting from the anti-women extremists: denial and distortion of women's lived experiences; threats of dire consequences based on blatant lies and fake care; impugning women's character;

and denying us our very humanity and human rights. The fact that religion was invoked to justify such cruel behaviour shifted the public gaslighting into a form of institutionalised gaslighting, which was reinforced by the anti-women comments by religious right federal politicians. So too, the silence and inaction of other authorities sent the message that it was okay to treat women this way, and probably, the message that those *bad women* having abortions deserved it—a version of *she asked for it*. Our patients, and by proxy all women, were humiliated and dehumanised.

The only antidote to such venomous abuse of power involved recognising the complexity of women's lives, validating the goodness of their intentions, and speaking up to ensure women's capacity and right to make their own decisions. We were experts at doing exactly that inside the clinic, but outside the clinic an evil snake poisoned the lives of women everywhere.

> *The female-specific concerns that men fail to factor in cover a wide variety of areas, but… three themes crop up again and again: the female body, women's unpaid care burden, and male violence against women.*
>
> CRIADO PEREZ (2019, P.XIII)

All three of these female-specific concerns met every day on a public thoroughfare outside the Fertility Control Clinic at a point where discrimination against women was paradoxically both blatant and invisible.

The psychologically intimate space of the clinic room was a wonderful classroom for me, but I had questions galore, and my developing woman-centred abortion language needed a wriggle on. As a scientist-practitioner, I decided I'd find answers to my clinical and language questions by enrolling in a PhD. Part-time. A scholarship. Flexibility!

The PhD was madness and tears, academic indulgence and wonder, superb juggling and shocking dropping of balls. My youngest was not yet two when I began and eight when I submitted *The Abortion Decision: Fantasy, Attachment and Outcomes* in 1999. My PhD was instrumental in maturing my understandings, language, politics, actions, network and clinical nous in this stigmatised but essential area of women's health.

My father had taught me the importance of 'defining your terms'. In the taboo area of abortion, I struggled just to *find* terms. I purloined facts, ideas and abortion language anywhere I could, but especially from feminist thinkers and researchers. A women-centred, pro-choice language was crucial to my work with women in the clinic room, my research, and would prove vital in the successful campaigns to decriminalise abortion and to introduce safe abortion access zones.

Facts and pro-women language provided a shortcut through the unfair myths, stigma and shame hovering over women seeking abortion. A year after I started at the clinic, I took the opportunity of our role as secretariat of the Abortion Providers' Federation of Australasia, to gather basic demographic data of more than 2,000 women attending seven private abortion providing clinics around Australia. Such data had never been available before and discussing such simple facts with our patients turned out to be myth-busting. This basic information challenged abortion stigma and stereotypes about the types of women having abortions and provided considerable relief to our patients. Journals considered it unworthy of publication.

In 1993 I wrote two booklets for women. The first, If You are Thinking of Having an Abortion & After an Abortion (available at www.fcc.com.au) proved invaluable to women and is a reminder of what this story is really about. The second, The Abortion Decision: Moral, Religious or Other Concerns, incorporated ideas from the religious pro-choice group Catholics for Free Choice and was provided to women struggling with such issues.

Abortion stigma and ignorance extended to the limited international and Australian abortion research. In fact, abortion barely rated a mention in Australian research. You'd be forgiven for concluding that women's capacity to control their fertility had nothing much to do with anything, when of course, the opposite was true: caring about and managing their fertility and sexuality is a central focus in women's lives. It was a clear gender gap, as Criado Perez would say, 'Men go without saying, and women don't get said at all.' (2019, p.XII)

Given that my clinic role involved assisting the relatively small number of ambivalent women, I was excited to find a book titled *The Dilemma of Abortion*

(Kenyon, 1986). Until I discovered the author, a doctor, was discussing his own ambivalence about 'allowing' a woman to have an abortion.

Such exclusion of women from a matter so uniquely affecting women was noted insightfully by Gideon Haigh in relation to the historic 1970 *Board of Inquiry into Allegations of Police Corruption in Connection with Illegal Abortion Practices in the State of Victoria* headed by Commissioner William Kay QC (aka The Kay Inquiry):

> *Not a single patient was heard from. The reasons abortions were sought went unaddressed. The place of abortion in the Crimes Act went undebated. A mainly female predicament was argued over in an exclusively male forum.*

HAIGH (2008, P.198)

More than twenty years on from The Kay Inquiry, as I settled into my Fertility Control Clinic role and began my PhD, women's voices still were far too often missing from abortion discourse and research. Feminist philosopher Caroline Whitbeck said it all in the title of her 1983 paper, *The moral implications of regarding women as people: New perspectives on pregnancy and personhood.* Gasp!

Research that did consider women's abortion experience often pathologised women as mother-and-victim within a grief and loss framework, or objectified women in terms of pregnancy-as-person and woman-as-uterus. A framework of misogyny and female pathology cannot conceive of research questions allowing for women's strengths, clarity of lived values, capacity to make tough decisions, pride and determination about their abortion decision, and ability to successfully get on with their lives.

Researchers like United States' Brenda Major and Catherine Cozzarelli (Cozzarelli, 1993; Major & Cozzarelli, 1992; Major, Cozzarelli, Sciacchitano, Cooper, Testa & Mueller, 1990; Major, Mueller & Hildebrandt, 1985) were a welcome exception, highlighting the relief and improved functioning most women experienced after an elective abortion, and the importance of women's self-efficacy, expectations, and positive abortion role models. Good luck with that last one when the abortion taboo made positive abortion role models invisible.

Other woman-centred research focused on the significant adverse impact of male physical, sexual and other violence on women's physical and mental health (Astbury 1996). This vital aspect of women's health, long ignored by mainstream research, was a specialty area of my brilliant PhD supervisor, Dr (now Professor) Jill Astbury. Jill's expertise was much sought after and she regularly disappeared to Geneva, home to the World Health Organization. Jill sat with other well-regarded feminists as a steering committee member of *The Health Costs of Violence/Burden of Disease* research by the VicHealth & Department of Human Services (2004). This report highlighted for the first time the huge burden on women's health of intimate partner violence and was a turning point in the recognition of an appalling gendered truth.

Public Health Association and La Trobe University academic Dr Angela Taft, also a friend, was researching at the intersection of violence and reproductive health: women were at significantly increased risk of intimate partner abuse when pregnant. Angela's work became focused on the pointy end where violence against women and abortion met (Taft, Watson, & Lee, 2004). Just like my work in the clinic room, there was little point carrying out research into women at all without including questions around women's experience of violence, especially from intimate partners. Angela and I always had far too much to discuss together.

Unfortunately, and like almost every arena in the world, researching humans was a male-dominated field. Female (and other-than-male) study participants were generally pushed into frameworks and topics relevant to men rather than women, or routinely excluded: women's bodies, psyches and lives were too complicated to be accommodated by scientific methods; women confounded and messed up research and its conclusions; and researchers were not particularly interested in women's issues nor in undertaking research in the interests of women. Criado Perez has written comprehensively about 'invisible women' and the tragic costs to women of the sexism that pervades research and data in a world designed by and for men.

But in the early 1990s, a growing cohort of women around the world, like Jill Astbury and Angela Taft, were researching in the interests of women.

These women shone a light on gendered violence, reproductive complexities, and women's entitlement to human rights. My PhD added to the slowly growing number of woman-centred and violence-informed exceptions in the research literature. Like Jill and Angela, but on a tiny scale compared with those two academic luminaries, I sent the fruits of my PhD, my research baby, out into the world (Allanson, 1994, 1997, 1999; Allanson & Astbury, 1995, 1996, 2001). While on any given day, just metres away, the real-life intersection of violence against women and abortion played out on a public street.

Sometimes you encounter a problem you know has existed but, if it is absent from our discourse, it is easy to deny its importance. Preparing to be an activist/advocate requires finding and listening to those people who 'get it', critically assessing the evidence base of rigorous research and anecdotal evidence and collecting the 'invisible' data and stories to drive your case. From there, you can develop the language and discourse to articulate the issue and its solution.

To make the invisible visible and be effective in speaking up for others who might not be able to do so themselves, you must listen, be well-informed, have the words to say it, and come from a position of respect and empathy for real people. I drew on both formal academic study and the real world—women who consulted me, and street-smart experiences. It helped me contribute to building a lexicon and framework for women's experience of abortion, which had been routinely ignored. The words we use are powerful.

CHAPTER 2

The Price You Pay

Late 1990s–July 2001

Remnants of the drama of abortion have trickled over from the 20th into the 21st century. Little of the moral panic and urgency of the issues remain, but legislative bones are embedded in ancient codes that provide provocation and occasional bouts of apoplexy.

JO WAINER (2008)

'It's not right, Lou. They have abortion buffer zones and bubble zones in some places in Canada and America. Keep the nutters out, and women protected.'

'Yeah, the only thing that'll work. But it will never happen, Susie A. It's the price you pay.'

In the late 1990s, I sat across from Medical Director Dr Louis Rutman in his patient consulting room. Lou's consulting room was one of several on the non-Virginia side of the clinic which also housed the pathology lab. The modern theatre complex was housed along adjoining corridors in grand old dame Virginia.

As a stand-alone, one-stop clinic, Bert and Jo Wainer and Lou had constructed a woman-centred model where every aspect of a woman's care was under one roof. Practice Manager Janice Nugent was a woman-centred star. We had a flexibility and continuity of care that was particularly advantageous with more vulnerable women. Like our doctors and counsellors, I could be available to a more vulnerable patient as they progressed through the clinic from consults, pathology, pre-theatre, theatre, recovery to post op.

For example, women highly anxious about needles or theatre could have their counsellor (or me) with them in pathology or theatre, and we could usually accommodate a woman with what she thought might be most comforting.

Based on my clinical observations, such debilitating anxiety was more common in women with a history of being sexually or physically abused, or of trauma related to adverse experiences of past medical treatment/accidents. I had little rigorous research to back my anecdotal understandings, although a quite rigorous research proposal of mine is still sitting in a drawer somewhere. Clearly there was not enough *flexibility* to get to that one, but it also suggests a certain sexist circularity in casualties and causes of 'invisible women'. Roll on initiatives for more women-focused research!

The extremists' abuse was hard enough on most women, let alone women who had a history of being a victim of violence. Being abused was *the price you paid* for being a woman. Or an abortion provider: Lou and his staff had already paid the price umpteen times over and were prepared to continue to do so. There was no way for patients or staff to avoid being targeted. As Lou pointed out in his 2014 Supreme Court affidavit:

> *I do not want to make patients feel like they have to sneak in through the backyard to enter the clinic. It brings to mind 'backyard abortions'... [and] has the potential to make patients feel uncomfortable and threatened, when they are already emotionally fragile. Nobody should be asked to enter medical premises in this way in order to avoid being harassed and intimidated.*

The extremists chased women down the bluestone laneway leading to the rear staff entrance and approached or followed women a hundred metres and more from the clinic. No one was stopping them.

So here I was working at an essential women's health service in the modern 1990s heading into the sophisticated noughties, following the feminist love-ins and contraceptive pill liberation of the 1960s; Gough Whitlam's progressive programs of 1970s, and women's big-shouldered career suits of the 1980s. In the 1990s was this the price that our patients and staff had to pay? Why weren't we putting up a fight? Why wasn't anyone else concerned and doing something? The answer, like so much in this world, lies in the resounding unnoticed, unheard repetition of events mistakenly relegated to history or discarded from human consciousness completely (see, for example, O'Shea, 2019).

In 1974, a young Dr Louis Rutman was tapped on the shoulder by abortion rights campaigner Dr Bertram Wainer. Would Lou like to come and work with him at the Fertility Control Clinic?

Bert Wainer had pursued a relentless and dangerous campaign for abortion law reform and forced two Inquiries into police corruption—the 1970 Kay Inquiry: *Board of Inquiry into Allegations of Police Corruption in Connection with Illegal Abortion Practices in the State of Victoria*, and the 1975 Beech Inquiry: *Board of Inquiry Into Allegations Against Members of the Victorian Police Force*. Gideon Haigh's book *The Racket* drills into the sordid history of abortion dominated by male criminality, control, ignorance, greed, warped religiosity and politics, corruption and misogyny. While women paid with their lives, Bert was lucky to escape with his own (Wainer, B. 1972; Wainer, J. 2004; ABC, 2012).

After the Menhennitt and Levine decisions on 'lawful' abortion, Bert established Australia's first abortion clinic in Victoria in 1972. Initially housed further along Wellington Parade, the clinic 'shared with unlikely tenants—the Liberal Party, Parents Without Partners, Alcoholics Anonymous and publisher Max Newton's porn empire' (Haigh, 2008).

The young and well-trained Louis Rutman was exactly the modern doctor Bert needed to lead the Fertility Control Clinic into a new era of women's reproductive and abortion health care. Lou had two to three years of Obstetrics and Gynaecology registrar training under his belt at the Queen Victoria Hospital for Women. He also had considerable abortion experience, thanks to the Queen Vic's recent abortion service, and the O&G trainees whose consciences told them to opt out of terminating a pregnancy. Lou's conscience told him that the evil lay in refusing to provide an abortion to a woman asking for one. Lou had witnessed Ward 1A—an entire ward at Queen Vic devoted to women dying and suffering from backyard abortions.

I remember very clearly that gynae ward there for people who had illegal terminations done by the backyarders. A whole ward was specifically for these patients. The ward was always full: sepsis, sepsis shock, some died.

None of the patients, no matter how sick they were, wanted to give up the name of the person who had performed the abortion. They were horrific stories and I felt sorry for them and I felt that something needed to be done about this.

Under the Menhennitt ruling they ultimately closed ward 1A, there was no need for it. I think that was probably one of the influencing factors in accepting the job with Bert Wainer. What I saw was an area of gynae that was on the outskirts, but it certainly wasn't on the outskirts, it was there.

I ended up doing most of the abortion lists at the Queen Vic. At that stage Bert was working with John Levin and Peter Bayliss, neither of whom were trained in gynae. He approached me and said, why don't you come and work for me a couple of days a week and see how it goes. I knew of Bert but had never met him. He was very charming. We got on really really well together. He liked the idea that I was trained, young and pro-choice. He saw me as the long-term future of this, whereas the others were still a part of the illegal days. He wanted to move it on professionally.

I enjoyed working with Bert. Bert was a very influential character. He could sway you. He had charisma. He'd make you feel good about what you were doing.

DR LOUIS RUTMAN (2019)

Gideon Haigh (2008, p 220) describes Bert as a complex man:

By his works in the late 1960s and early 1970s, Bertram Wainer won iconic status. He was thought headstrong, erratic, egotistical and self-serving—not without justification at times. But some of these same characteristics made him the kind of leader around whom people rallied... Wainer was a man of his time, a crash through or crash leader, whose very intractability was what made him effective.

In 1974, Dr Louis Rutman left his O&G training and stepped into the role of Fertility Control Clinic Medical Director. Lou would work with Bert until Bert's death in January 1987, and continues to run the clinic to this day.

The corrupt and criminal atmosphere around abortion was calmed some-what by the 1969 Menhennitt ruling in R v Davidson, the 1971 Levine ruling in NSW case R v Wald, and the completion of police corruption Inquiries. The bad old days seemed to be gone: no more backyard abortions, corrupt police, police raids, criminal prosecutions of abortion doctors or of women having abortions; no more death threats and murder attempts on the lives of abortion providing doctors like Bert. But the clinic, staff and patients con-tinued to be firmly in the sights of anti-abortion extremists and occasionally the police.

During the 1970s, there were few if any protests at the clinic. But the price paid by the clinic in the 1980s included major 'right to life' protests descending on the clinic, sprawling onto the road, trespassing inside the clinic, and generally causing mayhem.

In those early days, protests were not on an everyday basis, but they were significant protests. They'd come around before you got to work and put chewing gum into the locks. I remember one day when we got them out of the waiting room. One of them wandering around ended up in Pathology. So we locked the back door and I stood against it and waited for the police to arrive. But those protests were once a month. So it was a large number of people, but not on a daily basis.

Dr Louis Rutman (2019)

Clinic Senior Counsellor June Dryburgh (Dryburgh, 2019) recalled an occa-sion in the 1980s when protesters stormed the clinic and sat on the theatre floor, which at that time was upstairs. Police said 'higher up' had told them they must not touch the protesters, but there was nothing to stop the clinic staff from moving them. So staff, and Bert's sons, lifted the protesters out onto the clinic back steps, where Bert proceeded to hose them down. 'I always wash off the dirt at this time of day', he said.

During these large marches and attacks on the clinic, there was little hope of either patients or staff entering or leaving the clinic. The police presence was considerable. but police concern apparently lay with ensuring the safety of the protest. Police took no action to ensure a clear path to the clinic for women wanting the clinic's health services, or for staff. That would basically remain the police priority until enforcement of abortion safe access zones laws more than thirty years later.

Smaller groups of anti-abortion extremists also began to beset the clinic in the 1980s. Out of these arose the Helpers of God's Precious Infants (HOGPI) who targeted the clinic daily until safe access zones were enforced in 2016. HOGPI was associated with Melbourne's Catholic Archdiocese St Patricks Cathedral and to a radical United States group of the same name. The latter's online anti-abortion rhetoric is too ghastly to repeat here. The group's aim was to shut down the clinic and all abortion services to 'save the unborn'.

Ironically, the actions of this zealous group would provoke a movement that instead saved women from the abuse of this and other groups and ensured women's right to bodily autonomy, dignity and agency. But before that day arrived, we travelled a tortured path of harassment by extremists and failure to act by authorities. Women and staff kept paying the price.

One day in 1981, with lawful abortion provision still hovering around the edges of the health care system, and perhaps with some egos still itching for retribution against Bert Wainer, Lou drove past the clinic late on a Friday afternoon to find police cars scattered outside. The Australian Federal Police was raiding the clinic and taking away the private health files of hundreds of women (Rutman, 2019). Clinic Practice Manager Janice Nugent's home was also raided.

What Lou lacks in physical stature he makes up for in a stubborn confidence. Lou was having none of it and demanded to be let in. The clinic took out an injunction to forbid the AFP from reading the confidential health files and to return them.

It turned out that some time after the clinic began using the new medical technology of ultrasound in 1980, the Medicare item number changed. For over a year the clinic had been using the wrong item—one with a higher rebate. Instead of just giving the clinic a call, Medicare, the Department of Health & Community Services or someone in authority chose to be heavy-handed in a manner unheard of with other health services.

After everything returned to normal and the Department requested the Medicare overpayments be returned, Bert refused: the Department's mishandling of the situation had caused financial and emotional costs to the clinic, staff and patients. Bert and Lou didn't hear any more about it.

Lou also tells of referring a patient, who was twenty weeks pregnant, to the Royal Womens Hospital's Dr Ruben Wein who provided abortions. The Fertility Control Clinic has always had an excellent working relationship with the Royal Women's over all its years, and this incident dates back to the 1980s or early 1990s:

> *For some reason somebody, probably a nurse, contacted the police. They arrived and said they were going to charge me with homicide. So I basically said get lost, this is ridiculous, and he never came back. It was just a try out.*
>
> Dr Louis Rutman (2019)

In the early 1990s, a man attacked Lou outside his house. Lou was punched and hit the concrete. Lou's wife, Shirley, found him on the ground with his head bleeding profusely. Not long after, a Molotov cocktail was thrown over the fence and into Lou's driveway.

> *It escalated to phone calls at work saying we're following your wife and kids. And they knew exactly what was going on: 'One in the car and two in the bus.' SOG [Special Ops Group] lived in the house for a week in the front room. It was pretty serious: cameras and guns. We told the kids if they hear anything you're not to leave your room. Police were out the front every day. Police organised for six months to follow me to work, come back and follow the children to school. Sometimes they'd come into the clinic and sit in the waiting room and wait and watch. Not too many of my friends were aware. The police had some good ideas who was responsible but never laid charges.*
>
> Dr Louis Rutman (2019)

By the 1990s, Lou had been targeted dreadfully by HOGPI, but his dedication to providing health care to women never faltered:

> *HOGPI activities have involved harassment by HOGPI members at my home and a period of police surveillance for my family's protection. It has been very harmful for me and my family… My family has sometimes encouraged me not to work at the FCC. I stay because this is my life and I believe that the clinic has achieved something important. When I started in 1974, family planning was a whole new area of women's health. I*

think that we have done an important job to provide access to services for women...

DR LOUIS RUTMAN (2014)

The two Prahran detectives became like family as they protected Lou and his family for six months on end. Later, Lou and Shirley were delighted to attend the wedding of one of the detectives. The lengths police went to, protecting Lou and his family then, were markedly different from Lou's previous experience of police.

It was likely that the same person who attacked Lou in the early 1990s was behind threats to other abortion providing doctors and their families, including our own Dr Greg Levin:

I'm sure you remember us, we came to your house recently to speak with your husband. We have sent him a letter requesting that he stop killing our brothers and sisters otherwise we will come to the street outside your house and distribute information and hold up posters and placards about abortion. He has one week to respond...

We (and many others) are completely committed to stopping the killing of between seventy and a hundred children per day in this city... Your husband is one of the killers... If your husband doesn't give us his commitment within one week we intend to show your neighbours and friends what little baby girls and boys look like after he has torn them from their mother's bodies.

LETTER TO DR GREG LEVIN'S WIFE

6 DECEMBER 1994

That letter from a *Catholics for Life* extremist six weeks after he visited Greg's home, was written one month *after* the extremist was sent a cease-and-desist letter by Grace Warren Hale Barristers & Solicitors on Greg's behalf. This outcome was not a ringing endorsement of taking legal action against fanatical people who believed menacing others was doing God's work. The legal intervention may have exacerbated the intimidation of Greg and his family. It certainly did not cease and desist.

In the small world of abortion providing doctors, Planned Parenthood doctor Max Sizeland and Melbourne Family Planning doctor Maurice Nissen were similarly targeted. Back in 1994, Max took legal advice from John Bull & Sons' Russell Bull (who would spend more than forty years in health law almost to the current day) and barrister Felicity Hampel (who would go on to an illustrious legal career including as a prominent human rights lawyer, judge of the County Court of Victoria, adjunct professor at Monash University and Victorian Law Reform Commissioner). The advice noted that this particular extremist tread a very fine line: not quite threatening and not quite stalking, apparently even when he pointedly commented on the doctor who had been recently (1994) murdered outside a Florida women's health clinic as 'deserving it' and 'wasn't that a good thing'. This religious fanatic's behaviour was apparently informed by the advice of Charles Francis QC, former parliamentarian and 'Christian' anti-abortion advocate.

On 23 February 1998, Galbally Fraser & Rolfe sent a letter to Detective Sergeant Pat Whelan, Melbourne CIB:

Re: Harassment of Fertility Control Clinic

We act on behalf of the owner and occupier of the Fertility Control Clinic.

The Fertility Control Clinic has for many years provided a number of services to women (and their partners and families)… under the clinic's license with the Department of Health and Community Services… many members of the community who seek and obtain such services.

Our client is extremely concerned about the activities and conduct, in the immediate proximity of the clinic, of certain people who are believed to be associated with the so-called 'Pro-Life Group'… They have for a considerable time obstructed, harassed and abused people attempting legitimately to enter the clinic… and resulted in substantial interference with our client's enjoyment of his premises and the conduct of his business. Our client is extremely concerned about his safety, as well as that of his employees and of the persons seeking to avail themselves of his clinic's services.

We believe that such activity… constitute a public nuisance, as well as the offence of besetting premises under s.52(1A) of the Summary Offences Act. They are ongoing, obstructive and dangerous activities; and accordingly we would strongly urge that the persons responsible be prosecuted in order to deter them from engaging in such conduct in the future.

No action.

Subsequently Lou commissioned Galbally Rolfe Barristers and Solicitors to explore the clinic's legal options. *In the Potential Matter of the Fertility Control Clinic v Pro-Life Victoria: Memorandum of Advice* (25 August 1998) was written by Jonathon P Moore (now QC) and considered four options: intervention orders against protestors for stalking; tort of nuisance (watching and besetting, making unreasonable noise, shouting); tort of intimidation; and conspiracy to injure. The advice was pessimistic about the helpfulness or success of any of them:

> *'As presently advised, I would describe the clinic's prospects of obtaining any-*
> *thing more than inconsequential and unsatisfying relief as "fair" at best.'*

Solicitor Rebecca Dean later observed in her 2004 *Journal of Law & Medicine* article, Abortion in Australia: Access vs Protest, 'The true conditions and experiences of clinic staff and clientele or the services the clinic provides were perhaps not fully understood by the male solicitor.' She questioned his conclusion that the circumstances at the clinic did not really make private nuisance a legal option against the protesters. Dean noted that in Hubbard v Pitt [1976] QB 142 at 172-173, picketing is defined as being lawful when it involves nothing more than:

> *An orderly and peaceful collection of persons outside particular premises*
> *where there was no obstruction, molestation or intimidation of persons en-*
> *tering and leaving the premises, the object of the picket being the communi-*
> *cation of information (Hubbard v Pitt, 1976)*

Dean's own experience of being harassed outside the clinic and her other observations indicated that:

> *Although the protesters outside the FCC claim the objective of their protest*
> *is to hold a vigil, and provide counsel, their protests do involve obstruction*
> *of the FCC entrance and the intimidation (at times including unwanted*
> *physical contact) of patients and staff entering the clinic.*

Dean considered both the Appeal Division in the *Animal Liberation Case* (1991): 'Besetting includes a surrounding with hostile demeanour so as to put in fear of safety' (*Animal Liberation (Vic) Inc v Gasser*, 1991), and the *Dollar Sweets Case* (1986), where Justice Murphy defined besetting as:

The occupation of a roadway or passageway through which persons wish to travel, so as to cause those persons to hesitate through fear to proceed, or if they do proceed, to do so only with fear for their own safety or the safety of their property' (Dollar Sweets Pty Ltd v FCAA, 1986).

And also noted:

The anti-choice protesters and their billboards outside the clinic constantly occupy the passageway through which patients and staff must travel in order to reach the FCC. In doing so the protesters make people hesitate and sometimes turn away from the clinic perhaps for fear of their own physical safety, but definitely for fear of their emotional safety. In contrast to the [Galbally Rolfe] solicitor's beliefs, I feel the environment surrounding the clinic created by the protesters can be described at times as nothing short of hostile.

Rebecca Dean had hit on the issue that would be a stumbling block for years: the eyes of observers, especially when those eyes were male, viewed the footpath scene as odd but harmless. Those eyes were unused, and unable, to see through a prism of women's experience, to recognise the true abuse, distress and harm women endured. As Dean pointed out in her 2004 *Journal of Law & Medicine* article (p.510), *Abortion in Australia: Access versus Protest*:

Recognition of the gendered and androcentric nature of the law means the law must constantly evolve to better meet the needs of women in particular.
Health law is no exception.

The his-story on which our society rests, means that the law is not alone in receiving such criticism. Our society in general, and arguably the entire world, is still cruelly and remarkably androcentric in the way Simone de Beauvoir observed back in 1949:

Representation of the world, like the world itself, is the work of men; they describe it from their own point of view, which they confuse with the absolute truth.

We all must question the pervasive beliefs and habits of male orthodoxy and challenge the status quo. We need more women in positions of influence and power to champion women's social participation and human rights. We need more men who agree with what is actually a very basic idea: that women are entitled to dignity and respect. We need more men to use their privilege to take a stand for women and perhaps nothing ensures respect and entitlement for women more than women-centred laws.

Fourteen years before the High Court of Australia's landmark decision upholding safe access zones, Rebecca Dean concluded that the inability of current legal options to address access issues at the clinic indicated 'a failure by the law to provide protection to women attempting to access a health service' (Dean & Allanson, 2004, p. 512); highlighted the existence of abortion safe access zones (known then as bubble or buffer zones) in areas of the United States and Canada; provided evidence of safe access zones laws being effective, consistent with human rights charters and having tested capacity to meet legal challenge; and recommended similar legislation be enacted in Australia.

A woman's right to access health services such as abortion free from harassment, intimidation and obstruction should be recognised by Australian law. Women seeking abortions represent one of society's vulnerable groups. However, thus far… government has afforded them no protection and women continue to be victimised.

DEAN & ALLANSON (2004, P.515)

But in the 1990s, Rebecca Dean was still a girl yet to take her place as a woman challenging the androcentric status quo in her academic work on abortion (2003, 2004 and 2007). Even then, it would be some years before her work would be heard over the noise of the very male entitlement she called out.

As Fertility Control Clinic Medical Director, Lou held grave concerns about the chronic presence of anti-abortion extremists, but also had good reasons not to challenge it.

First, the clinic faced bleak 1998 legal advice and a track record of other expensive legal failures and police inaction that made our bad situation worse.

Second, in comparison with what had gone on in the bad old abortion days of the 1970s and 1980s, the monthly large protests and daily HOGPI intimidation of the 1990s were at least predictable. Police generally attended the clinic on request and were polite, while unwilling to take action that might change the status quo.

Third, the only effective approach would be government legislation to introduce a buffer zone to ban extremists from around the clinic area. At the 1992 Victorian election, the Liberal Jeff Kennett-led coalition had ousted Joan Kirner's Labor government. Kennett would remain premier until late 1999. Either way, both Labor and Liberal-National parties had Catholic members and constituencies where abortion was considered a political death knell. Though, it must be said, Catholic women then attended for abortion in numbers similar to their representation in society generally (Allanson, 1994). Oh, for a woman's gaze.

Fourth, publicly drawing attention to our plight might aggravate the situation for staff, patients and the clinic. The extremists might ark up further. Media attention might attract even more dangerous people and deter women desperate for the clinic's services. Both staff and patients might be put at greater risk. We were already targets; why would we want to stand out even more by stepping into a media spotlight?

Lou had good reason to espouse a philosophical acceptance, rather than succumb to pessimism, anger or public advocacy, his high blood pressure notwithstanding. While we waited for the world to catch up and put a stop to the woman-hating outside the clinic, inside the clinic we continued to make the world a better place by delivering woman-centred health care.

Occasionally Lou's frustration with the situation spilled over into an idiosyncratic 'direct action' approach which made me think of the 1986 movie *Three Amigos!* About to face the murderous El Guapo, Steve Martin's character cheerily advises, 'Relax and have fun with it'. So with a big grin:

> *Lou strolls out to the protestors, 'Hey, Dave. Is your wife pregnant?'*
>
> *'None of your business,' comes the indignant reply.*
>
> *'Exactly,' says Lou. And seeing that the penny doesn't drop, Lou adds, 'Just like it's no business of yours to know about the women coming here.'*

ALLANSON (2006, P.100)

It was rare for a staff member to take her cue from Lou to express frustration, helplessness and fear in a similarly 'have fun with it' manner, but one of our nurses, Gina, did just that:

Gina is fed up with them. She is a ball of cheeky anger. She pushes her way through the protesters, her flaming hair flowing in her wake. 'Get out of my way. Pregnant woman coming through.' Her belly protrudes round and huge. She looks almost ready to deliver. She nurses it proudly with her two arms. 'Pregnant woman coming through. Get out of my way.' And she enters the clinic.

Five minutes later and Gina leaves the clinic the same way. Out the front door, down the path and through the front gate. Struts past the protesters again. 'Ooh that's better,' she sighs. Pats her flattened tummy where the plump cushion had been.

ALLANSON (2006, P.100)

But aside from such occasional shenanigans, Lou succinctly recognised the gravity of his role:

[I am] involved in all aspects of the clinic, from management to consultation with patients [and have] ultimate responsibility for what happens at the clinic.

LOU RUTMAN'S 2014 SUPREME COURT AFFIDAVIT

That 'ultimate responsibility' came with a cost not borne by any other health service or workplace. For good reason, I had neither Lou's optimism nor blessing to agitate for change to the fraught environment directly outside the clinic. But ten years after I began working at the clinic, 16 July 2001 would bring a more horrifying clarity. That day would change us forever.

'Now's the time, Susie A,' said Lou. 'Now's the time to lobby the government.'

It was the day after 16 July 2001. The day after our security guard, Steve Rogers, was murdered by an anti-abortion fanatic. Steve was shot, and died, in the clinic's reception area. The killer had planned to burn the clinic and everyone in it to the ground: staff, patients, companions, children and pregnant women. He had taken the religious fanatics' rhetoric to its logical and hypocritical conclusion by lighting the powder keg the extremists danced around every day. But for the intervention of Steve and two men attending the clinic with their partners, there would have been a massacre by gun fire and flames.

After the frantic exhaustion of managing a critical incident workplace subsided to a semblance of normality, and on Janice's suggestion, I wrote about that horrendous time in my book *Murder on His Mind* (2006). My writing was driven by fury, despair and the naïve idea that people would share my outrage and demand protection. People would demand a buffer zone. The story told in *Murder on His Mind* is inextricably tied to the story of the abortion safe access campaign, but it is not a place I wish to return to here.

Suffice to say, on 16 July 2001, incendiary rhetoric turned to incendiary action, and I knew with a crystal clarity that extremists' daily harassment and rhetoric was an incitement to an even more extreme violence. Every day they pointed their pious fingers at the clinic, its patients and staff, and made us targets: the clinic was a slaughterhouse where babies were murdered. This time a killer had turned up and the worst had happened. The price was too high, and we were not going to pay it anymore.

Well, that was the plan.

Police were outside the clinic the day following Steve's murder. Police continued to 'balance rights' by allowing HOGPI to 'protest' in their usual fashion, including chasing women down the laneway running the length of the clinic to the rear entrance. Staff and patients were highly distressed and felt cheated of the protection the police should have provided. We were a trauma-affected staff in a trauma-affected workplace. Our patients were women with diverse backgrounds, strengths and vulnerabilities seeking help on the day after a high-profile murder. It was the first Australian abortion clinic murder, following in the footsteps of the extreme violence of United States anti-abortion groups, but Police still did not protect women or staff.

Nine months later the gunman was declared guilty—an ironic timeframe in the pregnancy business—and sentenced to life imprisonment with a minimum non-parole period of 23 years (*R v Knight* [2002] VSC 498). But in every other way, authorities meant to protect women from murder, arson, and violence, had failed to act, and continued to fail us. Authorities meant to uphold women's right to be let alone and to go about their lives with safety, dignity and privacy, did not want to know about us. Organisations with the power to intervene could not, or would not, recognise that extremists were crossing normal boundaries of decency to target and hurt women. Nor that the very presence of the extremists crossed the line from free speech to incitement. In its tragedy, surely a murder of a man must also bring a reckoning. Surely now we would see action from authorities.

That day, Lou decided the cost was too high and shifted gears: it was no longer enough to deliver an excellent woman-centred service in a hostile environment, the environment had to change in order to properly deliver the service. Lou had dedicated his career to giving women the opportunity to make their own decisions. Men like Bert Wainer and Lou Rutman had created the groundwork for women to be able to speak up, for women to be able to congregate and advocate for their interests. A man who embodied the opposite qualities to Bert and Lou had violated womankind, humanity and the caring, unsilencing space of the clinic. Now Lou had given me the green light to speak up and advocate for our patients' interests.

Would society's male gaze continue to dominate and blinker a more progressive and humanitarian vision? Would we continue to be chastised as a dirty business and a bloody stain affronting to men's ego? Or would a murderous crusade to 'save the unborn' paradoxically become a catalyst for action that would lead to women's unambiguous entitlement to reproductive choice and respect?

The business-as-usual approach from local police, the day after this shocking violence, did not bode well. It should have been a clear heads up that nothing was going to change quickly. I would like to be able to say that Lou and I were expecting a long journey. I would like to be able to say that we saw this as the start of extensive preparations so that when the opportunity presented itself, we could seize the moment and we would finally have our safe access. But no one knew it would take another fourteen years to get there, and another four on top of that to secure the High Court's adamant endorsement. No one knew that, least of all Lou and me. In fact, soaked in tragedy and naive desperation, I thought it would happen quickly. I thought that the start of abortion safe access preparations occurred decades ago, way before I arrived at the clinic. It felt to me like everything leading up to this tragedy was the preparation, and Steve's murder was the ghastly moment we would seize to make it happen for women. We would memorialise Steve's life with something incredibly powerful.

The day after the shooting, we wrote to Labor Premier Steve Bracks thanking him for his supportive comments in the media. We respectfully asked that in the wake of this tragedy he consider our concerns and do all in his power, 'whether through legislative or policy initiatives, to allow our staff and patients to go about their business in a safe environment and unfettered by threats and harassment'.

My advocacy for safe access zones had begun. It would be spectacularly unsuccessful.

The murder just took it to a whole other level, didn't it, because it just showed how dangerous it was. And then to have all of your team continuing to go in to work and nothing's changed? Someone died and no one is trying to protect you. No one, no one! How could that be? I mean that was a real tipping point, wasn't it? It really highlighted that nobody cared. The worst thing possible happened, and it changed nothing. What the hell! I still can't believe that. That changed nothing.

REBECCA DEAN (2020)

How much should people put up with before deciding that enough is enough? If we had spoken up sooner, might Steve's murder have been prevented? Or might we have provoked other tragedies?

In our case, before and after Steve's murder, we kept on delivering expert and kind women-centred medical care to women who otherwise would struggle to access what is still a limited abortion service in our society. Every woman who consulted us was one more woman who had a positive and holistic health experience where contraceptive needs, sexually transmitted infection treatment, routine pap test, pregnancy termination and other reproductive health issues were addressed. Many women presenting to us with fertility control issues, but also with significant psychosocial issues, may never have sought out help before, or may have been deterred by a less than sympathetic consultation elsewhere. Hopefully a woman's positive experience with us made it more likely that she would be linked to appropriate services or was more likely to reach out for psychosocial help in the future.

So our care of women was valuable, but it was not enough. The outside world had a way of undermining our efforts to provide women-centred care. Rightly or wrongly, we had been biding our time, and when we thought we could not bide our time anymore, and we began to agitate for change, we could not have foreseen that our efforts would take years more.

When, and how, to embark on activism is not necessarily straightforward. How long it may take to reach your goal, or if you will reach it at all, is unknown. It can be frustrating, demoralising, exhausting, and occasionally exhilarating. It was less of a decision for us, but rather an inevitability. You may have your own moment when you no longer have a choice.

CHAPTER 3

Born to Protect: The Council, Police & God

2001–2007

> *To change the story that ends in violence against women, we must begin with gender equality and respect for all women.*
>
> NATASHA STOTT DESPOJA AO (2019)

Prior to the shooting, I was focused on my work with Fertility Control Clinic patients and staff, my private practice clients, and in 1999 resumed occasional sessional work at the Children's Court Clinic under the indefatigable and eminent Dr Pat Brown. I sat on the Board of Family Planning for a couple of years, completed my PhD in 1999, published academic articles on abortion, and occasionally spoke at conferences and with various health professional groups. These all were a form of feminist learning and advocacy. I built rich relationships with academics and health practitioners. Women's reproductive health and fertility control was a fascinating area long neglected. In that neglect, there was never a shortage of abortion issues catching my attention.

After the shooting, I naively thought that if only more people knew what was really going on, someone or something would put a stop to the harmful targeting of women accessing abortion. With that in mind, I wrote *Murder on His Mind*, continued my clinical work, provided supervision to colleagues and clinical psychology masters and doctoral students on placement or researching at the Fertility Control Clinic, gave occasional lectures and workshops to health professionals and students, and engaged with media opportunities. Over the next fourteen years (yes, fourteen!), with Lou's astute backing and Janice and Susan's unflagging encouragement, on behalf of the clinic I also would appeal for a remedy from two major authorities.

The first authority was the Victorian Government who held the power to provide the well-proven overseas, most effective and our preferred solution: legislation for an abortion buffer zone, that is, an abortion safe access zone. Such legislation would ensure that protestors were excluded from a defined zone around abortion providing clinics, so that women would be protected from harassment within the zone. The second authority was our local council, Melbourne City Council, whose powers suggested they could, and should, act quickly to ameliorate the harm being perpetrated on women in its precinct.

Melbourne City Council (MCC) is the subject of the current chapter, while the state government is covered in the next chapter. In reality, these two avenues for a solution occurred simultaneously across the same time frame in what, to me, felt like a zig-zagging and intersecting experience. We could not know that it would be years before our work targeting these two authorities would finally intersect at a point that meant success.

After Steve Rogers was killed, we began a fight with Melbourne City Council (MCC) that eventually reached the Supreme Court. That 2015 Supreme Court judgement should send shivers down the backs of every rate payer in Victoria. It sure explained a thing or two about local councils.

Municipal Councils can be huge bureaucracies. Its elected officials, Councillors and Mayor perhaps can be likened to a company Board of Directors headed by its Chairperson, and primarily concerned with policy and governance matters. The Council's corporate organisation/bureaucracy is more like the 'company', headed by a CEO, and carrying out municipal functions for the benefit of its rate payers. Collecting garbage and recyclables is the tip of the Council iceberg.

With the expectation of a solution, you can complain to your local Council about a host of problems. So that's what we did. But my knowledge was clearly a penny short of a pound when it came to understanding the workings of local government.

Lord Mayor John So reigned over Melbourne from 2001 to 2008. The MCC throne then hosted the ample bottom of ex-Liberal leader Robert Doyle (who would resign in 2018 as he faced sexual harassment allegations).

From 2001 through 2015, clinic correspondence, phone calls and meetings with MCC were many. Lou, Janice and I observed that throughout such meetings, MCC staff were polite, patient and quite lovely. MCC threw significant resources at our concerns. Bottom line, MCC did whatever it needed to do *not* to do anything about the chronic harassment of women on a public street within its municipality.

Perhaps MCC feared offending the Catholic Church whose Melbourne Archbishop was located at St Patricks Cathedral in East Melbourne; wanted to avoid the inevitable push back by the Church and anti-abortion extremists and what that may cost MCC financially, at the ballot box and in the court of public opinion; did not want to be tainted with the 'stain' of abortion; was succumbing to blatant, plain old sexism and misogyny that relegated key women's issues opaque and trivial.

A July 2003 letter to Lord Mayor So was unusual in being a lengthy four pages. We surmised that 'The Council's lack of action may be because councillors have not had adequate information provided to them'. We provided details to rectify that and invited Lord Mayor So and his councillors to visit the clinic to see the situation firsthand.

By more fully appreciating the chronic and serious nature of this appalling situation, we hope that you and your councillors will respond to our urgent request to introduce a Council by-law to exclude demonstrators (and their paraphernalia) within a 50-metre radius of any health clinic.'

An exclusion zone? Ahead of our time? No, Melbourne was just years behind. MCC never caught up. Until we could convince our state government to enact a robust law providing a buffer zone around abortion providers, we pushed for a local government version.

Meanwhile, we continued to carry out our duty of care to our patients with one hand tied up in rosary beads. *Get your rosaries off our ovaries!* We heard the same comments from our patients and their companions over and over, day in day out: 'How can they upset my wife like that; It's just not right; They gave me such a shock—I nearly turned around and went home without coming in; S/he chased me down the street/wouldn't let me get out of the car/wouldn't let me alone/jostled me/blocked me from getting in the gate; How can they say such disgusting things? They shouldn't be allowed to be here; They are gross; How can they call themselves Christians when they are so mean? Why don't they get a real job? Bunch of f@$#%ing b@#$!% b@#%$s!'

And, 'You really should do something about them.'

The holier-than-thou group from St Patrick's congregation was definitely not following in Jesus' footsteps. Yet they were bestowed status, encouragement and blessing from Archbishop Denis Hart as if they were going off to dole out kindness and alms to the poor. Throughout this whole long saga, it never crossed my mind, or Lou's mind, or Janice's mind, to lobby the Archbishop to curb his followers' behaviour. Why would it? Most people within the Catholic church are good people doing good work, but I didn't have a high opinion of the church hierarchy: self-entitled, punitive beliefs and hypocrisy; amassing and hoarding of an obscene wealth that could have been used to ease mass suffering; abuse of children and heartless discrimination against so many; incapacity to hear with kindness a humanity and womanhood excluded from its sexually perverse, high-walled towers...

So, Melbourne City Council it was.

The current situation does not befit a modern, caring City Council which has a duty of care to its constituents and to members of the public accessing Melbourne services or visiting Melbourne. This duty of care takes on greater seriousness given the murder of our security guard in July 2001. We hope that it does not take another death for the City Council to act.

LETTER TO LORD MAYOR SO

JULY 2003

The last was a truth and a threat. If the Council was concerned that intervening with a sensible safety zone would provoke legal action from the

Church and its more extreme congregants, then by crikey let Council be concerned about being sued for failing to do so.

Ho hum. Who was I kidding? The Lord Mayor replied politely in August 2003 that the Council could not act, and a lovely male Community Liaison Officer phoned us to discuss and reiterate: *right to protest, communication of religious and political matters...*

'Balancing rights' must have been so much easier when the conflicting rights, that is, women's rights to access health care with safety, privacy and dignity, didn't even exist.

As I put together our 2004 submission to the Public Health Legislation Review: *Review of the* Health Act 1958: *A new legislative framework for public health in Victoria,* I came across laws that to my unlearned eye were made for our situation. In 2004 I reminded Lord Mayor John So of this law:

> *Municipal councils have clear duties in relation to nuisances under the current Health Act, where nuisances are defined as 'nuisances which are, or are liable to be, dangerous to health or offensive' including 'any state, condition or activity' which is liable to be dangerous to health or offensive, where offensive is defined as 'noxious, annoying or injurious to personal comfort.' (Section 38A Health Act 1958, Vic). Municipal councils have the right and obligation to issue an order to abate the nuisance...*
>
> *Ensuring that protesters are removed a reasonable distance away from the clinic entrance would sit well with a municipal council's obligation to 'remedy as far as reasonably possible all nuisances in its municipal district' (Section 41 Health Act 1958).*

A 'noxious nuisance', 'annoying', 'injurious to personal comfort'? This law was speaking my language. But MCC was not, and never would. Ten years later, these same nuisance laws in the hands of the clinic's learned legal counsel would be used to sue MCC in the Supreme Court of Victoria.

But in 2004, unlearned me didn't have a clue what I was doing. But I did it anyway. I also reminded Lord Mayor So that previous correspondence had: provided real life examples and set out clearly how the protest behaviour was offensive and injurious to the psychological and physical wellbeing of patients; explained that we believed in protesters' rights to express their views, but that it was inappropriate, offensive and harmful for them to continue this style of protest directly outside a women's health clinic and workplace; and (in the dark ages of 2004, years before the advent of online campaigns garnering thousands of signatures in the time it takes to tap a button) included a petition signed by hundreds of people declaring they found the protesters' behaviour offensive, intimidating and upsetting, and demanding the Council remove the protesters.

Hooray, MCC immediately saw the error of their ways and removed the extremists. Well, no. In fact, never. But we kept trying.

In 2004, lateral thinking Lou argued that everyone else had to apply for a Council permit if they wished to place an A frame poster or any other display on the public thoroughfare. Shouldn't the picketers have to also? Simple, sensible logic.

But according to MCC:

The City of Melbourne's commercial activities policy operating statement clearly states that it is Council policy not to require persons distributing or displaying political or religious material to obtain a permit to conduct these types of activities… no recourse under the Local Law with regard to censoring the material…

We valued people's democratic rights to protest and to communicate about political and religious matters. We struggled to see the political or religious nature of displays and leaflets depicting, for example, dismembered foetuses and Nazism, and falsely claiming the contraceptive pill was a 'toxic pill' and that abortion caused breast cancer. We struggled to see how humiliating and blocking women accessing a health service was either political, religious or communication.

MCC never did answer our questions about what definitions and guidelines informed MCC's view that graphic, offensive and frightening medical misinformation and images were deemed political or religious.

The chronic targeting we copped went far beyond protest and was arguably neither religious nor political. Even if it were, we were asking for only a small geographic limitation to be placed on those rights: anywhere else just not outside the Fertility Control Clinic. We had no intention of allowing a woman's right to safety, dignity, privacy and access to a health service to be relegated to unimportant.

But that is exactly what MCC was only too happy to do. Into the gendered too-hard basket or the tired-and-trivial file we went, again. Lord Mayor So reassured us that Melbourne Compliance Officers would 'keep monitoring pedestrian access on Wellington Parade to ensure that Council Local Laws were adhered to by the protestors'.

Over the years there was a great deal of MCC 'monitoring', sometimes a 'talking to', but even with repeated breaches, not even a fine ever eventuated. The closest MCC ever got to taking action was a written warning to pro-choice group, *Radical Women*. Hmm.

We built good working relationships with police: from Security and Intelligence to Homicide, from East Melbourne Constables to Chief Supers, even to the Police Commissioner. I don't mean to malign any of those dedicated officers when I say that everyone at the clinic rather wished we didn't have to have those relationships with police. No other health service did.

Security and Intelligence discussions with Lou, Janice and me about arrangements for the next large monthly 'save the babies' protest, or being told they would be keeping their eyes out for a known violent radical, were both worrying and reassuring. East Melbourne Police visits to the clinic for meetings or because of an incident meant our patients' thoughts could turn to all sorts of unsettling matters: *Is there a bomb? Is this clinic dodgy? Is this a raid? What about my privacy? The police have finally caught up with my boyfriend.* Not what our patients needed. Plus, no one ever wants to have to meet Homicide detectives, even if those detectives are kind and hardworking.

Call me naïve (again) but I had not foreseen that police liaison would be a routine aspect of my role at a women's health clinic. My predecessor clinical psychologist Kath MacPherson's cheerful, absurd and ominous words all those years ago when I applied for the clinic role all came to pass in my dealings with police. For Practice Manager Janice, liaising with police had probably involved many 'Let me stop you right there' moments. For Lou, police were part of the wallpaper. Lou had been targeted by police and had liaised with police for decades. A police visit was probably just another, 'The price you pay, Susie A'.

Police were hamstrung by laws not designed to deal with this unique form of gendered violence. With a 'we-said-they-said' scenario, Police rarely considered the behaviour complained about to reach the level of a chargeable offense or crime. I began referring to the extremists' actions as 'noncriminal violence against women', an oxymoron if ever there was one. Our laws, and many external observers, were either blind to this peculiarly female experience of abuse or misunderstood it as benign. But the many layers of violence against women in our society is an insidious cancer that needs to be cut out. Many a Wellington Parade passer-by apparently agreed: 'Cut it out, ya morons!'

Police action was also stymied by understandably reluctant complainants. Our patients attended us for deeply private matters. They had no wish to be exposed in public court proceedings, media attention, and a process that could continue for years. For similarly good reasons, staff weren't keen either. This was the last thing Lou wanted for our patients or staff. Plus, Lou, Janice and I knew that individual prosecutions were never going to provide the preventative, long term solution we needed.

In the old days, police had advised Bert Wainer that higher ups had ordered that police not move the pious people staging a sit-in in the middle of the operating theatre. No doubt police action was still obstructed by higher ups' orders involving an array of issues I had no idea about. I imagine it could be quite a headache to fine or charge zealots likely to view the legal process as an opportunity to spread their version of God's word from a courtroom pulpit and likely to pursue every avenue of legal appeal.

Both the clinic and police station were situated in the Catholic Archdiocese, and our chronic abusers received Saturday mass blessings from the Archbishop of Melbourne in St Patricks Cathedral before they set out on their large monthly parade to the clinic. The religious extremists' affiliation with the wealthiest institution in the world via St Pats, made for unique frustrations for everyone I expect. No doubt VicPol higher ups were keen to smooth things over and keep a lid on it all without laying charges.

But nothing was going smoothly for women and staff—it was rough. And lids were not being kept on at all—we were blowing our stacks. The revelations of long-standing sexual abuse of children by the Catholic Church provided the most appalling example of damage that ensues when authorities do not call a powerful institution to account.

> *The police were a rather religious organisation. A large number of Catholics were in senior positions in the police force. That has changed. But even in the 1970s and '80s, some cover ups of sexual abuse in the church were allowed because the police were complicit. That was certainly the case in Ballarat and Mildura…*
>
> Fiona Patten (2019)

In July 2005, the extremists were caught filming women and staff entering and leaving the clinic. Again, our laws had not yet evolved to deal with this unique form of technological revolution intimidation. Apparently such filming was not an offence unless the vision was publicly disseminated, and even then… There were gaping legal holes in the age of the internet and free-for-all camera operators.

I guess I shouldn't have been surprised that in 2005, filming women on a public street as they were accessing an abortion providing health clinic was legally deemed neither a crime nor an offence. But Victorians did take offence. The discovery provoked a public furore and a media storm. I was kept busy with media interviews in the typically sharp publicity sting that lasts a few days before it wears off and is forgotten.

'Media spokesperson' had not been in my job description either but, with Lou's blessing, it was a *flexible* mantle I took on after Steve's murder. I juggled media between patients at the clinic, my other clinical psychology gigs, and amongst home office papers, children, domestic chores… Many an interview with a print journalist occurred over the phone with me in my dressing gown—the best type of interview. The worst type of interview was TV, especially when they'd want film footage of me walking or working or staring or… I was not a model nor an actor.

The media role was not one I exactly warmed to, but if something needed to be said, I would say it. In this invisible, taboo area of women's health there was plenty needing to be said, far too much. Like the harassment leading up to our doorstep, most related to barriers to affordable, timely, comprehensive contraception, abortion and reproductive health services, and related to an idea that women were objects to be controlled and fucked over.

I rarely knocked back a request for a background chat or an interview, including with journalism students. I was not undiscerning though. I was careful to assess that the opportunity was one which would be useful and not one in which I would be used. I refused to be involved in any media requiring me to appear with, or debate, an anti-choice activist, and refused those journalists who were clearly pushing an anti-choice barrow—usually easily discerned. Journalists wanted 'a good story', but most also wanted to understand an issue. Speaking with journalists was an opportunity to educate, change the abortion discourse, keep the focus on women's experiences, women's rights, and women's access to the full range of reproductive and family planning options.

Just like the psychology students we took on placement at the clinic who would one day be psychologists working out in the big world, journalism students who knew about this essential women's business would end up making the world better for women, and that meant better for children and everyone else. Plus, the way we were going, or *not* going, who knew if the next time I spoke with someone I'd met when they were just a student, they'd be sitting in a senior and influential media position?

I had neither the smarts nor the ready-and-waiting army of seasoned advocates and campaign strategists to convert these buzzing media opportunities to a safe access zone solution. But being available to media was all part of a chipping away until serendipitous events, people and leaders arrived to harness the media, the law and popular opinion in a sophisticated manner. We would finally hold our society to account for a proper recognition of a woman's right to live her life as she saw fit.

In the meantime, there was no smoothing over for us, no balancing of rights, and no extant law that would protect our patients. There was just the damage. It is difficult to describe the amount of emotional energy, work, time, teeth-clenching, rising blood pressure, migraine, empathy, patience and skill that staff expended to avoid or undo the harm caused by the extremists. Similarly, the utter waste of police resources caught in a futile reactive approach. We needed people who really *got* our situation.

During 2005 to 2007, East Melbourne Sgt Mick Wilmott was one police officer who really got our situation. Lou enjoyed his conversations with Mick and held him in high regard, as did Janice and I. Mick went above, beyond and undercover. He popped in regularly to see how we were going, instigated an undercover operation, facilitated meetings, sussed out potential solutions and wrote a 2006 Police Issues Paper. Mick's Paper noted that buffer zones were not currently under consideration by the state government, and concluded:

> It is possible that current Melbourne City Council bylaw provisions and precedents could be applied (e.g. Activities Bylaw 2.1 re nuisance) to disallow picketing in the area. This needs to be researched. Currently the Council has shown little interest in acting to protect the privacy, well-being and safety of constituents or visitors living, working or passing through this area of chronic picketing.

Solicitor Rebecca Dean's August 2006 paper, prepared pro bono for the clinic, observed that MCC's *The Activities Local Law 1999 (ALL)* had a number of provisions relevant to the conduct of the picketers outside the Fertility Control Clinic. *Part 2: Behaviour, Activities Local Law* aimed to:

> Protect the amenity of public places for all citizens by prohibiting persons from acting in a socially unacceptable manner.

Points 2.1.(a) to (d), and (g) nailed the precise behaviour occurring on the public thoroughfare outside the clinic and within MCC's precinct:

> 2.1 A person must not in, on or within the hearing or sight of a public place:
> (a) cause or commit any nuisance;
> (b) adversely affect the amenity of that public place;
> (c) interfere with the use or enjoyment of that public place or the personal comfort of another person in or on that public place;
> (d) annoy, molest or obstruct any other person in or on that public place;
> …
> (g) use any threatening, abusive or insulting words.

Rebecca noted MCC's use of by-laws to curb the presence and actions of other people within the City of Melbourne:

Melbourne City Council by-laws have been applied to buskers and people who litter... prevented Aborigines from camping in the Domain... used noise abatement by-laws to prevent Hare Krishna from protesting with music and chanting. The Council has not yet applied its by-laws to prohibit picketers outside the Fertility Control Clinic on Wellington Pde... By enforcing Activities Local law 1999, Part 2, the Council fulfils its duty of care to residents, traders, workers and visitors to the Wellington Parade area, while also ensuring picketers' rights to protest elsewhere.

Her final paragraph:

Proposed Course of Action: Theresa Grilling from the Melbourne City Council has suggested the clinic lodge a complaint with the Council outlining the provisions of the Activities Local Law 1999 which it believes are applicable to the picketers conduct. The complaint should request the Council to explain why the applicable provisions are not being enforced by the Council and request that they be enforced.

MCC's reply included nothing they had not already said before. Sigh. But strong allies pushed the MCC by-law option to the next level. On 15 September 2006 Democrats Senator and local federal member, Lyn Allison, organised a meeting of key stakeholders at Lyn's political office (also located on Wellington Parade). I invited Sgt Mick Wilmott, Women's Health Victoria (WHV) and an East Melbourne (residents) Group member who had been most helpful. Lyn invited the big players: Lord Mayor So and our first female Police Chief Commissioner, Christine Nixon. Ta da!

Christine Nixon had only just taken up the Police Commissioner role when I had first written to her about our situation in 2001 and again in 2003. For this 2006 meeting I had never been so well prepared: agenda, incident reports, photos, complimentary copies of *Murder on His Mind*, Rebecca Dean's legal advice, handouts, and my introductory comments which optimistically concluded:

A win–win solution is possible. By enforcing its bylaws and working with the police, MCC can fulfil its duty of care to the people of East Melbourne and preserve picketer's right to protest. In Australia it is not an absolute right to protest anytime, anyhow or anywhere. At present the picketers' rights are being privileged above everyone else's rights.

Lord Mayor So didn't show. He sent underlings who I had had mutually respectful conversations with previously, like solicitor Mr Kim Woods.

Police Chief Commissioner Christine Nixon did show. Pardon the pun, but she was a gun. Straight to the point. Let's solve this thing. The plan? For police to become MCC authorised officers to enforce the bylaws. The Police Commissioner was clear that this cooperation between police and MCC would provide a solution.

But, follow up and follow up, delays and delays, the lack of progress in training police to become authorised MCC officers was a mystery. Years later a police officer told us that MCC reneged on the deal. Sounded like MCC to me, but who really knew. We were never told. We were just outsiders, unable to see how this large, slow and torpid institution worked. Ah, the bliss of deniable deniability?

Our hope had been that if Police enforced Activities bylaws with individual picketers, then both extremist numbers and harassment would diminish. Of course individual legal targeting tended to be reactive and piecemeal, and the courts might be clogged up for years with HOGPI appeals, but maybe it might persuade MCC to introduce a protected area for women. A feminist version of a clearway of sorts. Councils did that for drivers. Why not for women? Fines for vehicles parked in road clearways. Fines for anti-women extremists parked in health service clearways?

This type of strategy doesn't reflect that this is a structural problem. Disrespect for women is baked into society such that large institutions, like the church, actively organise around mistreating women in this way. Other large institutions, like MCC, Police and so on, feel permitted to ignore this. This bigger problem of societal disrespect for women requires relentless, tenacious activism to reverse. Small individual legal actions against individuals, while minutely effective potentially, would permit the larger structural problems to continue.

Ultimately, an individual case could work only when there had been years of advocacy work that shifted the structural ideas about respecting women.

LIZZIE O'SHEA

A year after that hopeful, but clearly failed, meeting with stakeholders, Sgt Mick Wilmott was still fighting the good fight. He and Inspector Duthie initiated a meeting at East Melbourne Police station in October 2007. In attendance were Sgt Wilmott, Inspector Duthie, East Melbourne residents, HOGPI members and their legal counsel, and me. It was more than unpleasant, and an example of what happens when you treat both sides as somehow equally valid. It felt abusive. Following the meeting I went home to shower off the words spat at me by the God-fearing bullies and their lawyer. With Lou's okay, I wrote a respectful letter to Inspector Duthie thanking him for the meeting and explaining why neither I nor any FCC staff would attend any future meetings with the people who abused us daily. It was basic Bullying/Violence Against Women 101. I was slowly recognising that I was a victim in all this too.

Police were well-meaning in both arranging that 2007 meeting and brokering a 'gentleman's agreement' with the extremists. One day we turned up to the clinic to find a gentleman's agreed white line painted along the footpath, parallel with the gutter and around one-and-a-half metres away from the clinic fence. That thin white line was supposed to have the magical power to stop extremists harassing women and staff. As if standing behind that line made God's soldiers any less intimidating or humiliating to women. And if they did step over that thin white line—which of course they did—no action taken.

Not only was that line the subject of curious questions from media, patients and residents, but many people seemed convinced that that white line had solved the problem. King not wearing any clothes here. Women walking here. Anyone?

Eventually, a God-fearing crusader turned the white line into a row of white crosses stuttering across the asphalt.

The following month, November 2007, Lyn Allison kept the pressure on speaking to the media about the chronic harassment of women outside the clinic:

> It does show the extent to which the far right will go to limit women's access to reproductive health services and outside there [FCC] today are members of the Family First Party.

Lyn was having a go at a rival political party, Family First, but fair enough. The whole Christian Lobby/Family First vitriol against women needed to be called out. Thank you, Lyn.

Lyn Allison's federal Senate career ended in 2008. The dedicated police officer who 'got it', Mick Wilmott, moved on in his police career, our situation even defeating this very determined and kind officer. Lord Mayor So made way for Lord Mayor Robert Doyle. MCC continued to dismiss women's experiences and rights. The Fertility Control Clinic maintained its excellent care of women. I proceeded on my muddled, befuddled way still wondering: Why was it so hard to get human beings to just do the decent thing?

Institutions can be slow and reluctant to change, and that was certainly our experience with MCC. The actions of HOGPI were not yet properly recognised by those in power as harassment, for which there ought to be zero tolerance in any rights-respecting society.

In retrospect, it took so much energy to just get the basics sorted, to undermine the legitimacy that HOGPI somehow had accrued, and which allowed people to look away. It can take an exorbitant amount of tiime to get human beings to just do the decent thing in part because, to varying degrees, everyone has been brain-washed in the tub of sexist dogma that it is okay to abuse women and trivialise their issues.

So, it's crucial to have your basic stress management skills relatively well sorted, otherwise you will never find the stamina you need, nor survive the vertigo-inducing merry-go-rounds, the brick walls you hit, and the crushing misogyny.

Naivety and hope defined my advocacy, and I often thought of them as my weaknesses, but I would not have gotten anywhere without them. I remain reluctant to use the word 'strategy' in relation to my advocacy, but successful campaigns have to start somewhere, and I realise that this is where I started: being naïve enough to hope for change against the odds. Denying the haters the opportunity to deter me, meant I eventually found fellow travellers to join on the path of reform.

PART TWO

DECRIMINALISING ABORTION

CHAPTER 4

Lobbying to Nowhere

July 2001–2004

*We kind of sat back and waited for it to happen.
But it didn't happen. You've got to change more than
the rules. You've got to change the culture... to get people
to recognise abortion law reform as a right.*

JOAN KIRNER (2010)

After Steve's murder in 2001, I wrote, phoned, met with, and had ongoing discussions with both state and federal politicians and their advisers and made submissions to state government inquiries, including those likely to be concerned about the chronic targeting of women by religious extremists, and likely to take seriously what we considered the best solution: a state legislated abortion buffer zone.

Similar to my failed efforts with MCC, while this could be termed 'lobbying', my lack of nous and lack of an advocacy team with a politically smart captain meant 'lobbying' would be a misleading term. My efforts were generally spasmodic and un-strategic. Despite our best efforts in the weeks after Steve's death, and followed up by various means over weeks, months and years, our entreaties to the offices of Premier Steve Bracks, Attorney General Hulls and key government ministers (some of whom were pro-choice women) were in the main dodged, handballed or ignored. To use a term from John W. Kingdon's (2011) seminal work *Agendas, Alternatives, and Public Policies*, I was a 'quaint irrelevancy' (p 16).

My quaint irrelevancy continued as I made submissions on behalf of the clinic to a raft of state government policies and strategies specifically focussed on women's concerns, but which neglected problem pregnancy and abortion. Our 1 March 2002 submission to the Department of Premier and Cabinet, Office of Women's Policy's Discussion Paper, *Valuing Victoria's Women: Key directions in women's safety: A coordinated approach to reducing violence against women*, described our situation as:

> *A peculiarly female experience where women's right to go about their lives and make their own health and vocational decisions is publicly challenged and threatened… a blatant violation of women's rights to privacy, respect and safety in accessing health services… This matter requires a serious and urgent response from those charged with a duty of care to the women of Victoria…*

Our 1 November 2004 submission to the Public Health Legislation Review: *Review of the* Health Act 1958: *A new legislative framework for public health in Victoria*, asked for the inclusion of legislation ensuring access to health clinics be kept clear of protesters and their paraphernalia, and noted:

> *Given the protesters 'right to life' agenda, health clinics or hospitals providing hospice care to the dying, fertility treatment, treatment based on stem cell technology, and so on, might also be targeted.*

Our 2004 submission to *The Vic Health & Department of Human Services (2004) The Health Costs of violence: Measuring the burden of disease caused by intimate partner violence*, stressed that:

> *Women with a history of violence attempting to access abortion providing services, face revictimisation… For the benefit of public health and to address inequalities, the review could bolster and clarify nuisance or duty of care provisions to exclude protesters from within 50-100 metres of any health service, without unreasonably restricting their right to protest elsewhere.*

A 2004 submission to the *Discrimination in the Law Discussion Paper* drew attention to:

> *Discrimination against women trying to access abortion-providing clinics in this state… a possible solution… adversely affects women…*

Mere months after Steve's death, the Victorian Department of Human Services' *Victorian Women's Health and Wellbeing Strategy Discussion Paper*, at least dot-pointed: 'effective, affordable contraceptives' and 'access to safe and legal terminations of pregnancy' (p.4). The Ministerial Advisory Committee membership read like a who's who of Melbourne feminists and included my revered PhD Supervisor and Professor Jill Astbury, Women's Health Victoria CEO Marilyn Beaumont, and MP Jacinta Allen. Our 13 February 2002 submission to Strategy Chair the Honourable Caroline Hogg, included a range of women's reproductive health and fertility control issues and:

> *Issues of violence against women, emotional and mental health, and access to services... women face heckling and harassment in their attempts to access abortion providing clinics... psychologically and physically harmful, especially when targeting people already feeling vulnerable and in a high state of anxiety associated with the stressors of facing an unplanned pregnancy, operation, or health-related medical or counselling consultation. High anxiety levels may increase the physical pain women experience during or following examination and surgery... In some areas of the United States, 'bubble' legislation has been enacted... abortion continues to be the only lawful surgical procedure in the Criminal Code rather than in the Health Act.*

All of our submissions fell on deaf ears. Our concerns did not even rate a mention. Nada. I thought I had just been pointing out the obvious: a serious problem for women—*and* a solution. The solution was about doing the decent and sensible thing. Melbourne was meant to be a modern vibrant city full of equal opportunity. With Labor in power, EMILY's List's ex-premier Joan Kirner as its matriarch, and EMILY's List women sitting in ministerial positions and on the back benches, such purposeful oversight and invisibility was bewildering, demoralising and infuriating. How could safe access to abortion not be recognised as a matter crucial to women's lives and health? How had Lou and Janice put up with this official ostracism for all the years they had run the clinic?

Maybe I'd become a rat bag and lost my manners. Become a vexatious letter writer and phone caller. Maybe I had misunderstood feminism and the meaning of being pro-choice. Maybe the words 'problem pregnancy, abortion, family planning', were figments of my imagination. The thousands of women who consulted the clinic each year were merely a hallucination on my part. I was mistaken in my belief that women's control of their reproduction was at the core of women's experience, capacity and relationships. I had become yet another hysterical, neurotic, mad woman who was also a 'quaint irrelevancy'?

Jill Astbury's (1996) book *Crazy for You* is a powerful historical examination of the physical and mental health costs to women of institutional silencing, belittling and pathologising of women and their experiences of hardship, abuse and exclusion. (Women are not alone, of course, in being harmed for being an 'other', that is, not a white heterosexual male.) Now, in the 2000s in a modern multicultural democracy like Australia, women and women's issues were still being relegated.

I had little idea about the workings of our state government and representatives. Was the inertia and apathy from state government and other authorities out of fear of offending the Catholic Church? Fear of the inevitable push back by the Church and the extremists, and the cost to authorities prosecuting that legal fight? Conflating the extremists' chronic harassment with 'protest' and fearing any action would jeopardise the protest rights of others? Fear of being tainted with the stain of abortion at the ballot box? Blatant, plain old sexism and misogyny that relegated key women's issues to the unimportant tray? All of these, or something else entirely? I was not a political animal. I was a Clinical Psychologist trying to do her best by her patients. None of it made any sense to me. Authorities, even supposedly pro-choice authorities, with the duty and power to protect women, instead ignored, silenced and trivialised our situation.

Past Labor Minister, Emily's List founding member and Upper House MP Candy Broad, whose 2007 private members bill ultimately led to the successful 2008 bill decriminalising abortion, *is* a political animal. Candy recently provided insights to me about our ignored submissions and advocacy:

> At the October 1999 Victorian election, the Steve Bracks-led Labor Party won government, defying expectations of a Kennett government return. I was a Minister where everything had to be negotiated in an Upper House comprising 14 Labor, 13 Liberal and 3 Independent.

In 2002 the Bracks government was returned with a landslide and a slender majority in the upper house. Expectations went through the roof, including the matters you had been making submissions about. Despite sky-rocketing expectations for the second term, there was absolutely no change through those seven years in relation to women's sexual and reproductive health rights. It was not possible to have it discussed in cabinet. The policy was clear, but there was no mechanism for that to be addressed through government. It wasn't on the agenda, full stop.

Given Candy's Ministerial experience governing with such a delicate balance in the Upper House, and governing by a party with a pro-choice policy but a refusal to discuss that policy in cabinet, rather than the questions I was asking, Candy considered:

There is a wider question to ask: Why do political parties end up with parliamentary representatives who are not representative of the make-up of the political party on these questions of public opinion? Research [at that time] consistently indicated that more than 70% of people supported abortion decriminalisation and safe access to abortion.

Oblivious to our unique political context at the time, but forever wary and mindful of the power and harms of sexism towards women, in November 2003, two years after Steve was killed, I went to the top of Victoria's feminist tree: Labor and EMILY's List matriarch, Joan Kirner.

Joan came back to me with the names of a variety of MPs she recommended I contact: Lisa Neville, Carolyn Hirsch, Joint Sec Labor Women's Caucus Helen Buckingham, President ALP Policy Committee on Women's Affairs Melanie McGrath, Office of Women's Policy Director Fiona Sharkie, 'Rhonda for Julia Gillard' (well that was the only pathetic note I made, but when that someone turns up years later as Australia's first—and so far *only*—female prime minister, then it deserves to be noted), Minister for Women's Affairs Mary Delahunty, Labor Women's Caucus Joanne Duncan, and Health Minister (from 2002-2007) and the clinic's Local MP Bronwyn Pike. Some we already had contacted and some we didn't even try to meet, but throughout 2004, meetings, phone calls, precis of problem and solution ensued with some of the honourable MPs on

Joan's list. One of our doctors, Dr Kathy Lewis, was a welcome addition to a couple of these meetings.

The clinic came to MPs with a problem, but we came with the solution too. Rebecca Dean's article, *Abortion in Australia: Access versus protest*, had been published in the 2004 *Journal of Law & Medicine*, and gave credibility to both the problem and the solution. Buffer zones would involve EMILY's List politicians doing what I expected they held dear to their hearts: legislating to protect and bolster women's rights.

But a notable avoidance and apathy continued to surprise us. Health Minister Bronwyn Pike seemed diligent and sincere in her active interest over several years, but it all came to nought. How could women copping harassment accessing an essential health service not spark a more active outrage in EMILY's A-Listers? Candy's activism in the Labor Party had focused on women's rights and affirmative action, including reproductive rights, with the expectation that:

> If women achieved parliamentary representation then it would be possible to address reproductive rights. That didn't happen. I had been a member of the Women's Policy Committee but it was not happening at the parliamentary level, or even when Labor was in government.

As first and only female Victorian premier, Joan Kirner's 2010 reflections are salient:

> When we worked hard in the Labor Party to get the affirmative action rule [in 1994] which would bring the number of progressive women into Parliament, we needed to make women's issues political issues and to shift them from women to the whole community. We kind of sat back and waited for it to happen. But it didn't happen. You've got to change more than the rules. You've got to change the culture… to get people to recognise abortion law reform as a right.

But changing culture can be incredibly difficult. People can agree in principle with a proposal but need to be pushed into actually taking action. It usually involves challenging dominant patriarchal structures and male-biased groupthink rotten with both intentional and unintended sexism (or other 'isms' like racism). Entitled white men still dominate positions of power. Creado

Perez (2019) uses extensive evidence to point out, with a generous politeness, the blatant sexism towards women and discrimination against women that is deeply embedded in so-called 'democratic' legislatures, including our own:

> *Democracy is not a level playing field: it is biased against electing wom-*
> *en... Women lead different lives to men because of both their sex and their*
> *gender. They are treated differently. They experience the world differently,*
> *and this leads to different needs and different priorities... a male-domi-*
> *nated legislature will therefore suffer from a gender data gap that will lead*
> *it to serve its female citizens inadequately. (pp 271-2)*
>
> *There are substantial gender data gaps in government thinking, and*
> *the result is that governments produce male-biased policy that is harming*
> *women... female perspective matters. (p 265)*
>
> *The evidence is clear: politics as it is practised today is not a female*
> *friendly environment. This means that while technically the playing field*
> *is level, in reality women operate at a disadvantage compared to men. This*
> *is what comes of devising systems without accounting for gender. (p 281)*

In addition, of course, the right to abortion may violate a potent male-biased norm of womanhood: the imperative of maternity and control by men. For this reason women's right to abortion may not be embraced as the feminist and human rights imperative that it is for promoting female autonomy.

We were continuing our muddled push for safe access when, in late 2004, the Offices of Attorney General Rob Hulls, Health Minister Bronwyn Pike, and Women's Policy all wriggled onto the same page: the clinic was expected to apply to the Supreme Court for an injunction against the extremists and utilise local police in the meantime.

We were aware that the Women's Hospital had a permanent injunction against anti-abortion extremists. Apparently that injunction was against Right to Life and specific people named in the schedule to a Supreme Court of Victoria order made on 20 July 1992. After speaking with the Hospital's in-house Legal counsel, Elizabeth Kennedy (now adjunct Associate Professor who continues to hold senior roles in health law), I understood the Hospital's situation to be quite different from the clinic's: a large public hospital where extremists trespassed on hospital property, were arrested by police, and faced significant legal and police clout; whereas the clinic was a small private hospital where the mischief occurred on a public footpath and where police 'balancing of rights' meant arrest was almost unheard of—unless there was a murder.

The clinic's own legal advice sought by Lou just a few years earlier had been pessimistic about seeking a Supreme Court injunction: lengthy, expensive, likely unsuccessful, and probably impracticable. This advice would be reinforced again in 2011 by the clinic's then learned counsel, and ultimately yet again in 2018 by High Court Justices' brief comments on the subject as they heard the safe access challenge.

Lou's 'Waste of time, Susie A' verdict on an injunction was also informed by what he knew of a NSW case occurring in the early 1980s which had attained abortion folklore status. It involved a serial harasser of women who, thanks to a bout of legal jiu jitsu, nearly ended up getting his hands on patients' medical files. Rebecca Dean (2006) subsequently detailed the facts of the case (Pre-term v Darcey [1983]) for the clinic:

In 1983 Pre-term, a NSW abortion providing clinic launched legal action against Patrick Michael Darcey, a man who protested outside the clinic and had also entered the clinic car park to take down patient licence plate numbers. The clinic sought an injunction against Mr Darcey creating a nuisance in relation to its premises by watching and besetting those premises and by hindering and impeding persons entering and leaving them.

Mr Darcey responded by issuing a subpoena on the clinic to produce all its records relating to abortions which had been carried out at the clinic for an identified period... the names of the persons upon whom abortions had been performed, their case histories, referrals and medical examinations, receipts from the Commonwealth and the health funds and payments made to doctors and others in relation to those abortions.

The clinic appealed to the Court to set aside the subpoena, however Waddell J refused to set it aside ruling the documents could arguably be relevant to a defence that the activities which the plaintiff sought to protect in the proceedings were themselves unlawful... the Plaintiff was forced to discontinue proceedings rather than hand over the documents.

The clinic pursued an alternative legal route by accusing Mr Darcey of trespassing on clinic land without lawful excuse of defence which is an offence under s4(1) of the Inclosed Lands Protection Act 1901.

Mr Darcey issued an identical subpoena to that issued in the previous discontinued proceeding. However, this time the clinic's application to have the subpoena set aside was upheld by Hunt J on the basis that 'there is no suggestion that a prosecution under the Inclosed Lands Protection Act, s4, can be defended by showing the premises were being used for an unlawful purpose' (at 501). Additionally Hunt J found that the clinic's application to have the subpoena struck down was supported upon the basis that the issue was not bona fide, that Mr Darcey, as someone who does not accept the legality of therapeutic abortions, intended to use the information which he obtained from the documents produced in answer to it in order embarrass the persons whose names were thereby disclosed... In so far as he hoped simply to find material in the documents which he could use in cross-examination of the prosecution witness, it was a fishing expedition of the worst kind, and it is obvious that the invasion of the private rights of the patients whose documents were involved far outweighed the need for such documents to be produced for that purpose: Waind v Hill [1978] 1 NSWLR 372, at 382 (at 502).

Although the subpoena was struck out, the charge against Mr Darcey was ultimately dismissed because the magistrate was not satisfied beyond reasonable doubt that Mr Darcey had actually entered the premises.

Yep, 'Waste of time, Susie A,' said Lou.

As to the advice to utilise local police, we already utilised local police, far too often. It was a lose-lose-lose move. Police attendance was distressing to our patients, their companions and staff; a waste of police resources; not a good look; and didn't change a thing. What is the definition of insanity again?

I pushed back at the government politicians, explaining our pessimism about the suggested courses of action, and asking that buffer zone legislation be reconsidered given its proven track record overseas. Both the Attorney General and Health Minister referred to the complexity of balancing protester and patient/staff rights. That old furphy. The Office of Women's Policy did not respond. I made an optimistic note—the result of my personality flaws of naivety, hope, and denial I guess—that the lines of communication were still open with the Attorney General and Health Minister Bronwyn Pike.

My uncanny political insights were, well, not canny. One minute, 2 March 2005, Health Minister Bronwyn Pike was in the local *Melbourne Times* newspaper deploring the antics of anti-choice protesters and suggesting bubble zone legislation. Less than a fortnight later, 15 March 2005, Bronwyn's adviser was advising me of the new party line: Before abortion buffer zones would be considered, the clinic must take out a Supreme Court injunction, *and* abortion must be de-criminalised. No biggie. Easy-peasy. Like that's been done before. I was realising that politicians are not inherently moral or logical but must be *forced* to act. But I didn't know how.

> *None of our legal advice has suggested that removing abortion from the Crimes Act is necessary for, or would improve the chances of, bubble zone legislation. The legal and practical issues are quite separate. Bubble Zone legislation is about ensuring women can access a health service without various human rights being violated.*
>
> *The probability of removing abortion from the Crimes Act appears to be less likely and more difficult than the introduction of bubble zone legislation. To have to wait on such a change is in my view delaying unnecessarily the serious responsibility the community owes to ensuring the safety and well-being of women in Victoria as they access a health service.*
>
> LETTER TO HEALTH MINISTER BRONWYN PIKE
>
> 5 APRIL 2005

None of my arguments were news to the Minister's office, but I put them in writing anyway. The day before I wrote that letter, a Magistrate had ruled against extending an intervention order taken out by our two security guards against one of the extremists. It was yet another instance where usual legal remedies did not provide a workable solution. Safe access zones legislation was the only viable option. Why didn't anyone want to get this?

This political argument of the early 2000s, that an abortion safe access zone could only happen *after* abortion decriminalisation in Victoria, would eventually be contradicted by the experience of other Australian states:

Victoria and The Australian Capital Territory (ACT) both would decriminalise abortion *before* legislating abortion safe access zones. Victoria would decriminalise abortion in 2008 and *then* successfully introduce 150-metre safe access zones in November 2015. The ACT decriminalised abortion in 2002 *then* in 2016 would pass laws to allow for 'protected areas', 'sufficient to ensure the privacy and unimpeded access for anyone entering, trying to enter or leaving an approved medical facility' which were updated in September 2018.

But New South Wales and South Australia would completely reverse the abortion decrim-safe access zones order: the NSW 2018 Public Health Amendment (Safe Access to Reproductive Health Clinics) Bill would provide for a 150-metre 'safe access zone' *before* NSW decriminalised abortion in 2019. South Australia enacted the Health Care (Safe Access) Amendment Bill on 20 November 2020 and decriminalised abortion in March 2021.

Tasmania would take a different chronological path. Building on other states' abortion decriminalisation and on Victoria's abortion safe access advocacy, Tasmania would earn the honour of becoming the first Australian state with abortion safe access zones by *simultaneously* providing for 150-metre safe access zones *and* decriminalising abortion in its Reproductive Health (Access to Terminations) Act 2013. At the time I passed on everything I had from our buffer zone lobbying to Women's Legal Service Tasmania CEO Susan Fahey, FCC made a supportive submission to the bill and FCC Dr Kathy Lewis, who ran an FCC abortion clinic in Tasmania, spoke with Tasmanian parliamentarians. I will be forever grateful to Susan Fahey for returning the favour during our safe access zones legislative campaign. Tassie paved the way for Victoria by enacting a 150-metre 'safe access zone'. In contrast to the relatively convoluted definitions of US 'buffer' and 'bubble' zones and the negative and extremist-centric perspective of an 'exclusion' zone, the term Tasmania used—'safe access zone'—clearly kept women and their safety as the legislative focus. I wished I'd come up with the term! The 150-metre boundary provided an unambiguous precedent.

But back in 2005, the prevailing political, and perhaps legal, view saw merit in prioritising decriminalising abortion.

It makes sense to me that you had to have the decrim first. That was the first step because until it was decriminalised you weren't going to get that buy-in to address this particular barrier to access, the footpath harassment of women. First you have to justify there being access, and the decriminalisation was that. Then once you've done that then, yes, abortion is legal, but what are the barriers to access? And they were significant. Working at the clinic you saw how significant they were when women came in and they were just distraught, and you heard about the protestors going after the children as well. It was disgusting, just disgusting.

REBECCA DEAN (2020)

With 2020 hindsight, the Victorian Attorney General and Health Minister were right. The abortion decriminalisation and Supreme Court legal action package was pretty close to what it took to finally persuade our legislature to commit to securing abortion safe access zones. Victoria's Parliament would decriminalise abortion in 2008 and, instead of the clinic seeking an injunction in the Supreme Court, the clinic would sue Melbourne City Council in the Supreme Court in 2015. Although it need not have been like this, clarity about the legality of abortion would ultimately strengthen and streamline the Victorian Attorney General's arguments in the challenge to safe access zones in the High Court (Walker, 2019).

But sitting in my Fertility Control Clinic office back in early 2005, I don't know which would have been more depressing: believing as I did that the government's precondition was impossible to meet or knowing then that securing safe abortion access would take an abortion decrim, a Supreme Court action and another ten years.

Did I feel I had failed at this point? Failed our patients? Our staff? Failed Lou? Yes. Did Lou believe I'd failed? Maybe. Did Janice and Susan believe I'd failed? Never. There would be plenty of these times to come, times of being weighed down by failure, times over the course of this saga that I felt I'd let down everyone. Lou never spoke in those terms, but I'm sure he felt it too. Could we have done things more effectively at that time? Probably. Maybe.

But was the failure really ours to wear? Powerful others were failing miserably too. Both MCC and the state government were failing women and letting us down badly. Our society was failing women. What else was new?

Through those times of feeling demoralised, Janice, Susan and my family were the cheer squad that kept me going, and Janice would keep Lou going:

> *I don't know how many times I said to Lou, we've got to make an effort, we can't just sit back and not try to do something. Here we were, a private organisation, as small as us. We weren't a huge Marie Stopes International. We were just a small private service for women. But Lou was prepared to go the extra mile. He put in when he needed to, and he was happy for you to do what needed to be done, Suse.*

JANICE NUGENT (2020)

In our 2005 world, Health Minister Pike's office was being pressured by groups concerned that buffer zone legislation would set a precedent for similar limits on their right to protest (e.g. animal liberationists). Concern about access zones infringing on protest rights of other groups was neither new nor minor. This concern was evident even in the days and weeks following Steve's murder, when various pro-choice groups rallied, including the Socialist Alliance and the Pro-Choice Coalition. They demonstrated at the Victorian Parliament House urging legislators to remove abortion from the criminal code, but deliberately missing the importance of ensuring women were kept safe from anti-abortion extremists. A public meeting held in NSW by Women's Abortion Action Campaign, *How will we defend abortion rights?* expressed concern that abortion buffer zones may lead to others' protest rights being curtailed. Radical Women, who 'defended' the clinic each month on a Saturday, was also against safe access zones and believed that 'direct action' was the only way to address the harm from anti-abortion religious zealots.

> *In response to the pressure being applied on your office by small interest groups, bubble zone legislation is legislation which: very specifically applies to women's health clinics; addresses… violence against women; stands up for women's right to choose and to access safe abortion services; and addresses*

a situation of chronic harassment of women, their families and staff. Such specific legislation would be overwhelmingly supported by the community, not just amongst the 80+% of the community who are pro-choice, but I suspect also amongst many who are anti-abortion… happy to speak with any group… so that they could appreciate our unique and unacceptable situation and be reassured about the specific and essential intent of such legislation.

LETTER TO HEALTH MINISTER BRONWYN PIKE

5 APRIL 2005

The solution was simple. The solution was common sense. What were people waiting for? Just do it.

I have contacted the Women's Legal Service and PILCH [Public Interest Law Clearing House], but both these organisations will not take us on because we are a private organisation, even though I reckon we are doing this for the women and families of Victoria. I've attached some comments.

We are still following up private lawyers who might have the woman-centred insight necessary to really get this issue. Yes, there's a whole string of legal tactics but really only to get it out there and put more pressure on the government to do something?

The anti-choice groups would delay and confound and subpoena and god knows what if we tried for a Supreme Court injunction—we'd be there 'til kingdom come and then some and the RC church's coffers would still be full and the clinic would be closed down. The RWH [Royal Women's Hospital] could not cope on its own—abortion access for women would be a pipe dream.

Canberra can get what it wants without having to do anything—just wait while the State does nothing. Legislation is the only way to go.

Ho hum same old same old. We'll plough on but…Where are the EMILY's List pollies? Where are the men and women concerned about women and families? Where are the pollies concerned about workplace bullying? Where is anybody who gives a…?

So that's how we're going.

EMAIL TO BRONWYN PIKE'S MINISTERIAL

ADVISER, 27 SEPTEMBER 2005

A shameful dummy spit from me in response to a kind query about how we were faring. My dummy spits were a barometer of the distress of our patients, staff, and me. An hour later I sent a sincere *mea culpa*.

My reference to Canberra getting what it wanted without having to do anything, spoke to the extraordinary politics at the time. It is worth detailing here the federal abortion politics of 2004-07, because arguably they uniquely influenced Victorian advocacy for abortion decriminalisation, and abortion decriminalisation was now apparently a prerequisite for achieving safe access zones.

Although abortion law rests with state governments, federal politics became entangled with women's access to abortion during the 12-year reign of Prime Minister John Howard's coalition government from 1996 until 2007. Howard's government signalled a sharp right turn into extreme religious right politics (Maddox, 2005). Progressive 'small L' liberals lost out to 'conservative Christian' politicians whose archaic, radical ideas about women (and others who were not white entitled men) were anything but conservative, and certainly were not progressive or kind. In my view they were radical 'Christians' who deserved to have their Christianity put into ironic and questioning quotation marks. They sure did not seem to be following the path mapped out by Jesus. Jesus Christ!

Arguably, religious right ideology still dominates the federal Liberal party today. The 'Vatican rules' leadership of Tony Abbott may have been usurped by a *happy clappy* religious leader, but both are just as far out there in terms of white male entitlement. Various feminist writers, for example, Barbara Baird, Marion Maddox, and Erica Millar provide insightful and frightening analyses of religious right governments' anti-women policies, including their links to a pro-baby-making 'anxious white nationalism' (Millar, 2015).

As Federal Minister for Health and Aging from 2003 until the end of 2007, 'mad monk' Tony Abbott appeared to be both blind to, and proud of, his blatant sexism and ignorance when it came to women and abortion and prosecuted a war against both.

As an ambitious politician, I had never had the slightest intension of be-coming a morals campaigner. Shortly after becoming the health minister, though, I'd been asked to justify Medicare funding for up to 75,000 abortions every year. It was a question that compelled an answer. The first instalment, delivered in March 2004 as a speech entitled 'The Ethical Responsibilities of a Christian Politician' distinguished between deploring the frequency of abortion and trying to re-criminalise it.

TONY ABBOTT (2009, P.180)

It is gratifying that such comments would likely attract widespread rebuke if made today, but at the time, Abbott was a powerful politician. To give some perspective to that time and Abbott's view that he was 'compelled' to answer the abortion 'question', it is worth noting that the government's Australian Institute of Health & Welfare (AIHW, 2008, p.248) figures indicated that 75,000 abortions would have comprised a mere 15% of the approximately 500,000 Gynaecological procedures carried out nationally in 2006-07. Total procedures in Australian public and private hospitals in 2006-07 came in at around 14 million. That means that Abbott was 'deploring' an inexpensive day procedure that comprised a mere 0.5% of all Australian hospital procedures.

Why not deplore instead the leading cause of death worldwide—cardiovascular disease. In Australia in 2006-07 (AIHW, 2008, p.248), there were almost 600,000 cardiovascular system procedures (affecting more men than women) and requiring more costly procedures and hospital stays. Where was Health Minister Abbott's outrage about this, and plans for improving the nation's diet, physical fitness and medical care?

I certainly share the concerns that many people have about the number of abortions that are taking place in Australia today. We have something like 100,000 abortions a year, 25% of all pregnancies end in abortion and even the most determined pro-choice advocates these days seem to be rightly concerned at the way that the abortion epidemic has developed.

TONY ABBOTT, ABC LOCAL RADIO,

1 NOVEMBER 2004

Most people in their ignorance, and health professionals who should have known better, agreed with Abbott's abortion myth of an epidemic of abortions and that everyone would like to see the number of abortions come down. Prime Minister John Howard chimed in declaring that Australia's abortion rate was too high. Disagree with the notion at your peril. It was the old politics of wedging-your-opposition and don't let facts get in the way of a good argument or policy. I decided that Health Minister Abbott was seriously afflicted with womb envy.

The silencing stigma of abortion made for rampant abortion illiteracy and ready gullibility by all and sundry to anti-choice myths. In an otherwise pro-choice 2007 article in *The Age*, Melinda Houston, was suckered into the false facts and rhetoric, declaring 'everyone agrees... a good thing if there weren't tens of thousands of abortions... Few (if any) who decide to terminate a pregnancy, ever fully put it behind them... traumatic... awful decision.'

Similarly, Susie O'Brien's 2007 article in *The Age*, an otherwise pro-choice piece about abandoned babies and the importance of sex education, deteriorated into language reflecting anti-choice propaganda, mythology and stereotypes: abortion was 'the best of a range of bad choices... the abortion rate is too high... not ready to be a parent... girls... young people'.

Rigorous longitudinal studies (David, and colleagues, 1988, 2003; Kubicka et al, 2003; and Sigal, 2004) indicated significant physical and psychosocial hardship for both mothers and children where women's requests for an abortion had been denied. Of course, women didn't need to look at rigorous studies to know this. Avoiding such hardship was the reason women decided on abortion. Our own evidence spoke to the fact that women would go to great lengths to do so: Lou's experience on Ward 1A, the arrival of women to the clinic the day after Steve's was murdered, and regional and interstate patients who surmounted a range of additional obstacles to attend us.

Tony Abbott's 2004 Adelaide University address set his anti-abortion discourse, and has been widely quoted ever since. Below are a few examples of what he said:

The problem with the Australian practice of abortion is that an objectively grave matter has been reduced to a question of the mother's convenience.

If half the effort were put into discouraging teenage promiscuity as goes into preventing teenage speeding, there might be fewer abortions, fewer traumatised young women and fewer dysfunctional families.

Abortion is the easy way out. It's hardly surprising that people should choose the most convenient exit from awkward situations.

No one wants to bring back the backyard abortion clinic or to stigmatise the millions of Australians who have had abortions or encouraged others to do so. But is it really so hard to create a culture where people understand that actions have consequences and take responsibility seriously.

This last quote about actions, consequences and taking responsibility provides an apt time to note that as a young man, Abbott basically walked away from his pregnant girlfriend while she endured the painful experience of relinquishing her child for adoption. It's not okay for a woman to 'walk away' from a pregnancy, but it's okay—although sad—for a man to walk away? In his 2009 biography, *Battlelines*, Abbott told this story as if it were a great love story where not bothering to use a condom was rather humorous and, unlike his statements about a woman choosing abortion for convenience, compassion took centre stage.

Kathy had been my first girlfriend. She was funny, clever, artistic and charismatic. At 19, we had been deeply in love. There was one problem, though. A part of me said that I should join the priesthood. So our romance was on-again, off-again and in the weeks when we were an item rather than 'just friends' we played what used to be called Vatican roulette.

One day, she tearfully announced that she was pregnant. For us, an abortion was out of the question. At first, we were going to be married. Then I got cold feet. I was too young and, frankly, too confused for that responsibility. She didn't think she could bring up a child on her own so she decided that the baby should be adopted. I had let her down, badly, so after the birth we went our separate ways. Still, we'd remained friends, stayed in touch and often wondered what would happen if our baby made contact. My reaction, I always felt sure, would be to 'dissolve into unmanly tears'.

In 2005, a year after his Adelaide University speech, Abbott had massaged both his anti-abortion language and the number of abortions—rounded up to a neat 100,000—in his address to Parliament:

I want to make it clear that I do not judge or condemn any woman who has had an abortion, but every abortion is a tragedy and up to 100,000 abortions a year is this generation's legacy of unutterable shame.

While purporting that he was not judging or condemning women, that's exactly what the Australian gaslighting Health Minister did. Over the years, Abbott's underlying anti-women, anti-abortion beliefs have been obvious in numerous cringe-worthy statements offensive to women. A small selection will suffice here:

What the housewives of Australia need to understand as they do the ironing is that if they get it done commercially it's going to go up in price.

SYDNEY MORNING HERALD, 9 FEBRUARY 2010

While I think men and women are equal, they are also different and I think it's inevitable and I don't think it's a bad thing at all that we always have, say, more women doing things like physiotherapy and an enormous number of women simply doing housework.

HERALD SUN, 6 AUGUST 2010

I think I would say to my daughters if they were to ask me this question... it [their virginity] is the greatest gift that you can give someone, the ultimate gift of giving and don't give it to someone lightly, that's what I would say."

THE AGE, 28 JANUARY 2010

I believe that there is a vast moral gulf which separates modern Australia from Nazi Germany. But can we be so sure that, under pressure over time, we will not slide down the same slippery slope. We only have to look at the abortion situation in this country.

AUSTRALIAN PARLIAMENT HANSARD
16 OCTOBER 1995

Abbott promulgated degrading, cruel and patronising versions of women. Women having abortions were: too young, just girls, irresponsible, too immoral, just to get out of an awkward situation... Abortions were: too many, too awful, too traumatic, too late in pregnancy, too convenient, an act of unutterable shame, a national tragedy... Victorian Liberal MP, Alan Cadman, was one of many right wing politicians who gleefully joined in Abbott's misogyny, 'I can't believe that women in this day and age are so dumb as to get pregnant willy-nilly' (*The Australian*, February 2005).

I knew who and what was really dumb. I knew who and what the real national tragedy was. I knew the facts: abortion was not traumatic, the problem pregnancy was the crisis and following the abortion the vast majority of women were relieved and got on with their lives; teenagers made up a tiny proportion of women accessing abortion; around 96% of abortions were early (prior to twelve weeks); the abortion rate was notoriously difficult to measure (Chan & Sage, 2005); and who says the number of abortions was too many—anti-abortion crusader Tony Abbott? In fact, the abortion rate reflected the number of women who chose abortion for good, moral reasons. Women had exactly the right number of abortions given the multiple unaddressed causes of problem pregnancy in our society.

But Abbott's opinions held more than a grain of truth for many people who, because of an abortion taboo and a pervasive societal sexism, were ignorant about the facts of abortion and well-practised at overlooking inherently offensive comments about women. Can you imagine the reaction if he suggested we reduce the incidence of heart disease by denigrating and publicly shaming heart patients, and cutting access to heart surgery and medication? If Health Minister Abbott wanted to reduce the number of abortions, then: stop violence against women; provide evidence-based sex education programs that include contraceptive knowledge (not 'Vatican roulette') and relationship skills like respect, consent and assertiveness; make contraception free; make equal pay genuinely equal and provide payment for all the 'unpaid' work of caring for children and others; change the workplace to truly champion work-children-life balance...

Women's Right to Choose – Again, the 2007 issue of *Women against Violence: An Australian Feminist Journal* showcased articles articulating the religious right's misinformation and gaslighting of women and abortion as a form of violence. Hayes (2007) provided a brilliant analysis of Abbott and the coalition's anti-choice discourse, concluding that it was designed 'to shame, blame and instil fear into women considering abortion' (2007, p. 27). Duvnjak & Buttfield (2007, p. 25) noted:

Underlying the argument that women are either in need of 'protection' (the women as victims of abortion argument) or education (women as 'ignorant

*fools') is, we believe, the very real fear that women, left to their own devic-
es, may indeed choose the 'selfish' route of an abortion or, indeed, a childless
life. Worse still, they may, without any moral dilemma, combine motherhood and abortion.*

Touché!

Tony Abbott was on the nose with many women. One of these was then Federal Senator Natasha Stott Despoja (elected to the UN Committee on the Elimination of Discrimination against Women in 2020) who as then Australian Democrats Leader had visited us one week after Steve was murdered. An impressive, kind and articulate woman, Natasha met with staff and then publicly championed buffer zones around abortion providers. Natasha would generously write about this tragic time in a hard-hitting foreword to *Murder on His Mind.* She would also write about the appalling treatment she faced by male parliamentarians, the media, and men in the community (Stott Despoja, 2019, pp 54-59, 81). I was saddened to hear from her that while happily pregnant in 2004, Natasha endured disgusting taunts from 'religious' right parliamentarians. A brand of Christianity similar to the clinic's footpath extremists, perhaps? Terminating? Continuing? Not really the point apparently. Natasha really should just know her proper place as a woman: home with her pinny on and getting the pipe and slippers ready for her lord and master.

But neither Natasha nor other women around Australia were sitting at home in their pinnies. Then Australian Democrats leader, Lyn Allison, was on her A-game in October 2005 when Health Minister Tony Abbott introduced a rather routine bill to amend the Therapeutic Goods Administration Act. Since 1996, the abortifacient RU486 had been the only 'restricted good' on the TGA's pharmaceuticals list under Health Minister Abbott's veto. Australian women had no access to medical abortion. Four senators, Lyn Allison (Australian Democrats), Judith Troethe (Liberal), Claire Moore (Labor) and Fiona Nash (Nationals) took the government by surprise by co-sponsoring a new bill, the *Therapeutic Goods Amendment (Repeal of Ministerial responsibility for approval of RU486) Bill 2005*, which successfully put control of

abortifacients back in the hands of the TGA in early 2006. Although for various reasons medical abortion would not become mainstream for Australian women until 2011.

Abbott and his anti-women crusade had been gazumped by four cross-party women. Women definitely were not going to take Abbott lying down.

Australian Democrats Senator Natasha Stott Despoja also fought against the government's radical anti-women, anti-choice agenda. With many other pro-choice organisations and individuals, I contributed to Natasha's 2005 private member's bill (introduced on 23 June 2005) to address the serious problem of 'false providers'. Anti-choice groups are mischievously skilled at creating confusion for women by commandeering pro-choice language as their own (e.g. 'woman-centred') and pro-choice sounding names for their free phone and face-to-face 'counselling' services (Allanson, 2007; Calo, 2007).

Free services are not captured by the Trades Practices Act 1974 which outlaws misleading or deceptive conduct and advertising. A woman accessed such services expecting, reasonably so, that she was the counsellor's client and that her needs and values would be prioritised. But the unambiguous agenda of such anti-choice organisations was that once conceived, a pregnancy was to be continued to term. In effect: the pregnancy was their client, not the woman; the 'life' and 'personhood' of the embryo or foetus had to continue, no matter the life or personhood, circumstances or wishes, of the pregnant woman; requests for referrals for abortion care were refused; and women were given frightening, harmful misinformation. I had picked up the pieces of too many women who had unwittingly fallen into the hands of anti-choice 'counsellors'.

The National Health & Medical Research Council's (NH&MRC) 1995 Draft Report, *An Information Paper on Termination of Pregnancy in Australia*, used the term, 'False providers' to describe anti-choice organisations purporting to provide pregnancy or post-abortion counselling to women. The term had been removed in the final NH&MRC 1996 report: the Howard-Abbott government succeeded the Keating Labor government in March 1996 and I expect the NHMRC was lucky to get a final version of the report out at all.

But Natasha's 2005 private member's bill and public consultations via a Senate Enquiry ensured widespread coverage of this anti-choice mischief to women. A revised version, *The Transparent Advertising & Notification of Pregnancy Counselling Services Bill 2006*, garnered cross-party sponsors: Democrats Natasha Stott Despoja, Liberal Judith Adams, Labor Claire Moore and Greens Kerry Nettle.

Meanwhile, to reduce the traumatic and tragic abortion rate, and I'm sure to teach his uppity, abortion-loving lady politicians a lesson, Health Minister Abbott knocked back tenders from reputable pro-choice organisations, and selected McKesson Asia Pacific and the Catholic Centacare agency to run his National Pregnancy Support Telephone Helpline. To repeat, a *Catholic* agency. In classic gaslighting speak, Abbott wrote:

At my instigation, the Howard government had introduced a new helpline to give more support to women facing an unexpected pregnancy. It seemed to be the best way to nudge the abortion rate down without affecting women's right to choose.

TONY ABBOTT, 2009, P 181

Minister Abbott also wielded his Medicare might to attack women's abortion access. In April 2006, the clinic shared its concerns with the Australian Medical Association (AMA), the Royal Australian & New Zealand College of Obstetricians and Gynaecologists (RANZCOG) and the Australian Psychological Society (APS) about the federal government's proposed *Pregnancy Counselling* Medicare Item. A formal policy paper distributed by Senator Santoro in mid-2005 to federal Coalition members, spelt out the eventual plan that all women wanting an abortion and wanting to be eligible to claim the abortion Medicare rebate, would be required to submit to the pregnancy counselling first and then a 72-hour waiting period before they could access an abortion.

This proposal contradicted best practice recommendations by the NH&MRC, the RANZCOG and other reputable organisations. It was a tactic straight out of the United States *ProLife* handbook and would stymy progressive abortion legislation by states and territories. It was frightening and plain wrong.

Over the years I was fortunate to receive encouragement from pro-choice members of my own professional body, the Australian Psychological Society (APS), like Heather Gridley and Associate Professor Grant Devilly. But the APS was not immune to the abortion political shenanigans in Canberra, when it made what looked like a Faustian deal with Health Minister Abbott: The government introduced both a revolutionary Better Access Medicare system of rebates for psychologists *and* the Pregnancy Counselling Medicare item number; while the APS provided the necessary online 'Non-directive pregnancy support counselling training' for psychologists and social workers. In line with Abbott's agenda, the training used anti-choice language and content that pre-empted a woman's own view of her pregnancy in favour of a 'right to life' version: the pregnancy was an 'unborn child', the partner in the pregnancy was the 'father', and the pregnant woman was the 'mother' and so on. 'Abortion' and 'pregnancy termination' were rarely mentioned and were associated with unfortunate and false characterisations of harm, pathology and good vs bad women. Even the term 'non-directive' counselling could not be equated to the term 'client-centred' which has a long history and usage in Psychology and should have been favoured in the training. Nor could 'non-directive' substitute for a woman-centred biopsychosocial crisis framework utilising effective psychological strategies and evidence-based sign-posting of risk and protective factors for women terminating or continuing a pregnancy (to parent or relinquish for adoption).

The APS eventually heeded my protests and input to make changes to the training, but it seemed impossible to remedy the potential harms. Fortunately, the uptake by health professionals was small. Ironically, by 2020 this Medicare item number had been reclaimed for women by skilled pro-choice and ex-Women's Hospital pregnancy counsellors in private practice.

Nonetheless, from 2009, the Howard-Abbott government was channelling millions of taxpayers' dollars to false providers, while reputable, expert pro-choice, pro-women organisations lacked funding. I was not alone in thinking it was time for a dummy spit:

The Church, the State and the Minister, *and* The Quest for Meaningful Help on the Other End of the Line *(The Age 6.1.07) were aptly titled. But like the abortion 'debate' both articles failed to feature the experiences or needs of those most affected—women facing an unintended, problematic pregnancy.*

The other day I was consulted by a refugee woman, still breastfeeding a child, in a marriage with a violent man and facing an unplanned pregnancy… This woman left intending to continue her pregnancy. Another woman in similar circumstances may well decide to terminate her pregnancy.

So, what do women need and want from a crisis pregnancy hotline?… an experienced person on the other end of the phone who efficiently, respectfully, non-judgementally and therapeutically prioritises that woman's experience, values and needs, provides pertinent information and reassures and directs the woman to the services she requests or needs.

My advice to Victorian women? The Royal Women's Pregnancy Advisory Service and Family Planning Victoria know how to provide women with what women want and need. But neither has the funds to run a 24-hour service—yet.

LETTER TO *THE AGE*
7 JANUARY 2007

Being chronically targeted by God-fearing, woman-hating extremists? No biggie. Having had a murder at our workplace? No worries. Being hand-balled around like a footy between local government, state government and police because no one wanted to do anything to ensure the safety and privacy of our patients and staff? Don't sweat the small stuff. But the fact that this was the quality of discourse from the Australian Health Minister was a smug, cruel joke on women that tipped me into a roiling, rolling dummy spit:

Before embarking on harsh judgements and cheap shots about 'convenience' when it comes to women who face an unintended and problematic pregnancy and decide to terminate that pregnancy, I wish you and your readers could walk a day in the shoes of the women who consult me at the Fertility Control Clinic. They are your readers' mothers, sisters, wives, girlfriends, partners, aunts and best friends. They are women facing a major crisis with the potential to turn their world upside down and jeopardise the welfare of their families or themselves.

They come to the clinic often with the proud support of their partners, family and friends, but sometimes in desperate secret and shame. They come because a woman's lot in Australia, compared with a man, is greater vulnerability to intimate partner violence, depression, poorer wages and job insecurity, and because when, or if, they become a mother (again) they want to be able to be the best parent they can be. They choose abortion because we do not have the 100% reliable, easy to use, affordable contraception and we are by our very nature ignorant, forgetful, passionate and imperfect.

But they also come because we have a federal health minister on an anti-choice crusade syphoning our taxes away from sex education, contraception and real support for women and their families.

LETTER TO *HERALD SUN*
8 JANUARY 2007

Tony Abbott's anti-abortion, anti-women crusade changed the landscape of federal abortion politics. In 2013, his misogynistic influence in this crucial area of women's health would be clear to our first female prime minister, Julia Gillard, who made another history-making move on behalf of women by calling out the Opposition leader and his party:

We don't want to live in an Australia where abortion again becomes the political plaything of men who think they know better.

ABC NEWS
11 JUNE 2013

I was unimpressed by 'feminist' voices that did not back PM Gillard:

Our prime minister is right to raise abortion as an important and gendered election issue. Abortion legislation is a state matter. But Medicare funding and PBS listing are federal government matters.

It is not at all ridiculous to conceive of an Abbott government removing the Medicare rebate for abortion, and blocking PBS listing of the medical abortion drug... Mr Abbott, and a disproportionate number of his colleagues, sit on the extreme religious right against women accessing abortion, contraception and sex education. I have heard nothing... to reassure me that they have any genuine understanding about the centrality of reproductive rights to the well-being and societal participation of women and their families.

> *Remove the Medicare rebate for abortion and women and their families are returned to the dangerous days when only wealthy women could access safe, timely abortion. 'Feminist' voices to the contrary are disappointing and naive.*

LETTER TO *THE AGE*

13 JUNE 2013

In October 2008, perhaps purposely timed to coincide with, and undermine, Victoria's parliamentary debate about decriminalising abortion, Health Minister Abbott was still at it with a Federal Inquiry into removing the Medicare rebate for later term abortion. Such a cut to abortion access would hit women facing the most difficult, saddest pregnancy circumstances and would have the most impact on those women with least financial means. During the frantic last-minute Victorian decrim lobbying and activity of those days, advocates had to find time to make submissions to this inquiry.

My submission was written with Dr Lachlan de Crespigny, the gentlest of men, most caring of doctors and an expert in post 18-week pregnancy terminations. Although I had been consulted by women experiencing this sad predicament, as a day procedure centre, the Fertility Control Clinic referred on the very small number of women presenting beyond 15–16 weeks gestation. I was probably relieved that on a day-to-day basis I had not had to wrestle with the complexity of such cases. In any event, that wrestle truly belonged to the woman concerned, and I just wanted to know that she received the best support possible.

In 2000 at the Royal Women's Hospital, Lachlan, with other colleagues, saved a woman's life by terminating her 32-week foetus (diagnosed with dwarfism). Liberal Senator Julian McGauran pursued his anti-abortion agenda by making this unusual and tragic case public. I will never understand how Senator McGauran came to have this woman's private health information, was allowed to bandy her private life about publicly, and yet was immune to any legal sanctions. In contrast, over several years, the doctors faced several investigations by the Hospital, Medical Board, Coroner, and Police (Nader, 2007). Lachlan and his colleagues eventually were cleared of any wrongdoing. The incident spoke volumes to the ambiguity of Victoria's Crimes Act abortion laws, and to the small number of desperate, complex cases at the pointy end of abortion care and women's experience.

Federal Health Minister Abbott was successful in getting his anti-women Pregnancy Helpline and non-directive counselling Medicare initiative—the first steps in his apparently grand plan to prevent women accessing abortion. But Health Minister Abbott's successes did not garner the compliant victims he had hoped.

Natasha Stott Despoja's *Transparency in Pregnancy Counselling Bill* was unsuccessful—it did not pass the Federal Parliament. But in concert with the success of Lyn Allison's cross-party bill removing the ban on RU486, the work of these two women and their cross-party colleagues was outstandingly successful. The 2006 Senate Hearing into Stott Despoja's bill revealed important truths about gaps and dangerous mischief in women's reproductive health care. Media coverage ensured that both women's health professionals and women themselves were wiser about their choice of pregnancy counselling services. A pro-choice voice from powerful cross-party women was heard loudly around the country providing role models and language validating women's reproductive experiences, decisions and right to both surgical and medical abortion. In the context of barriers to women accessing reputable, evidence-based healthcare and timely, affordable surgical and medical abortion, women's abortion rights were placed firmly on the nation's agenda.

Both Australian Democrats-instigated political campaigns were facilitated by pro-choice reproductive health advocate and ethicist Dr Leslie Cannold. Leslie and I originally met when we were both studying at the Key Centre for Women's Health in Society at Melbourne University where I was completing my PhD in Juggling. The successful cross-party bill removing the Health Minister's veto powers over RU486, and *The Transparency in Pregnancy Counselling Advertising* campaign set a new benchmark in cross-party collaboration between predominantly female politicians. Creating trust across usually competitive and mistrustful party lines can be difficult. But to stop harm to women, and with Leslie's smarts, the federal parliamentary sisterhood transcended traditional ways of functioning. Such a publicly vocal and popularly connected cross-party model would prove crucial to securing future state abortion rights.

Over the years, federal Democrats senators Natasha Stott Despoja and Lyn Allison and Liberal's Judith Troethe also transcended federal and state lines to visit the clinic and offer their wisdom and encouragement in our efforts to find a way to protect our patients and staff from religious zealots.

Tony Abbott had provoked a loud female-led pro-choice uprising around Australia. But in Victoria, Labor Premier Bracks was Catholic as was Attorney General Rob Hulls, whose wife was 'pro-life' lawyer Carolyn Burnside. Catholic women made up a large proportion of women having abortions (Allanson, 1994), and the majority of Christians and Catholics were likely to respect women's private decisions, but to be out there and public about abortion was an entirely different matter. No doubt for Rob Hulls, the old adage would apply: *happy wife, happy life.*

Greens MLC Colleen Hartland was in Parliament for 11 years, spanning both the abortion decrim and safe access zones. With a ready sense of humour and honest strength, Colleen became an ally and friend to me. Speaking with Colleen in 2020, she viewed Rob Hulls' long role as Victorian Attorney General, and the stigma surrounding abortion, as the major barriers blocking abortion decriminalisation and safe access zones:

> *You approached Rob Hulls. Our office did too. But he just didn't see it as an issue. He wasn't concerned. I think that goes along with the fact that his wife was a leading light in the right to life and he voted against the decrim bill. The wrong minister was in their for a long time. So that was a major barrier.*
>
> *The other major barrier was the stigma around abortion. People didn't feel that they had the right to complain about being harassed. If it was any other service and they were being harassed, then they would have felt capable of making a complaint, but because it was an abortion service they didn't feel that they could complain. The abortion stigma was so strong.*
>
> COLLEEN HARTLAND (2020).

None of this was promising for abortion law reform and perhaps reason for reluctance even from EMILY's List politicians. But other aspects of the political climate in Victoria suggested to Joan Kirner that the time to push abortion law reform was nigh. Joan was a consummate political performer and leader, both behind the scenes and out in front, with longstanding hopes and plans for abortion law reform.

I was to discover that for Joan, like so many others, 'abortion law reform' meant removing abortion from the Criminal code so abortion would be treated no differently to other medical procedures. Good. Great. Need that. But what about the rest? Sigh. Abortion safe access zones was not the big reform ticket item. A successful Victorian abortion decriminalisation would have to come first. Abortion safe access would be left on the shelf. There was still yet a hefty price to pay to elevate women to the status of persons.

Deep down, a part of me believed that if I just kept looking and kept on speaking up, I would eventually find the person whose job it actually was to solve this problem: a champion who knew what to do and would get the job done.

But politicians and institutions of power are rooted in deep-seated male-bias. They are sluggish and self-perpetuating. Individuals within them might say they are unbiased, moral and logical; they might say they stand for this that or the other and will take the fight on; but the reality is that they have to be forced to act, even when they know that action is needed and justified.

It's hard to think of an issue that exemplifies the idea of a political football better than abortion: a vitally important issue to women that most politicians and the public agree should be legal and safe, but which uniquely challenges patriarchal control over, and notions of, womanhood.

It was difficult at times to come to terms with this institutional reticence, especially after everything—the daily harassment, Steve's murder, women's distress, the decades of feeling under seige. It was a relief to find the occasional ally inside these institutions, but it was also clear that patient, polite advocacy, trying to get the people in authority to do the right thing was not going to cut it.

My work with the media and with women's organisations was a part of a growing movement that sought to challenge structural ideas that treated women as second class citizens. My little corner of that work was insufficient, but still necessary, tiring and fuelled by the inspiration of other women. So too, working with clinic patients always bolstered my advocacy resolve and stamina. Keeping in touch with your base reminds you of how much is at stake and what your work is really all about.

As we chased down each potential avenue for change, and the problem remained, it became clear that it wasn't enough for those in power to leave it to us. We were just one, relatively small, women's health service. We needed a coalition, a collective of advocates, to force the change we were seeking. Abortion is an issue that is personal and ostracised, so finding this coalition was hard. It needed to be built by key women and organisations. Maybe dummy spitting was the answer—finding others who were prepared to spit the dummy like me, and in doing so, put pressure on those holding power to act.

CHAPTER 5

Decriminalising Abortion

2004–December 2008

Her right to decide whether or not to bear a child... is central to a woman's life, to her well-being and dignity. It is a decision she must make for herself. When Government controls that decision for her, she is being treated as less than a fully adult human responsible for her own choices.

RUTH BADER GINSBURG (1993)

In 2004, three years after Lou decided the price was too high, leaders and advocates with the will and nous to ensure a cross-party legislative push for safe abortion access were not yet in position:

The Human Rights Law Centre (HRLC) was not even born yet. Emily Howie's credits were growing as she worked as Senior Associate with Allens Arthur Robinson and an associate to Justice Allan Goldberg on the Federal Court.

Maurice Blackburn legal dynamo, Lizzie O'Shea, was midway through her studies, stirring up trouble as the only genuine activist in the Melbourne University law school.

Dan Andrews, Jill Hennessy, Jenny Mikakos, Kris Walker, Claire Harris, Peter Hanks, Therese McCarthy, Susan Kiefer, Virginia Bell, Michelle Gordon... all yet to take their abortion safe access zones positions. The fireball of feminism and safe access zones that would be Sex Party MP Fiona Patten would not come along for another ten years. Fiona Patten was busy in Sydney as Chief Operations Officer of an internet adult sex company. She had resigned from her *Eros* CEO role and had already written, with Robbie Swan, *Hypocrits*, an expose on child sexual assault by priests. Fiona and Robbie called for a Royal Commission into child sexual abuse by religious institutions. Yep, that's the outrage, foresight and action we needed.

Meanwhile, my unsophisticated chipping away perhaps at least provided an occasional pro-women abortion voice and discourse in the clinical, political and public spheres. Eventually it led me to women who were sophisticated in the ways of advocacy, politics and the media. Standing on the shoulders of feminists who had come before, these women established strong pillars on which abortion safe access would be built.

The years 2004–8 were abuzz. Coinciding with the state government's advice that abortion safe access zones had to wait its turn behind abortion de-criminalisation, the clinic was advised of a Pro-Choice Coalition Meeting at Trades Hall on 18 November 2004. Curious to know what was going on, FCC Practice Manager Janice Nugent, Senior Counsellor June Dryburgh and I went along.

As old feminists working in an isolated and stigmatised area of women's health, our entrée into that meeting was a step into a delightful parallel universe. Instead of being vilified for our work, loud pro-choice voices were demanding that abortion be de-criminalised. Women expressed anger at Federal Health Minister Tony Abbott. The anti-abortion Howard-Abbott government's threats to abortion access and Medicare rebates had provoked outrage and action.

I had found Abbott almost too much to bear, he pushed me to the edge, a source of motivation that came from a place of boiling rage. But clearly I wasn't alone. Would the triumphalism and aggression of anti-choice voices end up being a precondition of their ultimate failure?

We would never have been as successful if we didn't have Tony Abbott. Because we had this incredibly anti-choice Health Minister, he was the one who got us mobilised, who got an entire nation of women alert and alarmed and very eager not just to defend their rights, but to actually push the agenda forward despite his resistance.

LESLIE CANNOLD (2010)

Following the Pro-Choice Coalition Meeting at Trades Hall, the Abortion Law Reform Association (ALRA) was resurrected by WHV and Joan Kirner's affirmative action/pro-choice Labor organisation, EMIILY's List. Political manoeuvrings were a mystery to me, although WHV CEO, Marilyn Beaumont, delighted in telling what it was like to have Joan Kirner phone her to say now was the time to 'have a conversation' about abortion law reform: 'When Joan Kirner calls, you jump' (WHV, 2010). Greens MLC Colleen Hartland was another to receive a 'classic phone call from Joan Kirner' (Hartland, 2020) and jumped into action. Colleen had already supported the clinic, and me personally, over many years. She and her Greens colleagues would be strong allies in securing both the successful abortion decriminalisation and ultimately the safe access zones legislation. Phone calls from Joan Kirner were no doubt jump-starting women's action across the political sphere.

Gideon Haigh's *The Racket* documents the first Victorian ALRA in 1968 when the likes of Gareth Evans, Peter Singer, Professors Carl Wood and Peter Brett, and Doctors Stan Gold and Sam Benwell, were amongst sixty others who adopted a constitution to press for abortion law reform:

> *ALRA's President was architect Bill Dye, and its committee included 25-year-old school teacher and novelist-to-be Helen Garner... [and] secretary Jo Richardson, a pretty Melbourne University undergraduate from a well-to-do family.*

Jo Richardson would later marry Bert Wainer and become Jo Wainer. Haigh notes that:

> *Most of the chief protagonists were men—it was perhaps the last exercise in female emancipation in Australia where this was so.*

> (HAIGH, 2008, P. 214)

The 2005 ALRA abortion decriminalisation campaign would be led, and won by, women. Women of the ALRA campaign were not bra-burning feminist radicals, but women who shared feminist ideals, held reputable positions in the work force, evinced a reasoned approach to the world, and our wardrobes wouldn't turn one head at a Sunday mass. Decriminalising abortion was not a radical thing to do. It was the sensible and right thing to do: update our laws to be consistent with current medical practices and societal expectations.

The battle *against* abortion law reform would not be won by so called 'Christians'. The pro-choice campaign had solid support from mainstream religion. The Young Women's Christian Association (YWCA) was in on the ground floor: fully behind abortion law reform; providing a venue for a forum in early February 2005; an integral member and backer of the 2007-8 ProChoiceVic successful postcard campaign; and giving a Christian tick of approval to abortion law reform. Sensible, mainstream Christians finally had a visible and viable alternative to the extreme anti-women rhetoric and bullying manner of the hard religious right.

The campaign also had support from other organisations including Liberty Victoria and the Public Health Association of Australia (PHAA). PHAA brought out a timely 2005 edition of its *Public Health Perspectives* entitled *Abortion in Australia* which provided much needed health facts and a reasoned voice for decriminalising abortion.

With other sensible women knowledgeable in the ways of abortion and politics, law and advocacy, I was invited to be part of ALRA. WHV CEO Marilyn Beaumont was the steady, can-do ALRA chair, with her hard-working assistant Kerrilie Rice. Grande Dame Joan Kirner toiled behind the scenes in capacities I had no idea about, her occasional attendance, charisma and advice always a morale booster. Jo Wainer's status as Bert Wainer's widow, involvement in previous law reform efforts and in earlier abortion provision and research rightly endowed her with media pull and capacity to open doors. Some gasps at Jo's occasionally more extreme language, but when you'd lived up close and personal with backyard abortion, *extreme* is just speaking the plain truth.

WHV's subsequent 2010 DVD, *It's about Choice: The Victorian Abortion Law Reform Story* provides interview excerpts from key players and a comprehensive list of all those involved in the campaign. My version below is just that: my own myopic and politically naïve version, and definitely not a roll call of campaign contributors. My abridged version speaks to the decrim campaign as a foundation from which the successful politics of safe access could spring—eventually.

The abortion law reform foisted politicians and campaigners into a bitter fight for women's rights that demanded soul-searching and emotional courage.

Victorian abortion law reform came with hefty public and private costs to our pro-choice parliamentarians as they confronted societal stigma, family secrets and intimidation from the (surely ironically named) 'pro-life' movement both within and outside Parliament. I expect that the public and personal costs to opponents of abortion decrim may have been almost as great, if not greater, given the eventual loss they suffered.

In a sense the abortion decrim blooded our pro-choice politicians for the safe access battle ahead. Except perhaps for the 2019 *Dying with Dignity Bill*, Victorian parliamentarians, especially women parliamentarians, would be unlikely to face another issue so personally and professionally testing. Seven years later, when finally the time came to secure abortion safe access zones laws, pro-choice politicians had already learnt their battle lessons well. They knew what to expect from extreme religious right institutions, groups and individuals, and trusted their party and cross-party pro-choice sisters and brothers. They had earnt seniority and displayed a steely determination and stamina. My advocacy was focused on the destination, but it was clear that sometimes the only way to convince people was for them to take a journey.

Before we reached that happy ending and new beginning, there would be this renewed and long campaign to decriminalise abortion, and a longer legal battle between one small clinic and the powerful Melbourne City Council.

It was a beautiful walk to Women's Health Victoria's (WHV) Abortion Law Reform Association (ALRA) meetings: through Melbourne's Fitzroy Gardens and along leafy Lonsdale street with its old world art deco buildings. I'd hasten my pace past the towering St Patrick's Catholic Church. Black and monstrous within its stark privilege, the place gave off a whiff of evil. Next door to WHV'S Lonsdale Street home, a little coffee shop provided a quick pick-me-up. Then up the lift, through the doors and down the corridor to the ALRA meeting room where seats around a long rectangular table were taken by exceptional and politically savvy women. Sometimes we were few in number, sometimes we were many.

I was nothing if not a diligent ALRA attender. But I was not politically savvy. I wasn't sure initially what I could offer. Academic, legal, political and strategic discussions played out while I quietly rued my ignorance, tried to keep up, and unvoiced questions nagged, embarrassed, and distracted me: *Who are they referring to? Is she a politician? But how would you do that? What does that word even mean?* and, *How does Kerrilie type all this so quickly and efficiently?* The last question was a complement to our minutes' taker and a reproach to my own overabundance of typing errors. So much of my precious *flexibility* was spent going backwards—to correct typos. Ah, life and its 'typos'.

Fortunately these exceptional and politically savvy ALRA women didn't know what was going on in my head. I was on my best behaviour, respectful, actively listening, looking intelligent? These smart women wouldn't have invited me in if I had nothing to offer. I must have something to offer. I was Dr Susie Allanson, clinical psychologist at the Fertility Control Clinic; a scientist-practitioner with an intimate understanding of the research/academic evidence and the day to day, practical and emotional experience of women having abortions, and of abortion providers.

And there it was. That was what I had to offer ALRA: the lived experiences, stories, and voices of women accessing abortion. Intrinsic to this was using a pro-women language, and facts/evidence to help inform the decrim strategy to counter anti-choice myths and misinformation that would be lobbed like grenades by opponents of abortion. I could leave the intrigue of politicking to others.

Personally and professionally, ALRA linked me to collaborative, generous, knowledgeable and strategic thinkers and advocates; broadened my political understandings; exposed me to different styles of leadership and team play; and buoyed me with pride and trust in a 'can-do' sisterhood of women.

ALRA was also another obligation, another trip to the city. ALRA was a slow burn over three years and another juggle. It was another one of Lou's 'Waste of time, Susie A', but accompanied by a shrug that meant, 'If you reckon, Susie A, give it a go.'

Candy Broad's 18 and 19 July 2007 first and second readings to the Victorian Legislative Council of her private member's Crimes (*Decriminalisation of Abortion*) Bill 2007 was a gutsy and defining moment.

The purpose of this bill is to ensure the provision of safe and competent health services to women having an abortion and bring legislation regarding abortion into line with community expectations by abolishing the offences of unlawful abortion in the Crimes Act 1958 and in the common law.

CANDY BROAD, SECOND READING SPEECH
VICTORIAN LEGISLATIVE COUNCIL, 19 JULY 2007

Candy had worked with Joan Kirner and others to establish EMILYs List and affirmative action in the Labor Party. Despite Candy's impressive credentials, her actions bringing this private bill courted hostility and danger politically and personally. Catholic Premier Steve Bracks was not alone amongst Candy's Labor party colleagues in not wanting abortion on the government's agenda. Plus, Candy had now walked into the sights of a movement of 'God's soldiers' who had murdered doctors in the United States, murdered our security guard Steve Rogers right here at home, and paradoxically were prepared to accept as collateral damage the deaths of pregnant women and the 'precious life' those women carried. It is one thing to speak with like-minded people about abortion rights and women's rights. It is another thing entirely to speak publicly and court the wrath of God-fearing terrorists. But Candy did.

There were differences of opinion and much cloak and dagger around the private member's bill strategy. I remember my chilling sense of that cloak and dagger when I arrived a little early for an ALRA meeting, turned the wrong way and ended up in a room where Candy Broad and Marilyn were in deep conversation. The plot thickened. Plans were afoot. I backed out of there quick smart.

Caucus would never vote to adopt a private member's bill. But the leader can decide, and give permission, to do it and advise cabinet that he has made that decision in his capacity as leader. Joan Kirner was incredibly persuasive and persuaded Steve Bracks to give that permission. But there were so many conditions attached: I wasn't allowed to talk publicly about the bill, so it had to be confined to a small number of people; I was not permitted to use the services of the parliamentary counsel, so that's where pro bono lawyers were just fantastic. A great many hurdles had to be overcome by being determined, finding a way, compromising, to keep the ultimate goal in view…

I had to work with women and some men who were prepared to work with those conditions. So usual collaboration just didn't apply. I was aware that some people worked for organisations that if their help became public could present issues for them. For example, Marilyn [Beaumont] was so supportive, generous, but also the CEO of Women's Health Victoria which was very dependent on the Victorian government for funding. Marilyn couldn't assume the Department [of Health & Human Services] would support WHV being involved with this private members Bill, or assume that Health Minister Bronwyn Pike supported it. Bronwyn Pike thought the way to decriminalise abortion was to codify the Menhennitt ruling and put that into the Health Act. That was the AG's view as well.

How were we going to do this when it came to talking to parliamentarians? Kay Setches, Jo Wainer, and Marilyn Beaumont came up with the idea of an organisation, ALRA, that would function purely for the decrim and then no longer exist. We spoke to parliamentarians by sending people, like Susie Reid, to electorate offices to have private conversations in the name of ALRA. This was very successful in gathering information and engaging with MPs.

When I was able to announce that I was introducing the bill, many MPs said, 'No one has spoken to me about this, how can I say what I think?' We reminded them that in fact they had spoken with ALRA about this. So we had a great deal of detailed information at that stage, but it was all done in a very siloed way… it was never seen as a collaborative approach, and it wasn't.

CANDY BROAD (2019)

Candy's voice and bill were bold, beautiful and they worked. Standing up in Parliament was a brave 'taking a stand' moment that provided a crucial model of courage subsequently taken up by other women (and some men) during the campaign and parliamentary debate. Candy had provided a voice to the silenced. Women could and would speak out about abortion.

For unrelated reasons, Premier Bracks resigned and handed the Premiership to Labor's John Brumby. Daniel Andrews was Health Minister. On 21 August 2007, Candy withdrew her private member's bill and newly installed Premier John Brumby referred the matter of abortion law reform to the Victorian Law Reform Commission (VLRC) to advise on models for a government bill decriminalising abortion. This was huge. Bracks had allowed the discussion to begin, but Brumby had given it the push it needed to become a real prospect. As Julia Gillard and Ngozi Okonjo-Oweala emphasise in their book, *Women and Leadership*, 'Men are not bystanders when it comes to women's *leadership*' *(2020, p. 106)*. Candy agrees:

> *The one thing no one foresaw was Steve Brack's resignation. Shortly after the 2006 election he informed me, after much work by Joan Kirner, he would allow me to do this... Much later, he stood up in caucus and said, 'I've given permission for this to happen', and there was a long gap between those two points in time.*
>
> *We ended up in that extraordinary situation where I had introduced the bill and it becomes the property of the House to decide what to do with it. And we have a new premier, John Brumby, and in his first week in office he had to decide. So the first thing I did was to go into the Upper House to seek permission for the vote to be delayed so he would have some time. Discussion went on at that time and cabinet backed it... That was a monumental shift. Certainly it was never possible to have that discussion in cabinet before... John Brumby made it possible. Everything changed in 2007, in the third term, when John Brumby took the helm. Cabinet made a decision to adopt a framework of decriminalisation in line with societal expectations, and the Victorian Law Reform Commission [VLRC] was asked to advise on how to do it, not if.*
>
> *I asked for permission from the Upper House to withdraw the Bill. It was a huge weight off my shoulders because I knew no matter how much work I and others had done, the limitations imposed were so constraining. The VLRC would be so much better resourced with a better framework and backing of cabinet. This now would have a so much better chance of not just succeeding but developing a really strong legal framework.*

It is chalk and cheese once you have a government bill. Even if some in the party have some reservations, they become more likely to support it through their loyalty, and it makes possible positive discussions with other parties. With a conscience vote you need to elicit that support.

CANDY BROAD (2019)

Lou was now fully committed to the decrim and we discussed our abortion decriminalisation submission with the VLRC Commission on 1 October 2007. We were impressed with the open mindedness and insight which greeted us. Our hopes for abortion decrim were buoyed.

Seven months later, 29 May 2008, I scrambled into Parliament House. With Greens MP Colleen Hartland, Leslie Cannold and others, I poured over the just tabled VLRC's *Law of Abortion: Final Report*. Seated around a large, polished table, we read and considered, discussed and cheered. The Report concluded that consent, safety, and other concerns around abortion were amply covered by existing legal, medical, ethical, professional and accreditation rules, regulations and guidelines applying to all medical procedures, and offered the government three slightly different law reform options. Effective abortion law reform was looking a real possibility.

Bright political minds started calculating votes and tactics. My bright eyes, but dull political mind, were drawn instead to the Victorian Law Reform Commission Report's final chapter, *Chapter 8 Other Legal and Policy Issues*, and its subheading *BUBBLE ZONES*. Yes, it was even in capitals. This section noted: the concern of several people about the safety and wellbeing of patients and staff being jeopardised by intimidation and harassment from protestors; the Women's Hospital's permanent injunction against Right to Life and people named in the schedule to a Supreme Court of Victoria order made on 20 July 1992; that Victoria Police can issue on-the-spot notices for breaches of Melbourne City Council by-laws for obstruction or public nuisance; the robust bubble or buffer zone legislation in British Columbia, Canada, and various areas of the United States; that 'bubble zone' legislation raises several complex and policy issues which fall outside the terms of reference'; and 'the Commission encourages the Attorney-General to consider options'. Woohoo!

As early as June 2003 we had written to then VLRC Chair Professor Marcia Neave about abortion buffer zone legislation. She had passed on our concerns to Attorney General Hulls and advised us to follow up with him— the round and round the merry-go-round. Now under VLRC Chair Professor Neil Rees, bubble/buffer zones had been considered in an official VLRC report. In the lobbying yet to come during the next seven years of advocacy for abortion safe access zones, I was grateful to garner additional credibility by referring countless times to the learned 2008 VLRC report. But it would take seven more years, so not quite the timely safe access triumph I had hoped.

But the decrim sailed on. On Tuesday 19 August 2008, Minister for Women's Affairs Maxine Morand introduced to the Victorian Legislative Assembly a bill 'for an act to reform the law relating to abortion, to amend the Crimes Act 1958 and for other purposes' and delivered her second reading speech. Lobbying for parliamentary members' conscience votes accelerated.

Still involved with ALRA, I had become more active with Leslie Cannold's ProChoiceVic. Following Leslie's successful facilitation of federal cross-party collaboration on abortion issues, she pursued a cross-party and grass roots campaign. Participants came from ALRA, state and federal politics, human rights, legal and health organisations, and the YWCA.

Both Lou and I were despondent about safe access but could detect the heady whiff of success with abortion decriminalisation. Lou agreed to the clinic as a venue for ProChoiceVic meetings, clinic staff for admin support, and bank-rolled setting up the ProChoiceVic website. Lou popped his head in at the meetings and then would leave us to it as Leslie cracked the whip, cajoled, ordered, smooched and harassed people till they toed the line and got it done.

The YWCA/ProChoiceVic provided T-shirts, and a postcard campaign that was an easy, effective way for constituents to convey their pro-choice wishes and support to politicians. The ProChoiceVic website was a sensational avenue for information dissemination, garnering grassroots support from the wider community, and directing easy email support and lobbying by constituents to their pollies. Although mainstream now, such websites were rare then. Onto the parliamentary table, anti-choice politicians still laid down old-school handwritten petitions against the reform bill. To keep the table balanced, Greens MP Colleen Hartland and Labor MPs laid down their own in support. But we all knew that the abortion debate was not going to be won with petitions.

ProChoiceVic emails flooded politicians' inboxes, and women from a multitude of organisations linked in with ALRA/WHV and ProChoiceVic hot-footed it into parliamentary members' offices to convince our elected representatives in person. Visits and advice to cross-party politicians were co-ordinated, as were ALRA/WHV and ProChoiceVic T-shirts, letter-writing and media interviews.

The parliamentary debates, and media campaign and coverage during September and October 2008 were hectic. Anti-choice, anti-women abortion myths were busted at every turn by a huge army of women fighting for women's reproductive freedom. They spoke out with evidence, expert opinion and humour. *The Age* cartoonist Tandberg illustrated the absurdity of the still-persisting notion that an abortion decision belonged to men, rather than to the woman concerned. Tandberg drew a pregnant woman saying, 'I'd like a vote,' while a male politician, doctor and priest said, 'You're not eligible' and closed the door on her. My own short letter to the editor appeared beneath: 'A conscience vote for politicians, doctors and priests. A conscience vote for a pregnant woman? Sorry, who's she again?'

The Australian Medical Association, other health organisations and individual doctors publicly supported the abortion law reform. Three male doctors Short, De Crespigny and Saveluscu (*The Age*, 2008) argued sensitively and insightfully that women have the moral capacity and right to decide whether to continue or terminate a problem pregnancy at any stage of pregnancy.

Social worker and Royal Women's Hospital Pregnancy Advisory Service Manager Annarella Hardiman and I co-wrote a *Herald Sun* op-ed headed, We Know Our Minds, arguing against proposed bill amendments put by anti-abortion parliamentarians.

It is unusual, patronising and insulting to legally mandate counselling for any adult—man or woman—around a personal, private health decision. Some women may want in-depth support, information or counselling.

Others, like those suffering violence have a right to strong informed support tailored to their specific needs. Others reach a clear decision in consultation with their partner, family, friends and often their GP. Between 80 and 90 per cent of women who come into the Fertility Control Clinic are already clear in their decision…

The Bill maximises a woman's choice up to 24 weeks gestation. In our experience this reflects the reality of delays in decision making and detection of some fetal abnormalities… It is unfair and dangerous to judge a pregnant woman, especially when she is close to 24 weeks pregnant, unless you have walked a mile in her shoes…

Abortion is no different to any other medical treatment in a hospital or clinic in the sense it is governed by stringent regulations covering safety, duty of care, informed consent and risk…

Those proposing mandatory counselling incorrectly depict modern elective abortion as dangerous to a woman's mental and physical health. That's contrary to research evidence.

Removing abortion from the Crimes Act is an important step away from ignorance, stigma and sexism. We support it. But we oppose legally mandated counselling for women considering abortion.

Annarella and I were both experts in problem pregnancy/abortion counselling, Annarella from the major public provider of abortion, and me from the major private provider of abortion. I reckoned it was hard to trump those credentials.

But perhaps the most powerful myth busters involved personal stories. Greens MP Colleen Hartland and Victorian Health Commissioner Beth Wilson spoke to the media about their own abortions. Completely blitzing Tony Abbott's insulting views, they spoke up as women whose abortions strengthened and liberated them from the difficult life crisis of an unplanned pregnancy. In 2020, Colleen recalled:

During the abortion decrim debate, I did that article in The Age *about my own abortion. It was something that had occurred over 30 years ago and I'd never spoken to anybody about it. It was actually something Leslie said to me: that unless we start talking about abortion openly, the taboo continues.*

Victor [Colleen's partner] encouraged me and I had some funny reactions from my aunts who told me they still loved me. My aunts are people who go to mass most days. I just thought because the article was in The Age, *and not the* Herald, *they wouldn't notice!*

COLLEEN HARTLAND, 2020

Both Colleen and Beth can tell anecdotes that make you chuckle while simultaneously revealing profound truths that can bring you close to tears. It is difficult to convey the enormity of these two intelligent, relatable women publicly owning and personalising a decision that society usually only heard about in frowning whispers, if at all. Stepping boldly into the sights of anti-abortion fanatics comes at a personal cost. So can revealing to family and friends a secret that was no one else's business, but once revealed has the potential to upset and estrange. Coming from an Irish Catholic family, Colleen had kept her abortion secret for *three decades*. Her bravery was rewarded when the Irish love from her family clearly gazumped cruel Catholic judgement.

Like MP Candy Broad, Beth and Colleen were formidable women clear in their values, determined to normalise, respect and validate women who chose abortion, and unafraid to take on misogynists, institutionalised religious bigotry, power brokers and bullies.

Meanwhile, Catholic Archbishop of Melbourne Denis Hart threatened to close the maternity departments in Catholic hospitals if the abortion decrim bill did not delete the obligation for anti-abortion doctors to refer women to a doctor who did not hold a conscientious objection to abortion (Zwartz, 2008). This, and other threats and amendments out of the anti-women handbook of Tony Abbott and the United States anti-abortion movement were similarly knocked down by pro-choice health experts and politicians using reason, facts, true stories and woman-centred and rights-based language.

On 10 September 2008, after ten hours of debate where almost three quarters of MPs spoke, Lower House parliamentarians voted 47–35 for the abortion decriminalisation bill sponsored by Women's Affairs Minister Maxine Morand. Divisions occurred in all parties. The usually progressive, but Catholic-and-married-to-an-anti-abortion-lawyer, Attorney General Rob Hulls voted against. Amongst those supporting the bill were Opposition

Liberals leader Ted Baillieu and Women's Affairs spokeswoman Mary Wooldridge, Health spokeswoman Helen Shardy, and Deputy Leader Louise Asher, Nationals Jeanette Powell and Independent Craig Ingram. The gender spilt was telling: 19 women voted for the bill, and 6 against; 28 men voted for and 29 against. Draw your own conclusions.

Next, the Upper House.

I was keen to see Parliament in action during the historic abortion bill debate, but also reluctant. In the public gallery I was never far from anti-abortion extremists (more than a couple who were clinic regulars), and during the debate prominent anti-choice politicians used vile language to describe both women and abortion providers. But our law makers were sitting all day and into the late night, and those publicly supporting the law reform had been lobbied and threatened by anti-abortion extremists in person, email and received ghastly objects in the mail. Our pro-choice politicians appreciated seeing friendly faces in the gallery. So on three occasions I flexibly juggled my way into Parliament House for hours on end. Clinic practice manager, Janice Nugent, managed to attend one of these sessions with me. It was a whole new experience for us.

Liberal MP Bernie Finn probably spoke longer than everyone else put together during the Legislative Council's debate on the bill on Wednesday 8 October and Thursday 9 October 2008. Embellishing with his own idiosyncratic passion, MP Flynn minutely detailed legal advice sought by Catholic Health Australia from DLA Phillips Fox regarding the application of the *Charter of Human Rights and Responsibilities Act 2006* (Vic) to the *Abortion Law Reform Bill 2008* (Victoria). No surprise that this advice contradicted the government's stance. ProChoiceVic had independently sought solicitor Rebecca Dean's conclusions of the DLA advice: DLA's advice regarding the application of the Charter to the bill was incorrect; Minister Morand was not mistaken in her belief that a statement of compatibility in accordance with section 48 of the Charter was not required at the time of the second reading of the bill; and the bill did not infringe upon the obligations contained within the Charter.

I decided yet again that 'Health' in Catholic Health Australia was an oxymoron of the worst kind. There was no room for real women and their real health needs in its definition of Health, just like there was little room for real women within the Catholic Church anywhere. Catholic hospitals accept government, tax-payer funding, but fail to provide for the full complement of women's reproductive health needs. I had been consulted by women whose health care had been refused and delayed because Catholic hospitals would not provide abortion and contraceptive services—and would not refer women to doctors who did. Sifris (2013) considered that forcing a woman to continue an unwanted pregnancy, by denying her request for an abortion, to be a form of torture that had been completely negated by the prevailing masculinised definition of torture. The reality of women's experiences bears this out.

> *The risks of abortion criminalisation are not minor and are not only that someone might suffer trauma and torture and the many burdens associated with having to carry an unwanted pregnancy to term—exceptions for Catholic health providers can end up killing women. The trigger for Ireland's successful abortion decriminalisation in 2013 was the 2012 death of Indian woman, Savita Halappanavar, who was living in Ireland and died because an emergency, life-saving abortion was denied to her.*
>
> Lizzie O'Shea

Back in Parliament House in October 2008, these realities for women were nowhere to be seen or heard as MP Flynn produced a sincere and grandstanding performance for his religious right supporters, and orchestrated a futile attempt at gerrymandering. He cherry-picked history, law and religion to equate abortion (and thereby women and health professionals) to Nazism, slavery and the genocidal murder of children.

I should have expected his rhetoric, but in that hallowed chamber, the sheer volume and insult of the offense still caught me by surprise. Our politicians had far more stamina and thick skin than I had. I vacillated between disbelief, rage, a sense of the ridiculous and a philosophical Zen. The parliamentary décor and Mr Flynn's antics revived memories of the Supreme Court trial of the man who murdered security guard Steve Rogers.

In the Upper House on Thursday 9 October 2008, one of my favourites, MP Jaala Pulford, spoke emphatically:

Opponents of abortion have had many, many years to develop their arguments and tactics around this issue. I would urge my colleagues to be wary of amendments to this legislation being put by proponents who are implacably opposed to abortion in all circumstances. In the other house 41 amendments to the bill were proposed.

That last long day, Friday 10 October 2008, sitting on the red, cushy public gallery benches so close to the Upper House action, I was dressed in purple stockings and purple jumper under a greyish pinafore. Ridiculous attire. But Green, White and Violet are the feminist colours linked by their first letter to 'Give Women the Vote'. Violet is especially viewed as the feminist colour. My wardrobe presented slim pickings when it came to the purple hues. But there I was wearing the colour of feminism and ensuring any pollie knew where my support lay, rather like attending a footy match.

As determined politicians stood firm against anti-choice bill amendments, to my right sat anti-women extremists, including some of the regulars who targeted the clinic. I was comforted by being amongst the pro-choice coterie. WHV CEO and ALRA Chair Marilyn Beaumont, a woman with a build to match her strength of character, turned to tell us how in earlier parliamentary proceedings she found herself sitting beside a right-to-lifer and she thought, *What will I do if he suddenly punches me in the stomach?* It was a surprising comment. But I knew exactly where Marilyn was coming from.

Late that night, the third reading of the bill to decriminalise abortion passed the Upper House unamended, with a conscience vote of 23 to 17. The cross party split: Labor 14 for and five against, Liberals 5–10, Nationals 1–1, Greens 3–0, DLP 0–1. Women having abortions and abortion providers would never be criminally prosecuted for doing what they thought was right and was a woman's right.

My respect soared for the strength and determination of our progressive parliamentarians, both women and men, who had stood up for women being autonomous human beings. My hopes crashed that so many people (especially men but also women who had internalised an archaic sexism) felt an entitlement to vote against legislation respecting women's right to make their own informed health decisions about their own bodies and lives: The Upper

House gender split: nine women for and three against; 14 men for and 14 against. To state the obvious, we need more progressive women in our houses of Parliament—and completing Gender Studies 101 should be a prerequisite for all MPs.

The decriminalisation of abortion was stupendous and deflating. The most wonderful passage of legislation that women should never have had to fight for. Does it really need to be pointed out that a man's right to make his own decisions about his health care (and most everything else) is never questioned? Then why so for a woman? A man would never be mandated to jump through legal hoops to access, say, a vasectomy or heart surgery. A man would never face criminal prosecution for walking away from a pregnancy of his making, as Tony Abbott once did.

A significant aspect of the abortion law reform was the parliamentary leaders in the Lower and Upper Houses all supported it including Liberals Ted Baillieu, Louise Asher, David Davis and Wendy Lovell...

Daniel Andrews was Health Minister. He's a Catholic, but the wonderful thing about Daniel was that he said that it was his job as Health Minister to do this. And he was just wonderful about that in a way previous Health Ministers hadn't been. He made a huge difference in making it happen... The National Party at the time was all men except for Jeanette Powell. There was huge significance in having the only National Party woman vote for the decrim.

CANDY BROAD (2019)

Through her private member's bill to decriminalise abortion, Candy Broad had set a model of feminist bravery that others followed. Seven years later, another private member's bill would do the same for abortion safe access zones.

But at the end of that last long day, Friday 10 October 2008, as abortion was finally decriminalised and we were suffused with disbelief and jubilation, we suddenly all knew where Marilyn was coming from when she had thought, *What will I do if he suddenly punches me in the stomach?* In that hallowed place of governance, anti-abortion extremism was showcased in a threatening display of irrationality and disrespect. Anti-abortion extremists in the upper gallery ranted and threatened, 'You've got blood on your hands! There will be retribution on the Parliament!' and on and on. The President observed that security was being far too slow removing the miscreants and restoring order—and did the President just say, 'Jesus, fucking bananas'? Jesus fucking bananas.

I was disturbed by the powerful societal dregs of hatred towards women. Towards women like me, women like Marilyn, women like those I saw every day at the clinic. Towards women, full stop.

Through the abortion decrim, I had witnessed just how much it took to champion essential, basic human rights for women and win. I was ecstatic, relieved, tired and a little despondent. I left soon after a celebratory acknowledgement with others. Looking over my shoulder as I passed the anti-abortion fanatics giving media interviews in the Parliament House foyer. Looking over my shoulder as I bounded quicker than I ever had down the long flight of parliamentary steps into the cool Melbourne night. Looking over my shoulder as I headed for the warmth of home and family. Looking over my shoulder. What a wuss I was.

Then I thought of Marilyn Beaumont.

Three days later, the first celebration of the decrim was hosted by ProChoiceVic. On Monday 13 October 2008, champions of women's abortion rights thronged happily in a city pub, not quite believing what had just happened for women's reproductive rights in this state: Victoria now had the most liberal abortion laws in Australia. Lou, Janice, June and I went along. Leslie Cannold gave a rousing speech mentioning everyone by name and their specific efforts—a gutsy effort, what if you forgot someone? But she didn't. That's our Leslie.

I arrived alone and a little late to the second celebration, hosted by Women's Health Victoria at the Queen Vic Centre on Monday 1 December 2008. I stood at the rear of a crowd of faces I knew and faces I did not: Politicians, practitioners, advocates, academics, lawyers. Women dominated, but key men were there. A champagne offered to me and accepted. The first—and so far only—female Premier of Victoria, Joan Kirner was somewhere in the middle of her speech. So relaxed, articulate and apparently off-the-cuff that I recognised all the hallmarks of meticulous preparation—unless, maybe, some people, like Joan, really can just speak perfectly on the fly. Certainly I was to stand in awe of another such woman in the years to come—a woman who was Minister for Health, Attorney General, and may become premier?

In that large and celebratory Queen Vic Centre room that evening as I arrived a little late, Joan had thanked various politicians, others, Leslie and then said, *Susie Allanson, are you here*? That's me. I excitedly waved my hand high and called, *I'm here at the back, Joan*. She *mentioned* me. Good grief Joan mentioned *me*. How kind, how generous. I was so chuffed and embarrassed, I don't remember a word of what Joan said about me.

At the end of that second abortion decrim celebration, I sought Joan out. She peered at me through those glasses which made her eyes loom large like the wise owl she was. Holding my gaze she asked, 'How is it now at the clinic, Susie? Do women say they are pleased they are no longer a criminal for having an abortion?'

I didn't want to dampen this celebration, this great achievement that took the years and the lives of so many women. I couldn't tell Joan that most women had no idea, and have no idea, about the lawfulness or otherwise of abortion—women were just grateful that we were there. I couldn't tell Joan that the decrim had not made any difference to the harassment women faced, the unique barriers for rural women, the lack of an abortion and fertility control training pathway for doctors, too few abortion doctors, the almost complete absence of younger doctors entering this crucial area of women's health, the poor access for women with pregnancies beyond 16 weeks, the low Medicare rebate for abortion...

So I smiled my biggest smile, 'Yes, Joan. The decrim is wonderful, amazing.' And it was.

It was important to reflect on how much women had achieved in the years leading up to 2008. Still, my impatience for more and faster change could be a source of frustration, but also energy and motivation. If you're interested in change, you have to be in it for the long haul.

I was learning what I could contribute and how to lean in. Clearly you didn't win reform on your own—you won by working with a team of people who had a spread of skills. You win by being part of building a broad coalition coming at the issue from all angles, prepared to find support and leverage it, and largely ignoring the haters and minimising their power. You win by being brave and being with the brave.

Achieving the decriminalisation of abortion was a necessary step, legally and politically, but also for the women activists who would go on to spearhead safe access zones. The abortion decrim prepared us all for the safe access battle ahead: we would know the tactics of anti-women enemies well, and be confident we had the know-how, stamina and thick skins to beat them. The decrim built a rare model of unbreakable trust amongst cross-party pro-choice colleagues. Despite party political divisions on other subjects, our pro-choice politicians trusted one another to prosecute the case for women.

CHAPTER 6

Garden Beds, Fountains & The Media

2009–2011

For too long we have positioned women as a deviation from standard humanity and this is why they have been allowed to become invisible. It's time for a change in perspective. It's time for women to be seen.

CRIADO PEREZ (2019)

With abortion successfully decriminalised, we had reached the end of our beginning.

Abortion buffer zones were next in line. Let's go!

Sadly, I was to discover that everyone else seemed to think abortion decrim marked an end, not a beginning. They had taken the abortion millstone hanging around feminist necks for decades, if not centuries, and laid it down, rightly, as a milestone of feminist success: abortion was finally decriminalised in Victoria, yay! Problem was, that milestone did not mark the end of the abortion journey. We were nowhere near the end yet.

To mix my metaphors here, while I was ready to ride that abortion decrim wave to freedom, the decrim wave had dumped pro-choice champions half-drowned and exhausted on the beach called Never Again. During the abortion decrim campaign and parliamentary debate, we had worried that the clinic might come under even more fire from anti-choice groups. Instead, a degree of heat was taken off us as the god-fearing ultra-right blowtorch was applied to Parliament House and pro-choice politicians. Politicians found anti-abortion extremists' tactics and language disturbing. They found them disturbing because they are. The successful campaign that saw abortion decriminalised in 2008 was so gruelling personally and politically that most had no inclination to revisit abortion any time soon.

I got it, I really did. They'd done more than their bit for now. And who knows, maybe decriminalising abortion might normalise and destigmatise abortion to the extent that it would solve our problem, although I wasn't holding my breath on that.

For me it just seemed a logical two-step that once you had abortion decriminalised, well of course, then nothing that is happening here is of any kind of criminal nature… I actually think that we thought it would just happen. I don't think any of us really thought it would be this huge new battle.

COLLEEN HARTLAND (2020)

Seven years after abortion had been decriminalised, and during the eventual 2 September 2015 parliamentary debate of Fiona Patten's private Safe Access Zones Bill, 'unfinished business' would be how Labor Minister Jaala Pulford referred to safe abortion access. But from 2008 until then, Joan Kirner's words would hold true for our pro-choice politicians, 'We kind of sat back and waited for it to happen. But it didn't happen.' Sigh. What followed the decrim would be more of the same: more of everything we'd struggled with since Steve's murder.

My clinical psychology theories of change were tailored to individuals or small groups who were brave enough and desperate enough to *want* help to change. I didn't have tucked up my sleeve some sophisticated *theory of change* to guide me in how to shift the values of a whole society who didn't want to change, or how to propel into action people who didn't want to move. What I did have was more along the lines of Life lessons from my father: *get your priorities straight, take a deep breath,* and *grit your teeth and keep going.*

Sigh. Yes, any good theory of change must include the Age of Big Sighs, which of course, overlaps with the Stages of Stamina, and must be informed by the Bible of Stress Management Basics. As an imperfect human being, but especially as a clinician, I had considerable experience with the last one. I relied on family, friends, other productive work and projects, music, exercise, sleep, good food, laughter, breathing in and out... And like so many women, and with varying degrees of success, I relied on plugging away at learning how to be more assertive, how to say *No*, how to say *Yes*, and how to be kind to myself.

Armed with this practice and knowledge, I reminded myself of the deep truths contained in old sayings: *There's more than one way to skin a cat, cook a chook, crack a religious nutter?* We had *more than one iron in the fire* and *finger in the pie*, and *bun in the oven*.

The eleventh of May 2009 was a good day. The World Health Organisation & United Nations Population Fund (Eds) (WHO & UNFPA) report, *Psychological Aspects of Reproductive Health: A Global Review of the Literature* finally was published. Professor Jill Astbury and I had written the chapter: *Psychosocial aspects of family planning: Contraceptive use & elective abortion.*

Writing something for WHO was its own nightmare of delays and political posturing. Given the burden of years and politicisation this had involved, I had been resigned to the Review, particularly the section I wrote on abortion, never seeing the light of day. Back in July 2005, clinical psychologist (now Professor) Jane Fisher, railed that 'this document is going to haunt us for life' as she explained WHO wished us to rewrite yet again and, given the delays to publication caused by WHO, include updated research too. By May 2007, as I sent yet another amendment of the chapter to Jane, I spat that dummy far:

> The original brief which I agreed to was to consider abortion and mental health within a human rights perspective—how that has changed... If I had known that I would end up having to write with the underlying assumption that abortion must not be considered a human right, I doubt I would have accepted. I grow weary and angry with the tolerance we show the anti-choice movement with its intolerant bullying intimidation, violent criminal and non-criminal behaviour and its demonising of women.

Now I feel I have been involved with something which has allowed anti-choice people to intimidate academic and humanitarian endeavour, my endeavour... I have received no remuneration for my work. I note the reviewers were paid... I can't imagine a man putting up with this. I am not prepared to alter the chapter anymore.

The WHO comments that fired me up included:

UNFPA cannot promote any types of abortion at all (due to decision of our member states)... We can say 'unsafe' abortion should be eliminated, but many of UN member states do not regard even 'safe' abortion as part of Reproductive Rights... Mental health itself is very ostracized, so we'd better be very safe and careful regarding abortion.

Apparently nothing is more political and likely to offend than family planning and women's reproductive mental health, especially if that includes abortion. Something to do with the sexist foundation of the globe rooted in a deep and primitive womb envy perhaps? The triviality of a woman dying? The androcentric religions that reach into every corner of the globe teaching a toxic mix of chaste idealisation, hatred and control of women—especially of women's sexuality?

But in May 2009, after a change of federal government in Australia and in the US ('That's right, I'm a lefty, get used to it,' US President Obama said as he signed his first executive order in 2009), abortion now decriminalised in Victoria, and a paid maternity scheme just announced, the WHO & UNFPA report and family planning chapter didn't look too shabby. Boring abortion facts can speak volumes.

That May 2009 day was also a good MCC day. No, really. After eight years of MCC fobbing us off, someone at MCC finally got creative on our behalf. Garden beds, yes garden beds, were the reason MCC intended, finally, enforcing removal of the extremists' displays with fines and confiscation. Garden beds, not women's safety or dignity or privacy or access to health, but garden beds, provided us with a small, odd and far too brief victory for the clinic women versus the religious extremists. Let me paint a picture.

Wellington Parade is a rather magnificent avenue. A major thoroughfare joining the city of Melbourne's bustling Flinders Street to the shopping mecca of inner suburb Richmond's Bridge Road, Wellington Parade is a broad carriageway where two lanes of traffic (plus on street parking) travel East and two lanes travel west. Slicing the road in half is a dual tram line.

Behind the southern footpath lies Jolimont station and the 100,000-spectator capacity stadium, the Melbourne Cricket Ground, or MCG, or simply, the G. The clinic sits on the north side of Wellington Parade, amongst the shops, cafes and businesses, and a hop skip and a jump away from a multistorey luxury hotel and the vast Fitzroy Gardens (also home to Captain Cook's Cottage). On Friday afternoons, preparations for an Aussie rules footy match or a concert at the G carries on the wind the blast of a footy siren or rock band. On any day, tourists swell the usual Wellington Parade hoi polio.

Wellington Parade footpaths are also roomy. So roomy that trees are set within elevated concrete borders enclosing a 'garden' more than a meter square. As well as placing their posters and displays on the footpath, the extremists leant them on the trees in the garden beds. On that day in 2009, an MCC officer warned that they must hold any displays, or face fines and confiscation of their displays. They were damaging the garden beds. Forget women, garden beds rule. Yay!

The extremists sought legal advice and intended mounting a legal challenge on the basis the displays were political or religious in nature. In the meantime, they toed the line. Instead of women (and others) confronting displays along the street, they now confronted them hanging from around god botherers' necks. Surely scraggy necks wouldn't hold up under that burden.

The embargo on setting placards against the garden beds didn't last long but, hey, it was great while it lasted.

We continued to badger the government, police and Melbourne City Council, but our squeaky wheel was not getting the oil. Other abortion providing clinics were attracting some attention from extremists, too. Not that I wished that on them, but being the clinic copping all the nasty attention all the time was exhausting and seemed to signal that it was all our own fault. One resident, a definite outlier compared with the other supportive residents I met, considered that the problem would be solved neatly if the Fertility Control Clinic just moved somewhere else.

I was not a leader like Marilyn Beaumont nor a captain like Leslie Cannold. I was just a team player needing a coach and a team. I would spasmodically 'give up' on abortion safe access. I had plenty else to occupy me in my life, I didn't need this.

But my clinic patients and private practice patients didn't need this either, nor did my colleagues. To see experienced staff shaking, in tears, sighing with helplessness, fuming with anger. To have a patient regress, therapy progress disrupted, a clear-cut pregnancy/abortion/contraception decision made distressing and unduly complicated, children crying, partners yelling, residents upset. Too many were harmed. My lot was to just keep trying. My family, friends and clinic colleagues Susan (Speaking) Hopkins and Janice Nugent were never short on emotional encouragement and practical support.

Lou would shrug. But Lou's shrugs had changed their meaning since the 1990s. Back then a shrug was his reluctant and philosophical acceptance of the horrendous abortion price that had to be paid by our patients and by our staff. Back then, Lou reckoned safe access was never going to happen in his lifetime. But, the murder of Steve had solidified Lou's determination to remove the religious extremists, and the successful abortion decriminalisation had shown that a political, legislative solution was possible. Lou's shrugs now communicated something entirely different from acceptance of the *status quo*.

Lou's shrugs meant, 'Fair enough, Suse, do what you want to do, go ahead.'
He knew you could manage it and he was giving you cart blanche to do
what you thought best.

JANICE NUGENT (2020)

So, with Lou's blessing, and many a discussion, I continued to do what I thought best, even when I was butting heads with an organisation like MCC that seemed to me to be expending far too many resources to avoid doing its job. The phone calls and meetings Lou, Janice and I had with pleasant, but purportedly powerless MCC personnel. The hours of 'monitoring' by MCC enforcement officers who sat in cars seeing *religious or political communication/ protest*; believing the extremists' delusion that their offensive actions were in fact benevolent expressions of helping women; not seeing the reality of gendered abuse; not seeing a noxious nuisance in action. The stopping, observing, doing nothing. Balancing rights? All I could see was MCC being wilfully blind, deaf and plain bloody-minded in its determination to do nothing.

In early March 2010, with yet another claustrophobic 40-day vigil, and with staff, patients and their companions deeply distressed by the god-bothering nutters, my gut-wrenching, teeth-clenching and hands-wringing body sent out pleas in all directions for pressure to be placed on MCC to stop the abuse. To Police Inspector Bernie Jackson, Joan Kirner, Marilyn Beaumont, Health Minister Bronwyn Pike, Minister for Women's Affairs Maxine Morand... *We respectfully ask that you encourage, and support, the Council enforcing its Local Laws to remove this group to the other side of Wellington Parade.*

A letter to the Right Honourable the Lord Mayor Mr Robert Doyle on 2 March 2010 was much less respectful—a hardly suppressed fit of anger. Well, okay, it was a dummy spit:

... No other hospital, business, school, church or organisation faces such an appalling, chronic situation. If this group were occupying a path outside a school, we are sure that MCC would act immediately to remove them... you have failed to act... you have upheld the rights of this group above all others and you are entirely disregarding the rights of the public, workers and visitors to go about their business without being insulted, intimidated, obstructed, confronted with offensive material and having their privacy and personal space violated. Wellington Parade East Melbourne is where we work, where people attend for vital medical care, shop, meet with friends and enjoy the amenities of East Melbourne. We are involved in important work. In contrast, there is nothing to stop the picketers conducting a proper protest across the road...

The MCC has a duty of care to its constituents, the public, workers and visitors to the area... we intend using every political, legal and media avenue to insist that MCC enforce its Local Laws. If MCC continues to fail to enforce its own laws, and another tragedy occurs—which is foreseeable given the circumstances—we will take legal action against MCC for failure to exercise its duty of care.

Lou and I signed our names neatly at the bottom of that furious letter.

I thought that the abortion decrim would give City of Melbourne that power to actually act. I've never quite understood City of Melbourne... I know when I spoke with Cathy [Oaks, Greens Melbourne City councillor], and I have high regard for Cathy, she felt that the council was completely tied up around the bylaws: they just couldn't do anything and that it needed state legislation to do something. Yet they never asked for that legislation, so what was the gap there?

COLLEEN HARTLAND, 2020

It is worth momentarily skipping ahead here to a 2015 freedom of information request made by MP Fiona Patten which revealed that on 14 December 2011, Lord Mayor Doyle did write to then (Liberal) Attorney General, Robert Clark, asking that the state government 'consider legislative amendment to enable a no-protest zone around the Fertility Control Clinic'. Mr Clark's 9 June 2012 reply referred to 'competing considerations' and to using existing laws as remedies, including MCC local laws:

...injunctions, criminal charges and on the spot notices for breaches of bylaws relating to obstruction or public nuisance. As you have noted in your letter, a range of infringement offences that could be used in relation to improper protest activities already exist in the Melbourne City Council's Activities Local Law 2009. For example, causing nuisance; affecting amenity of a public place; interfering with the use or enjoyment of a public place or the personal comfort of another person, annoying, molesting or obstructing any other person in that public (clause 2.1)...

I note your view that use of these local laws have to date been unsuccessful. I suggest that the Melbourne City Council may be able to work with Victoria Police to improve the use of these infringement penalties in appropriate circumstances.

Exactly. But wait, MCC had *used* the local laws to address this problem? Not on my watch. Not ever. So how could the Lord Mayor possibly say the local laws had been unsuccessful to date? Handball, sham ball. Back and forth the clinic patients and staff were thrown, battered and bruised by such reckless mishandling.

In October 2010, the VLRC *Surveillance in Public Places Final Report* arrived in the mail for me, a page ear-marked and a VLRC slip of paper from VLRC Chair Neil Rees. In 2008, Neil Rees had released the VLRC Report providing the successful model for abortion decriminalisation and had raised 'bubble zones' for consideration. I was rather a fan of Neil Rees. The ear-marked page 125 included the following:

> *6.106… use of a surveillance device to intimidate, demean or harass another person is unacceptable.*

And:

> *6.107 The new offence should apply in two situations. First, where a surveillance device is used to intimidate, demean or harass a person of ordinary sensibilities. Secondly, where a surveillance device is used to prevent or hinder a person from performing an act they are lawfully entitled to do. This latter situation includes, for example, using a surveillance device to discourage people from entering places such as abortion clinics or gay bars.*

In this latest VLRC report, I saw a possibility of achieving our goal via a back door. The Report's glossary defined surveillance as 'Deliberate or purposive observation or monitoring of a person, object or place'. Maybe there were possibilities beyond the surveillance 'device'. Perhaps in our case religious extremists were 'devices'. They were certainly tools.

Aw, made me feel all warm and fuzzy that someone like the VLRC Commissioner had so kindly kept us in mind and taken the trouble to send us this report. I didn't care how we stopped the harassment, just that it stopped. After all, notorious gangster Al Capone, aka Scarface, was finally brought down not for his violence and racketeering but for evading federal taxes. And to draw on a case a smidge closer to home, the 1969 Menhennitt abortion ruling 'had to slip between the cracks and occur when no one was looking… there wasn't a single journalist in the courtroom the day that Menhennitt gave his ruling'. (Haigh, 2019). Could the VLRC Surveillance report solve our problem while no one was looking? In 2010 I shopped around the *Surveillance in Public Places Final Report* and idea to my political network.

At the same time, and with no sign of MCC being under any additional pressure whatsoever, on 18 October 2010, *The Age* published an article by Julia Medew highlighting our push 'to create an exclusion zone around the clinic and others across the state to balance people's rights'. Other media interviews followed, and I spoke with, and wrote to, various MPs and advisors. I kept mum about the VLRC Surveillance Report.

Political eyes and minds were on the December 2010 state election. Some say a good time to lobby. Others say, 'Nah, no way'. 'The latter it was. In December 2010, the Labor state government fell, and apparently the VLRC Surveillance report fell too—off the political radar. Pro-Choice Liberal Ted Baillieu became Premier of Victoria. Labor was relegated to the Opposition benches. Abortion had been decriminalised, but local councils, police, justice and parliamentary systems were never built on the pillars of women's experiences and needs.

> *Really, it was an area that nobody wanted to touch. MCC didn't want to know about it because it was too hard. Politicians didn't want to know about it because it was too hard. So basically everyone was saying, 'If you want to work in this area, this is what you have to deal with. They're out there. You're in there. Do your job.'*
>
> Dr Louis Rutman (2020)

Solicitor Rebecca Dean had noted in her (2006, 2007) advice on MCC's by-laws that MCC displayed no reservations about taking action against other human 'nuisances'. In 2011 MCC's reluctance to address our chronic noxious nuisance, while stopping other arguably legitimate protest, would be cause for one of my dummy spits, which ended with:

> *... in contrast to the peaceful Occupy Melbourne protest, the situation in East Melbourne apparently does not warrant the Lord Mayor's attention. Are water features more important than women? Shame on you, Mr Doyle.*
>
> Letter to *The Age*
25 October 2011

That 2011 letter in *The Age* garnered a swarm of follow up media interviews. Buzz buzz buzz. 'Are water features more important than women?' had struck a chord. But no chord sounded with tone-deaf Melbourne City Council.

But I wondered… Fountains? Garden beds? MCC was prepared to protect fountains and garden beds. If only women were just silent, pretty and inanimate. Not human at all. Just for men's amusement. Like a fountain, a garden bed, a pretty flower. Maybe then MCC would care. Would somebody please care.

A tough time in women's lives continued to be made worse. Society continued to tolerate the abuse dished out by religious extremists. Women were held hostage to people whose bizarre and unkind mindset represented the tiniest proportion of our community. And the extremists' power was amplified both by authorities' passivity and warped idea of 'balancing rights', but perhaps also by the media's approach to it all.

Marriage equality campaigner, former GetUp Campaign Director, and Executive Director at change.org, Sally Rugg (2019), points out both the public's and the media's thrall to the drama of a triangular conflict story comprising a villain, victim and hero. 'A clear villain in the story also reminds us that injustices don't just happen, they're perpetrated by people' (p.189).

At least, clearly, we weren't the villain in this story. Were we?

'But that is exactly the dastardly point, nye, nye, nye,' the evil villain laughs, twirling his rosary beads and clasping his gold cross with glitzy-ringed fingers, Amen. The long silence around women's histories and lives had historically cast both abortion-providing health professionals and women having abortions as villains: greedy, heartless murdering monsters of doctors; and selfish, God-less, cold-blooded child-killing sluts. Sometimes women were cast as the victims of 'the abortion industry' villain. Add to that, society's penchant for blaming the victim, especially when the victim is a woman (Stott Despoja, 2019, p.86–101). Whether we did, or no longer fit a villain, victim, hero framework, a persisting complexity in our situation allowed people to look away.

Despite the delusion and cruel impracticality of the extremists' anti-women, anti-abortion, anti-contraception, anti-sex education language and actions, the media's penchant for a conflict, if not a conflict triangle, had dominated reports. Couched as an ethical obligation to report all sides of a story, it was yet another weird interpretation of the word, 'balance'. To give equal airtime to a group representing a tiny percentage of the population? To give credibility to deliberately concocted 'facts' that were untrue? To provide a megaphone to bullying, bigotry and lies that we knew to be harmful? The media and the public would more openly grapple with these issues in the American Trump years to come.

This idea that the ventilation of fake 'facts' and lies helps resolve them is too often a way of perpetuating injustice. When does it become real for people, rather than just some intellectual debate? I think it undermines the media's credibility. It's why extinction rebellion talks about 'telling the truth'—it's been a massive problem for climate activism and the world tackling the reality of climate change. More recently, during the COVID-19 pandemic, we have seen the preventable deaths of millions of people worldwide caused by science-denying leaders and conspiracy theorists who hypocritically and unquestioningly enjoy and rely on the fruits of science in every other area of their life.

Maybe this dangerous distortion of reality and human rights can only come to an end with a combination of being selective as to the journalists you work with and broader social shifts that make faux notions of balance look outdated.

LIZZIE O'SHEA

Journalists knew they could come to me for comment, and I knew I could turn to them with potential stories. I was generally impressed with their passion and insights. We developed productive relationships of mutual trust and respect. Clashes with journalists, or journalists who made it onto my black list, I can count on two fingers. Print and radio journalists were the best. TV were another breed altogether. But the power of the box to bring attention to an issue was undisputed.

I never was much good at speaking in the short sentences with a headline wow factor that made a journalist's job easy. But journalists were expert editors and generally were adept and hungry to learn. Left-leaning and rights-minded journalists became well-versed in a woman-centred abortion language and viewpoint. The media was the conduit to public opinion and political pressure, and crucial in the campaign for safe access zones.

Women's Health Victoria, and many others, were instrumental in shifting the media coverage around women's reproductive health and violence against women, towards a more boldly woman-centred frame. Over decades of pro-choice activism, and even in the more recent time since Steve's murder, I felt a gradual shift in the media representation of conflict, or of villain-victim-hero in our story. Extremists' quotes in the media tended to come off as offensive and irrational. They shot themselves in the foot and were left wearing the villain's blood-spattered shoes.

My memory is that the media did report the views of some of the Helpers as a part of their coverage. But I think that was not necessarily detrimental because those views were clearly so extreme and not views that are shared by the majority of people, so that reporting probably increased the level of understanding about what was going on and also sympathy for the case we were bringing.

RACHEL BALL (2020)

In some reporting, the harm of the extremists was now a given with no need to include their delusional view that they were 'saving lives' and 'counselling' women. Most people in the minority who thought abortion wrong, also found abhorrent the extremists' bullying of women on a public street outside a women's health service.

Occasionally, Melbourne City Council may have been wearing the mantle of villain, although I suspect that was just my own frustration-driven fantasy. As far as MCC was concerned, anti-abortion extremists' rights continued to trump women's rights. Easily done when women's rights didn't merit a mention.

But there was a growing public realisation that women were no longer the abortion villains. They were our mothers and partners, daughters and friends, sisters and neighbours. They were the women loved by the men and women of Australia. They were us and we were them. Good women who should not have to run an ugly gauntlet just to receive medical care. And one day, women would become the hero.

Women had worked hard for the right to abortion, but translating that right into a genuine choice, made without copping public humiliation, felt daunting—a bureaucratic stasis had set in, to the point where garden beds were better protected than women.

The overt message of such bureaucratic evasion was: you're someone else's problem, someone else's responsibility, and it's okay for us to look away. The covert message was that women's issues were unimportant and not worth the trouble; women had only themselves to blame for being born women!

Contradicting such messages was a shifting public discourse and mood pushing for women to be respected. It was driven by women and health professionals speaking up to tell their stories and to challenge the lies of anti-women extremists; the increased number of female journalists whose personal and professional consciousness-raising about the issue translated into a societal consciousness-raising; and strong links between our issue and a broader movement that demanded respect for women and women's rights. That movement had already achieved changes in women's societal participation—representation in positions of power, greater investment in education and career, later age at having children, changing gender roles, and more visibility (and outrage) about violence against women.

PART THREE

SUPREME COURT ACTION

CHAPTER 7

Lawyers Can Be Handy

December 2010–January 2012

Lawyers can be handy. What I don't know is who came up with the idea of using the duty under the Health and Wellbeing Act back before the safe access zones. Who came up with that legal argument?

KRIS WALKER (2020)

Over the years I had approached a range of people I thought might be able to help push along our advocacy for safe abortion access. There'd been academics, politicians, lawyers and women-centred organisations (like Women's Legal Service Victoria). Delightful, but ultimately futile, conversations with delightful but hamstrung women. During the abortion decrim, WHV and ALRA head honcho Marilyn Beaumont and her side kick Kerrilie Rice had kindly found time to tee up and attend with me a meeting with a QC, advise us around an application to the Public Interest Law Clearing House (PILCH), and been present at the 2006 Lyn Allison/Mick Wilmott meeting with the Police Commissioner. Over the years, people had approached the clinic too.

Everybody who came—Telstra in the building next door, then the GP College—and saw this, thought: 'We've got to do something. My staff, who have nothing to do with this, walk past and they're harassed and upset.'

So they all came with the right intentions, but when they came to the process, they all hit the same brick wall. Nothing happened. Go to the police and nothing happened. Go to Council and nothing happened. So really, nothing ever happened. Human nature is that when you try and try again and don't succeed, eventually you just have to accept it.

Dr Louis Rutman (2020)

But I was not going to accept it, no matter how badly my head hurt from hitting that brick wall. I kept trying and kept looking—finally, I found the game changer. I found Emily Howie and the Human Rights Law Centre (HRLC). Without Emily there would be nothing to report. Abortion safe access zones would still be an abstract idea in Victoria and Australia. Big call, but fair call. Em was how the safe access zones magic began.

One Saturday in December 2010, I was having a coffee and reading the *Saturday Age*, sitting in my special place on a comfy lounge chair in a corner of our house where two windows meet with plenty of light and greenery. Every woman needs her comfy place, or as Virginia Woolf put it, 'a room of one's own'.

Australia's first female prime minister, Julia Gillard, didn't seem to have a comfy place. Installed on 24 June 2010, Julia Gillard would remain in the top job for three years and three days until 26 June 2013 when she would lose a leadership ballot to both her predecessor and successor, Kevin Rudd.

One might have thought that having a woman finally ascend to the position of Prime Minister of Australia would bring greater respect to women and girls—human rights for all. But instead, Australia seemed to have become a religious redneck backwater. Tony Abbott in his budgie smugglers, and with his posse of men in blue ties, hounded Prime Minister Gillard for her sin of being born a woman. And not just the usual womanly sins. Our first female PM had sinned by being born a woman who didn't meet their expectations: Julia Gillard had triumphed in a man's world and rejected her God-given roles of wife and mother. The sledging abuse was disgusting, chronic and will not be repeated here.

How could anyone speak that way about any woman, let alone Australia's first female PM? How could a father of daughters snigger that way? If it was okay for the leader of the Liberal Party to abuse our prime minister like that, what hope any other woman in Australia? What hope our patients? Our staff?

It was a despicable display of misogyny by the blue ties that would go unchecked until Prime Minister Gillard gave her 'misogyny speech' in Parliament on 9 October 2012. That speech would immediately be lauded around the world and go viral online. Except in Australia where its significance would barely be recognised. At the following year's federal election, the electorate would vote for *mad monk* Tony Abbott to be prime minister. Adding insult to injury, Abbott would appoint himself Minister for Women.

Australia had not grown up by installing its first female PM. It had regressed to being one of the most puerile and sexist countries in the world. The lesson was clear: women stand up at their peril, and bullied women must stand up for themselves. Nobody else will.

December 2010 was both a depressing and celebratory time for feminists, humanists and me. Sometimes I felt like I might as well just lie down and give up—for a little while anyway. So, that Saturday I sat comfy but uncomfortable with the state of the world and the state of our country and the state of the street outside my workplace—and the state of me—when an opinion piece caught my eye: *Human Rights Must Not Be Party Political* by Emily Howie and Phil Lynch. The article discussed the new state Coalition Attorney-General Robert Clark's comments threatening the 2006 Victorian Charter of Human Rights. The article's underpinning human rights values caught my mind and my heart. Who was this Emily Howie? What was the Human Rights Resource Centre? What did its Director Advocacy and Strategic Litigation actually do?

I was to discover that in 2006, Phil Lynch became the founding Executive Director of the Human Rights Law Resource Centre (which eventually was rebranded as the Human Rights Law Centre, HRLC): an independent, not-for-profit, non-government organisation and a registered charity supported by various like-minded philanthropists. I didn't ever meet Phil who left in 2012 to become the CEO of International Service for Human Rights. But I had numerous chats with his charismatic, intelligent and kind successor, Hugh de Kretser. Solicitor Emily Howie had been only the third person employed at the Centre, and back in December 2010, the HRLC had just four staff in total.

I'd been doing a great deal of pro bono work for the Human Rights Law Resource Centre when I was a commercial lawyer. I worked on a constitutional case in the High Court about prisoner's right to vote. The HRLC had initially been our client for that. Then I did a variety of other pro bono work and I was asked to be on the Board of the Centre. A job came up and I applied for that job. So I've been involved with HRLC since almost the beginning, and a staff member since 2009 [until 2020 when a role at the Victorian Equal Opportunity & Human Rights Commission beckoned].

The HRLC's focus was on capacity-building and providing resources to the community, and sector more broadly, about how to engage with the human rights systems and legal rights system and advocacy.

Emily Howie (2020)

By 2020, HRLC staff would more than double and its positive impact would grow exponentially:

Ensuring that in Australia everyone is free to lead a decent, dignified life; where our laws, policies and institutions promote fairness and equality; and where people and communities have the power to address inequality and injustice and ensure that governments always act in the public interest.

The Human Rights Law Centre uses strategic legal action, policy solutions and advocacy to support people and communities to eliminate inequality and injustice and build a fairer, more compassionate Australia.

We work in coalition with key partners, including community organisations, law firms and barristers, academics and experts, and international and domestic human rights organisations.

WWW.HRLC.ORG.AU

Back in December 2010, knowing next to nothing about what the HRLC was then, or would become in another ten years, and purely on the promise of *The Age* opinion piece, I cold-called Emily Howie, HRLC Director Advocacy and Strategic Litigation.

Cold-called? Apparently that's not how things are done. Yep, that'd be me and my desperate naivety. Fortunately, there are some times when desperate naivety is just the ticket. Up until 2019, and perhaps even today, my cold-call was the only cold-call case the HRLC ever took on.

I doubt that butting up against the wall until a brick comes loose, would be found in any respectable publication about advocacy, but hey it finally worked! Serendipity meets tenacity: following up endless leads that are dead ends—until one isn't! Maybe that is exactly what activism is about.

Em's response to my call was welcoming interest, insight and can-do manner. From that first call I rightly pegged Em as intelligent, kind, a great listener, a delightful and funny human being, and an expert in championing a model of the law where women's rights are human rights and human rights are women's rights. Even then, Em made of our situation exactly what it was: a wrong needing to be righted.

We just had a new Victorian Charter of Human Rights. We talked a lot about how to use that Charter to try and gain some progress on human rights issues. One thing that Charter does is set out the human rights protected. That includes free speech and assembly, but also rights to non-discrimination, equality and to security of the person, and it requires public authorities to balance those rights.

When you called, I remember thinking, yes, well it is a free speech issue, but free speech doesn't trump women's rights all the time. I think too often in human rights, women's human rights are subordinated to other more traditional interpretations of rights like free speech. It's an outdated framework that presupposes that there is equality in the marketplace of ideas and everybody has equal ability to speak freely. Of course in real life, some people are much more powerful than others, and speech can do harm.

I can remember thinking, this is one of those cases where we need to think about what the appropriate balance would be between the legitimate rights of free speech and assembly, and the rights of women to access medical services without discrimination and harassment, and privately and safely, not knowing exactly how we'd do that.

Emily Howie (2020)

Individual rights exist in a structural context. The gradual shift in power towards women has helped put a new gloss on our understanding of individual rights. What is a vote, a job, the capacity to speak—if you are a second-rate citizen? If your membership of a group designates you as so inferior that others get to make decisions on your behalf? The commitment to individual rights, when too strongly adhered to, allows these broader injustices, inequalities and oppressions to carry on unaddressed. So maybe it wasn't until we got that broader shift that the rights in question in this particular case—reproductive/privacy v speech/association—came into a better light for the purposes of fixing the problem the FCC faced.

LIZZIE O'SHEA

On the afternoon of Tuesday 18 January 2011, Lou, Janice and I met with Emily Howie (and solicitor Zara Durnun on short secondment to the HRLC) in the clinic post-op lounge.

The post-op lounge was a beautiful room in old Virginia—lounge chairs and high ceilings, fireplace and grand mantelpiece, large windows and artwork. There was also the obligatory nurse's work station and small kitchen. Following theatre for an abortion, long-acting reversible contraception, or a D&C (following miscarriage or for other reasons), women transferred from their post-op bed in recovery to the post-op lounge. There they usually were met by a loved one, a nurse, a cuppa and a snack. My preferred go-to room for meetings and media interviews, the post-op lounge was only available in the afternoon once all our patients had left. The voices of women and their stories hovered in that room—a reminder to me to speak up for them.

Directly above the post op lounge on the first floor was its staffroom twin: a lounge of similarly large dimensions, high ceilings, fireplace with a framed photo on the mantelpiece of the late Steve Rogers. Windows looked out over a foreground of the clinic's tall trees and garden, the backdrop of the MCG and, in between, the broad and bustling Wellington Parade. This section of Wellington Parade was home to traffic, trams, pedestrians and the God-bothering gauntlet. Having a morning cuppa, staff had a good view of the extremists and their antics. We had a view of Steve's memorial plaque resting on a rock at the garden pond too.

The pond was a quiet spot where patients, partners, mums, dads and friends sat at times to ponder the world and its unexpected turns and trials. Well, quiet except when the extremists' singing, yelling or noisy arguments followed patients and staff through the gate or over the brick fence, often all the way up to the staff room. My consulting room in the building next door to Virginia was upstairs at the front too, and so similarly accosted.

I was never sure what people who were neither patients nor staff made of the clinic. The great divider and decider was whether that person arrived, as Emily initially did, during the quiet and calm or had to navigate a path through the weird and disturbing morning ritual or 40-day vigil of intimidation. Turned out Em had experienced both:

> When I was a teenager, and in my 20s, I had at least two friends who had an abortion at the Fertility Control Clinic and who were really traumatised by the people out the front. So when you called me it was an issue I was familiar with because I supported those friends through that time. I can remember at the time being so angry that these strangers were allowed to stigmatise people who were going to do something that was deeply private at such a difficult.time in their life.
>
> So when you called I can remember thinking, wow, this is still going on? I probably hadn't thought of it for a while, but I definitely had some insight into the trauma that the anti-abortionists created in women accessing the service and the real sense of injustice of that. I remember thinking, someone's got to be able to do something about this…
>
> I think that public-private divide was maybe part of it, but in human rights law, governments have a positive duty to create safe places for women to be free from discrimination. This was something that had been going on for so long. I can't remember if you put the whole case for it happening on a public street, but whatever you said Susie, I thought, this can't go on. I thought, we have access to people who can provide really good, strong advice and strategy around what to do for this and I think it's worth at least scoping it for what might be possible.
>
> EMILY HOWIE (2020)

Turned out Em was experienced and confident in women's reproductive health rights—including abortion. In fact, unlike so many people I had turned to before, Em was not shy about tackling this stigmatised area, she was excited:

I would have been confident because in 2008 when the abortion decriminalisation was going through, [HRLC solicitor] Rachel Ball had done some work on behalf of the Centre, so we had a position on abortion...

At that time we were also looking into quite a few reproductive rights issues. We had the Assisted Reproductive Technology Act. When they allowed single women and lesbian women to access the service, they also introduced a requirement to undergo a criminal record check... They changed the law, but one of the concessions that the Church secured was to address its view that the system was now open to these 'unsavoury elements' that need to be vetted. That was one issue. And then there was the Medicare for IVF, and Rachel Ball had successfully run a case of access to IVF in women's prison. So we were really interested in some of the social issues for women around reproduction and stereotyping women.

This FCC case also was like, oh wow, it's another reproductive rights issue. At that time HRLC was so new—there were only four of us. As things came in, we had strategic areas, we had things we were working on, but we were still exploring: the landscape of issues that existed; where we fit in; how we add value; and how we work best. So there was a lot more latitude to explore different issues...

EMILY HOWIE (2020)

Given Lou's past experience of receiving pessimistic and rather androcentric legal advice, Em's approach was a breath of fresh air to us all, and we were all enlivened.

When we met Emily she knew what she was talking about, for once, because we'd had a lot of dealings with legal people over the years, men mostly, and they were no help at all.

JANICE NUGENT (2020)

Lou agreed. 'Run with it, Susie A.'

Em was all over our two options: legal action; and advocating for new parliamentary legislation to create a buffer zone. At a Parliament House meeting on Tuesday 1 March 2011, I introduced Emily to cross-party politicians: Liberal MLC Andrea Coote, Labor MLC Candy Broad, Greens MLC Colleen Hartland and her adviser. Seated around a table, a range of possible solutions were canvassed: existing 'move on' laws (recent, inapt for our situation, human-rights-unfriendly, and since rescinded); VLRC's recommended surveillance laws (Candy thought that no surveillance legislation had been considered or passed yet); injunctive relief; align our problem with the fight to end violence against women; a coordinated pro-choice campaign; exclusion zone precedents (e.g. dredging, forestry, the upper steps of Parliament House), gazetting geographical areas using MCC by-laws/permits or by introducing state bubble zone legislation.

Candy emphasised the need to clarify the legal options first, including the new context of Victoria's Human Rights Charter. We had an expert on that sitting right with us in Emily. But the most deflating part of that meeting were the nodding political heads concurring with Liberal Andrea Coote's clear advice to implement an approach *not* requiring new state legislation. Wha-a-t? The most effective, well-tested, long-term solution brushed off the table? The solution within the ambit of these pro-choice politicians, buffer zone legislation, splat, off the table. Why?

Since the 2008 abortion decrim, the political landscape in Victoria had changed. In December 2010 a Liberal government was elected. Led by pro-choice Ted Baillieu and with strong pro-choice Liberal women like Mary Wooldridge, Georgie Crozier, Andrea Coote and others, nonetheless there was strong right-wing anti-choice influence within the government and Parliament, including a religious right Attorney General. Plus, I reckoned that a two-and-a-half-year breather from abortion politics may not yet have been enough. We had been the victors with abortion decriminalisation, but in fact 'once bitten, twice shy' teeth marks still stung for pro-choice politicians.

Five months later, on 18 August 2011, Em and I again met with pro-choice cross-party women MPs and with pro-choice advocate Dr Leslie Cannold. Even after Greens' Intern Hilary Taylor's 2011 report indicated various legislative precedents for exclusion zones, these politically savvy women were in agreement that any political push could see the abortion issue blow up and risk the gains we had secured in 2008.

Sigh. That same argument had been made for years to put off pursuing abortion decrim: leave well enough alone; we might end up with something worse than Menhennitt; be a good little girl now... We also knew from our experience with abortion decriminalisation that those arguments were wrong. But these were champions of women, and Andrea Coote's spit spot manner still scared me a little. The advice was to focus on MCC: enlist residents' support, re-visit police as MCC authorised officers, petition MCC again... Round and round and round we go. I felt dizzy and despondent about ever securing buffer (safe access) zones. We've done all this before.

But we had never done this with the HRLC. In fact, by early March 2011 when we first met with pro-choice politicians, Em had been busy chasing our second option, which was fast becoming our only option: legal action.

One of the strengths of the HRLC is that often what is really needed is that connection between people like you who present cases, and really expert lawyers who can argue them in courts. Or, connections to competent campaigning advice. That kind of hub is really created by the HRLC.

Emily Howie (2020)

The Victorian bar is very good at doing pro bono work and really getting on board. But as a general rule, we're not proactive: we don't go and look for cases; we don't know the people; we wait to be asked. So taking the step of asking is so important because once you ask you will find that there are barristers who will help and hopefully, as in this case, come up with an argument.

Solicitor General Kris Walker QC (2019)

Soon after we first met, Em had tilted the world on its axis towards a fairer go for women by securing the clinic generous pro bono legal representation. And not just any legal representation but esteemed doyens in public health and human rights law: Peter Hanks QC, Claire Harris (now QC), and Therese McCarthy (now a Judge).

How had Em conjured magic like this, and so quickly? I had been grilled and mocked by a QC some years ago in a well-meaning WHV initiated meeting. We had been passed around from one government and one organisation and one person to another like soiled goods. We were the lepers of women's health and women's rights. And now we were being represented by such luminaries? Free of charge? Turns out that for Em, such magic tricks were a routine part of her HRLC work. Behind every connection there was an Emily story, like Em being seated with Peter Hanks QC at a wedding, and off the back of such a fortuitous meeting (and also Em being aware that Peter's wife was a strong supporter of women's rights), Em calling him to ask if he would be involved in our case.

Throughout March 2011, Em and I worked on a *Memorandum to Counsel: Advice for the Fertility Control Clinic in relation to ongoing picketing at their premises on Wellington Parade*. Lou, Janice and I met with our learned legal representatives at Peter Hanks' Owens Dixon West chambers. Information was exchanged. Ideas tossed around. Laughs and serious discourse were had. Latin and legal terms I had no idea about rolled splendidly off Peter Hanks' tongue. Claire and Therese breathed reassurance, calm, grounded care and welcomed us into this new world. We were flying with extraordinary legal eagles experienced and expert in public health and human rights. Our trajectory had taken a decidedly positive arc. Emily Howie knew how to deliver.

Another smart and delightful HRLC solicitor, Rachel Ball, joined Emily Howie. Rachel was completely on board and also well-versed in abortion after completing abortion work for HRLC during the 2008 abortion decriminalisation. Under the direction of Phil Lynch, and subsequently under CEO Hugh De Kretser, HRLC excelled in attracting and nurturing the very best in human rights law and the very best in human beings.

By mid-August 2011, our learned counsel had provided us with an initial *Memorandum of Advice*. Phone calls and emails zipped back and forth between Emily, Rachel and me. Written feedback was sent to counsel. While we waited on the final advice which would clarify the best legal approach to take, Rachel asked us to also think about how much we wanted to take the gloves off versus maintain a 'good working relationship' with MCC. I wasn't sure that we'd ever had a good working relationship with MCC. I reckoned after ten years of (mostly) polite letters, phone calls, meetings and not getting anywhere, like me, Lou might be all for not pulling any punches this time round.

While all this was taking some time, it was clear to Lou that this was the most orderly, professional and determined approach to date. Lou was all in and prepared to back the action financially if we ended up having to pay the costs of the other party.

On 28 October 2011, the Memorandum of Advice was complete. It is impossible to precis detailed, learned advice, but by lifting some direct quotes here and there, here goes. Counsel primarily considered two legal causes of action and remedies available to the FCC.

The first was the common law tort of nuisance where the case law from courtroom judgements back through the ages set precedents about how a matter like nuisances was to be treated by our legal system.

A public nuisance is an act or omission which materially affects the reasonable comfort and convenience of the life of a class of the public… those liable for such a nuisance would be the persons who created it, and also persons who unreasonably failed to end it. Hodgson CJ in Wallace v Powell [2000] NSWSC 406 at 32.

Our counsel advised that generally *a public nuisance action is brought by the Attorney General acting on behalf of the public.* Exactly! I reckoned that although the nuisance had everything to do with the clinic, in so many other ways the extremists were nothing to do with us. This abuse was happening on a public street. Government inaction was the whole reason for resorting to our own legal action. No Attorney General had ever led the charge against this gendered nuisance, nor were they ever likely to. I could not presage that seven years later, feminist Attorney General Jill Hennessy would triumphantly lead the charge against this gendered nuisance in the highest court in the land.

Our 2011 counsel's advice continued:

Of most assistance are the cases where public nuisance has been found in the many 'protesting cases'. In those cases, injunctions have been granted in a wide range of circumstances… analogous to those involved in the protests against the FCC.

Reference was made to various cases familiar to me from Rebecca Dean's work years earlier. Round and round the whirlwind goes. Like Rebecca Dean, our counsel recognised the serious harm of this nuisance. They noted that the

Royal Women's Hospital was granted an injunction against Right to Life and others in the late 1980s, and Carlton abortion provider Dr Christine Healy was granted an injunction on 12 February 1987:

Restraining Right to Life Inc and a range of individuals on the basis that the 'defendants have participated in the commission of nuisances and various trespasses and a conspiracy to commit nuisances in respect of the operation of her practice as a medical practitioner.' In that proceeding, Nathan J took into account, in assessing the balance of convenience the fact that 'Dr Healy conducts a practice to which women in some distress have recourse' and to which they were entitled to 'be free to proceed in a calm way.'

Sounded perfect. Amass and update a range of evidence—again—and head for the Supreme Court to get an injunction. An injunction was perhaps a different style of buffer zone? Barring individuals from being a nuisance, just like Attorney General Hulls and others had advised us all those years ago.

But how would it actually work in practice? Despite abortion provider Dr Chris Healy's success in the Supreme Court, and perhaps after an immediate and pleasant injunctive relief, her clinic and patients continued to be targeted. The Fertility Control Clinic and Chris's clinic had both security guards and religious extremists in common.

If we were granted an injunction, would the relief apply only to the entrance of the clinic, or the clinic boundary, or further? Would it apply only to some behaviours and not others? Who would it be directed against? Would we need to engage in rolling court actions as we were beset by new extremists not on the injunction, or old extremists who became members of organisations not on the injunction? A reprieve of any sort would be welcome, but we wanted a long term, effective solution. Well, we wanted a buffer zone, but a state legislated exclusion zone didn't look like happening in our lifetime.

The FCC is likely to have a basis on which to obtain injunctive relief from the Supreme Court to restrain the commission by protestors of the tort of public nuisance... It will be necessary to identify the appropriate defendants to a claim in the Supreme Court... the individuals who sponsor, organise and take part in the protests outside the FCC.

Unlike the Royal Women's Hospital case, we couldn't rely on police to gather identifying information. How had Chris Healy gathered that identifying information? A private detective?

There was more to our reluctance. Apart from my non-learned reasons above, both Lou and I continued to have reservations about seeking an injunction. These days, 'gut instinct' or 'listening to your gut' has been given greater street cred: experts now refer to our gut as a 'second brain' (Gershon, 1999; Schneider, Wright, & Heuckeroth, 2019). In my clinical work I always valued the body's signals and the importance of listening and working out what they might mean—both for my patients and for me! There was something about going down the path of an injunction that both Lou and I didn't feel was the way to go. There were some clear reasons and then there were gut reasons more difficult to work out. With all Lou's experience, I trusted his gut on this.

As victims of the extremists' abuse, we did not want to be responsible for gathering their names and addresses for an injunction. We were a visible, prime target for religious extremists. We were targeted like no other abortion provider—daily vilification, large monthly protests, 40-day vigils, biffos and death threats, a murder. There was no appeal in providing courtroom air-time to our persecutors. There was no appeal in taking them on one by one. We had had a gut full of them as it was. No wonder our guts were arcing up.

It is at least possible that the grant of the interlocutory injunction would encourage the protesters to agree not to continue with their actions.
Hmm, I didn't think so. Our experience of the fanatics was that they were just that—fanatics. They would agree to nothing, other than having the clinic shut down. Ever tried to engage reasonably with religious fanatics? The usual rules just don't apply.

Testament to this were the evolving strategies of two professional gentlemen, Psychotherapist Torrey Orton and Futurist Charles Bass, who initially approached me with an offer to mediate an agreement between the clinic and the extremists. We sighed and declined. But Torrey and Charles were keen to try negotiating with the extremists. I voiced my concerns about the physical, emotional and legal danger Torrey and Charles might expose themselves to in what they intended to do. Retired obstetrician and gynaecologist Dr Pieter Mourik was beginning a fierce campaign for women's safe access to abortion in New South Wales. As the only abortion providing clinic in a vast rural region, the Fertility Control Clinic's Albury clinic was the focus of his challenge to the religious right. While his courage and fight bolstered women and me personally, the religious extremists ultimately made Pieter pay dearly both in the law courts and in his life generally. Engaging with anti-abortion fanatics tended to be a deeply taxing experience.

Clearly we had no power about what others decided to do on a public footpath and, like the presence of Radical Women, despite potential negative consequences for our patients, Torrey and Charles might bring positive ones too. Still, it was hard not to feel like we were just accruing more death-defying circus acts outside the clinic.

Torrey and Charles began a group called 'Friends of the FCC'. Initially they spent time on the footpath talking with the extremists and trying to persuade them with reasoned arguments to behave more in keeping with the true ethics of Christianity. But as Torrey and Charles witnessed the extremists' abuse up close and personal, their 'mediation' evolved into a form of direct action: they interposed themselves between the extremists and the women running the gauntlet.

Our original intention was to go and talk to the protestors and find out why they were doing what they did. We did that for six months and made a genuine and profound effort to listen to them and debate the pros and cons of the way they were going about it.

In the last two and a half years, we have had to intercept them because they were not willing to listen... We see our job now as to provide some physical protection to clients so we interpose our person between the protesters and the clients wherever we can. The protestors are usually very persistent so that is when we step in... and by then the clients are able to get into the clinic.

CHARLES BASS (2014)

I knew Charles had reached the point of no return when a rainy day spent on Wellington Parade inspired him to use an umbrella as a defensive weapon to shield women from the extremists, and the idea alit of attending every day with a pink umbrella emblazoned with 'Friends of FCC'. Oh-oh.

How much did the Friends add to, or subtract from, the gauntlet experience for women? The mere fact of being a man on the footpath outside the clinic (even if he wore a sign saying Friend of FCC) could create a frightening ambiguity for women. But Torrey and Charles became expert bird's eyewitnesses of the abuse and, like Radical Women, they stood up for women when no one else would.

Negotiate with extremists? The police couldn't. Torrey and Charles couldn't. Why would we?

I think there were a couple of issues with that option [injunctive relief]. One is that, the injunction would only operate against named parties. We could injunct the regulars if we found out their names, but they are part of a bigger movement and could just send other people. It would just be injunction after injunction against whoever turned up out the front.

I think the other really important factor in the decision not to pursue an injunction, was the clinic's sense that you didn't want to escalate the confrontation with the people out the front; that you already lived every day with this low-level threat that seemed like, particularly after Steve was killed, something that could blow up. That seemed like the best reason not to do it.

A case against the council also positioned the issue not as a private issue between you and the Helpers, but something that was genuinely the responsibility of government to do something about. There is this sexist idea that women in general should protect themselves from the violence of men. This strategically seemed like a really good and important thing to transfer that responsibility onto the government, even though we could see the reluctance of any government authorities to really take that responsibility.

EMILY HOWIE (2020)

Exactly.

In a legal context there can be powerful influences towards compromise. But at that time, we knew that we were the experts on our nuisance, and we wanted change as close to our own terms as we could. So, our grumbling guts and ill-defined reservations, questions and discussion met the learned kindness of our legal counsel. An alternative legal avenue was offered up: a creative use of a law not used in this way before, but with a reasonable chance of success, and avoiding the whole us-them confrontation. Given our adversarial legal system, it was still a legal us-them battle, but with a different 'them'. This alternative provided a legal buffer between us and the extremists, and rightly positioned eradicating the nuisance as the responsibility of government.

In addition, in this second legal approach, it was not likely that a Court would allow legal intervention from the religious extremists, the Catholic Church, the Christian Lobby, HOGPI... All of these hard right religious entities had well-earned reputations for sticking their long Pinocchio noses into areas that were none of their business.

This alternative course of action lay with the statutory law, that is, the laws written and enacted by Parliament. Specifically, our legal action lay with nuisance under the Public Health and Wellbeing Act 2008 (Vic) and enforcement through the statutory mechanism, or via the remedy of *mandamus*. Part 6 Division 1 of this Act, sets out the *Regulatory Provisions Administered by Councils* applying to nuisances:

A Council has a duty to remedy as far as is reasonably possible all nuisances existing in its municipal district. (s. 60)

The Council must investigate any notice of a nuisance. If, upon investigation, a nuisance is found to exist,

the Council must exercise specific powers conferred by the Act including issuing an improvement notice or prohibition notice, and bringing proceedings for an offence against the Act. (s.62).

A nuisance was any state, condition or activity which are, or are liable to be, dangerous to health or offensive. Where dangerous to health likely includes physical or mental health, and where offensive means: noxious or injurious to personal comfort (s. 58).

This sounded familiar: Almost ten years earlier in 2004 I had reminded Lord Mayor John So in my non-learned way that Municipal councils had clear duties under Section 41 of the *Health Act 1958 (Vic)* '*to remedy as far as reasonably possible all nuisances in its municipal district'*. We were summarily rebuffed then by City of Melbourne CEO David Pritchard who considered the extremist nuisance did not fit the definition of nuisance under the Act and that there was insufficient evidence to prove beyond reasonable doubt a nuisance within the limited types of nuisance in the Act.

Since then, and in order to update and modernise, the *Health Act 1958 (Vic)* had been repealed and replaced by the *Public Health and Wellbeing Act 2008 (PHW Act)*, which had taken effect from 1 January 2010. Our 2004 submission to that law modernisation recommended the inclusion of buffer zones around health clinics. Let that go. Water under the bridge. Whoosh. Sail on with our bright, eminent legal counsel.

> *This is so fascinating in retrospect. You put in a submission and then over ten years later, counsel made the same argument. It's like lining up the holes in Swiss cheese. You finally found counsel that shared the view you had for decades and had actually expressed over ten years before. Whereas, previous legal advice, handicapped by a 'male gaze', hadn't even truly recognised the problem. Patience, tenacity and selectiveness in your legal team seem like the ingredients of a great legal strategy for social change.*

Lizzie O'Shea

Yep, Em was a human rights match maker: a perfect Swiss cheese match. Our counsel pointed out that:

> *The MCC, and its councillors, are 'public authorities' for the purposes of the Charter of Human Rights and Responsibilities Act 2006 (Vic) (The Charter): s 4(1)e… The MCC would, therefore, in exercising the power to investigate, and in determining whether to prosecute, be required to consider relevant Charter rights, and not to act inconsistently with those rights…*

Counsel highlighted protester rights of *peaceful assembly* (s 16 of the Charter) and *freedom of expression* (s 15). Like all Charter rights, these may be subject to reasonable limits to ensure a democratic society based on human dignity, equality and freedom.

The freedom of protesters to express their views in relation to abortion may be limited by lawful restrictions reasonably necessary, relevantly, to respect the rights of patients and staff of the FCC, and to protect public order and public health... There is a strong privacy interest in all personal medical information, and the privacy interest of women who are accessing the services of the clinic in relation to the termination of a pregnancy are arguably even stronger than in relation to other medical matters...

There is in our view, no basis on which the rights in the Charter would prevent the MCC fully investigating and prosecuting protesters for nuisance under the Act.

Other provisions [of the PHW Act] establish a process by which the MCC may be notified of a nuisance and the MCC must then investigate that notice: s62(1) and (2). If a nuisance is found to exist, the MCC must take certain action: s 62 (3) and (4)... Section 60 of the PHW Act imposes a clear duty on the Council, not only to investigate nuisances, but to remedy them so far as is reasonably possible.

Somewhat worrying, counsel noted that they had:

Not identified any judicial authority which considers or applies the sections of the PHW Act or the Health Act.

And:

The difficulty with the [notification] scheme established by the PHW Act may be that the Council may investigate but decline to prosecute, or may make a minimal investigation... There is not specific provision in the PHW Act as to whether action could be taken against the Council if it investigated, but again declined to prosecute.

With these issues in mind, where there is a refusal to exercise jurisdiction conferred, or to perform a duty imposed, by law, counsel pointed out that a more effective and convenient remedy to pursue may be to:

Bring proceedings in the Supreme Court of Victoria to seek an order of mandamus against the Council requiring it to remedy the nuisance constituted by the protesters' activity.

We had no idea then that when we finally made it into the Supreme Court seeking an order of *mandamus* against MCC, opposing counsel would derail our case by mounting a technical argument around the very same worrying PHW Act provisions, or lack of provisions, or misunderstood provisions, or prone to being spurned provisions, or... Our remedy would prove not as effective as we had hoped.

I think part of the difficulty of doing human rights litigation in Australia is that we have limited human rights protections in law. Victoria is one of the outliers in having a Charter of Human Rights. If you aren't using human rights, often you're running cases for an outcome that is going to be supportive of human rights, but using a different legal vehicle. It can be like putting a square peg in a round hole. You are seeking to address harm using a cause of action in the courts that seems distant from, or unrelated to, the human element of why you're there...

Public law arguments, like the ones that we were running in that case, are really about trying to restrain government power or require government action to discharge their obligations. Government is often the entity that is going to abuse human rights and also protect them. So public law is a really important site for protecting human rights.

So on the one level, it made perfect sense to me that we would use that intellectually.

EMILY HOWIE (2020)

There is considerable criticism by legal scholars about social movements and their 'turn to law'. The claim is that a turn to law can be a conservatising influence. Of course on the one hand that's true, but it's also a critical way in which social change happens. The example commonly referred to is gay marriage, where in the US at least, the people who fought in courts were very conservative, that is, the plaintiffs were always presentable, nuclear family types. But my view is: they got the law changed, and we all benefit from that. Of course the fight isn't over once you secure law reform. But it's hard to continue to fight if you are up against legal barriers all the time.

LIZZIE O'SHEA

We had arrived at an extraordinary turning point in the campaign. Our problem was starting to be framed legally in a way which was structurally correct, identified the correct 'them' in 'us v them' and, was couched in a woman-centred language and human rights perspective. We were at the beginning of a strategy that would ultimately bring success. I had sprinkled a little water in Em's direction and she had become the seed sprouting the special people who would become our team, and the arguments that would bring our case.

Butting your head against a brick wall might eventually loosen a brick. If you can't find a way around or over that wall, keep head butting. Agitating for change is an act of faith, a constant rehearsal with the hope that it might one day be a performance, work done with an optimism of the will, even though there is a pessimism of the intellect (Antonio Gramsci, 1929).

Patience, tenacity and a select legal team are ingredients of a great legal strategy for social change. The law is conservative, slow and formal. It doesn't like to be changed, so forcing such change is a monumental effort. The temptation to compromise in a legal context can be immense. Recognise you are the expert on your issue and within reason, wherever you can, seek change on your own terms.

And, whatever you do, remember Lizzie's Swiss cheese rule: Does your legal counsel get you? Do they share your view? Are you preparing to take advantage of opportunities coming your way? Do your Swiss cheese holes align?! You don't want just anyone coming on board. You need to find the right cheese, er, people.

CHAPTER 8

Who's Running the Case?

February 2012–November 2013

> *You have to be in a marathon, not a sprint.*
>
> LIZZIE O'SHEA (2020)

Finding a law firm for our legal action against MCC turned out to be tricky. For almost a year, Rachel approached law firms to find one who would join our pro bono case:

Rachel Ball, Human Rights Solicitor, has tried five law firms re pro bono representation with no success so far.

One firm is really interested and could take on for a nominal fee... Another firm has pro bono coordinator who is keen but has been stymied from above because they also represent various protest groups. Rachel is still pushing and arguing that FCC situation quite different.

Rachel has now exhausted Human Rights Resource Centre's pool of legal firms. Rachel is still pushing the above options.

MEMO TO LOU RUTMAN &
JANICE NUGENT, 3 FEBRUARY 2012

I guessed we would never shake the old abortion taboo. Was everyone but HRLC worried about being smeared with the sinful stain of abortion? Come on now. We were talking about real women's lives here. Women's strength and self-efficacy when confronted with our imperfect, complex and sexist world. Our case oozed with real, meaty human rights arguments. Join us.

I think law firms are partnerships, so even law firms who do pro bono work need to have the support of their partners to do that work. Usually they would have guidelines about the kind of pro bono they can or can't do. Some who do work for the Department of Immigration, for example, won't do work for asylum seekers on the other side. So there can be relationship reasons why they won't take on a case. I suspect that it was not an issue of a conflict with a client, but more an issue of abortion that was seen to be raised by the case. I think even if you had just one member of the partnership who felt very strongly on that issue, that would be a reason not to take it on...

Mostly with their pro bono practices lawyers do really great work, but there wouldn't have been much work on this kind of issue. It's a hot button issue. Unfortunately it still was then, and I think it is much less so now. I think it shows that the legal profession is really progressive in parts, but firms are made up of diverse groups of people. Probably it comes down to a cross benefit analysis in pushing that through at the firm level.

EMILY HOWIE (2020)

By early 2012, Rachel Ball was on her own in the challenge to find us a law firm. Encouraged by HLRC Phil Lynch, Emily Howie had taken up an opportunity to do a Masters in Law from Columbia University—civil rights, human rights, public international law subjects—right up Em's alley. Once in New York, Em successfully applied to do a Leebron Human Rights Fellowship research project looking at the asylum seekers going from Sri Lanka to Australia. I was both dismayed and elated at Em's success. I wanted Em here to continue her work with us, but for an old feminist like me, seeing this new generation of young women taking on the world was inspiring and cause for great optimism.

Meanwhile Rachel Ball, a gentle, generous soul with a fierce determination, pushed our case along. Eventually, somehow, Rachel secured the pro bono services of Maurice Blackburn (MB) Lawyers. We were perhaps not an obvious or natural fit, given that MB was a champion of protest rights. MB would not be the first to struggle with the idea that the 'protest' outside the FCC was in fact *not* a protest, but chronic, insidious and harmful behaviour trampling on myriad women's rights.

I remember the initial struggle to find a law firm to take on our case. I think it was more than five in the end that we had gone to. It's not unusual for firms to say no to a request for pro bono assistance for a variety of reasons, including where there might be a conflict. I think that was the case for some of the firms.

But we usually didn't need to go to that many firms for a case that had legal merit like this one did. I can only speculate and read between the lines of what I was told by the pro bono managers at the firms, but I expect that at least in some cases there was a concern that running a case about abortion, which is how it was seen, was too controversial, too hot, for the firm to take on. From memory, the request was one that resulted in some robust debate amongst the partnerships about whether or not it was a good matter for various firms to pick up.

I think working with Maurice Blackburn was a great match and it probably was to our benefit that we were working with a firm with such a clear demonstrated commitment to free speech and protest rights because we were able to use that expertise and profile to ensure that we were finding and communicating the right balance between the competing rights at play throughout the case.

RACHEL BALL (2020)

During a March 2012 introductory phone call with Lizzie O'Shea, I learnt that Lizzie ran MB's pro bono cases, and she had already discussed our matter with Rachel, Peter Hanks, Jacob Varghese and MB's Sydney-based Principal, Rebecca Gilsenan. Much more had been going on behind the scenes, too.

Rachel first approached us at the end of 2011. There was a flurry of emails between us while the offices were closing. In January, I put a referral to our Social Justice Committee which was made up of different lawyers from across the firm, representative of different practice areas that were indicative of people's interest in this field of work... I'd circulate a referral, people would talk about it on an email chain and we'd have a meeting, or a vote, or similar.

The first time I circulated it, the main concern that was raised was that we acted for Greenpeace in NSW, for example, who often protest and get arrested for protesting. Committee members were very concerned that potentially this kind of precedent or legislation or order by the Court might be used against protesters in other settings. Our industrial department felt similarly concerned. There were many people on the email list who were keen to take on the case but were concerned about that issue. We talked back and forth about why this was slightly different to protest.

It wasn't particularly controversial, but I think Rachel needed a decision very quickly. I think it was because there was a decision made by Council that we wanted to try and challenge within a certain time frame if we took that path to seek to overturn Council's administrative decision. She was asking for a decision, but we decided that we couldn't make that call in that time, so we turned it down.

Terri Butler, now an MP in Queensland, was a Principal in our Queensland office at the time. She has a long history of working with Children by Choice in Queensland and advocating for abortion rights there. She got back well after the deadline. 'Sorry I'm late to this but,' she said, 'I really think we should do something about it'. I have such a strong memory of that, having another female in a position of power did make a big difference.

So Jacob [Varghese], who is the CEO of the firm now, and was responsible for managing me then, said let's have another talk about it, then we can go back to Rachel. Jacob is very skilful at making those political dynamics work and making decisions in institutional environments, very good at getting people on board, and because he was a senior staff member he had the gravitas to make it work. So Jacob got everyone over the line and then we agreed to take it on. So it was really probably Terri sticking up for it as well.

We went back to Rachel, 'Could we talk with the barristers about these concerns and explore it. We would like to act but we are worried about these things.'

And then it unfolded from there.

LIZZIE O'SHEA

So was the old abortion taboo a hurdle as well?

No. There was a view that we'd have to manage it from a comms perspec-
tive. But there was an overwhelming view that this type of behaviour
[from HOGPI] was unacceptable, even if you were against abortion.

LIZZIE O'SHEA

Late afternoon on 15 March 2012 in the clinic lounge, Rachel, Lou, Janice and I met with Maurice Blackburn (then Associate) Lizzie O'Shea and her supervisor, MB Principal Jacob Varghese. An afternoon appointment usually would protect Lizzie and Jacob from running into extremists out the front, but the Easter Lent vigil was on, and as an apparent couple in crisis, Lizzie and Jacob drew some attention.

They saw a man and woman walk in together and you could tell they were
scowling at us because they thought that Lizzie and I were going in there
for 'bad' reasons. In reality the real reason we were there was much worse
for them in the long run!

JACOB VARGHESE (2020)

In our meeting, Jacob Varghese's calm and affable presence indicated MB's commitment to our case. Lizzie O'Shea's feminist energy and brain space spilt from her petite frame into rapid and exciting words. Over the years I grew both to expect and still be amazed by Lizzie's prodigious productivity—running marathons, authoring books, fighting the good fight here and overseas, running cases, running our case. I received emails from Lizzie from around the world: 'Hi Susie, I'm in Canada for a few days... I'm running in the New York marathon tomorrow... I'm in Ireland working on their abortion decrim...' When I eventually attended the 2019 book launch of Lizzie's genius take on modern technology, *Future Histories,* I thought the title apt for both author and book. Lizzie would always be a woman ahead of her time. Lizzie would never be out of date.

I recall meeting with you in that stately room at the front of the lovely peri-
od building, looking out over a peaceful garden towards Wellington Parade.
The whole place felt like a sanctuary, which it must have seemed to people
who arrived there after running the gauntlet to get inside.

We spoke about how we might proceed legally. You were clearly deter-
mined, and you could tell you'd been doing this kind of advocacy work for

years. We were coming to it legally for the first time, but you were carrying the experience of decades of exhausting work, and the frustration of being ignored. You were very professional and respectful about it all, but it was clear to me that we ought to be sensitive to that.

My objective was to ensure you understood the legal process, so that we could work collaboratively, as equals, because the legal process could be tedious in its own way. I wanted to make sure you understood the parameters we were working within. I was very keen to make sure you trusted that we were on your side.

LIZZIE O'SHEA

We had our law firm and a legal team!

Emily and Lizzie were both all over it and no one was going to put anything over them. To hear these young women speak, I was in awe.

The moment we met with Emily, Lizzie and the barristers, you thought if this is going to happen, these people are going to make it happen. There was no doubt in my mind that with you driving this and these exceptional people fighting for us, there was never any doubt. They were so on the ball, and we were in such good hands, that if anything was going to work it would be this. Susan felt exactly the same, and at the end of the day, you only had to hear them speak, and you knew they would make it happen.

JANICE NUGENT (2020)

Whenever we met with our legal team, Lou, Janice and I would be reminded of their brilliance, and the fact that they totally got our situation as an important women's rights, human rights and public health issue. But it was the kind care shown to us over and over again that meant I knew, without a doubt, we could trust that our legal reps were on our side. I personally felt immense gratitude for how generously and patiently our legal team shared their time and learned advice in the face of our less than legally-minded questions and comments.

That didn't mean that there weren't challenges along the way. Being involved in this legal action was foreign territory for us and we were not exactly a straight-forward case. By that first meeting in March 2012, our instructions were already out of date. Sigh. Over and over again, nothing changes, but we're always out of date. Gather new evidence, again, which will end up being the same. Groan.

Six months later, 5 September 2012, we were all together at MB's offices at the court precinct end of Lonsdale Street: Our learned counsel Peter Hanks QC, Claire Harris and Therese McCarthy, MB's Lizzie O'Shea and Rhiannon Reid, HRLC's Rachel Ball, and FCC's Lou, Janice and me. A part of me smugly pictured us suing the socks off Melbourne City Council. Picture it, a case about protest rights versus women's rights, and we walk into Court with champions of protest rights and human rights: Human Rights Law Centre, Maurice Blackburn Lawyers and our learned team of giants in human rights law. Slam dunk!

It had taken us eighteen months to reach this point. We left with plenty of homework to do. I felt exhausted by the amount of up-to-date evidence we needed to amass, especially when: nothing's changed.

Well, in fact, one thing had changed. We had new evidence. Exciting, fabulous, awful evidence. Turns out our learned counsel didn't share my excitement. Apparently *evidence* through a clinical psychology lens is quite different to *evidence* through the prism of the law. But, here's what I was excited about, and it had everything to do with women's voices being captured in research. As Criado Perez (2019, p 314) points out:

> *Failing to collect data on women and their lives means that we continue to naturalise sex and gender discrimination—while at the same time somehow not seeing any of this discrimination… It's the irony of being a woman: at once hypervisible when it comes to being treated as the subservient sex class, and invisible when it counts—when it comes to being counted.*

The new research evidence also had everything to do with the FCC being more like family, in more ways than one. Mother and daughter, Rhonda and Tash, were FCC charge nurse and admin respectively. Susan's daughter, Georgie, filled in on FCC reception/admin duties. In earlier years described above, warm-hearted, clever, hard-working Rebecca Dean provided invaluable pro bono legal advice to the clinic. My descriptors betray the fact that Rebecca is in fact my own daughter, who as a uni student had worked casually at the clinic. Plus, through me Rebecca had an inevitable exposure to the clinic's fascinating and challenging issues overlapping with the law.

Similarly, while completing her studies, Janice Nugent's daughter Allie Humphries worked casually at the clinic. Allie too had absorbed our woman-centred ethos. Allie worked her way to topping her University of Melbourne's coursework Masters in Clinical Psychology—the course I'd completed 32 years earlier. I'd been amongst the second or third year of intake for what was then a new progressive Masters course.

During Allie's Masters studies, I was delighted to co-supervise both her clinical and research work. Such roles were not uncommon for me. I was even more delighted that she chose and devised an elegant and rigorous study on a topic so lacking and so vital to our campaign for safe abortion access. I had taken simple audits of clinic women's experiences before, but Allie's research was a methodologically rigorous, theoretically anchored and cohesive work that would prove invaluable in our advocacy for safe abortion access. *Stigma, Secrecy and Anxiety in Women Attending for an Early Abortion* (2011) provided crucial, previously unknown, data about women's experience of the extremists.

In considering whether the anti-abortion picketers could be considered a form of 'enacted stigma', Allie reported on 158 pregnant women attending the FCC in 2010 for an early pregnancy termination for psychosocial reasons. From this: 135 (85%) women reported seeing the picketers outside the clinic; 118 (75%) had seen anti-abortion displays such as posters and props; 95 (60%) reported that the picketers had tried to hand them anti-abortion information; 87 (55%) had picketers say things to them and 32 (20%) had picketers attempt to block their entry into the clinic. Part and parcel of the usual neatness/limitations in research design, a range of other extremist behaviour (e.g. stalking, photographing/filming, praying, singing) was not enquired about.

Women completed the statement, *When I was confronted with anti-abortion protestors today I felt...* by choosing a word from the well-validated and researched Positive and Negative Affect Scale (comprising 10 positive feeling words e.g. strong, proud, determined; and 10 negative e.g. upset, guilty, scared; rated on a 5-point Likert scale from 1. very slightly or not at all, to 5. extremely).

Despite all of the anecdotal evidence to the contrary, a part of me hoped that we would find women unaffected by the extremists. Then we could just leave things be, knowing that women were not being harmed at all. But Allie's research corroborated and extended our anecdotal evidence with most concerning truths. There was no doubt now that every day on a public footpath, religious extremists were causing significant numbers of women considerable distress.

Allie's study found that women's mean Negative Affect score was more than two standard deviations higher than for normative samples and was comparable to psychiatric samples. Their mean Positive Affect score was less than half that of normative samples. Other well-validated measures indicated that higher levels of pre-abortion anxiety in our patients were associated both with more exposure to the anti-abortion picketers, and with experiencing more negative affect in response to the anti-abortion extremists (e.g. higher levels of guilt, shame, and anger).

Seventy-one per cent of women reported feeling personally stigmatised by their decision to have an abortion. All women were asked to consider various sources of that personal abortion stigma. Women perceived the greatest amount of stigma to come from the picketers, and from the picketers being allowed to protest outside the front of the clinic. Women reported feeling the least stigmatised by the partner in the pregnancy, their friends, and the healthcare system.

Higher overall ratings of perceived abortion stigma were associated with having women feeling that they could not tell anybody about their pregnancy or abortion, which in turn was found to undermine women's well-being.

SOURCES OF PERCEIVED ABORTION STIGMA (% of *n* = 158)

Is abortion stigmatised by:	Very Much So (%)	Moderately (%)	Somewhat (%)	Not At All (%)
The picketers	78	4	5	13
Allowing protestors	71	11	10	8
Religious groups	54	20	12	15
Society	22	29	32	17
The media	11	34	37	18
Your family	21	18	30	31
Partner in the pregnancy	5	10	25	60
Your friends	6	17	39	38
The healthcare system	5	17	33	45

% of *n* = 158

Allie's research had provided disturbing but solid world-first, methodologically rigorous evidence. But apparently *legal* evidence is first-hand witnessing and testimony of the nuisance and harm, so Allie's research was not strictly helpful to our case. Compared with my own anecdotal, first-hand witnessing evidence, I probably placed as much, or more, value on Allie's robust research which was basically reporting the accounts of the too-many women who suffered harm at the hands of the religious extremists, but whose first-hand accounts of the harm were usually not heard because part of that harm included silencing women. Ugh.

Allie's research ultimately was included as an attachment to my Supreme Court affidavit. Years later, her work would find its way into parliamentary debates about the Safe Access Zones Bill and, when the Office of Public Prosecutions would defend the challenge to the zones law, Allie's work would go all the way to the High Court. And so would women's voices.

Women's voices were also being gathered with extreme sensitivity by Rachel who was focused on winning our case both in the courtroom and in the court of public opinion.

The media coverage was critical to the ultimate success of the campaign because initially the problem wasn't just inaction from the police or from the council. They were both symptoms of a deeper problem which was that women's voices were not being heard, that their concerns and their rights were not being respected. Shifting that was always going to be critical to any success that we might achieve. So getting the media interested and implementing a smart media strategy was as important, I think, as the legal matter in this case.

One of the things that made such a difference in terms of the media coverage was our ability to work with staff at the clinic and some of your clients who generously offered to tell their story as part of the media coverage. I remember calling up a small handful of clients who were so affected and felt so strongly about the injustice that they had experienced, of having to run the gauntlet to get into the clinic, that they were willing to share their experiences. In the face of those stories it became impossible for the Helpers to maintain this false narrative where they were the only players with rights in the story that gave their rights to hold and express religious beliefs as the sun that the world revolved around. There were other people who were part of this story: the women and their children coming into access health services whose voices also needed to be heard. It was the media coverage that allowed that to happen and that ultimately helped us to shift the narrative so that the urgent need for action was so much clearer.

For some of the women it took great courage because there is still so much stigma around abortion. Even though they all requested that they be de-identified in any media coverage, it was still for some of those women quite nerve-racking.

But having those women's voices in the media was really important because decision makers and the public needed to be hearing both sides of the story. We, the clinic's clients and clinic staff who gave evidence and spoke to the media ensured that happened.

And staff like Janice [Nugent]. I know that the whole experience for her was probably quite gruelling, and people wouldn't necessarily *understand or see that, see the kind of personal commitment that was required from her, and that steely determination that she had to have to get through it all.*

RACHEL BALL (2020)

Yes, you had to admire the likes of Janice, a woman from my own generation. You had to admire feminists of earlier generations. But you had to love this new generation of young women with the heart and know-how to push forward the agenda for women: women conducting woman-centred research, like Allie Humphries and Rebecca Dean; women demanding protection and respect for women with a carefully planned legal and media strategy, like Rachel, Em and Lizzie; and women, like some of our clients, defying abortion stigma and demanding respect by bravely and publicly speaking of their own experience.

All of these young women filled me with such hope that I could feel a dance coming on. Serendipitously, another inspiring woman, then Reproductive Choice Australia's Leslie Cannold, obliged with a well-organised *Let's End the Stigma* (around abortion) flashmob dance in Federation Square. Yes, a flashmob dance! On Sunday 30 September 2012, I was happily reacquainted with Leslie's fun-filled, grass roots campaigning. Beside Melbourne's upside-down Yarra River, and accompanying the new generation of happening young activists, old feminists like me, Colleen Hartland, Beth Wilson, Annarella Hardiman, Janice Nugent and so many others, men and women, shimmied our shoulders and extended our best jazz hands. We were hip. We were cool. And rather unco. We were dancing our way through abortion rights history.

A month later, October 2012, I still felt refreshed remembering that inter-generational, gender-inclusive flashmob, and I had completed my new Affidavit. Well, I thought I had. Other FCC staff, *Friends of the Clinic* Charles and Torrey, and East Melbourne Group residents were all working on their statements. Residents were troubled and frustrated by Police and MCC inaction against the extremists. The East Melbourne resident below was one suck away from a dummy spit:

We had great hopes of the police and City Council who seemed to be saying they had a solution to the protester problem. But I gather not so. Why they can move on beggars and homeless people sleeping in local parks, not to mention the Occupy Melbourne squad yet do nothing to resolve the protester issue in spite of volumes of complaints I do not know. The people who sent in complaints recently are a bit miffed that apparently their complaints don't count. Now the police are saying we have to go through the process all over again with people who are prepared to go to court asked to submit complaints of actual harassment. Nothing so far seems to have been good enough. It really is a ridiculous situation.

It was always nice to know that I was not alone in throwing the odd dummy spit over our situation. 'The pen is mightier than the sword', I hoped, and my dummy spits landed as Letters to the Editor, in private correspondence, and even in a formal police statement that eventually found its way into the exhibits attached to my Supreme Court affidavit:

I have been the Clinical Psychologist at the Fertility Control Clinic (FCC) for more than twenty years. The FCC provides a range of essential family planning and reproductive health services including contraception, PAP test, sexually transmitted infection screening and treatment, pregnancy termination (abortion), pregnancy and contraceptive counselling and health referrals...

East Melbourne Police has again asked for a statement from me. But Police already have a huge file on unpleasant and violent incidents on the footpath, and staff statements about the impact of the picketers on them personally. I have met with numerous dedicated police officers over the years... hundreds more [complaints] do not reach the police or MCC because women do not wish to cause a fuss or become embroiled in a more stressful situation, or have their private health concerns made even more public...

A proactive preventative solution would see police and MCC freed up for other pressing matters. Recently MCC and police acted swiftly to move the Occupy Melbourne group.

We are the only workplace having to endure this... There is no 'good enough' excuse to sit on our hands and allow such disrespectful mistreatment of our daughters and mothers, our partners and friends.

EXCERPTS FROM A STATEMENT TO EAST MELBOURNE POLICE
16 FEBRUARY 2012

Police and legal action required evidence from staff and residents. Evidence required taking note of specific, recent examples of what the extremists were doing, saying and displaying. Media wanted that too. But my usual go-to coping strategy was avoid; if unable to avoid, ignore; if unable to ignore, delete. I did not want to observe and note, and I definitely did not want to go out the front and take photos. Why would I want to have to add to the mountain of examples of extremists' behaviour that I, other staff and patients found disturbing? But, occasionally for the 'greater good' of getting the message out there, or gathering evidence for our legal action, I would force myself to pay attention and make detailed notes afterwards of events I really did not want to become part of me. The example below, included in my book, *Murder On His Mind*, gives some idea of the tension between wanting to avoid-ignore-delete the experience versus the importance of gathering the facts:

I take in the trees. We're so lucky in Melbourne with our tree-lined streetscapes.

Yep. A protester is coming my way.

Guess at the weather—wonderfully changeable. Notice a car coming out of a basement car park.

Yep. Here she is.

There's the building where Simmo used to work.

She sidles up beside me. She is walking along with me now. There might be a hair's breadth between us.

I look in the travel agent's window at Balmy Phuket... Sizzling Spain.

'You are wearing the colour of the blood you spill.'

Oh, look a little bird picks up a crumb from the pavement.

'You are wearing the red of the blood of the precious children you murder.'

I notice a drop of coffee bubbling out of the take away plastic top.

'Don't kill the babies.'

I wipe the coffee drop with my thumb as it slides down the cup towards my hand.

'Don't kill the precious children. Save the precious infants.'

Ah, there is Steve.

'You're the last of the few doing the dirty work.'

Steve sees me and gives me a grin.

I see the glint of a cross hanging around her neck. I walk past the others now. Two men and another woman. They are standing on the footpath facing the clinic. Their heads are bent in prayer. Bibles are open in their hands... 'Save the little children. Do not go in there. Do not murder the children. Call on Jesus' name...'

But I don't see her. I don't hear her. I don't see them. I don't hear them.

ALLANSON, 2006

Staff, patients, residents and passers-by all coped in their own way. Many were like me: first line of defence, avoid; if that's not possible, ignore what was going on outside of us and the feelings threatening to erupt inside of us. It was the opposite of what you want clients doing within the safety of the therapy room, but sometimes the only thing left to do in the big bad world.

Then there would be an event, a patient, an action, a prop, a day where it had all just gone too far. One more extremist step violating new, or old, territory. Whatever it was, it would tip us over the edge into rage and hopelessness. We would re-visit the decades of abuse. Re-experience the day Steve was murdered.

Being asked to detail specific instances seemed to sell short the whole long shemozzle of our experience of siege. After decades of nuisance calls and death threats Susan Speaking endured while working at the clinic switchboard, did it help to observe that on the day of 17 November 2012 Susan counselled women who found the extremists particularly aggressive, the extremists sang directly outside the consulting rooms by standing in the laneway that runs the length of the clinic, police were called, and HOGPI continued on doing exactly what it wanted. The laneway nuisance became a regular occurrence. 'Our workplace is becoming even more besieged,' Susan cried.

Did it help that on a particular day, Susan wound up shaking, indignant and in tears after she was doused in coffee?

Sometimes I worry when I see a new person standing with the HOGPI. I think that my nervousness is related to the murder of the FCC's security guard in 2001. Peter James Knight, who was convicted of that murder, was seen standing with the HOGPI... A couple of months ago I saw a HOGPI member that I had never seen before. She had covered her face and her body with clothes so you couldn't see her and she was holding a baby doll. When I went out to get a coffee with a colleague I saw this woman. When I returned she was still there. I went inside. I got my camera and returned to take a picture of her. When she saw me trying to take the photo, she flipped a coffee she was holding which went all over me.

Affidavit of Susan Hopkins,

18 December 2013

Did it help to point out from Janice's years of confronting extremists, comforting patients and staff, calling police and MCC to attend... did it help to describe just one incident in early March 2013 of Janice challenging an extremist displaying a particularly offensive poster, calling police, to have nothing done, Janice following up with me, me following up with police and finally, miraculously, police charging the woman with displaying an obscene figure in a public place contrary to s 17(1)(b) of the Summary Offences Act 1966 (Vic) (2013). Janice would be a witness in lengthy court proceedings spanning four years!

Out of all of the grubby goings-on, did it help to highlight that one of our security guards was taken to court by an extremist seeking an intervention order to stop him attending the clinic? That is, an intervention order to stop our security guard attending his own work place? Needless to say, the extremist's threat stopped just short of the courtroom door. But the emotional and time costs to our security guard (the financial costs were carried by the clinic) were hefty and unwarranted. Legal intimidation of FCC employees was just another one of HOPGI's strategies.

Did it help to note that another security guard left her job with us because of an extremist's death threat? Did it help to comment on a particularly nasty extremist who, charged with threatening to kill our security guard, was banned from being in the vicinity and 'retired' to Queensland, only to return years later and cause havoc on Monday 27 February 2012: a patient's companion pushed him away and he fell over; ambulance, police, a circus, Lou telling police, 'the picketers cannot expect to continue in this vein and there not be any consequences'.

Hell, it didn't even help to note 16 July 2001: Steve's murder.

And what about pointing to just one instance out of thousands of a vulnerable or assertive patient, companion, resident or staff member being involved in a clash and having to chance police censure and charges as Police 'balanced rights' and bewildered bystanders decided to spit the dummy:

Dear Minister,

This morning I was walking east on Wellington Parade… I placed myself between the woman and the couple and asked the woman to refrain from accosting the couple further. The protestor accused me of assaulting her. Another with a crucifix tucked into the front of his pants, like a cowboy, brandished a cane and hit me twice. A heated discussion ensued as I tried to explain the damage they were doing to clearly vulnerable members of the community…

Standing nearby were two young police officers who then stepped forward to diffuse the deteriorating situation… I learned that the police officers had been told by the protesters that I had been involved in previous altercations. I am a Qantas pilot staying overnight, unaware the premises was a fertility control clinic before today…

As a visitor to Melbourne I was appalled by what I witnessed this morning… Give your police the powers to move these protesters on or arrest them for public mischief.

LETTER TO MINISTER FOR POLICE & EMERGENCY
SERVICES FROM VISITOR
15 FEBRUARY 2012

If this man had succeeded in action being taken against the extremists, he would have made history. No history made that day, or any other day. HOGPI devotees continued on their merry way using whatever form of intimidation they could to secure their goal of shutting us down: No staff means no FCC.

No patients means no FCC. No security guards means no FCC. Just women and families abandoned to torture and hardship.

On rare occasions, I'd think I should assert myself with the extremists. Speak up. Don't be such a wus. What a mistake that always was. My most shameful was the day I went outside to point out that having small children sitting on chairs on the footpath was not appropriate. This was not a situation for children to witness or be party to. Lessons in bullying?

But I ended up yelling, in front of the children. Swallowed up by a dummy spit out of my control, I returned inside the clinic mortified, shaking, ashamed. No, nothing good ever came from thinking you could reason with fanatics.

We couldn't argue this alone or rely on individuals to continuously be appalled and raise it with authorities. We needed to make an argument that confronting this problem was a collective responsibility. For us, that meant following a legal path with our elite legal team who could speak our language, but also speak a language to power that would be understood. It meant trying to win in a court of law, trying to win in the court of public opinion, and trying to win over the powers that be.

Of course, legal challenges are always going to make you present your case in a particular way, perhaps lacking nuance and almost as representative of an ideal rather than as a real person. But we managed to do it on our own terms. We avoided the struggle of women and the clinic being objectified as a party in a court matter because we had an excellent hand-picked team, you were a determined and uncompromising party, and we never lost sight of the human stories.

LIZZIE O'SHEA

It is exhausting to constantly repeat yourself and not be heard. But treat everyone with respect and kindness. You have no idea the pressures they may be under.

While it may be difficult to extend quite the same respect to those who do not share your values, like anti-abortion extremists on our doorstep, losing your cool does not help.

We had creative and intelligent researchers with us to make visible the facts and set out what needed to change and how. Such research partners are invaluable at different times and worth seeking out for collaboration.

Slowly turning what we knew, and often viscerally felt, to be true into credible, methodical evidence for a court process speaks to power in a different way. In our case, our arguments and evidence were formalised and given power by taking a legal pathway with a team who 'got' us and our situation, and who shared our feminist and human rights values. Our legal team took good care of us, and empowered us to make choices, inform the strategy and strengthen arguments that could be put squarely and formally to the power structures.

Without hope there is no advocacy, and without advocacy there is no hope. Find hope in the successes of advocates past, the inspiration of present old hands, but perhaps especially, in the younger generation of bright, good-hearted people. Advocacy demands a collective, rather than an individual, response.

CHAPTER 9

In the Eyes of the Beholder: Obscenity

March 2013–March 2017

I find that the figures displayed by the appellant in the context of a protest outside a medical clinic when viewed objectively are obscene because they might properly be described as disgusting.

LACAVA J (2015)

There seemed to be an assumption among people we encountered—the council, police, politicians and others—that we could sort this problem out through individual prosecutions. But rarely were the actual and practical realities recognised. We at the clinic knew these realities inside out, and it is instructive to consider one individual prosecution to debunk the myth that rolling individual prosecutions could ever provide a workable solution. In order to present this case from its beginning, March 2013, to its end, four years later, the otherwise generally chronological order of our story must stray here. But by the end of this chapter, the moral of this element of our story should be clear: individual prosecutions using existing laws were unworkable as a way to protect women.

A charge of obscenity against one of the extremists was a relatively rare instance of police laying charges against an extremist. A woman outside the clinic was charged in early March 2013 with displaying an obscene figure in a public place contrary to s 17(1)(b) of the Summary Offences Act 1966

(Vic). She was convicted in the Magistrates Court on 5 August 2014 (Fraser v Walker), her appeal was heard *de novo* in the County Court on 7 October 2015 (Fraser v Walker, 2015 VCC 1911) where she was convicted again on 19 November 2015 (Lacava J delivered written reasons). Her 1 August 2016 application for a Supreme Court review of the County Court decision (Fraser v County Court of Victoria and Constable Brenton Walker and Attorney General for the State of Victoria intervening, with Emerton J presiding) was dismissed on 21 March 2017. Conviction and penalty stood. Another salutary lesson in the futility of current laws to protect our patients and staff also stood.

I have attached a photo of a graphic and offensive poster displayed by one of our less regular female picketers. I've been told by our staff that we contacted MCC, then police arrived, and the picketer concerned was given a warning. I don't think that staff really ever know what has happened. I hope that in fact police exercised their power to issue an on-the-spot fine for violation of s.17(1) (b) of the Summary Offences Act 1966 which makes it an offence to 'exhibit or display an indecent or obscene work, figure or representation'.

It appears to us that MCC and police talk to, or warn, the picketers on numerous occasions. The picketers then might alter their behaviour or display for a short time, but eventually do it again, just like this woman who returned on a subsequent day with the same display. There are so many other picketer displays and leaflets I consider offensive (let alone picketer behaviour), but surely there can be no question about this one.

Email to East Melbourne Police Officers

8 March 2013

The legal words in my follow-up email to local police had been provided by HRLC's Rachel Ball. On that March 2013 day, almost every patient and their companion arrived distressed and referring to this particularly offensive poster. A staff member took a photo of the display. Practice Manager Janice asked that the woman remove the poster or Janice would call the police. Janice called the police.

History told us that Janice and I had wasted yet more of our time on a lost cause. History told us there was no hope of police action. But if we didn't speak up and at least try to right this wrong, it felt like we were as good as colluding with this entrenched abuse; agreeing that nothing untoward was happening and accepting that women didn't really count as full human beings. So it was not okay for us not to say something. Speaking up and not being heard is lousy—but muting your own voice to demur to an unfair and harmful system always felt worse. Then we were diminishing our very selves, as well as every other woman on the planet. And anyway, you never know, you gotta be in it to win it and throw your hat in the ring.

Shock, horror! Police subsequently, and uncharacteristically, swooped on the woman with the offending poster, confiscated the poster and charged her with obscenity. Really? Janice and I could feel the world tipping a little in our favour—in women's favour.

Janice made a police statement. Lizzie noted that if the woman with the obscene placard had not denied she held the placard, police should ask her to accept Janice's statement so Janice did not have to attend court. Ah, the old tease of an agreement of facts. HRLC solicitor Rachel Ball and I accompanied Janice to court.

It was so comforting to have someone like Rachel literally in our corner. When the defendant took to smiling fixedly at Janice, Rachel positioned herself to block that rather creepy line of sight.

That court case really riled me because it was turned around by the defence to her [Fraser] being a poor old soul, and I knew that wasn't the case. No, she did it in a way to hurt the women coming to the clinic and that was the last straw.

JANICE NUGENT (2020)

Well, in fact, over the years I reckon we'd had hundreds of last straws, but this one got to court. The hearings and judgements in this case to a small extent presaged the style and arguments which would arise in the eventual 2018 High Court challenge to safe access zones. The Victorian Government Solicitors Office *Case Summary—Fraser v Walker* provides learned insights to this obscenity case. My own non-learned account is below.

In the Magistrates Court on 5 August 2014, the defendant pleaded not guilty. Janice was cross examined in anti-choice language which I thought offensive and obscene too. Prosecutor Ms Elizabeth Ruddle (now SC and Senior Crown Prosecutor) was exemplary. The Judge pointed out that the defendant was 'misguided' if she thought it was okay to express her 'religious beliefs' in the way she did: there was a distinction between holding religious beliefs and how (and where) you express them. The woman was convicted of one charge of displaying an obscene figure in a public place.

Before sentencing, Her Honour asked about any mental ill health issues she should know about, and noted the appellant had not expressed any regret, her likelihood of reoffending and how severely she would be treated if she did. I have to admit I particularly enjoyed that exchange. The defendant was fined $600 to be paid in monthly $100 instalments in light of her government-dependent status of 'carer'.

A Notice of Appeal was immediately lodged against her conviction and sentence pursuant to s254 of the Criminal Procedure Act 2009, to be reheard *de novo*. In the 'redo' hearing at the County Court in October 2015, the Appellant barrister arrived with boxes piled high on trolleys. His Honour Justice Lacava placed firm and sensible limits on the relevance of both the Appellant's baggage, style of questioning, and his misunderstandings of the court proceedings. I cheered inside.

Janice carried the burden of being cross-examined twice, holding her own armed with my little cherries of wisdom plucked from my own court experience—look at and address your answers to the Judge, ask for water/blow-your-nose/ask-for-the-question-to-be-repeated-or-clarified/take-a-breath/take-your-time, and if all else fails, ask the Judge! More importantly Janice was armed with her own considerable down-to-earth nous and asser-tiveness, her sincere disgust with both the display and the woman's antics, and the distress caused to our patients. Nonetheless, being a witness brings its own stress.

Respondent/Prosecutor Ms Ruddle was fabulous again. In his written Reasons, Justice Paul Lacava (19 November 2015) at 9 described exhibit 'A':

> On each placard is a photograph of what appears to be a small aborted foe-tus covered in blood and displayed in such a way as to give an indication of the size of the foetus by a comparison with other objects also displayed in the

*photograph. For example the photograph on the right-hand side of the ex-
hibit displays the head of the aborted foetus lying on top of what appears to
be a one dollar coin by way of comparative size. The photograph on the left
also appears with some parts of a human finger included in the photograph
giving some impression of the size of the aborted foetus.*

His Honour noted at 20:

*The use of the word 'obscene' in s 17(1)(b) of the Act is not confined or, to be
read down so as to refer only to acts displaying figures of a sexual nature.
The word 'obscene' where used in the Act relevantly, also includes displays
that are offensive or disgusting and that embraces the ordinary and natural meaning of the word. For these reasons, I reject the first argument
advanced by Mr Brohier on behalf of the appellant.*

At 31:

*I find that the figures displayed by the appellant in the context of a protest
outside a medical clinic when viewed objectively are obscene because they
might properly be described as disgusting.*

At 43:

*Here, the figures displayed… are so far beyond what should appropriately
be displayed in public as to render them obscene within the meaning of the
section.*

Lacava J went on to consider arguments similar to some that would be raised
in the High Court challenge to safe access zones. At 48:

*I am not satisfied on the facts of this case that what the appellant was dis-
playing could properly be characterized as political communication. That
which was displayed by the appellant was not directed at government or
those charged with legislative responsibility. In my view, it was nothing
more than a communication directed squarely at those who operate the clinic in Wellington Street and those who attended as patients. Section 17 of
the Act exists for the purpose of ensuring, where possible, good order in
public places such as the footpath in Wellington Street. In the circumstances
here, proper application of the provision does not, in my view, burden in
an inappropriate way the appellants' right to political communication and
is thus enforceable.*

At 49:

> *I accept Miss Ruddle's submission that the appellant's right to religious freedom does not provide a legal immunity permitting her to breach the provision of the Act in question. Assuming the appellant's stance on abortion comes from her religious belief, the display of obscene figures is not part of religion nor can it be said the display is done in furtherance of religion.*

At 51:

> *I remind the appellant... that I have the power to impose a sentence that is more severe than that imposed by the Magistrates' Court.*

I loved those written reasons. If Lacava J wasn't a J I'd have set up a fan club.

At a personal and clinic level, the lengthy legal process at least delivered vindication. Janice and I found it immensely satisfying to see police take this action, to hear two judges deal so adamantly with a woman who had caused unnecessary distress to our patients, to hear also the Prosecutor, Ms Ruddle, deliver her case so expertly, and to delve into issues around Obscenity, political communication and religion.

The intervention of the Attorney General in the woman's 1 August 2016 application for a Supreme Court review of the County Court decision (Fraser v County Court of Victoria and Constable Brenton Walker and Attorney General for the State of Victoria intervening, with Emerton J presiding) was gratifying and consistent with the government's clear pro-women stance by then, and its successful 2015 safe access zones legislation.

To think that we could have been having the extremists charged via this Summary Offences Act for decades given the Act's prohibition of 1 (c) and (d) which inter alia states:

> *Any person who in or near a public place or within the view or hearing of any person being or passing therein or thereon—*
>
> *Uses profane indecent or obscene language or threatening abusive or insulting words, or*
>
> *Behaves in a riotous indecent offensive or insulting manner.*

The obscene joke was that for decades no authority recognised the extremists' displays, behaviour and language as indecent, threatening, abusive or insulting. Even if they had, clinic staff, police and prosecutors would have spent all their time enforcing the law via the courts and we would still be beset by extremists. Police charging individuals for specific breaches was never going to solve our problem. This four-year legal saga might have drawn a line in the sand in terms of extremist displays and provided proof that police could, if they really looked, see the harm occurring to women accessing a health clinic. But except as an argument for safe access zones legislation, or more creatively using the legal process, this case was almost irrelevant.

While this episode demonstrated a failure of the existent law for our circumstances, the case was also a resounding victory. There are champions for women's rights residing in all manner of places, and you never know when you will meet someone like Constable Brenton Walker, Lacava J, or Ms Ruddell, and let's not forget Janice and Rachel...

So while you need to take time out to recharge, never give up fighting the good fight, and continue to speak up, because that next time might be the time you win. That next time might be the time your voice is heard.

CHAPTER 10

Suing Melbourne City Council

March 2013–December 2014

> *We all have to be bold in speaking out against sexism,*
> *gender inequality and violence.*
>
> NATASHA STOTT DESPOJA (2019)

Back in March 2013, when the obscenity case was just beginning, progress towards the legislative option of abortion safe access zones remained blocked. So we were about to embark on a creative use of the law. A year after our first meeting with Maurice Blackburn, and two years after our first meeting with eminent counsel, Maurice Blackburn wrote to MCC:

> [We] act for the Fertility Control Clinic... [and] request that the City of Melbourne take urgent action pursuant to Part 6 Division 1 of the Public Health and Wellbeing Act 2008 (Vic)... this is a formal notice that a nuisance exists in the City of Melbourne... We request per s62(2) of the Act, the Council investigate this notice and take immediate action...duty to remedy as far as is reasonably possible all nuisances...
>
> LETTER FROM MB's RHIANNON REID TO MCC
>
> 5 MARCH 2013

The one-page reply, from Mr Russell Webster, Manager Health Services as delegate for the Melbourne City Council, was prompt and efficient:

> Firstly, I take issue with your assertion that the Fertility Control Clinic has contacted this organisation on numerous occasions and that we have

taken no action in relation to the activities of the protestors. As the
Council's Chief Executive Officer noted in a letter to Dr Allanson dated
21 December 2012:

> *There has been a long history of correspondence between the clinic*
> *and Council on the activities in front of the clinic, the right to protest*
> *and the limited role the Council has in respect to these activities. Over*
> *the years Local Laws officers have been in contact with protesters to*
> *address unauthorised items placed on or over footpath areas but our*
> *officers do not have the right to direct protestors where to protest nor*
> *can they impinge upon the right to protest...*

As a delegate of Council under the Act, I have investigated the matter... I
have determined that whilst most of the actions of the protesters do not fall
within the specific definition of nuisance in the Act, it is arguable blocking
entry into the clinic is such a nuisance... the matter is best settled privately
through the referral of such behaviour by the aggrieved individual to the
Victoria Police. I advise the person to refer such complaints to Insp Lisa
Winchester, the Melbourne East and St Kilda Local Area Commander of
Victoria Police.

7 May 2013

This opening gambit of letters is a key part that sets up the legal process and legal arguments. Our letter essentially said: we think it's your job to deal with this nuisance. They came back and said: we don't agree; it's not our job; and we think it's up to you to complain to the police. This was just as we thought. This would be the terms with which we would go to court and thrash it out in front of a judge.

Yes, all as expected. But I felt this opening gambit in a far more emotional way. I guess I had been secretly hoping that a letter from our lawyers would suddenly turn MCC around and they would do the decent thing. I felt MCC's letter as an insult. I wondered for whom it was 'best settled privately' by referral to police. Certainly not us, and certainly not our patients. I wondered about the process and detail of Mr Webster's investigation. How had he investigated the matter? Perhaps his first step was to unconsciously pick up those gendered glasses. Sigh.

I eventually phoned Inspector Lisa Winchester, as Mr Webster had recommended, to find that MCC had not discussed the matter with Inspector Winchester. She had arrived in 2004 and told me that, 'we have gone around in circles for years, going nowhere'. Yep, she was on our roundabout all right. Police wanted a safe area for women, Inspector Winchester said, but needed appropriate legislation or by-laws in place. She generously suggested that we should all sit down together. Hmm. Ride that merry-go-round round again with all its ups and downs and ending up right back where we began. MCC was never coming to that party with anything new. Talk was cheap. Court cases not so much. Enough of the round and round. Onward and upward!

We gathered statements from staff, residents, and others, video evidence and an excel document describing the video footage that security guard Tariq had taken over the last few months, photos of placards and paraphernalia, pamphlets handed out to patients by the extremists, HOGPI web pages from here and overseas, patient surveys, letters, Allie Humphries' research—you name it, our team collated it.

Journalist Suzy Freeman-Greene had written a fabulous article about our predicament back in November 2011 and alerted me to photographer Mario Borg's work. Mario had been taking photos of the streetscape conflict for a photo essay. Mario and I happily met for coffee. His photos had an intimacy and immediacy that were powerful in communicating the emotional distress triggered by the extremists' intrusion, rites and paraphernalia. As a professional photographer, Mario had put his high calibre skills to work with women's rights in mind. His pictures really were worth a thousand words.

My photojournalism career began as a cadet with The Herald & Weekly Times in 1976. The organisation published The Herald *and* The Sun, *before Rupert Murdoch acquired it and created the* Herald Sun. *In 2014 when I took those photos, I was transitioning to a new career as a family mediator, and studying psychology, after realising that the media landscape was changing.*

Although I was raised in the Catholic church, I believe there is enough evidence to show that those institutions harm human rights, and the causes of gender equality and women's rights in particular. In my view, religious institutions oppress and attempt to control women (among others) and, moderate adherents enable big religion's abuse of human rights to endure by supporting that religion and its underpinning superstitious beliefs and patriarchal tyranny. When the clinic challenged the Melbourne City Council to act against the protesters' harassment of vulnerable women it was in the news regularly. I realised that the situation outside the clinic had been going on for thirty years and nothing had been achieved to protect the clients who attended the clinic, even when a sympathiser to the anti-abortion cause murdered a security guard!

I'd always felt that photography, done well, can change the world. The mission of photojournalism was to reveal the world to us all. When cameras and reporters would attend the clinic, it was periodic and brief, and the protestors would behave then. You never saw what really went on. I wanted to document and explore the reality that was reported in Suzy's [Freeman-Greene] story. I wanted the harassment to be exposed. Not just a photo of that day, but a universal picture of cowardice, harassment and oppression meted out on vulnerable people. I wasn't getting paid, but I thought I might use my time, in between jobs, to cobble together a photo essay just to give a taste of what was really going on.

I ended up attending each morning, pretty consistently, between August and December 2014. I took a small, unobtrusive camera and I thought, I'll just stand around and see what happens. I'll fold myself into the everyday. I wanted to be able to get up close and give an impression of what it was like for the victims without identifying them.

Initially I developed a working relationship with the protestors, but then my views came out. For example, I expressed concerns that their diagrams and plastic models misrepresented fetal development: they were larger, oversized, and not biologically accurate. A couple of them, including a priest (who actually believed that Adam and Eve existed, yes, we had a few 'discussions'), went right off at me. They weren't the loving and kind people that their faith demanded and I still naively expected. They started intimidating me with their own cameras. I was threatened with police action when one of the protesters showed me the hidden video camera he *used to intimidate those who challenged them. They were so angry. They kept threatening me with calling the police, yelling at me. I had no problem as I knew I wasn't doing anything wrong or illegal. I knew the law about taking pictures in public places.*

The irony of the situation was breath-taking, when they said, 'don't photograph me, don't come into my space'. They were blocking people in the street and thrusting alarming pictures in the clients' faces any opportunity they had. I thought it insane that they claimed harassment from me, considering their abusive behaviour.

MARIO BORG (2020)

I was sensitive to intellectual property issues and Mario's ownership of his work product. But by the time it came time for our evidence to be submitted to the Supreme Court, Mario generously offered to include his photos. The Supreme Court, concerned to protect our patients' privacy and confidentiality, assured us that our videos and Mario's photos would remain confidential.

One of Mario's photos had serendipitously captured the wife of HLRC media guru Tom Clarke walking with their small children through the anti-abortion group. The photo exquisitely depicted the layers of harm. Thanks to Mario's generosity, and the Clarke family's support, the image figured prominently in the public campaign for safe access.

Master storytellers, from diverse walks of life and employing diverse methods, were telling our story, telling women's stories. Would the Court really hear those stories? Would the public?

The gathering of our evidence and witness statements took months. Hundreds of hours were spent by me and our legal team on evidence and statements by eight staff: Drs Louis Rutman and Kathy Lewis, Practice Manager Janice Nugent, Susan (Speaking) Hopkins, Senior Counsellor June Dryburgh, Vicki Sweeney, security guard Tariq, and me. Most of this evidence eventually was included in my affidavit which was to grow to two inches thick.

Through 2013 our case moved at what seemed like a glacial pace. Maybe that was just how these things were—slow. But over the years I had lost count of how many patient surveys, video evidence and statements became obsolete. Now we had gathered so much evidence, we couldn't afford further extended delays before we issued proceedings. Hell no, we didn't want this latest evidence trove to become outdated and need to be done all over again.

People come to work at MB because they want to work on good matters for working people. One of the philosophies of our practice was that as much as possible we refer this work to other lawyers who are doing other areas of work, and who put their hand up to take on a pro bono case. I would support them, but largely they could run matters themselves. It was a noble idea, but it can be really challenging in practice, especially for lawyers from other departments with a lot on their plates.

Now the practice is not structured like that. All our pro bono work is now run by a specialised team of lawyers. Victories for the firm, victories like safe access zones, belong to everyone in the firm.

LIZZIE O'SHEA

By the end of September 2013, Rachel sped things up. Rachel got Lizzie O'Shea back working directly on our case. Lizzie O'Shea, MB solicitor and young woman extraordinaire brimming with intelligent energy and a big heart, prioritised our case and stayed the distance. Lizzie was not a person to stroll. She ran. Lizzie ran marathons, in excellent time. MB's Emeline Gaske came on board too.

This case is actually one that required a fair bit of work and preparation for the Supreme Court. That can be the difficulty of doing these cases pro bono. But I think ultimately once Rachel got Lizzie back on the job, the case proceeded well.

EMILY HOWIE (2020)

MB had a busy practice and our matter was difficult for a range of reasons. Then there were the more usual decisions to make about: a cause of action; what additional evidence was required; deciding upon a process and timeline of finalising evidence and issuing proceedings; how to manage the workload for this matter over the coming weeks and months... Counsel needed to feel confident with the level of instruction they would receive.

Liberty Sanger ended up being the supervisor, technically, for the matter the whole way through. Liberty is a very senior member in the firm, a very talented lawyer, but extremely busy. She was very encouraging, and she let me drive the matter. But if I needed guidance I could track her down.

LIZZIE O'SHEA

While ultimately Lizzie would look back on our case in years to come and feel deeply satisfied, the weight of running the case was a heavy one.

At the time, I felt very stressed because I felt that I owed you this enormous responsibility to do the right thing by you, which means preparing as much as possible, coordinating a team of counsel often who have their own views about how they run things, preparing documentation in short turnaround times...

My worst nightmare was to fail you as clients because you are so important. You go above and beyond what is required by anyone else in their working lives for their clients, for your patients. So many people are prepared to turn a blind eye to this issue, to pretend that it's not really something that affects them, to pretend that they don't know anybody who's been in this situation before, to pretend that it's only an issue for women who are bad or to be derided and stigmatised.

To have advocates like you who are empathetic, both personally but also in a professional sense, makes such an enormous difference, and none of this is possible without that energy and drive. I knew that you had been campaigning for so long around all sorts of issues—including abortion decriminalisation, let alone this kind of issue—that I didn't want to take that very precious energy and enthusiasm for this cause and pour it onto a case if it wasn't going to be useful.

So that was my primary worry and it's a big motivator. In retrospect, I think wow, this has all worked out so well! But at the time, oh God, I didn't want to fail you. I do remember saying to you once, 'I just don't want to disappoint you, Susie.' And you said, 'Oh no, you couldn't disappoint us.' And I remember thinking, I hope you're right, Susie.

Obviously, the law is what it is, and if it needs to be reformed, then you can only do what you can with that. I really felt like you deserved the best possible representation from lawyers who couple their passion for the cause with technical excellence. I just didn't want to be the person that let you down.

I was motivated by the honour and the privilege of being able to act for you, and to be at a firm that supported you. There's a reason I wanted to work at MB as opposed to other firms. It is a real privilege to be put in this position and be able to do this work for a cause you think is important.

Lizzie O'Shea

Brilliant minds and generous hearts. I could believe that the world would be in good hands into the future, but I really wished this particular burden was not so great.

Before the end of 2013, a couple of events occurred with the potential to positively impact on our prosecution of both our legal case and our political case.

First was the early October 2013 Supreme Court decision about the lawfulness of MCC taking action against Occupy Melbourne [Muldoon v Melbourne City Council [2013] FCA 994]. My non-learned understanding was that MCC had relied on camping and parks Local Laws to remove Occupy Melbourne protesters. Only three out of eight MCC notices were considered invalid, and the Court seemed to back the use of MCC Local Laws.

In terms of the Constitutional and the Charter rights of freedom of expression, peaceful assembly, political expression and political communication, MCC local laws were apparently considered to be: not incompatible with these rights; not an impermissible burden; not drastic means; and not incompatible with requirements of natural justice. Freedom of expression required special duties and responsibilities and the right may be subject to lawful restrictions reasonably necessary to respecting the rights and reputation of other persons, and for the protection of national security, public order, public health or public morality. The Charter's limits on expression of speech also included insulting someone's reputation. I reckon HOGPI standing on Wellington Parade day-in-day-out telling people we were murderers certainly insulted our reputations.

The Occupy Melbourne decision referred to the importance of the impact on other people (or public spaces). It noted other regulations (being ignored by MCC in relation to HOGPI) forbidding a person from placing or erecting a portable advertising sign or other thing in, on or over a public place or allowing that to occur, where advertising is the promotion of any person, company, organisation or thing, and prohibiting displaying or distributing a handbill in a public place—excluding any handbill of an exclusively political nature.

My unlearned reading of the decision suggested to me that MCC could, should and would more confidently intervene to remove HOGPI. But that was just me. While the work on our legal case continued, Melbourne City Council continued to refuse to act on the clinic's requests that its Activities Local Laws be enforced to address the harassment of clinic patients and staff on a public footpath within the Council's boundaries. We also called police. Business as usual then. By the end of September 2013, HOGPI had begun another 40-day vigil. Sigh.

The second important event occurred on the 21 November 2013 in our island state:

Hi Susie,

Sorry about the belated email. I guess by now you've heard that yester-day we achieved decriminalisation and managed to keep the 150m access zones!

Thank you for all your help in this. Your work played a really big part in convincing the MLCs that these zones were critical.

SUSAN FAHEY, CEO WOMEN'S LEGAL SERVICE TASMANIA

EMAIL

22 NOVEMBER 2013

Tasmania had passed the *Reproductive Health (Access to terminations) Bill* to both decriminalise abortion and provide 150-metre safe access zones. I was giddy with happiness and green with envy. Lou began revising history on Victoria's 2008 abortion decrim—we coulda, shoulda got a zone then too! Tell him he's dreamin'.

But two years later, our dream would finally come true. The Tasmanian 150-metre safe access zone would provide an Australian legislative precedent for Victoria's own, new and improved we thought, 150-metre abortion safe access zone.

Two days before Christmas 2013, MB's six-page letter to MCC CEO Kathy Alexander, detailed an orderly account of the facts, and attached statements from eight FCC staff, a summary of Allie's research, and:

In our view, Mr Webster's assessment of the nuisance, of which he was notified in our letter, is too narrow. We nonetheless note that he found that it is "arguable" that a nuisance has taken place and is ongoing... [and] "better settled privately through the referral of such behaviour by the aggrieved individual to the Victoria Police'... staff members of the clinic have attempted to remedy the nuisance in the manner suggested by Mr Webster on numerous occasions. To date, this has been unsuccessful...

If the Council persists in its refusal to take action to remedy the nuisance created by the activities of the sidewalk counsellors, the clinic intends to apply to the Supreme Court for an order in the nature of mandamus to oblige the Council to take action against the sidewalk counsellors... The clinic is committed to engaging in open and constructive dialogue with the Council...

MB LETTER

23 DECEMBER 2013

I for one had had a gutful of dialogue with the Council. Unstoppable force and immovable object would meet in the Supreme Court of Victoria.

The right lawyers can definitely be handy to navigate the confusing corners of our legal system. So can the right photographer able to take pictures that speak thousands of words.

Getting a case off the ground takes incredible energy, time, brain space and teamwork. I have no idea how our legal team pulled everything together so beautifully. Setting up litigation is painstaking work, so you want to ensure it is all worth it.

CHAPTER 11

That's the Game

March 2014–July 2014

> *Step back Mum. You will find everything offensive about MCC's approach. That's the game!*
>
> REBECCA DEAN (2014)

Wednesday 12 March 2014

Law firm Maurice Blackburn and the Human Rights Law Centre will today commence Supreme Court proceedings on behalf of the Fertility Control Clinic seeking to compel the council to enforce existing laws that would protect the clinic's patients and staff from harassment.

Susie Allanson, a psychologist at the clinic, said the decision to take the council to court was not made lightly, but was the only option left given the council's inaction…

The head of Maurice Blackburn's social justice practice, Elizabeth O'Shea, said existing laws enable the council to act on the anti-abortion group, but the council was simply failing to enforce the law. "It's disappointing that the council continues to turn a blind eye to this kind of ongoing harassment, despite the fact we have brought it to their attention on numerous occasions," Ms O'Shea said. "Our client shouldn't have to launch legal proceedings just to get the council to do its job and make sure patients and staff can safely access medical services at the clinic."

Charlotte (not her real name), who attended the clinic in 2013, said she was intimidated and distressed after being rushed by a group of strangers telling her she was a murderer, that she was going to hell and that she was a whore. '...they shouldn't be allowed to stand right out the front and treat people the way they do. They could stand on the other side of the road or at least provide a larger area of space. It's just common decency," Charlotte said.

The Human Rights Law Centre's director of advocacy, Rachel Ball, said that safe access to reproductive healthcare is an important women's rights issue. "No one is suggesting that people should be prevented from expressing their opinions. We'd simply like to see an arrangement in which women can safely access health services without being harassed and intimidated," said Ms Ball... 'sensible measures to ensure safe access to health services would not excessively limit the right to freedom of expression and assembly.'

The legal case will argue that the self-described 'sidewalk counsellors' meet the definition of nuisance as outlined in Victoria's Public Health and Wellbeing Act. Under the act, the council has a duty to address issues of nuisance within its borders. The Supreme Court action to be launched today seeks an order requiring the council to perform its duty...

FCC, HRLC & MB Press Release

12 March 2014

In more legalese terms, pursuant to Order 56 of the *Supreme Court (General Civil Procedure) Rules 2005*, the Plaintiff, the Fertility Control Clinic seeks an order in the nature of *mandamus* compelling the Defendant, the Melbourne City Council, to perform its duty under s 60 of the *Public Health and Wellbeing Act 2008* (Vic) to remedy an alleged nuisance existing in the Council's municipal district.

That morning at MB offices, Rachel, Lizzie and I faced a bank of cameras and journalists to announce FCC's court case against Melbourne City Council, and to field questions. It was finally happening. For the rest of the day, we responded to media. I still found myself surprised by the interest, and relieved to now be just one cog in a well-oiled media machine that comprised communications HRLC Tom Clarke and MB Chee Chee, and media savvy speakers like Rachel and Lizzie.

I had signed my Supreme Court affidavit the day before, 11 March 2014. It was two inches thick, bulky with 16 attached exhibits. Subsequently adjourned from 30 April 2014, a 6 June 2014 Directions Hearing by The Honourable Associate Justice Mukhtar (Supreme Court of Victoria at Melbourne, Common Law Division, Judicial Review and Appeals List) set out The Court Orders by Consent:

> *Any further evidence from FCC to be filed by 25 July 2014;*
>
> *MCC to file affidavit evidence by 29 August 2014;*
>
> *FCC in reply by 5 September 2014;*
>
> *Agreed facts by 22 September 2014*
>
> *FCC file submission not exceeding 15 pages and list of authorities by 6 October 2014;*
>
> *MCC to file submission in reply by 27 October 2014;*
>
> *FCC in reply not exceeding 5 pages by 3 November 2014;*
>
> *FCC file and serve a court book by 3 November 2014.*
>
> *Proceedings fixed for hearing on 1 December 2014.*

A clear, methodical, scheduled process then. It was to feel anything but, to me. In a case like ours there was a multitude of issues to be submitted to, and negotiated with, opposing legal counsel: Directions hearings, proposed consent orders and agreed consent orders, proposed facts and agreed facts, proposed orders and agreed orders, discussion, writing, discussion and re-writing. MB's Emeline Gaske's 3 June 2014 email was an example speaking to the ongoing saga of agreed facts:

> *I have just been advised this afternoon that MCC will not agree to any statement of facts at this stage. We will need to put in all of our evidence, and they may agree down the track. On that note, please see attached draft directions I wish to propose to Hunt and Hunt about the further timetabling of this matter.*

I learnt not only that 'lawyers can be handy' (Walker, 2020), but lawyers have very big brains, massive, humungous brains that methodically work through every little piece of matter that matters. I mean you wouldn't know it to look at them. Our lawyers were perfectly pleasant looking people. It's not like their heads got stuck going through doorways. Their heads were more like Mary Poppins' bag or Dr Who's Tardis: quite normal on the outside, but inside a brilliance that touched infinity.

Meanwhile, my puny brain ripped open at the seams and spilt onto the floor like fluff 'n' stuff from a cushion. Sometimes it just exploded, splat. Through it all, my brain told me that MCC was not playing fair. MCC asked for this, that and the other thing only to ignore, renege or ask for an adjournment. Putting forth human rights arguments, only to withdraw them. Asking the Court to delay the hearing so we could mediate, then declining to mediate. Of course as well as a legally deficient brain, I had a particularly one-eyed view and a tendency towards the odd dummy spit or two.

Everything blurred, a brain cloud. MCC seemed to go beyond legal craft to a game of one-up-brinkmanship played out on the back of women's pain—a cliché echoing down the eons of 'civilisation'.

Lizzie said she had never seen anything like it before.

'Welcome to our world,' I said.

I have a distinct memory of issuing the case, and the next day in the media [Lord Mayor] Robert Doyle said that he also thought that what they were doing outside the Fertility Control Clinic was terrible and so, seemingly, it was the administrative arm of Council that didn't want to do anything about it.

I have a distinct memory of that evening: the Council's lawyer from Hunt and Hunt was on the phone for a long time, talking about the case. I think she was trying to be comradely and in a very pleasant way, yet mildly fascinated by the curiosity of bringing a case like this, which I found a bit discombobulating.

But now in retrospect I think I understand about where it was coming from. They didn't see it as their job as a public authority to protect people who are accessing a medical service. My impression was that they thought these powers were there to protect people's safety in the wake of a chemical spill, or sinkhole, not to protect people's safety that was jeopardised by structural sexism and lazy stereotyping. To take on that task would require nuance and bravery and they seemed to prefer to treat it as a problem that was beyond their remit.

It was a convenient attitude to have, particularly because the people in question were people who could be easily stigmatised. The Council really

saw it as not a function of a public authority to do the work of protecting
these people. That's an interesting concept in this particular moment where
we are relying on public authorities to take all sorts of serious and wide
ranging actions that interfere with our liberties and our daily lives to pro-
tect us from a health hazard, COVID-19.

Lizzie O'Shea

Amidst the tremendous work (of MB, HRLC and counsel) and frustrations (mine) of our case, various legal threads crisscrossed in time. One of
those threads concerned 'agreed facts', due 22 September 2014. In amongst a
dizzying array of possibilities, 'agreed facts' weaved into another thread: psychiatric assessment of staff.

Peter [Hanks] has now had discussions with [MCC legal counsel] Richard
Niall. It appears that some matters on our proposed agreed facts can be
agreed to but importantly, the issue of the effect of HOGPI on the health of
the staff is not agreed. Therefore, we will need to make the appointments
with the psychiatrist so we can receive expert evidence about that…

Therese McCarthy Email 26 May 2014

I reckoned I knew which people really should be consulting a psychiatrist in
this whole scenario, and it was not staff and not patients!

The whole focus of our advocacy and legal action had always been about
protecting our patients from harm and protecting their privacy. Asking
women who attended the clinic to take legal action or give evidence would be
an unethical and unacceptable intrusion into their privacy, and the antithesis
of the very goal we were trying to achieve. So we, the staff, would have to be it.

As staff, we tended to just get on with our work. Nonetheless, we also knew
that our physical and emotional health was deeply affected by the extremists.
We all suffered a variety of stress symptoms and preoccupations unique to
our siege-like workplace. There had also been times when threats or assault
had followed staff members into their personal lives away from the clinic. We
needed evidence to put to the court and to MCC to prove that HOGPI's
activities were 'noxious' or injurious to a person's personal comfort, and posed
a risk to health. Those persons had to be the staff members of the Fertility
Control Clinic.

As a clinical psychologist who had done my share of court assessment reports, you might think I would be comfortable with the idea of attending for a psychiatric assessment. You'd be wrong. I was antagonistic to the whole idea. I knew how a skilled mental health professional could drill down into deeply personal matters. To then have such deeply personal matters enter a public forum like the Supreme Court of Victoria for the extremists to exploit to bully us further in the service of their relentless religious crusade? I was never a convert to the whole 'turn the other cheek' approach to life. Clearly neither were our HOGPI 'Christian' soldiers. Armed with the cross, 'foetuses', rosary beads, and stand-over tactics, they quite happily kept slapping away at our cheeks instead.

Our learned counsel were patient and kind in addressing my concerns. On 28 May 2014, Therese McCarthy noted safeguards developed around the psychiatric assessment, and provided me with a much-needed reality check:

> It is our assessment that this evidence is critical to the outcome of the case and that to refrain from obtaining it, or then using it, would be to compromise the litigation strategy such that failure would be likely.

That last paragraph really hit home. Therese McCarthy was a woman with a gentle aura and a brain for clarity about the law and people. Throughout our court case, Therese always made me feel safe and calm. If Therese said it was necessary, then, yep, we were heading to the psychiatrist.

Psychiatrist Dr Gregory White had a CV as long as your arm and his credentials were beyond reproach. On paper he was the ideal expert. Still, I was going to sus this psychiatrist out first, before Janice, Lou or our security guard, Tariq, took part. Gentle and quietly spoken Tariq was an important member of the clinic team. As our security guard, his gentleness suited us and our patients, and his calm manner defied the extremists' cruel judgement. Not tall, but well-muscled, Tariq loved working out in the gym with weights. He hoped one day to find a job building things from wood – carpentry, furniture making. I noted an endearing sense of both humour and loneliness about Tariq. I was happy for him whenever he had a girlfriend. I had no idea how Tariq had reached Australia from war-torn Iraq, nor any real knowledge of the experiences he had faced there or here. I didn't think it was my place to ask. But now Tariq was going to be asked all sorts of questions by a psychiatrist. The questions weren't even for Tariq's own benefit. The assessment was for the benefit of our case: our patients and staff. I thought a psych assessment might be pushing Tariq's dedication to his job, and his affection for us, a bit far. But Tariq was all in with us. Tariq strengthened my resolve to sus out this psychiatrist first.

I attended as the first appointment with psychiatrist Gregory White in early July 2014. My paranoia—or sensible self-protection—stepped up from the get-go. A routine form to fill in with the most basic personal details had me worried that even this information could be made public and expose my family and me to additional harassment. The wise and kind Dr White immediately deleted any information I was not comfortable with. As my session progressed, my concerns dissolved. Here was an eminently experienced and respectful man who would treat all of us, especially Tariq, with the utmost care.

By 22 July 2014 Dr White's report was complete. Individual assessments were kept confidential within the Court process, but Dr White's report Summary could potentially be released more broadly:

The four employees of the Fertility Control Clinic assessed by this examiner have each described in detail their experiences in relation to reported activities of protestors, namely members of the Helpers of God's Precious Infants (HOGPI)...

Dr White noted that while individual affidavits and interviews differed in detail, and staff described a variety of life experiences and coping mechanisms:

There were marked similarities... regarding bullying, harassment and threatening behaviours towards patients and staff... common themes include symptoms of heightened physiological arousal, as well as frustration, and periods of significant emotional distress and/or anxiety...

Professionally dedicated and holding strong beliefs about their roles in caring for and providing a safe and supportive environment for their patients, as reflected in the longevity of their tenures at the FCC, they report having experienced strong feelings of powerlessness in relation to HOGPI...

Their fear and hypervigilance has particularly been relevant, in so far as three of the individuals were employed at the Fertility Control Clinic at the time of the traumatic murder of a security guard eleven years ago by an anti-abortion activist.

The four individuals also all described intermittent or ongoing medical conditions or stress symptoms which, whilst not meeting criteria for a formal psychiatric disorder, would appear to be significantly likely to be stress related.

Whilst these stress symptoms, such as anger, frustration, sadness, anxiety, tension, agitation, tremulousness, hypervigilance, worrying, chest and abdominal tightness, increased heart rate, palpitations, hyperventilation, and irritability; as well as the ongoing medical conditions, including insomnia, bruxism, migraines, and hypertension are perceived by the individuals to not be entirely related to workplace events, there is also a significant likelihood that repeated stressful experiences related to the abovementioned activities of the protestors could be a significant contributing factor...

A range of features noted upon mental state examinations of the four individuals were consistent with the symptoms described... ongoing and unresolved mental and physiological reactions to the reported protestor activities... cause regular distress and discomfort, and resonate with the shooting at the Fertility Control Clinic. These features included sadness, anxiety, demoralisation, change of voice tone, tension, guardedness, defensiveness, and tearfulness or being close to tears.

Dr White discussed in more general terms the adverse effects of stress on health, before noting:

Research has demonstrated a link between the experiences of staff working in a range of medical settings such as the FCC, and dealing with repeated stressors, and the development of personal health problems... caring staff empathise with their patients, and are often more aware of being affected by the distress of their patients, rather than their own vulnerabilities...

Stressors that occur repeatedly or daily have impacts that can be enlarged... the experience of discrimination and hostility from others in relation to their situations or roles, may impact more upon their health than their actual traumatic experiences… the four staff members from the FCC perceived themselves to be hostage to the HOGPI protestors and the nature of their daily activities…

The HOGPI activities may well already be causing significant adverse health effects, and if these activities continue, the health risks are likely to increase.

All our years of advocacy had been focused on protecting our patients. But Lou was on the money when he pointed out that it was both confronting and strangely validating, to see in black and white, the stresses and harm to Lou, Janice, Tariq and me. To all of the clinic staff.

Would MCC challenge psychiatrist Dr White's opinion with their own?

It's very difficult for us to say whether MCC will file anything in response. As you know, they had originally said to me that they would not file any evidence, but they then subsequently sought a longer schedule, suggested they may have changed their mind. It's a compelling report, so they may have difficulty arguing there is no nuisance without any evidence of their own.

My gut feeling is that they are more likely to file evidence about what they have done to remedy the nuisance (however scant and futile) rather than continue to deny that it is occurring. But we will have to see.

Lizzie O'Shea, July 2014

The psychiatric assessment was evidence we would never have acquired without our court case. The fact was, without our court case and the passion and generous diligence of our legal team, we would never have so methodically amassed the diverse and high quality evidence we ended up with, and there was yet more highly reputable and supportive legal evidence to come. Ultimately, all that evidence from our court case would prove to be a ready store of advice to the campaign, media and parliamentarians when it mattered most. The payoff would be breathtaking.

Legal cases can be tiresome because lawyers are exacting, asking for tiny details to be proven, details which you implicitly, instinctively know to be true. But putting evidence out there, even when it's burdensome and exhausting to collect, can have significant worth. The excruciating detail of such cases serves a crucial purpose by putting on the public record the harm being done, and by providing validation. Even if ultimately the judge didn't think it was a problem MCC was required to address, the fact it was on the record meant that eventually it could not be ignored by that other branch of government that holds power: the legislature.

LIZZIE O'SHEA

In mid-2014, barrister Claire Harris had to withdraw from our case for family reasons. We were disappointed to lose Claire. We did not know then that Claire would again graciously step in to expertly represent the clinic as *amicus curiae* in the 2018 High Court Challenge to safe access zones.

The upside to Claire's withdrawal was that we had the opportunity to work with yet another learned, kind and generous barrister, Kris Walker QC. Kris also would go on to the High Court challenge, as the Solicitor General for Victoria, the key advocate leading Victoria's successful preservation of safe access zones.

Before my involvement of course, there was a team of Peter Hanks, Claire Harris and Therese McCarthy. Then Claire couldn't continue... Peter Hanks asked me if I would be involved and I was more than happy to do so. I've always done a reasonable amount of pro bono work. I think that's a really important part of practice as a barrister. So I was really quite delighted to be involved. What had been going on was so horrendous. That we might be able to bring some slightly creative legal proceedings to try and provide some redress, I thought was really important.

When I was first asked, I didn't know about your experience as a worker at the clinic. But I knew about the protests, and my thinking, I suppose my focus, was on the women who had to run that gauntlet to get medical treatment. I'm a strong supporter of the right of women to choose whether they have an abortion or not. I had been aware of the protests and thought they were outrageous and something needed to be done about it. For that reason I was really happy to be involved in trying to do something.

SOLICITOR GENERAL KRIS WALKER QC (2020)

Kris's academic and professional credentials were extraordinary: winning the 1991 Supreme Court Prize as top law student; becoming an Associate to High Court Chief Justice Sir Anthony Mason, and then pursuing both academia and the Bar (Keaney, 2018). Lizzie was fortunate enough to be taught by Kris at Melbourne Law School:

> *I got my best mark of my entire degree in Kris Walker's course. And the subject? Law and Sexuality—looking at all the ways in which law tried to regulate sexuality from a theoretical and practical perspective. Ten years later, there we were going to court representing the clinic. Full circle!*

Kris had been becoming our ideal champion since kindergarten:

> *My father's a lawyer, so growing up I was exposed to many legal concepts. He was a criminal defence barrister so that was very much the perspective. I always used to say I would never be a lawyer, largely because everyone expected I would be. And as it turns out I am a lawyer! I spent a bit of time at a law firm as paralegal before I got to law school. But when I got to law school the range of subjects I chose to do included human rights law, law of discrimination…*
>
> *I was a feminist from very early on apparently—kindergarten, prep! I do have a vague memory of being chastised by the teacher for doing something the boys were also doing. So early on I was a feminist. Then getting to law school, then seeing some of the problematic aspects of law, as well as the potential for law to do good things, I knew that the law was by no means a perfect system.*

But Kris's most unexpected credential in her background?

> *My grandfather was a doctor who provided abortions when they were illegal, so I was aware of that as well. The history of the way abortion has been regulated in Australia is in hindsight quite problematic. I guess at the time that's how things were. Women had been having abortions for millennia, but could not have them safely. The fact that doctors were prepared to break the law to provide women with safe abortions was very significant. That was probably relevant not so much to my general trajectory, but partly to my interest in this case.*
>
> SOLICITOR GENERAL KRIS WALKER QC (2020)

Lou and Kris literally dined out on that association. Lou liked to refer to Kris as 'Rising Star Kris Walker'. He was right.

Amongst everything else on her plate, in early July 2014, Rachel wrote up a case note for the HRLC bulletin (Ball, 2014): anti-abortion extremists had successfully sued the United States Massachusetts Attorney General (McCullen, et al v Coakley, Attorney General of Massachusetts et al. 53 U.S. 26 June 2014) on the ground that the Reproductive Health Care Facilities Act, that is, abortion safe access zones, violated the First and Fourth amendments.

Reading the decision, my blood boiled. Sorry Dr White, I couldn't help it. The Court accepted the extremists' description of their own behaviour as curb-side counselling, providing information, help and so on. There was no consideration of the fact that those for whom the Act was designed to pro-tect—women—experienced and described the extremist behaviour as quite the opposite. Nor was there recognition of abortion access as a health issue rather than a political/ideas issue. Women were unseen and unheard. But Rachel was not, and her case note spoke up for women.

Evidence in reply is designed to address any points raised by their evidence. Given they have filed none, we are not in a position to reply to anything with further evidence. This omission on their part cannot in my opinion be the basis of an extension of the timetable. Courts are generally amenable to amending timetables to allow people to put forward their case, for obvious reasons. But in this instance, we can assume the MCC deliberately does not want to file evidence and won't be seeking any delay or extension. The MCC will have to explain why they did not file any evidence to the judge at the appropriate time.

Their lack of evidence puts them in a difficult position in my view, as we've discussed, but I'm still a bit unclear what their strategy is. We will obviously point out that they could have filed evidence, and have not done so, in our submissions (amongst other things). The MCC will be able to file their own submissions which will presumably explain this. That's in the timetable already…

I am preparing an updated proposed agreed statement of facts which incorporates extra points from the evidence we filed. That is the next step in the timetable. It's not controversial, but I am sending it to counsel on Friday to show to the other side's counsel to re-start that discussion.

LIZZIE O'SHEA

EMAIL

4 SEPTEMBER 2014

Even Lizzie was a little puzzled that various deadlines went by without MCC filing any evidence with the Court. The Court orders by consent indicated that 27 October 2014 was the final date for MCC to file any material they wished to rely on. Instead, on 3 November 2014, the date listed for our final filing in reply, MCC filed its 11-page submission. I guess they had misread the schedule, or the Court had changed the dates. No biggie. Our counsel still filed a reply that day, in time.

MCC'S beautifully written and fascinating legal arguments were rather lost on me. I found too many sentences offensive to women and to us. My wise daughter's words echoed, 'Step back, Mum. You will find everything offensive about MCC's approach. That's the game!' Even now as I write this, it is better that I heed Rebecca's advice to step back. I really do not want to get into it all again: our team working flat chat to meet another deadline, just to wait endlessly; seeing the ongoing tragedy of authorities' inaction on our patients' faces; wondering if we would ever make it happen; anger flaring with the injustice of it all, and dying with the hopelessness. On and on.

I don't agree with the Council's philosophy, but I understand where they're coming from: [MCC] didn't think that that's what was required of them at law; they didn't think that that's what the function of the Public Health and Wellbeing Act, which we were relying on, was their due. They were kind of bemused by this piece of litigation and didn't really see it as really substantial.

I can see how these things end up happening. I think probably we're similar in this sense, Susie, I feel so strongly about these matters. I don't re- ally empathise with people who oppose doing something about this. Well of course you should be doing something. This is on your turf. You can't expect others to do it. We have to look after people who need services, not just let the clinic do it, or let clients have to manage this themselves. You don't get to get away with shirking this responsibility. You think because the cost and consequences are hidden so you can shirk it?

But I get what they mean in retrospect. It emerged over time as well, this was going to be rather challenging litigation. I think clinic counsel were surprised how hard it was to get this argument up in court. The Court didn't seem to be into this argument at all.

LIZZIE O'SHEA

Leading up to our Supreme Court case, we hammered the air waves. As HRLC Communications Tom Clarke and MB Communications Chee Chee Leung pointed out on numerous occasions, winning the court of public opinion was as important, or more important, than winning the court case. Lizzie, Rachel and Em were seasoned media performers, and whether I had wanted to be or not, I guess now I was too.

As a human rights lawyer, I view litigation as one tool in the tool box of a much bigger strategy that you have to bring to an issue. This kind of case was probably one of the first where the Human Rights Law Centre actually had bigger ideas. We knew that we wanted to have those bubble zones, but we didn't have the political will at the time. Nonetheless we started to do some of the things that have become more the hallmarks of what the Centre does now. That communications piece, and having our lines about women running the gauntlet and it being about intimidation and abuse, was the first time that we really developed a good strong communications strategy and stuck to it. We knew: these are our talking points; we stick to this; and this is how we want to frame the issue.

We had done some of that preparatory work and messaging and narrative-creating with you and MB. That, I think, set us in good stead because even though inside the court they were talking about esoteric parts of law, when we were outside in our press conference we had great messaging and great people delivering the message as well: three women, you there with all your experience, MB there as you say with its history of protecting protest, and the HRLC.

I wouldn't say we had a pre-arranged whole strategy that we filled out to get to the legislative reform. But I think the thing we did best there was to use that case as an opportunity to build those messages and define the issue. We couldn't have just called a press conference and got all those cameras there. But we used the moments that we could and that was important.

EMILY HOWIE (2020)

A fight can happen in two courts: a court of law and the court of public opinion. Each court runs according to different rules of engagement. The argument that unfolded inside the courtroom in our case would prove to be dry, confusing, and deliberately sanitised of women and their suffering. It was about technicalities rather than harm and how to fix it.

But running the court case created media moments to shift public opinion our way. The real argument for us happened outside the courtroom where we were ready with our messaging, stories, visuals and spokespersons able to meet media demand.

Litigating in court, with its detail-focused legal rules of engagement, also forced us to methodically amass a raft of evidence, including our psychiatric assessment. that we would never otherwise have had. It helped us to frame the issue on our terms, and to make the need for change—whether through the court or through the legislature—an undeniable reality. Ultimately all this evidence would prove to be a ready store of advice to inform campaigners, media and parliamentarians when it mattered most.

CHAPTER 12

When a Lord Mayor Comes Calling

September 2014–March 2015

> *I see nothing. I know nothing.*
>
> CORPORAL SCHULTZ, *HOGAN'S HEROES*

Despite Lou having wangled a meeting for us with Robert Doyle when he was the state Liberal opposition leader, over the years our invitations and requests for meetings and direct pleas to MCC Lord Mayors So and Doyle had been declined. What a surprise it was when Lord Mayor Robert Doyle dropped by the clinic one morning in September 2014, completely unannounced.

Lizzie sensibly saw the Lord Mayor's visit as a positive gesture and encouraged us to think about whether it would be helpful to propose a meeting with MCC, with or without lawyers. But when I told Lizzie the whole story of his visit as relayed to me by Susan Speaking, Lizzie quipped, 'Oh God, if he's there for a vasectomy, feel free to keep it to yourself.'

Apparently Mr Doyle had been having a coffee in the area and decided to pop in to see us. Of course, why not.

The first member of staff the Lord Mayor met was Tariq, carrying out his security duties at the clinic gate. Tariq had no idea who this round man was and so asked him. The Lord Mayor then asked Tariq who *he* was. Tariq asked the round man who *he* was. Mr Doyle asked to see Tariq's ID. Tariq showed him his ID.

'I want to speak with the manager. Offer my support to staff.'

Tariq showed him into the clinic.

At reception, Robert Doyle said, 'I'd like to speak with the manager.'

'Do you have an appointment?' sensible receptionist Tharma asked, not having a clue who he was either.

'I'm here to offer my support to staff.'

Practice Manager Janice was not in that day. I was not in that day. Tharma led the man to the next best person, Susan Speaking, working at switch that morning.

Susan knew exactly who he was. The Lord Mayor of Melbourne had finally deigned to visit us when we were in the thick of suing Melbourne City Council? Extraordinary.

The Lord Mayor apologised for HOGPI and offered his best wishes.

Susan gave the Lord Mayor a piece of her mind, elegantly of course because Susan is always elegant.

The Lord Mayor said, 'Well, it would be good if residents complained.'

Susan, incredulous but polite, said they had complained to MCC.

He asked, what about to the police?

Susan said they had, and silently wished Janice or I were in.

Susan suggested that he speak with Medical Director Dr Louis Rutman and led the Lord Mayor of Melbourne back through the waiting room to the consulting rooms and a seat outside Lou's room. The Lord Mayor sat and waited for the doctor like any other patient. Except that he had not been heckled or obstructed by HOGPI, and it was unlikely he was pregnant or wanted an IUD or a Pap screen. Other health screens or contraception? Maybe.

A short time later, Lou invited the Lord Mayor into his room. Mr Doyle apologised about HOGPI and wished staff well. Unlike Susan who took her opportunity to let the Lord Mayor have it, Lou was not at all sure about the protocol here. We were suing MCC and here was the Lord Mayor. Lou was convivial. He and Robert had acquaintances and interests in common. The conversation quickly meandered into horse-racing and footy.

Why did the Lord Mayor pop in? Guilt about the court case? Thoughts of having a vasectomy? A problem pregnancy? The plot thickened. Sometimes we just needed a little levity.

Following the Lord Mayor's visit, and on counsel's suggestion, Lou aimed to set up an informal mediation with Robert Doyle. If Lou didn't succeed, counsel could propose directly to Hunt and Hunt a mediation with 'clients only' in the room. I was disinclined to mediation. I'd had enough of that already. I couldn't imagine MCC being genuine. Let's get on with the court case. Our team had worked so hard to reach the point where we could say, see you in court!

Big wigs can say what they like, but those who have to execute on this always seemed to be putting you off and wriggling out of things. There can be satisfaction in saying: well, you've had your time to try and fix this, you've failed to do so, see you in court. That's what the hard work is about really, using the legal process, however alienating, to force them to behave if they elect not to voluntarily. Empowerment can come from having worked hard to get to this point, to shift the power dynamic in the bargaining.

LIZZIE O'SHEA

Turned out, we were not going to see MCC in court quite yet. Our Supreme Court hearing was scheduled for Monday 1 December 2014. At the last minute, MCC asked for a delay to allow mediation. Of course it did. Our hearing was rebooked for 3 and 4 June 2015. MCC reneged on mediation. You had to give MCC credit for being consistent. Another six months for MCC to avoid their duty to protect the public from noxious nuisances. Another six months for women to suffer that noxious nuisance.

With MCC's request for an adjournment to mediate, Rachel Ball had been robbed of attending the case hearing. She had toiled diligently to get us to this point. Embarking on maternity leave, Rachel accepted our best wishes as she entered that special cocoon of breathtaking love.

Tash was locking up and a woman in her 60s came to the door. She had rosary beads in her hands and said, 'You're going to end up like your security guard—all dead.'

Tash called the police. Police didn't take a statement.

Friday morning, this same woman drove up and Tariq got her rego. I followed up with East Melbourne Police and they're looking into it.

JANICE NUGENT 12 JANUARY 2015

When I was a kid, I used to watch a TV show called *Hogan's Heroes*. It was a crazy, farcical comedy (and of course sexist) set in a German prisoner of war camp in World War II—where else would a comedy be set? In conjunction with my other teenage TV viewing, *The Goodies, Get Smart* and *Monty Python's Flying Circus,* this confession might shed some light on, and evoke some forgiveness for, my more irreverent and ridiculous remarks throughout what is an exceptionally serious matter. One of the characters in *Hogan's Heroes* was the hapless and lovable Corporal Schultz, whose favourite line in his rich German accent was, 'I see nothing, I know nothing'. Schultz's motto echoed in my brain after a 15 January 2015 meeting with two City of Melbourne Safety Committee members. Manager of the Women's Hospital Pregnancy Advisory Service and good friend, Annarella Hardiman, had astutely suggested this sideways approach to MCC to raise the lack of safety for women accessing abortion and reproductive health services. Setting up the meeting, Annarella had informed Anne Mulloch and Nancy Pierorazio that WHV CEO Rita Butera and I would also be attending. We would be attending as members of the Abortion Working Group. Clearly our wardrobe included multiple hats, and given the court case, Annarella was very clear about my FCC clinical psychologist headwear too.

Thanks so much for organising the City of Melbourne meeting—quite eye-opening but may well provide a productive avenue to actually get something done. Our MB lawyer was quite shocked that they knew nothing about the legal action and we wondered just who the CEO had spoken with before she responded to our correspondence. Bit depressing really that the people within City of Melbourne who might have some expertise with such issues were not brought into the loop. Weird in fact.

EMAIL TO ANNARELLA,

22 JANUARY 2015

But who really ever knew anything about anything when it came to MCC.

'That was all a bit strange,' said Annarella.

In early February 2015, our court case generated more high-quality evidence. Like the rest of the treasure trove our case had spawned, not only was this latest evidence important to our case, but it would also be put to excellent use in the campaign's future legislative push. As required in cases raising human rights issues, the Victorian Equal Opportunity & Human Rights Commission (VEOHRC) provided a learned and measured submission by Kate Eastman SC, Counsel for the Commission. The 9 February 2015 VEOHRC report (pp14-15) proffered conclusions helpful to our case:

> *Restrictions on protests will undoubtedly limit the right to freedom of expression in s 15(2). However, assuming that the Plaintiff's characterisation of the factual issues is correct, permitting restrictions on a nuisance caused by the manner and form of the protest (together with its content) would fall within the internal limitations in s 15(3), particularly respecting the rights of other persons and protecting public order and public health.*

And:

> *Not only must Council give proper consideration to relevant Charter rights, but it must also act compatibly with them. In that sense, what matters is the result.*
>
> *A breach of either obligation renders conduct unlawful unless, under s 38(2), the public authority could not have acted differently as the result of a statutory provision. Section 38(2) is not applicable here.*

Finally:

> *The Commission generally submits that the Defendant would be acting compatibly with Charter rights by permitting the protests, but using the functions, duties and powers available to it to regulate the manner and form of those protests—provided that such measure are carefully and appropriately tailored so as to be reasonable and proportionate.*

Discussion began with our learned counsel around Draft Orders: 'carefully and appropriately tailored' measures MCC could use to remedy the nuisance.

The first Order was for MCC officers to attend Wellington Parade and once they reasonably suspected that a person had committed a nuisance, or was about to do so, an officer would issue a notice prohibiting the person from abusing, or interfering with, those accessing or leaving the clinic. The abuse or interference would be prohibited whether it occurred right outside the clinic or further along the street (e.g. at the tram stop). The target of the prohibition could not simply be a list of activities that in general the clinic did not want to occur.

The second order, tightly confined in terms of geography, identified a 20-metre zone where the person who committed the nuisance could not enter at all, regardless of purpose. This area was kept so small so as not to weaken our case. It was unlikely that Council could prohibit a person from entering Wellington Parade to conduct lawful business at adjacent premises.

Therese McCarthy advised:

In our view the Court is very unlikely to make an order that sought to prevent a peaceful protest that did not involve abusing, harassing, intimidating etc. Again, this would weaken the overall case the clinic seeks to make—that is, it would reduce the overall prospects of success if we overreach in terms of the order we are seeking.

THERESE McCARTHY
EMAIL
19 FEBRUARY 2015

Our Orders were intended to stipulate a legally defined and legally valid process which hopefully over time would end with our patients and staff no longer copping abuse. Given our lengthy history with MCC, Lou, Janice and I wondered whether in practice, this order might end up being just more of the same, even with the Supreme Court's say so. We suspected that the problem again would be that the determination of what constituted abuse or nuisance would be left to Council officers looking through gendered glasses. Could the evidence to the Supreme Court and a request that officers undergo relevant training, nudge those patriarchal glasses off and provide them with some modern women-centred frames instead?

Our learned counsel proposed providing the Draft Orders to MCC with a view to settling the matter.

Using the legal process can be confronting and time consuming. It demands a great deal from those involved, and often feels like managing technicalities rather than issues of substance. But a court case is also a struggle for power. A court case can shift a power dynamic that had headed only in one direction for decades.

CHAPTER 13

Let's Just Write a Bill: Fiona Patten

January 2015–August 2015

Common values, orientations, and world views form bridges, at least to some degree, between those inside and those outside of government.

JOHN KINGDON (2011)

'Fiona Patten? The Sex Party? Waste of time, Susie A.'

'Have you seen her, Lou? She's classy, articulate, and gets it. I'm calling her back,' I said.

Lou shrugged.

The state election on 29 November 2014 had delivered a win to the Daniel Andrews-led Labor party and installed Sex Party MLC Fiona Patten. Fiona was one of the independent MPs holding balance of power in the Legislative Council and, just two months after the election, Fiona had shot out of the parliamentary gates into the media limelight demanding, of all things, exclusion zones around abortion clinics!

Fiona's passion for the issue was ignited as a young woman when Fiona had an abortion. Relatively unperturbed herself by the antics of the anti-abortion extremists outside the clinic, Fiona's mother was deeply distressed by them. Acknowledging this personal experience, and with considerable expertise working in other stigmatised health fields (detailed in Fiona's 2018 autobiography *Sex, Drugs and the Electoral Roll*), Fiona had ascended to balance of power MP in the Victorian Parliament. Fiona was the perfect advocate for safe access zones. It didn't take long for Lou to agree:

'Susie, the Sex Party? Fiona Patten? The last people I need. I'm trying to keep this very professional, I don't want the Sex Party. I knew nothing about the Sex Party or Fiona. Not long after, here is Fiona Patten being interviewed by Derryn Hinch. I thought Sex Party person? She's all over it. I was so impressed I couldn't wait to get Susie on the phone, 'Yes, we are very interested in getting her support.'

LOUIS RUTMAN (2019)

Fiona's agenda included wonderful antidotes to our androcentric world. But as a first time MP, her decision to pursue safe access zones was also an astute and politically calculated decision:

I knew I couldn't legalise cannabis. My decision to pursue abortion safe access zones was a calculation. It seemed to me actually quite low hanging fruit and something that I could do, get support for and get through. Looking at all the different issues we had on our list, this one seemed the most current as well. It was the currency of the court case, it was a simple piece of legislation, we had Tasmania to follow, and this was something we were able to do, really, in that first instance.

FIONA PATTEN (2019)

Low hanging fruit? Simple? Easy? We finally had a champion inside Parliament who saw that safe access zones were not just effective and relatively simple but were necessary and doable. We had become easy pickings! Hooray for the charismatic, newly minted politician, Fiona Patten.

If you look at John Kingdon's policy window, we finally had the hallmarks of what could be successful. We had a simple policy ask with an evidence base. We had the solution starting with Rebecca's research all that time ago. We had created public support through the advocacy around our case and raised the awareness of the issue. Then, it was a matter of getting the political support.

EMILY HOWIE (2020)

Given Fiona's push for safe access zones, I was initially surprised that the clinic had not heard from her before. I had not met Fiona and she had never come onto my radar. I was more surprised when Fiona reached me via a rather circuitous route: from Leslie Cannold to my daughter Rebecca, and finally to me. Rebecca had spoken with Fiona by phone and wisely warned me, 'Mum, she is excited and thinks it will be easy—she'll need to get the reality from you.' Since Steve's murder, we had seen plenty of initial excitement about solving this problem before the latest crusader would toss in the towel. But we hadn't reckoned on MP Fiona Patten.

Our Supreme Court case was creeping along—a hearing due in four months. But we had experience over far too many years of other efforts that had led precisely nowhere. We were not going to put all our eggs in one basket—the Supreme Court basket—especially when Fiona's basket offered the legislative panacea we had always known was the only way to secure genuine, safe abortion access. I'd whinged to Lou about needing a buffer zone back when my PhD studies first acquainted me with their existence overseas; Rebecca's research teased out the overseas legislation, showcased its effectiveness and how much it was needed here in Australia; and Em, Lizzie, Lou, Janice and I had never taken our eyes off the legislative solution during all the hard work on our court case. Now, Fiona Patten was brushing aside stubborn obstacles that had blocked us from the legislative solution for the last 14 years!

After chatting with Fiona by phone on 3 February 2015, I followed up by throwing Fiona's way every piece of information, advice and woman-centred language I had about our situation and solution, as well as introductions to legal, abortion and women's health experts in my network. Fiona caught everything without so much as a fumble and ran with it. This new cool kid on the block was a media and cross-party darling who had an insightful, sensible and respectful approach, an infectious can-do enthusiasm, and a fascination factor. Fiona Patten was compelling. Okay, so I might have had a little crush. It seemed everyone else did too.

On Wednesday 4 February 2015 I emailed Em and Lizzie about this latest hopeful avenue towards safe access. Moments later I received an email from Fiona:

Thank you so much for this information and taking the time to speak to me yesterday. I suspect you saw that the issue was reported in the HS [Herald Sun newspaper] today. I have had considerable support from my colleagues

on both sides of the house as a result. I am hoping to talk to the Health
Minister about this soon. It would be great to get the govt to take the lead...
Would love to catch up.

Yes, it would be fabulous to get the government to take the lead. And great
to catch up. Emails, attachments and phone calls whizzed back and forth,
while Fiona worked the media, her colleagues and the pro-choice network.
How had Fiona moved so quickly? Had she discussed her push for safe access
zones with Labor or Liberal parliamentarians in the lead up to the election?
Turned out, no:

It all came afterwards. I used to go up to the Clinic Defence on Saturdays
at least once or twice a month. Quite a few of our party members would
go up there even during the week to provide that chaperoning for women
attending the clinic. So it was front and centre in my mind: the need for
what we were still calling bubble zones at that time.

Certainly I was aware of the work of the court case against Melbourne
City Council. The Melbourne City Council case was fundamental in rec-
ognising that we needed legislation.

I'm only half joking when I say I didn't have a clue what I was doing,
because literally, well, let's just write a bill. And that's what we'll do and
we'll work on getting support.

Dr Rachel Carling-Jenkins had been elected and there was a real fear
that she was going to work very hard to pull back abortion laws. That
was a double-edged sword. When I first talked about proposing safe access
zones, there was some fear that would open up the abortion debate. But
when we realised we didn't have to put it in the abortion legislation, and
we could actually put it in the Health & Wellbeing Act, that allayed many
fears. At that stage I spoke to Jill [Health Minister Hennessy] and Jill was
largely supportive...

There's a photo of the early days of one of those early meetings—Rita
Butera, you, Emily, Mary Wooldridge... We saw support right from the
start from women on both sides of the chamber. And look, who could say no
to it? With a prochoice Health Minister it was going to be really hard for
her to say no to this.

The campaign was good and the organisations came together so well. We all ran a very good campaign. It was almost naivety that I just thought well, I know, I'll just write a bill.

FIONA PATTEN (2019)

I was suddenly living in a new world. We finally had a dedicated champion for safe access zones inside Parliament. Sex Party independent Fiona Patten brought a refreshing pro-choice, pro-women vitality to State Parliament. Maybe the Andrews government would join her.

It seemed like a tipping point, a moment when all the holes in the swiss cheese lined up in a good way! You need people who put in decades of effort, like you, and you need people like Fiona who come in as outsiders and act as the catalyst.

LIZZIE O'SHEA

We now had two strong options. On the one hand here was this stunning, determined woman inside Parliament whose only speed settings were fast and faster towards what we knew would be effective legislation. On the other hand, we had the slow, unpredictable drip-feed of our Supreme Court action, but with the smart legal and media know-how of our champions: the Human Rights Law Centre, Maurice Blackburn Lawyers and our distinguished legal counsel.

Our court action had publicised the issue, seen us amass and organise material crucial to persuading the government and other parliamentarians about the need for safe access zones legislation, and had delivered the Victorian Equal Opportunity and Human Rights Commission's (VEOHRC) submission to the Supreme Court. The VEOHRC submission was powerful in assuaging human rights concerns about legislating abortion access zones. The excitement generated by the VEOHRC report and MP Fiona Patten was obvious in Lizzie's 10 February 2015 call: 'This has been a great week for this issue!' Lizzie urged us to progress the meeting with Fiona, the Greens and others.

In mid-February 2015, a couple of weeks after Fiona and I first spoke, a large meeting of pro-choice women took place around a Parliament House table. Used to the more measured and agenda-focused meetings of the small Abortion Working Group facilitated by Women's Health Victoria CEO Rita

Butera, I was surprised by the relative chaos and noise of this safe access zones meeting. Pro-choice advocates included strong and vocal personalities. Like me, Rita was relatively quiet, given that it was sometimes hard to get a word in edge-wise. I had to remind myself that Fiona had bucket loads of experience with all sorts of personalities and would not be put off.

Hi Fiona,

It was lovely to finally meet you and your adviser today…

Rita [Butera] is well informed with a solid network and will be a strong ally.

While Colleen [Hartland, Greens MLC] works in quite a different way to you, she also has a huge depth of knowledge in this area and about the political 'beast'.

You have re-ignited this issue beautifully and are bringing key players to the table. I'm not sure whether you realise just how uplifting your advocacy has been for our staff and for me, let alone for women everywhere.

I do hope that our legal action does not mean government will avoid/delay the issue. Meanwhile I think City of Melbourne is avoiding/delaying, hoping the government gets in first! Ultimately, a state legislated access zone would be the most effective outcome.

Please let me know what else you may want from me or our legal reps—they are wonderful, learned young women.

EMAIL

20 FEBRUARY 2015

In the dead of night I found myself composing arguments urging that the political push for safe access zones move along and not wait on our Supreme Court case. The next day I emailed my thoughts to Fiona, Em, Lizzie, and Greens MLCs Colleen, Sue Pennicuik and Nina Springle, proffering arguments we might put as to why legislating for an access zone should occur irrespective of the court case and as soon as possible:

FCC may not win the Court action. Even if FCC wins a Court Order against Melbourne City Council, the Council may appeal (is that right Lizzie, Emily?) The Court Order would apply only to FCC. Any Court Ordered 'solution' will have unproven effectiveness and sustainability.

Whereas, access zone legislation provides:

LONG-TERM, PREVENTATIVE, EFFECTIVE & WORKABLE SOLUTION FOR ALL PROVIDERS

A strong evidence base has accumulated over decades from various abortion access (exclusion, bubble, buffer) zone legislation overseas. Jurisdictions which have faced legal challenges to access zone legislation have generally withstood such challenges, even in the USA where right to free speech and self-expression is strongly privileged.

TIGHTLY FOCUSED & SPECIFIC LAW

Evidence from other jurisdictions indicates that such legislation does not 'flow on' to put at risk other forms of protest/self-expression.

PRACTICAL EXPRESSION OF GOVERNMENT CONCERNS & PRIORITIES AROUND WOMEN'S RIGHTS:

Safety, privacy, health service access/choice, reproductive health rights and more.

WOMEN'S ACCESS TO ABORTION & OTHER REPRODUCTIVE HEALTH CARE

Most abortion providers, like FCC, also provide contraception, pap tests, sexually transmitted infection assessment/treatment and more.

PRACTICAL EXPRESSION OF GOVERNMENT CONCERNS & POLICIES RE ENSURING RESPECT FOR WOMEN & FREEDOM FROM VIOLENCE

POPULAR LAW

Surveys indicate that the right to abortion is supported by 85% of the community. Some of the 15% either opposing abortion or endorsing 'don't know' may oppose the current intimidation of women and be in favour of access zones.

Email

21 February 2015

At the clinic it was business as usual. There had been another death threat. Our sweet-hearted protector, security guard Tariq, was looking drawn. Plus the media attention and court case had hyped up the extremists. Perhaps they were finally wearing Tariq down. We didn't want to lose him.

Hi Fiona,

Thank you so much for your bolstering words!

I also wished to let you know that four staff were assessed by a learned psychiatrist. That psychiatric report is before the Court and so we have to take some care in any distribution of it. If however the premier wishes to see the report's conclusions we could provide them…

Our Medical Director, Dr Louis Rutman, is most appreciative of your wonderful advocacy. It is so uncommon for someone to really 'get' and artic-ulate our situation, but you do. Lou would love to speak with you, meet, or attend any meetings with you if you felt that might be helpful…

EMAIL

FRIDAY 6 MARCH 2015

By early March 2015, Fiona had met with Premier Andrews in a productive meeting and by the end of May 2015, Fiona advised me that:

Trades Hall has come out in complete support which is very useful with this government. I am meeting the Deputy Commissioner of police on Tuesday to discuss how we make this happen. I am quite optimistic at the moment.

What a coup. Trades Hall had joined the growing throng recognising that what our patients and staff endured was not a protest but chronic abuse of women and trampling of women's rights. Surely now we could finally put to bed any doubt that safe access zones legislation might pose a threat to the right to protest. We had three human rights giants—HRLC, MB Lawyers and Trades Hall—all agreeing that women's rights to safety, privacy, dignity and abortion access deserved to be prioritised over a relatively small geo-graphical limit on where a religious group could 'express' their views.

Fiona can say that it was all done, but she did so much. I remember the first time I spoke with her and she said, I've spoken to Police, spoken to Trades Hall, and a number of very important others. I thought, wow, she had already done the lion's share of lobbying to get major institutions over the line.

Fiona had just entered Parliament after being a lobbyist for years. She is a great operator because she's so smart, so likeable, and she knows how to get things done. Everyone loves her, including us. She's wonderful. She's using all of her powers for good.

Emily Howie (2020)

But even for the charismatic Fiona Patten, surely it must have been difficult to win over Trades Hall?

No, Trades Hall really got it. Luke Hilakari was newly anointed at that stage. He was supportive right from the start, and that was really hopeful. We had the Nurses of course. We had the AMA. There was no one it was going to upset except perhaps the SDA—the shop distributors, but I don't think they are even affiliated with the Trades Hall anyway…

I spoke with the Police Association's Ron Ingles and Bruce McKenzie the Deputy. I'd been meeting with Bruce since he'd been Deputy Secretary in the '90s. I had known him for a very long time, so I could speak to Bruce.

A lot of the people who were in my chamber were staffers and many of them came out of Rob Hulls office. Rob really did mentor women in particular, so many of them had actually responded to letters I'd written and sat in meetings with us. Even though I didn't know them very well, they were familiar with us, and I think that throughout this we were reasonable.

It was great having Tassie. They contacted us, and that was fantastic. Susan Fahey [Legal Services Tasmania CEO] was fabulous and she stayed all night for the debate as well which was great.

Fiona Patten (2019)

While Fiona previously had been outside my rather blinkered field of vision, she clearly had been doing extensive work in other sexual and gender rights areas for years. It seemed that everyone, no matter where they sat politically, liked her as a lobbyist, and now loved her as an elected politician. Fiona was an outsider from mainstream parties, but her work over the long term meant she began her parliamentary career already an insider. Plus, as one of the independent MPs holding balance of power in the Legislative Council, the major parties were no doubt happy to both court Fiona and be courted by her.

Fiona is awesome, amazing. She doesn't seem like she's afraid. It's as if she's got nothing to lose. And she cares about people, she cares about women, and she has got charisma in spades. So Fiona had that perfect mix. There was Natasha, wasn't there, and she cared about this issue too. But she didn't have the right pull then: she was federal and it was a different time.

Being an independent, Fiona didn't have to worry about the party lines. Labor had EMILY's List politicians coming through, who ultimately helped get the legislation through, but because they were part of the Labor party they couldn't instigate this somehow. They had to walk this balancing act between more conservatives in the party and the more liberal in the party, plus the fact that they were women too.

REBECCA DEAN (2020)

People can be doing work on an issue that might seem totally unrelated, but over the long term can align with the work and strategy of other activists. It's really lovely to see it all play out so nicely. Imagine, say, Fiona had not been elected, or she was elected ten years earlier or later, or you were no longer doing this work.

LIZZIE O'SHEA

Let's not imagine that!

Fiona was a feminist and humanist to her core, with vast experience enacting those values for the benefit of others and to create a fairer, kinder society. Her bravery lay in knowing her own mind and the inequities and injustices she wanted to address. Respectfully speaking strength and reason to power was Fiona's *raison d'etre*. Getting good done by bringing people along with her, was her superpower.

Walking with Fiona from the parliamentary foyer to her office could take a while: you'd lose count of the people she stopped to speak with on the way, offering encouragement, a kind inquiry or fillip of fun to everyone from high powered pollies and lobbyists to kitchen staff and security.

Fiona poured all her political capital and charismatic magic into our issue. *Lenin, of all people, has a great quote: There are decades where nothing happens; and there are weeks where decades happen. It must have felt a bit like that. Without patience there is no change. But even the most en-thusiastic and charismatic change maker cannot make wine out of water. By generating the right conditions for reform, you laid the terrain in an invaluable way. You just needed an advocate in the right spot to come along to get things moving.*

LIZZIE O'SHEA

The brutal murder of Steve Rogers in 2001 triggered our campaign for abortion safe access zones. The 2008 abortion decrim turned out not to be the turning point we'd all hoped, but Em in 2010, and Lizzie and our pro bono legal team in 2011, were both crucial turning points in the campaign. Fiona Patten was the catalyst who finally made it happen.

A campaign is not necessarily a chess game where you have to be six moves ahead. Nor does a campaign have to be rooted in pre-conceived ideas about the right way to be an activist or the right way to get things done. Activism can be more about keeping options open and never assuming you will succeed in a particular way. We always had safe access legislation as our preferred solution to our problem because it had been proven to work in situations like ours overseas. But given major political roadblocks over many years, we also were prepared to try the unproven option of taking creative legal action against a public authority we thought should take responsibility for this noxious nuisance, in the hope of securing a de facto safe access zone.

I relied on my instincts, knowledge and values to know who I could trust, who I might be wiser to tread carefully with, or who not to engage with at all. Someone's track record of reliability, honesty, intelligence and how they treat others speaks volumes. A sense of humour and a passion for the cause was essential. Like our legal team, Fiona felt like home.

CHAPTER 14

Our Day in Court and a New Day in Parliament

3 June–August 2015

> *'Curiouser and curiouser,'*
> *cried Alice.*
>
> LEWIS CARROLL, *ALICE IN WONDERLAND* (1865)

On 3 and 4 June 2015, we were detoured from Fiona Patten's Wonder Woman World into a strange *Alice in Wonderland* world: Our date with the Supreme Court of Victoria had finally arrived.

Supreme Court Justice Michael McDonald presided. Appointed to the Supreme Court less than eight months earlier on 16 September 2014, Michael McDonald QC had been an experienced barrister specialising in administrative law, employment law, industrial law, discrimination law, sports law, industrial torts, contempt, restraint of trade, other employment-related proceedings and high-profile industrial litigation cases including Grocon in contempt proceedings against the CFMEU. Impressive.

But did that legal background fill us with confidence? Not really. Public health? Women's issues? Abortion? Gendered Violence? At least discrimination law was in his CV, although I didn't get the feeling it was of the gendered type. Fingers crossed, here goes everything.

In the grand old Supreme Court of Victoria we sat in the usual wedding seating style: MCC counsel and legal reps on one side; Em, Janice, Lou and I behind our learned counsel of Peter Hanks, Therese McArthur, Kris Walker and Lizzie O'Shea. After all her hard work, Rachel Ball was missing the main event. By the end of the two days in the Supreme Court I'd be relieved that Rachel hadn't had to endure it.

I took the stand to testify that nothing had changed in our circumstances since my affidavit, and to face cross examination. As I stood in the witness box, an ephemeral curtain closed in on me: I was exquisitely present in that moment, and not really there at all. Get a grip, Susie, breathe. It wasn't like I'd never testified before. But all the hours and years of laborious work by so many people for our patients and staff was all culminating in this.

As it turned out, apart from taking the affirmation, which I knew automatically from my days in the Children's Court, I uttered just two words on the stand: 'Yes' and 'No'. There was no cross examination, at all.

In the lead up to the hearing, MCC had provided the court with no evidence about the key facts of what went on out the front of the clinic. Until the day of the hearing, they had declined to accept our evidence, and they had declined to talk to us about providing the court with an agreed set of facts. We were working overtime to set the scene of what was happening, they didn't engage with that at all. I think this was probably a small target strategy—they wanted the case to be about the legal duties owed by council, and their very narrow interpretation of them. By the time they made their written legal submissions, just before the hearing, they claimed that various things had happened, conveniently, in the passive, that is, they say 'the activities of HOGPI are said to be...' Then in court, they elected not to cross examine you about your evidence at all, they just accepted it. It's a clever way to acknowledge factual matters without giving them much airtime, to run the case on their own terms.

LIZZIE O'SHEA

I was too relieved about not having to face cross examination to wonder what that may mean for our case. All I knew was that my evidence, all of our evidence, had been accepted unchallenged and uncontradicted. Now let's relax and enjoy it. I was looking forward to incisive arguments about the definition of nuisance, women's rights, Council obligations. This would finally be a payment of sorts to our learned pro bono counsel, where they could strut their stuff and make history with their fabulous human rights arguments. Peter Hanks, Therese McCarthy and Kris Walker were dolled up in their flowing gowns, ready to rock and roll.

But the only thing that rock and rolled that day, and the next, were incredulous, eye-rolling looks between Lou, Janice and me. Even before we got out of the blocks, the Judge had us chasing a white rabbit down a hole into Alice's absurd Wonderland. He was not a big picture kind of guy—he was a legal technicalities type of judge. In the face of him pursuing minute detail round and round in ever constricting circles, Peter Hanks' and Kris Walker's polite and articulate patience was extraordinary to behold.

We were sitting in court, and court is never a great spectator sport, but I do recall sitting there, with you and Lou getting increasingly fidgety. It's hard to follow court if you don't have all the documents in front of you, and I was trying to follow those proceedings and I remember thinking, how are Susie and Lou with this?

I suppose we were trying to achieve an outcome in court that would have required some action by the council on an issue that had been neglected and on which moral responsibility had been denied for so long. It was the legal way to do it.

But we were so far removed from talking about women's experiences, and even the staff's experiences. You had all been so courageous in providing information to the expert psychiatrist to put on that expert evidence. That was something that I just admired so much. That's a huge amount to ask of staff in an organisation.

We were very careful with that evidence ensuring that it wasn't distributed any further. But we knew you and the staff well enough to know what you went through on a daily basis, and the debate in the Court seemed overly technical and removed from the human issue that we needed to address.

EMILY HOWIE (2020)

The law has this tendency to make even the most visceral of human suffering seem like an abstract concept. It's really terrible in some ways to force people to debate, in such a formalised way, what ought to be done about the abuse of women seeking to lawfully access a health service, and the decades of misery that these people inflicted on you and the staff. This is the dark side of the law. The whole point of the case is to elevate the argument to principle, with properly constituted evidence and facts, to strip it of its human aspects to allow a judge to opine on it. That's a very frustrating process!

I too felt your pain, as at heart I'm an activist. I used to get so frustrated in all these cases, just wondering why someone couldn't immediately understand why we were right. It was obvious! The upside of law is that when you win, you get to force people to do something they don't want to do without violence. But it takes enormous reserves of patience and abstraction, and it's important not to lose yourself in the process.

Lizzie O'Shea

More detailed thoughts on the court case are included in the next chapter's discussion of His Honour's eventual decision. But at the end of those long two days in the Supreme Court of Victoria, we still believed that MCC had both an obligation and the power to stop the extremists' abuse of women. We were wrong.

Our date with the Supreme Court had come and gone. We'd put our best foot forward for the June 2015 Supreme Court hearing. Now we had to wait for Justice Michael McDonald's judgement. We couldn't dwell on what might happen, firstly for the sake of our sanity, and secondly because the Supreme Court verdict was diminishing in importance. The battles outside the courts— in the court of public opinion and inside Parliament—were starting to matter more. Work with Fiona continued apace. Political advocacy, meetings, emails, discussion and media ramped up. Women's groups and advocates from around the country mobilised.

Our court case had successfully amassed exactly the type of information needed by our parliamentarians and was readily disseminated. Safe access zones emails were zipping through cyber space, like the one Emily Howie sent to Fiona Patten's determined adviser:

Thank you for the meeting this morning. It was great to hear how far progressed Fiona's team is on access zones for Victoria!

I attach for you the Human Rights Law Centre's submissions to the Tasmanian abortion law reform inquiry:

http://www.hrlc.org.au/wpcontent/uploads/2013/07/TAS_ReproductiveHealthBill_HRLC_Submission_July2013.pdf.

The VEOHRC's submissions in the Fertility Control Clinic case are the best analysis of the balancing of rights and proportionality arguments under the Victorian Charter. Their submissions are online here.

http://www.humanrightscommission.vic.gov.au/index.php/training/item/1197-fertility-control-clinic-v-melbourne-city-council.

Finally, I attach a table that compares the US and Canadian decisions on access zones. The Canadian case is best, as their law is very similar to the Victorian Charter, so they apply a similar test. They upheld a 50m buffer zone. The rest of the cases are US ones and all but one upheld access zones. As I mentioned this morning, the access zone that was struck down was very restrictive. However, I don't think US law is the best guide anyway as they apply a very different legal test to any that an Australian court would apply…

As we mentioned today, please don't hesitate to contact us if you have any further questions or if we can be of more assistance.

17 June 2015

On 18 August 2015, Fiona Patten's *Public Health and Wellbeing Amendment (Safe Access) Bill* 2015 was introduced into the Victorian Parliament. The next day Fiona delivered her second reading speech:

I rise today to speak to the Public Health and Wellbeing (Safe Access) Amendment Bill 2015… designed to create safe access around premises offering reproductive health services, in order to protect and promote women's reproductive health. It's about medical privacy and the rights of women who are accessing a legal medical service to do so without fear of intimidation or harassment.

This bill, the first I have proposed since becoming elected to this place, won't be a surprise to anyone coming from me. It is an issue The

Australian Sex Party campaigned heavily on at the last election. Safe access to reproductive services is something that I have championed for a long time and I am proud to be able to bring this bill forward to the house today.

This amendment to the Health and Wellbeing Act is quite simple. It inserts a new part that creates safe access zones of 150 metres around reproductive health clinics wherein prohibited behaviour can be met with criminal remedies including financial penalties and imprisonment. Prohibited behaviour is to include: distribution and display of materials pertaining to reproductive health services, communications—yelling, singing, chanting, and what some call 'counselling'—harassment, intimidation, threats, and recording of any variety...

It is our job as law makers to help protect the people of Victoria from such threats of intimidation and violence... Women have been known to delay attendance for essential health care and follow up appointments because they have been so apprehensive and scared of who they will face when they attend the health centre... [This] poses a serious threat to women's health and wellbeing.

Women with a history of domestic violence or mental ill health can feel particularly threatened. This is a significant problem for individuals who may be traumatised and face depression and anxiety in the face of stigmatisation, and staff who may fear coming to work, a valid fear considering a staff was murdered—yes murdered!—in Melbourne due to their work in one of these centres...

This problem and these issues are highly specific to premises offering reproductive health services... Currently, Victoria Police and councils can issue on the spot notices for breach of Council by-laws for obstruction and public nuisance... [these] simply have not been working... It places an enormous amount of strain on Victoria's police services, and there has been discussion from Victoria Police advising a preference for specific legislation to provide clarity—exactly what I am proposing here... also places a strain on Council resources, with some councils having to send out representatives two or three times a week.

A more comprehensive, targeted approach than disconnected interventions and infringements is required. This would not only recognise the highly specific, gendered nature of this kind of offence, but also provide clarity for enforcement, and avenues for remedy.

Access to lawful medical treatment can be so clearly linked to gender equality, economic and social stability and mental health... overseas jurisdictions have similar laws. Tasmania has a similar type of legislative arrangement providing for 150 metre safe access zones similar to what I am proposing today—and it works. The Australian Capital Territory Government is currently considering a similar bill.

In 2008 the Victorian Law Reform Commission stated:

'The safety and wellbeing of women using abortion services, and any other medical facilities, is a matter of significant importance (8.271, p 139). There is understandable community concern about safety and well being of staff and patients at the hospitals and clinics where people protest or stage vigils because of their views about abortion. The Commission encourages the Attorney-General to consider options for a legislative response to this issue. (8.273, p.140)'

So this isn't new and nor is it really controversial—it's just common sense... individuals have a right to medical privacy and the right to go about their lawful business without fear of intimidation or shame. This is the right thing to do.

The Bill does not seek to impede anyone's right to protest it only seeks to prevent people being harassed and intimidated. I welcome the daily debate with people who greet us at the carpark gate each morning... I ask that over the next few weeks before this matter is brought to a debate, that fellow members search their conscience and ask themselves the question, regardless of their religious or other views—'Is it ok that women of this state are harassed and intimidated every day on my watch when I have the option to do something about it?'

The answer is surely a resounding 'no'.

I commend this Bill to the house.

Yes, that's our Fiona! Debate on the bill would commence during the next sitting week in two weeks' time. All hands were on deck for lobbying, media, consultations and all manner of support. Fiona continued talking the talk and walking the walk with spectacular results.

Campaigning for this bill among my parliamentary colleagues quickly became 'not-so-secret women's business'. A small cross-party group of women emerged to lead support for the bill, including Mary Wooldridge (shadow health spokesperson and leader), Jaala Pulford (Minister for Agriculture), Colleen Hartland (the Green's health spokesperson), Georgie Crozier (shadow for children's health), Jaclyn Symes (government whip) and myself. It was my first taste of cross-party collaboration and it was a wonderful feeling to be united around an issue with a group of women that all had vastly different political affiliations. Since it was all about women's health, I suspect that it would have been a different process had men been involved.

FIONA PATTEN (2018)

Fiona just had a really positive meeting with female MPs from both the Gov and Opposition. They have basically said change 'reproductive health services' to 'abortion' per the Abortion Law Reform Act, which will still cover advanced contraception, remove claims by pro-lifers that this would include pharmacies etc, and allow the Libs a conscience vote. Between Greens, Liberals, and what is looking like possible Gov support, this is fantastic.

FIONA PATTEN'S ADVISER
EMAIL
20 AUGUST 2015

The courts and Parliament are two different sites of social change. They need different approaches and can yield different outcomes.

In many ways the court was our last option: the final stage of years' long advocacy. As that door started to close, as it became clear that court was unlikely to fix our problem, another window began to open. Parliamentary reform had always been the right thing to do, and it was increasingly clear to many that it was the only way this problem could be meaningfully addressed. Finding a change-maker like Fiona Patten was essential to generating this paradigm shift. Fiona was a relative newcomer but, in reality, her life experience and her own advocacy meant she both totally got it, and was in a position to do something constructive and, ultimately, momentous. It was a relief for us to see that others were able to see the world as we had known it for decades.

Once you've found someone you trust, you can ride the wave of change they make.

CHAPTER 15

Tears...

26 August 2015

A square peg in a round hole.

EMILY HOWIE (2020)

Supreme Court D-Day was 26 August 2015. His Honour Supreme Court Justice Mr McDonald delivered his decision in the Fertility Control Clinic v Melbourne City Council [2015] VSC 424.

In my non-lawyerly language, the Fertility Control Clinic had asked the Supreme Court to compel Melbourne City Council to carry out its duties under the Public Health and Wellbeing Act 2008 and deal with the nuisance of a group chronically harassing and harming staff and women accessing the clinic's health service. Since the court hearing in early June 2015, we had waited a mere two-and-a-half months for the decision. I had been waiting for a decision for more than two decades. Lou, Janice, Susan, June and other FCC staff for even longer.

On the eve of Justice Mr McDonald's decision, at 8:48 pm, HLRC Tom Clarke sent through two media releases: one for if we lost our Supreme Court case the next day; the other for if we won. Regardless of the outcome though, Tom sensibly reckoned that two key messages needed to be put to the media:

1. This case was about trying to ensure that women can access health services without being harassed and intimidated.

2. Today's decision once again highlights the pressing need for Victoria to introduce safe access zones for fertility clinics.

Win or lose, we wanted safe access zones. We needed safe access zones.

On the morning of 26 August 2015, Lou, Janice, and my daughter Rebecca and I squeezed into the packed Supreme Court room. It felt wrong that we, as a party to this case, struggled to get a seat to hear the judgement. Lizzie was overseas, MB's sub, Katie Robertson, was yet another delightful, learned young woman.

At 9:30 am, Supreme Court Justice Mr McDonald, brought down his decision.

We lost.

No matter Tom's media release about win or lose—we lost and I was gutted. Outside the Supreme Court, Em, Katie and I faced media on the Williams Street footpath. Trams and traffic hurtled by. I held it together for the cameras, but as I walked away with my daughter's arm around me, my tears fell. Failed. Our patients. Let down. Our staff. Disappointed. Our legal team.

My lay, unlearned, non-lawyerly, not-a-jot-of-law-school and emotionally subjective judgement was exactly the same as legions of people before me: the law is an ass. A legal technicality had gazumped women.

The case did not fail in terms of the human rights issues involved. Melbourne City Council (MCC) initially made submissions under the Victorian Charter of Human Rights and Responsibilities 2006 and the Commonwealth Constitution but did not pursue the Constitutional freedoms and Charter in Court. While the human rights issues remained untested, our own human rights evidence was prepared by the Victorian Human Rights Law Centre, Maurice Blackburn Lawyers, and our QCs/barristers—all outstanding experts and champions of human rights. Plus the Equal Opportunity and Human Rights Commission submission strongly supported the clinic's view that women need access to health care without intimidation, and that it was legitimate to impose limitations on others' rights to achieve this end.

Nor did the case fall on recognising as harmful nuisance the types of behaviour women endured as they accessed a health service. MCC left unchallenged and uncontradicted the extensive evidence we offered to the Court about the nuisance and the harm inflicted on staff and patients. Of this matter His Honour Mr McDonald's judgement concluded:

Much of the conduct complained of by the clinic, including the blocking of the entry to the clinic's premises, potentially constitutes both a private and public nuisance… It may be that the Protesters have engaged in conduct which supports a conclusion that persons attempting to attend the clinic have been beset with insults or messages in ways which offer discouragement to their attendance.

And yet, ultimately, His Honour Mr McDonald also concluded:

There was no actual or constructive failure by the Council to perform the duties imposed upon it by the Act.

How could that be? If the case did not fall on human rights grounds or on recognising the extremists' behaviour as being a harmful nuisance, where did it fail?

The case fell at the second of two 'legal technicalities' relied on by Melbourne City Council. It was a legal technicality which should explain much to rate payers struggling to get their local council to act on their complaints. So, here's my lay woman's view of the technical loophole that got MCC off the hook and kept women on the hook.

Our lawyers' formal complaint to MCC in 2014 received a one-page letter from the Council stating that it had investigated the matter and did not find the extremists' behaviour to be a nuisance under the Act. The Council therefore was not going to take any action.

Justice McDonald decided that under the *Public Health & Wellbeing Act 2008 (Vic)*, which provides for the duties of local councils and on which our Supreme Court action hung, as long as a Council investigating officer 'investigates' a complaint and 'asks the right question', it does not matter if s/he comes up with the wrong answer. And clearly, even after a Supreme Court action, there is no legal compunction for the Council to correct its mistake.

Council investigator Mr Webster relied on a narrow and out-dated definition of nuisance to both ask and answer his question of whether a nuisance existed. I reckoned he didn't even rely on MCC's own definition of nuisance in the Activities Local Laws created by MCC to aid in carrying out its duties under the Health & Wellbeing Act:

Any person using threatening, abusive or insulting words, or annoying, molesting, obstructing or interfering with the personal comfort of others.

No matter. Never the point. Unimportant. Irrelevant.

The Supreme Court judgement held that using the correct definition of nuisance was not part of 'asking the right question'. And, even if using the wrong definition of nuisance in the question led to the wrong answer, the investigator was entitled to come up with the wrong answer. And, the Council is apparently under no obligation to correct its mistake. And...

Surely common sense would say that the investigator asked the *wrong* question *because* he used the wrong definition of nuisance. Surely the investigator then got the wrong answer because he had asked the wrong question.

The investigator's answer to his question was that, apart from the blocking of the clinic entrance, no nuisance existed. As His Honour McDonald concluded:

If the decision makers did erroneously conclude that the conduct was neither offensive nor dangerous to health, any such error was one within jurisdiction... It is unproductive to speculate as to the process of reasoning which underpinned the Council's decision that the only conduct which arguably constituted a nuisance for the purposes of the Act was the blocking of the entry to the clinic's premises. In circumstances where the Council's reasons for decision disclose that the relevant decision makers addressed the question required by the Act, there is no utility in going behind the stated reasons for the decision.'

During the hearing Justice McDonald had pondered this technicality, around and around and around again, down, down, down until I fell dizzily into the rabbit hole leading to absurdity. Hearing Justice McDonald's judgement, I fell again. We all fell. My colleagues raised eyebrows at the different responsibility we shouldered in our workplace, and probably most other people in their workplaces: If we make a mistake, we do what we can to rectify that mistake. Plus, to maintain our professional pride and our accreditation we are expected to be up-to-date with 'best practice', which might mean, say, keeping up with the most recent definitions of important procedures and words.

Justice Mr McDonald did note a mistake in the advice that the investigator provided to the clinic. The Council had an obligation to advise the person notifying the Council of the nuisance of any available methods for settling the matter privately. Council's advice that the clinic should seek to settle its dispute with the protesters privately 'by aggrieved individuals making a complaint to Victoria Police was misconceived... the advice was erroneous.'

But again, as long as the Council directed itself to the right question (even using an incorrect definition), it didn't matter if the answer was incorrect, and there was no legal requirement for the Council to correct their error. Eye rolling in Wonderland again from we laypersons.

In the end, to this laywoman (who may be asking the right question but may be making a mistake in both her question and her answer), our eminent, fabulous legal team was like a thoroughbred racehorse falling just as it leapt out of the gates because some idiot failed to clear an archaic barrier of bastardry and sexism.

I felt devastated for our legal team who had put in so much work over several years just to have the important human rights and public health arguments brushed aside; to have women brushed aside; to have our staff brushed aside; to have our community brushed aside. We were all nothing but a pesky, tiny piece of lint given the brush off.

If Gideon Haigh were updating his 2008 abortion tome, *The Racket*, he could add this judgement as yet another example of women being excluded from deliberations directly affecting them. The McDonald judgement was focussed so exquisitely on the technical, that women's voices were muted. The judgement could have at least given greater acknowledgment of the facts of the harm happening to women, even if the final decision is that the law can't give us a remedy. The judgement could have at least let women know that they had been heard and believed.

It is difficult to understand any of this, even when I had been present during the lengthy, tediously technical, but apparently crucial and clever legal arguments raised in court by Melbourne City Council; the clever legal arguments that so intrigued the Judge; clever legal arguments with nary a woman in sight; clever legal arguments that got MCC off the hook. Is getting MCC off the hook really the only name of the game?

Not according to MCC's media statement on 26 August 2015, following the decision:

> *The Supreme Court has today found the East Melbourne Fertility Control Clinic has been unsuccessful in its attempt to have the City of Melbourne reconsider complaints of nuisance under the Public Health and Wellbeing Act (2006).*

The City of Melbourne takes no relief or pleasure in this result. The City of Melbourne sympathises with the women targeted by protestors at the East Melbourne Fertility Control Clinic and acknowledges the impact the group's presence has on the health and wellbeing of the clinic's patients, staff and management.

For more than 20 years, the City of Melbourne has worked within its limited powers to protect the interests of women who attend the clinic. Although we have wanted to do more, we have not had the authority to do so.

Although we respect people's right to a peaceful protest, we consider that the groups who assemble at the clinic show little respect for the rights of women who attend it. Despite what the group might say, we have no doubt the gatherings at the clinic intimidate women at what is a vulnerable time in their lives.

The City of Melbourne accepts the findings of the Supreme Court in this matter. We recognise the court has found that we made an error in referring the clinic to Victoria Police in order to resolve the issues. We will reflect on the decision and its implications as a matter of priority.

Today's finding by the Supreme Court leaves unresolved the broader issue of managing protestors at the clinic. Our ultimate aim is ensuring that the health and wellbeing of the women who attend the East Melbourne Fertility Control Clinic is not jeopardised. We will continue to engage with all relevant stakeholders including the East Melbourne Fertility Control Clinic and its clients, Victoria Police and the State Government in order to develop a coordinated and effective approach.

Wasn't that a lovely and perceptive media release? I would have quite liked having mediation with *that* MCC. After this long legal saga, it appeared that MCC did have feminist insights after all. It was just that this great institution with massive resources and the powers to, for example, put a stop to the Occupy Melbourne protests, was helpless to do anything about this abuse of women; prepared to throw resource after resource, dollar after dollar, officer after officer, to evade, delay, mislead and play the pass the parcel game: someone-else's-problem.

Why should I have hoped for anything different at the court case? It was not about doing the right thing or making our society fairer or better. The law, like too much of our world, was derived from an outdated, but still powerful, patriarchy; a competitive game of football whose macho contestants were out to win at all costs; to win no matter the cost to women, and no matter that these very same women were also the mothers, sisters, daughters, partners… of these Tin Men. 'If I only had a heart,' the Tin Men should sing mournfully, and then do all they can to go and find one. Plus every lawyer, councillor, judge, justice, CEO, you name it, should have to complete Gender Studies 101—and pass.

I guess I had been hoping for a touch of the old Clifford Menhennitt who, back in 1969, had cleverly and legally recognised the desperate necessity of abortion for women. Retired Appeal Court Judge Marcia Neave's description of such 'judge-made' law, speaks to what I had hoped would result from our Supreme Court case:

> *A novel case comes before the courts and the existing legal principles don't fit perfectly to the situation and therefore the court has to decide whether to extend a principle or to find a new principle which you can do because there may well be other examples or situations that are analogous, but not exactly the same.*
>
> MARCIA NEAVE (2019)

Now that my outrage at this gross miscarriage of justice is out of the way, let's hear from calmer, brighter minds than mine. And let's also dip into a happy preview of how well this failed Supreme Court action set us up to finally gain the legislative solution we had always wanted.

> *The case did run in an odd way in the end. We had some human rights aspects and the constitutional argument had been floated. Then Richard Niall, who was on the other side at the time, abandoned various arguments. If the other side abandons an argument we can't then just decide to make gratuitous arguments about a point that's no longer an issue.*
>
> *Richard is a very good litigator—was, now of course he's a Court of Appeal judge. I think there was a bit of strategy in him focussing down very much on the way the scheme operated in relation to councils and the particular decisions that had been taken. It became a very technical case.*
>
> *We still thought that we had a good case even in that much narrower sense. But it was always a creative argument. It was an attempt to use the*

legislative framework that was available at the time in a way that no one had really come up with before, in trying to require the council to act.

There had been some historical attempts, and successfully, to get injunctions against particular people who were creating the nuisance, because they are the people actually creating the nuisance. This was more removed, because obviously it is really impossible to injunct individual after individual. So this was an attempt to get the council to act. But the council wasn't the entity creating the nuisance. It was a much more indirect way to try and manage the problem.

I think the judge took a very narrow view of the nature of the Council's duty and also of the nature of the decision that the Council had made. In the end he accepted that there had been some errors made, but not sufficient to give us the remedy that we were seeking.

But in the end it was actually a much better outcome because if you had to sue the council every time things started getting out of control that's not practicable in the longer term sense. Of course we wanted to win the case at the time, but in hindsight, really it was a great thing that we didn't win because it was the impetus for the Safe Access Zones Bill. And what we have now is a much, much better regime…

In the absence of that legislative scheme, the safe access zones scheme, it is hard to know what are the parameters of the council's duty that we were seeking to rely upon. Is it a duty enforceable by the remedies? There was a very good argument I thought, to say that it's not. Yes, it appears to be a duty, but not every duty is a duty capable of enforcement by mandamus.

So I got the arguments on the other side from a technical perspective. Because the regime just didn't have in mind how this would work with this kind of activity, it was much more difficult to find a pathway where you would have a concept of, well how does it work? Does the council have a duty every time someone rings it to send someone out? Then what does it have a duty to do? Does it have a duty to arrest people or fine people or issue them with notices? It was quite hard to work out quite how it worked. Whereas what we have now is social change that we've now seen nationally, but completely tied up with legislative change.

SOLICITOR GENERAL KRIS WALKER QC (2020)

My memory of the Supreme Court was that it was a legalistic exercise with very technical arguments. The barristers were arguing about jurisdictional error and error of law, and very little time was spent on the staff and patients' everyday lived experiences of harassment and abuse. At that time we didn't have a law that squarely addressed the issue, so the case had to apply more orthodox legal actions to the set of facts at the clinic.

That Supreme Court experience was so different to our experience of being in the High Court because once we got safe access zones law, we had a law that directly addressed the issue. Then, we could talk about what was actually going on and we could talk about what the case was really all about: insisting that women are entitled to human rights.

EMILY HOWIE (2020)

The actual argument that was going to unfold inside the courtroom was probably always going to be dry and confusing and be deliberately sanitised of the suffering that was going on. In retrospect, I always thought we had a decent shot of winning, but I also thought that these processes have a way of making things convenient for the powers that be, that the law is too often about preserving the status quo rather than upsetting the apple cart. But I always thought it was worth a shot because, what have you got to lose? Maybe it was hard to watch your experience transformed into evidence in that way, but I think we knew that we were playing the long game and using the court process as a vehicle for legislative reform. We had our eye on the main prize, and the real argument was happening outside the courtroom.

LIZZIE O'SHEA

At the time, HRLC and MB quickly perceived the positives of Justice Mr McDonald's decision. On 26 Aug 2015, at 10:21 am, and based on tweets coming out, HRLC Communications Tom Clarke advised that AAP and others were reporting a straightforward loss, so if we did want to push the partial win line we should get this out ASAP:

Partial win in Melbourne Fertility Control Clinic case highlights need for safe access zones

A Melbourne abortion clinic is looking to Spring Street to create safe access zones after the Supreme Court of Victoria this morning found that whilst the Melbourne City Council had not applied the law properly it could not be compelled to take action to prevent women being harassed and intimidated as they entered the clinic.

The Human Rights Law Centre's Director of Advocacy and Research, Emily Howie, said whilst the case should lead to some improvements on the ground, more work was required to find a broad-based and lasting solution.

'Whilst in some ways this is a partial win for our client, it does not provide an adequate solution. This case focused on one clinic, what we need now is a clear law to ensure that all Victorian women can access health services without being harassed or intimidated. It's time for the Government to introduce safe access zones for abortion clinics across Victoria,' said Ms Howie.

The Fertility Control Clinic's Psychologist, Dr Susie Allanson, said intimidation and harassment was an everyday reality for the clinic's staff and patients. 'It shouldn't take a court case to ensure women can safely access our services. It's clear from this limited win that more is needed. We need clear laws that protect a woman's right to access medical services and I strongly believe that safe access zones are the most sensible way to ensure that,' said Dr Allanson.

A proposed law was introduced last week by cross-bench member Fiona Patten MLC which would create zones around reproductive health services in which people would be prohibited from harassing, intimidating or impeding people entering the clinic, as well as communicating with or recording those people.

Katie Robertson, associate at Maurice Blackburn, said the clinic had been subject to years of bullying and harassment by anti-abortionists who were deliberately preventing women from safely accessing health services. 'This decision goes some way in addressing the problem but its impact will be limited unless it's followed up with practical action from the Victorian Government to stand up for women's rights,' said Ms Robertson.

In 2013 Tasmania introduced access zones around clinics in which terminations are conducted. Similar zones also exist in the United States and Canada. The ACT government has also released an exposure draft of a Bill *to create patient privacy zones that support women's rights to access health services privately and free from intimidating conduct.*

'Safe access zones are an easy and sensible solution. They are about respecting the privacy and dignity of women accessing terminations. UN human rights bodies as well as courts in the US and Canada have all found that sensible measures to ensure safe access to women's health services do not excessively limit the right to freedom of expression and assembly,' said Ms Howie.

The case has been run with the generous assistance of Peter Hanks QC, Kristen Walker QC, Therese McCarthy and Claire Harris, who also provided their services pro-bono.

How great was our team? How great was Justice McDonald? Justice McDonald had in fact given us just what we needed: a last-ditch legal fail; a throwing down of the gauntlet to our government and our parliament to protect women with safe access zones.

I always thought winning the case against the Council was never going to get us want we wanted. How was it going to work in practice? There were issues all along with the Council. We'd end up calling the Council every day to deal with the nuisance—fining and prosecuting individuals. A lot of legal work went into reaching 'agreed facts' with the Council, including an access zone. But it was unlikely the Council would ever bring in its own access zone. It would have been small and probably unworkable. I said to Susie A a few days before the decision, with Fiona's bill in play, probably the best outcome is if we lose the case.

DR LOUIS RUTMAN (2019)

It emerged over time as well, this was always going to be rather challenging litigation. I think clinic counsel were surprised how hard it was to get this argument up in court. The court didn't seem to be into this argument at all.

But one of the things I constantly return to in talking about this case is that you don't actually need to win to be successful. Part of the job of this piece of litigation was to show that you had done everything you possibly could do to fix this problem, including going to the Supreme Court. You've taken responsibility for your clients. You took responsibility for your staff. And you also showed the public that the law is inadequate to protect people accessing a legal medical service. So what are we going to do about this now?

In essence you could say: we've tried to discharge our obligations as good corporate citizens, as good medical practitioners, as good employers, in all those faculties we've done our best. The law needs to change. And I do think that was a compelling argument that made it easier for someone like Fiona Patten to come in and propose safe access zones, and for this to be ultimately taken up by others.

LIZZIE O'SHEA

For the rest of the day, the whole team was involved in a raft of interviews. I sank into the blur of my interviews, hidden away at the clinic and then at home: *ABC News, That's News Daily, Raph 774, The Age*... We continued to fight the good fight; we continued to give women a voice:

I was doing a triple j interview, and one of the opposers, who was quite eloquent, was saying that that never happens: we never harass, we do this, we do that. Call after call came in, women calling in saying, 'Well that's bloody not true', this is what happened to me and this is what happened to me'. It was just time and time again. No one called in to say, 'No, they were very polite, helpful,' or 'I was very pleased to have had that prayer'.

FIONA PATTEN (2019)

We had had a loss/partial win in the Supreme Court. But we had an outright win in the Court of Public Opinion.

Court cases generate that interest, and so it not only generated the political, the Bill, but it drew public attention to what was going on. It had been going on for decades, but you didn't get regular public attention. When you run a court case about it you do get public attention. You also amass all that evidence, and the Minister can say, well we tried to use existing law and it didn't work, so we have to do something. That was actually really important to show that we didn't have a legal framework that worked to deal with the problem.

KRIS WALKER QC (2020)

Women and women's issues are notoriously undermined by a societal system that has a built-in poverty factor for women—a topic too huge to detail here. This is why affirmative action and EMILY's List (Early Money is Like Yeast) is so necessary and effective. Money makes the world go round. We would never have got this far without pro-choice women politicians. We would never have got this far without Emily Howie's feminist lawyering and that of other lawyers at the independent Human Rights law Centre. We would never have got this far without lawyers like Lizzie O'Shea, law firms like Maurice Blackburn, and barristers like Peter Hanks, Claire Harris, Therese McCarthy and Kris Walker who all were committed to pro bono work. A commitment that in fact eschewed money to fight the good fight for fairness and decency.

Our court case had amassed supporters, evidence and opinion that was on our side and beyond reproach. We had the support of Fiona Patten and cross-party women.

I think Fiona deserves a huge amount of credit. It wasn't like we had been in cahoots about this grand design or scheme. If she hadn't got into office, I don't think we would have gotten the reform. But equally I think this work we did together had to be done. Even if Fiona had been elected four to five years later, she would have been reliant upon this example of the deficiency in the law and used it to justify stepping in to fix it.

So I think there is the role for the litigation to do that. It's very challenging for the individual. You don't want to run litigation to make a point, you want to run litigation to win. But I do think we have situations in public interest litigation quite commonly where a loss like this actually facilitates a win in the long term. You have to be in a marathon, not a sprint.

LIZZIE O'SHEA

It sure felt like a marathon to me, but I could finally see the finish line, I think, maybe, hopefully. Well, given my marathon exhaustion, it could have just been a mirage.

Especially when I talk to a younger person, they think a social media campaign can be successful in six weeks. They don't understand that these campaigns can go on for decades. I actually think stubbornness is essential. People will call me stubborn and obsessed. Yes, that's me.

So you can't give up. In between the moments, you just have to keep chipping away at it and keep on trying to force it into the public arena and keep talking about it. I think that even though it wasn't successful, the action you took in the courts against Melbourne City Council, even though you didn't win, I think it was pivotal. I think it was about people organising, and also then every single avenue had been gone down and the only thing that could be done was legislation.

The lessons are very much that you can't give up. You were right. These were religious bigots. They were dangerous. It wasn't just that they were religious bigots, I think it's that they were dangerous, both physically and psychologically, to staff and people coming into the clinic. So you actually had no choice but to continue your campaign, because nobody except for you and the clinic were keeping people safe. I think it's a really important moral lesson that you can't walk away from people's safety... As well as providing the service, you've got to keep fighting for it to be free, safe and accessible.

COLLEEN HARTLAND (2020)

We had no idea that within days we would have the public support of the Minister for Health, Jill Hennessy, and the Victorian Government.

Law cases can be extremely difficult work if you expect it to be like other forms of campaigning. But a day in court can make your issue stand out to media, the public and the powers that be.

With the right team and with helpful media advice, you can work to shape these outcomes in ways that suit your longer-term goals. HRLC Tom Clarke's reframing of our court loss as a 'partial win', and as the final proof that new legislation was needed, was both accurate and effective. You need media/communications people who understand the guts of your issue, can creatively and steadfastly keep your language and goal front and centre and, in the case of a legal action, understand the law and work with the lawyers.

PART FOUR

ABORTION SAFE ACCESS ZONES

CHAPTER 16

From Tears... to Cheers

27 August–1 September 2015

---

*The aftermath of that case did translate
so relatively quickly into legislative change.
Not every case that has a bad outcome
results in legislative change.*

KRIS WALKER (2020)

We didn't spend much time crying over the spilt milk and smashed eggs left in our Supreme Court basket. All our eggs now lay in the legislative basket. The morning after the Supreme Court Decision, 27 August 2015, HRLC Em, MB Katie Robertson and I attended Fiona Patten's *Public Health and Wellbeing (Safe Access) Amendment Bill 2015 Brief and Discussion Forum*.

Fiona's St Andrews Place office was housed in a large building opposite the rear of Parliament House, a lovely walk from the clinic through the Fitzroy Gardens and up past Peter Mac hospital. But the torrential rain got the better of my umbrella and me. I arrived soggy and drippy-nosed to find everyone who was anyone in the women's health/abortion field: Health Commissioner Beth Wilson, WHV CEO Rita Butera, Jo Wainer, Liberty Victoria's Anne O'Rourke, Adelaide Pregnancy Advisory Service's Brigid Coombe, Legal Services Tasmania CEO Susan Fahey, Reproductive Choice Australia Jenny Ejlak, FPV CEO Lyn Jordan, Marie Stopes Loren Bradley, and other women's health VIPs. It was particularly heart-warming to see interstate colleagues who had flown in to generously offer their support within our mutual relationship of sharing and encouragement.

Present also was an impressive group of cross-party parliamentarians including: Labor MLC Minister for Agriculture, Minister for Regional Development and Deputy Leader of the Government in the Legislative Council Jaala Pulford, Liberal Shadow Minister for Families & Children Georgie Crozier, Greens MLC Nina Springle, and of course Sex Party MLC Fiona Patten and her advisers.

It was a convergence of champions that happens just before these moments of transformative change, and the air sparkled with possibility.

Given that we were on Fiona's turf and Fiona was able to court anyone for a good cause, I shouldn't have been surprised that also present was Shooters, Fishers & Farmers MLC Danny Young. In our mysteriously muddled preferential voting system, Danny received just 3.5% of first preferences. His co-party MLC Jeff Bourman received a mere 2.44%. Go figure. Fiona invited Danny into this bastion of women's business in an effort to sway two more votes for her bill. In Victoria, duck shooters would become protected from animal rights protesters by legislated buffer zones in 2018. Our staff and patients might better identify with the hunted ducks than the duck shooters, but in any event, Danny Young was not persuaded of the need for safe access zones for women accessing urgent health care.

Friendly chats were had over tea and coffee before we took seats around the conference table. I sat back taking it all in, happy and silent. I didn't need to say a thing. After years of being a voice in the wilderness, a chorus of voices sang from the same hymn sheet.

There's something rather satisfying using religious metaphor here. I might be a heathen, but as a little girl I attended Sunday school at the local Presbyterian church (eventually becoming the Uniting church). After Sunday school, I snuck upstairs to the church's choir gallery in awe of my mother singing solos. I joined in the singing, my lungs and voice bursting but feeble in comparison with the strong and tutored voices of the mature women and men choristers. Through a Sunday school song I learnt the names of First and Second Testaments books—well almost all of them. The parables made me think and wonder. I vividly remember walking home from Sunday school one day with a skip in my step and a determination to be as good as Jesus for the rest of my life. That ambition lasted maybe half an hour.

When I had my first child, Rebecca, my hand reached for that special book of epic stories and life lessons. No, not the Bible. The myths of the Greek Gods and Goddesses. I could select stories where women were active and strong, rather than of the Bible's ilk: meek and invisible, saint or whore.

But there is something to be said about having time in the week, like that afforded by a church service, to think about how to be a good person. Unfortunately, institutionalised religion has always been tainted by evils. It seemed to me that the Truth and Goodness in Jesus and Christianity (and probably in every other religion created from the minds of men) was never meant to be about rigid rules and pious judgement, cruel arrogance and ignorance. Truth and goodness demanded that we be kind, think and ask questions.

The women around the table, brought together by Fiona Patten, were all thinkers and questioners. You couldn't be a feminist otherwise. That thinking and questioning means being a feminist can be frustrating and infuriating, but also challenging and satisfying, and on days like this it can be glorious. Outside the rain poured down. Inside I was drenched in a festive sense of relief. No matter that private members' bills are notoriously unlikely to pass. Safe abortion access was finally going to happen. I could feel it. Would it?

The abortion decrim seemed so long ago now, and so different. Then, women had mobilised on the back of their rage at the cruel misogyny of Catholic Federal Health Minister Tony Abbott. Although Abbott was now the sitting Australian Prime Minister, in this brave new Victoria the likes of Tony Abbott were irrelevancies. Perhaps one might even call him a 'quaint irrelevancy'.

The abortion decrim had ultimately seemed like a tough necessity in preparing our pro-choice politicians for the safe access fight ahead. But here we were, now being led by a first-time MP who had not been 'blooded' by that fight, and perhaps that was the point. Fiona Patten was not scarred from the abortion decrim legislative battle, nor did she carry any world weariness about 'the abortion issue'. Fiona's optimism and can-do confidence was a breath of fresh air that breathed new life into the political campaign for safe access zones and re-ignited the trust in a cross-party sisterhood. She had revived enthusiasm and determination to ensure women's right to abortion and right to respect. Fiona turned out to be the perfect leader for our times—the perfect woman for our times.

At the conclusion of the meeting, more collegial conversation was had with these lions of women, before I popped into 'the ladies' to prepare myself for the wintry walk back to the clinic. In the mirror, I was greeted by a face with a bright red moustache and frizzy hair. A drippy day, a drippy nose, and me a big drip. In front of all those fabulous women! Shaming exercise 101. Who cares, we're really going to do this!

My recollections of the next three months cannot convey the enormous work carried out by an army of women—and more than a few good men—who fought the good fight to get safe access zones over the line.

Victorian Government confirms support for abortion clinic buffer zone laws.

The establishment of buffer zones to keep protesters away from Victorian abortion clinics looks certain to become law, after the State Government confirmed it will support the move...

'This will be Fiona's bill, largely reflected and represented in the government bill,' [Health Minister Jill Hennessy] said. 'We just have some of the boring enforceability and administration issues to make sure we get it right.'

Ms Hennessy said the new bill would be introduced to Parliament by the end of the year.

ALISON SAVAGE

ABC NEWS

1 SEPTEMBER 2015

Six days after our failed court case, and fittingly on the first day of the spring in 2015, the most wonderful, and the most sensible, thing happened. On the steps of Parliament House, and standing with Fiona Patten MP, Health Minister Jill Hennessy announced a bill for abortion safe access zones. Yay! Yay! Yay!

Suing MCC had been an exercise that exposed both the worst of local councils, and the failings of our legal system—a system arguably established by and for white male privilege above all 'others', in this case women. But ultimately, suing MCC catalysed the potential and power of the media, public opinion, and our law-makers to secure safe access zones legislation. Our court case got us what we had wanted from the beginning. Well the court case *and* a feminist whirlwind called Fiona Patten *and* a Labor government that decided it was not going to 'sit back and wait for it to happen' (Kirner, 2009).

I think there were a few things going on at the time. One was the flavour of government at the time. You had as a general proposition that the Labor party would be more interested in abortion rights than the Liberal party. You had Fiona Patten who was like a dog with a bone who just pushed it. You had a female health minister who was obviously also committed to it. Private members' bills rarely get up, yet this one did because the government backed it. Full credit to Jill [Hennessy] for her role there. We've got women in those positions. Two decades ago, there were fewer women in positions of power who would be interested in the issue.

KRIS WALKER (2019)

During that time when Labor was in opposition up to 2014, a great deal of work was going on in policy and agenda. I was secretary of shadow cabinet and there were many new shadow ministers who joined the team led by Daniel Andrews, like Jill Hennessy and Fiona Richardson, who had very strong ideas that if they became ministers, rather than shadow ministers, those policies would translate into action. They were very influential, with this determination to not muck around, to get on with it straight away.

It was important that men were part and parcel of this too. Attorney General Martin Pakula was very supportive. Dan Andrews was keen to get on from day one.

This was the continuation of unfinished business. The 2008 abortion decrim was a means to doing other things. I always had the view that the decrim would make it possible to address a whole lot of other issues, open some doors, and opponents would no longer be able to shelter behind the Crimes Act.

CANDY BROAD (2019)

With this issue in particular it seemed that if it wasn't for Fiona safe access zones wouldn't have happened. But the campaign had gone on for fourteen years. To me, it was the right time and the right minister. Yes, Fiona had a role but that issue around violence against women was really pivotal. You can campaign and campaign and then suddenly everything turns around and everyone thinks this is an overnight success, but it's not.

I think you can see a similar situation with Andrew Denton and the end of life debate. He had a high profile and knew how to use the media. Andrew was that fresh face and he could lead the charge. But with Dying with Dignity, again there was a change of minister and the premier changing his mind. So many of these campaigns happen around just these moments of change.

COLLEEN HARTLAND (2020)

Probably the work that Fiona Richardson was doing and saying, that we don't accept violence against women, did help us. It would've been somewhat hypocritical to have said we're on a mission and yet we're allowing that intimidation and humiliation outside the abortion clinics. A Royal Commission, and yet we're allowing this abuse to occur? The government couldn't say no.

FIONA PATTEN (2019)

I don't disagree on one level, but I think the Labor party has to be pushed to do most things. I don't mean that as a moral observation, though it is frustrating from that perspective, but more as a statement of practical reality. I always felt the amazing thing about Fiona was that she was happy to set things in motion and then let Jill take over and take credit. I'm a bit cynical, but I think it's important to remember that Labor is a big beast (a broad church!) and getting them to act is hard, even if individual people within it have good intentions.

LIZZIE O'SHEA

All the balls had to fall at the same time, along with people that were so enthusiastic and dedicated. But the balls had to fall at the same time.

LOUIS RUTMAN (2019)

Excited by the news, Lizzie contacted me from New York where she was now completing a Masters in Law at Columbia University, the same course Em had completed a few years earlier.

'I'm sorry we couldn't win our battle,' said Lizzie, 'But we are winning the war!'

I replied that Lizzie had been a key to all this and 'I do hope New York was ready for you—it might not be able to keep up with you!'

In the Big Apple, and ever on the ball, Lizzie asked whether the judge had heard submissions on costs yet. This was her biggest concern. But given the decision went a bit in both directions, she was hoping that he would decide to order that each party bear their own costs.

And after all that, MCC said why don't we just pay our own costs! I wasn't sure why. Maybe we did have some 'declarative relief' given that: our evidence had been unchallenged; MCC abandoned the human rights arguments; and the MCC investigator had wrongly advised us to settle the matter privately with police. Maybe asking us to pay their costs would involve more work for MCC. Maybe MCC wanted to rack up some brownie points with the public, or the government. Or maybe, MCC just wanted to do the right thing. In the end, it was also good for them to have the law settled.

Certainly I did find some irony, probably not felt by those *au fait* with the ways of our legal system, that the distinguished Richard Niall QC— who represented MCC in our Court case—had by this time been appointed Solicitor-General for Victoria. I now had a strong sense that we were all in this together. We were all on the same side—on the side of women and safe access zones. This was finally, truly, fingers and toes crossed, touch on wood, going to happen.

In any event, the most important thing about no costs? Relief for Lou, and a celebration with our team!

The day after Jill's announcement, I asked Susan to arrange thank you flowers to be delivered to both Fiona Patten and Colleen Hartland. While Fiona had been in this for months, Colleen had been there for us through years of headbutting brick walls. Both deserved special thanks. A thank you email to Jill Hennessy went the next day. But don't worry, there would be a beautiful and blooming gift for Jill in the near future. If I mentioned all the thank yous and dinners and drinks and celebrations throughout this campaign, there'd be no room for much else.

The point is, if you're going to run a marathon like this one (a la Lizzie), and if you're asking others to run it with you, you've got to recognise, share and enjoy the good stuff. And let's face it—it is the people who are the good stuff. Over the years, during and after my miserable Fs for Advocacy, and my questionable grades for dummy spits, I always achieved A-pluses for my thank yous. After every meeting I would touch base with a thank you. Bigger thanks were a team effort: my genuine appreciation expressed in words; Janice backing and improving my ideas; Susan Speaking's know-how with arranging dinners, parties and flower deliveries; and Lou's genial backing, social charm and sense of fun.

This is so important. This was one of the reasons why people went the extra yards to help you. Making campaigns pleasant, polite and an exchange of good faith is not superfluous, it's a foundation for success! Women are usually better at it than men too.

LIZZIE O'SHEA

The first time I had an inkling that perhaps a thank you like ours was not the norm was early on in our collaboration with HRLC and MB, when Lou and I invited Em and Lizzie for Christmas drinks at The Botanical in South Yarra—as a thank you. And, well, because they were so much fun to spend time with. Em told us the story of leaving work to meet us. HRLC staff had waved her goodbye a tad enviously and sadly because clients taking an HRLC solicitor out for Christmas were unheard of. Most HRLC clients were asylum seekers shut away in 'detention centres'.

Out and proud Christian leaders of the federal government? Christmas? Bah, humbug.

But our experience of a thank you was not just one way. Our patients regularly thanked us with words, cards and flowers. But again and again, at pivotal times—Steve's murder, our Supreme Court case and loss, media highlighting our awful predicament—we would hear from our patients, colleagues and complete strangers expressing their appreciation of what we were doing and encouraging us to keep going. Those thank yous meant the world to us.

It is important to recognise, celebrate and share the good stuff. Never take others for granted and always thank them with an A-plus thank you that can be an ordinary follow up, small gesture or splendid celebration. A thank you is one way to change campaign work, which can be a slog, into a mutual exchange of good will and inspiration. We need to make it easy for each other to help each other.

This campaign had now transformed into a diverse and substantial force for change, with people from different backgrounds finding common cause. We worked together and built allies, found shared experiences, and ultimately prioritised our objectives above any differences.

Together, women can do anything.

CHAPTER 17

Proud Women

2 September 2015

It's when women are able to step out of the shadows with their voices and their bodies that things start to shift.

CRIADO PEREZ (2019)

Although the government was working with Fiona to table a bill, the parliamentary debate proceeded in the Legislative Council as scheduled at 2:30pm Wednesday 2 September 2015, the day following the government's announcement.

From the get-go, the debate on abortion safe access zones was completely different from the 2008 abortion decrim debate. Despite notable, deeply personal reflections by a small number of MPs, the abortion decriminalisation debate rested on more abstract, though powerful and important, ideas around women's autonomy and rights. The decrim had no current individual or case study at its centre: no abortion provider or woman having an abortion being prosecuted, say. And thank goodness for that.

Whereas the safe access zones debate could hang its hat on a contemporary case study. The Fertility Control Clinic was front and centre—our patients, staff and our failed, 'partial win' Supreme Court case.

It may sound disingenuous after everything that had gone before, but until I sat in Parliament to hear the debate, I hadn't realised just how central we were to all this: that the clinic, our patients, staff, Em, Lizzie and me would figure in individual speeches; that the clinic, our court case, and so many of our advocates would be named in Parliament; that it would all feel so personal.

I was taken by surprise. The second day of spring turned out to be as extraordinary as the first.

As I sat again on those red cushioned public gallery seats, I felt self-conscious, exulted and validated as pro-women language and women's real, lived experiences were spoken by our government representatives. Woman-centred words of advocacy of the past fourteen years echoed around the chamber. The experiences of women that had for so long been summarily dismissed and trivialised, made invisible and unheard, were now being told by our parliamentary representatives with the authority, kindness and respect they had always deserved. Determination to secure safe access zones was plain to see.

No one better exemplified this than MLC Jenny Mikakos who since championing abortion decriminalisation, had risen to Minister for Families and Children in 2014. Soon she would stand in the Upper House for hours, unerring and indefatigable against the final anti-choice, anti-safe access zone onslaught. But before then, Labor's Jenny Mikakos set the ball rolling:

The introduction of a government bill will be in direct response to the Supreme Court decision last week. These proceedings were brought by the Fertility Control Clinic against Melbourne City Council... I particularly want to refer to the witness statements and the other evidence the Supreme Court received... The safe access zones legislation seeks to prevent this ongoing level of harassment that existing laws have failed to address... this is not just a problem at the East Melbourne clinic... Emily Howie from the Human Rights Legal Centre has said...

At this point I stifled a gasp and texted Em who was running late, 'Jenny Mikakos just mentioned you!' Quickly followed by another stifled gasp and text, 'She's just mentioned me!' And that pretty much says all that needs to be said about my schoolgirl excitement. Public speaking, court cases, media, journal articles, you name it, had nothing on this! Jenny Mikakos continued:

Emily Howie... Dr Susie Allanson... The Royal Women's Hospital... Rita Butera, the executive of Women's Health Victoria... Beth Wilson... We will work with Ms Patten to ensure that the bill addresses the objectives of her private members' bill... important that we strike the appropriate balance… appropriate for Parliament to address deficiencies in the current law to address circumstances where people are clearly intimidating and harassing people going about their business and seeking access to what are legal medical procedures.

I was blown away.

Next to speak was the sensible and delightful Liberal Shadow Minister for Health and Leader of the Liberal Party in the Legislative Council, Mary Wooldridge,

I am pleased to inform the house that members of the parliamentary Liberal Party will have a free vote on this matter… For 20 years, people of opposing views have been in conflict about access to a clinic in Wellington Parade, East Melbourne… I particularly thank the Minister for Police for facilitating a briefing from the police… given by the station commander at Melbourne East, Acting Inspector Huntington, and Superintendent Millen. We talked through the reality of the situation… The message from them was very clearly that… there is intimidation and harassment going on… Going to the clinic is one of the top priorities of the police each and every day, as it has been for the best part of 20 years… Essentially what they were saying is that they want to break away from a front door siege mentality—and those were their words… very helpful to have a mechanism by which they could act…rather than the victim, after the fact, having to undertake what can be a retraumatising experience in the process.

There has been interesting research done such as the dissertation Anxiety in Women Having an Abortion—The Role of Stigma and Secrecy *by A. Humphries in 2011…*

Yay, Allie. Quick text to Janice. Mary went on to mention a man she had met whose office was near the clinic and every day he felt nervous and anxious just walking by because of the presence there. She noted the views of Women's Health Victoria, the Rationalist Society, the Victorian Equal Opportunity and Human Rights Commission's submission, and Fiona:

I give credit to the work of Ms Patten in raising this issue and doing the work to bring a legislative model before the chamber…

I wanted to stand up and cheer.

Greens' Nina Springle was up next. Nina is a woman you like instantly and feel like you have known for years:

Since the government yesterday made its intentions very clear, the real discussion is about the issues, the need for reform and the risks of delay more than anything... Ms Patten has placed this issue squarely on the legislative agenda and I think we are all grateful for that... The government must also be commended for its response...

Nina extended her condolences to Steve Rogers' family and said:

It is a testament to the resilience, tenacity and commitment to the health and wellbeing of Victorian women that clinical psychologist Susie Allanson and the staff of the East Melbourne clinic have continued their work under such stressful conditions over such an extended period of time with, until now, no end in sight.

I thought I might cry. I could not believe all this.

I did not have my termination at the East Melbourne Clinic and so did not experience the harassment and intimidation that women experience there on a daily basis, although I do witness it regularly when I pass the clinic, which I probably do a couple of times a week. However, I know firsthand what it is like to be in the vulnerable space that a woman occupies when she is considering abortion as an option. It is a vast breach of our duty of care as lawmakers to allow this perpetration of trauma over some of our most vulnerable to continue...

I would like to acknowledge my parliamentary colleague Colleen Hartland for all her years of work on abortion reform... [Greens parliamentary intern] Ms Hilary Taylor's [2011] report titled Accessing Abortion – Improving the Safety of Access to Abortion Services in Victoria was an excellent report... [that] recommended the creation of bubble zones, or safe access zones, around clinics...

It was not Victoria, but Tasmania, that was the first Australian state to take up the [Victorian Law Reform] Commission's urging on safe access zones...

Time is of the essence... every day the government delays the introduction of this bill is one more day that women at clinics like the one in East

Melbourne will not be protected from harassment and intimidation...
Last week's decision by the Supreme Court was a technical one, but some
anti-abortion protesters have interpreted it as a green light to continue
causing what the existing law calls nuisance outside the East Melbourne
Clinic. It was not a green light, but that Supreme Court decision did high-
light the inadequacies of the current law regarding this particular issue...
we in this Parliament must hold the government to its word.

I loved Nina.

Next was Liberal anti-abortion crusader Dr Carling-Jenkins who most eloquently told stories about violence against HOGPI protesters in order to further her argument *against* safe access zones. I reckoned those stories were a good argument *for* safe access zones. Still, sitting through her speech once was enough for me. 'Balance' shmalance. Available in *Parliamentary Hansard*.

Liberal Margaret Fitzherbert spoke in favour of safe access zones. She spoke of the hundreds of recent emails that referred to the Victorian Human Rights Charter's right to freedom of expression but that neglected to mention the Charter's duties, responsibilities and lawful restrictions attached to the freedom of expression:

(a) to respect the rights and responsibilities of other persons; or
(b) for the protection of national security, public order, public health or pub-
lic morality.

Amidst her support of safe access zones, Margaret expressed concern that a zone of 150 metres may be too big. Later in the day, Liberal Simon Ramsay, the only man to speak, also supported women and safe access zones, but considered 150 metres too far.

Labor Minister for Agriculture Jaala Pulford stood to support safe access zones and reflect on the 2008 decriminalisation of abortion. Over the years I had missed opportunities to speak with Jaala, sometimes I'm sure to the point of appearing rude: despite the weighty demands of her job and a tragic personal loss, Jaala always appeared to me to be far too young to actually be Jaala. No, that's not Jaala I'd say to myself. I whispered to Em about Jaala's generosity in meeting with me many years ago, when I suddenly realised Jaala was talking about our first meeting too:

Diary alignment being what it was, we met at about 8 o'clock in the morning before Parliament... around the time of day people were turning up for their terminations or perhaps consultations with medical staff as they contemplated the choice that they might make. I had to run the gauntlet of the protesters. I had to do so without being faced with an unwanted pregnancy, and without contemplating termination. But just turning up for that meeting, I experienced heckling and posters being waved in my face...

As members will appreciate, resources are available to government that are not available to non-government MPs, and I am confident that we will be able to introduce legislation that acquits some of the concerns members have raised about Ms Patten's bill while being absolutely faithful to the change Ms Patten is seeking to bring about...

This is not a question of people's right to choose; that was resolved a number of years ago in this Parliament. This is a question of people being able to access this legal medical service as they would any other legal medical service—without fear of harassment or intimidation.

Excitement and validation surged in me and all over Em's face:

I was struck by two things. One was the messaging, that so much of the messaging we developed was just adopted by the supporters of the bill. The language we had developed was all in there. The other thing was that so much of the work that we'd done for the Supreme Court, including the evidence of the impact on you guys, was useful in persuading MPs who were concerned about rights, or who needed to understand that the harm was real. We had simple explainers of US cases and expert evidence of the harm being done outside the clinic.

And because we'd researched all those different options even before we decided on the Public Health and Well Being Act, we'd looked at the human rights issues. So we were really able to just leverage all that work that had already been done to a fairly receptive group.

EMILY HOWIE (2020)

One after another, speaking with dignity and with respect for those expressing contrary opinions, cross party parliamentarians stood up for women and abortion safe access zones: Liberal Georgie Crozier, Labor Jaclyn Symes, Liberal Simon Ramsay, and Liberal Wendy Lovell.

At 5pm, Acting President and anti-abortion campaigner, Bernie Finn, unceremoniously interrupted Ms Lovell mid-sentence to move on to other matters. Nina, Colleen, Fiona and her advisers, Em and I retired happily to the parliamentary dining room for afternoon tea. It was a refreshing hiatus before the collective of women and a few good men would put the pedal to the floor to ensure that in a couple of months' time we would see the passage of a historic government bill for women.

A real-life case study can propel a campaign, a legislative debate, and a new law. We were a real health service in a neighbourhood just down the road from Parliament. We were living, breathing staff, patients, events and stories. Our failed court case was part of our story, as was the clinic's historic establishment, Steve's murder, the extremists' ongoing harm, and our long campaign for safe abortion access.

There's no doubt that having us as the case study at the centre of the campaign meant others could relate to our situation and understand better the wrongs needing righting. Everyone knew a woman who had been, or could be, harmed if our Parliament did not act. Politicians could see that the powers they would confer on authorities to deal with the problem were necessary and proportionate.

While the community can become jaded with political scandals and obfuscation, many politicians are in Parliament for the right reasons: to make the world a fairer, better place. They might need an almighty push to get there, but once they're in, they're all in.

CHAPTER 18

The Bureaucracy

September–October 2015

*Excessive multiplication of, and concentration of power
in, administrative departments or bureaus; a system
characterised by power without responsibility
and by resistance to change.*

MACQUARIE DICTIONARY

Out of the ashes of a Supreme Court loss we had bolted straight into law reform like a phoenix on steroids. Women's groups and pro-choice politicians were leading the charge. I was ecstatic. Until I discovered that the legislative process involved the Victorian Department of Health & Human Services, that is, DHHS, or merely and mightily, The Department.

Apparently when you seek to insert an amendment into the *Victorian Health & Wellbeing Act*, or when the health minister is responsible for enacting new legislation, DHHS 'consults' with key stake holders. Given The Department was the executive part of government ultimately responsible for putting various parts of the bill into practice, this was a consultation to work out how this bill would work in practice if passed. Call me naïve again, but I wasn't expecting this and, call me unkind, I didn't want this.

The Department and I don't necessarily have a good history. It is fair to say that I consider DHHS to be an unwieldy bureaucracy employing many good people, but whose culture can at times be cruel and tipsy on its own power. DHHS is: good staff doing good work; good staff burnt out by the overwhelming nature of humanity's problems up against the sheer bloody mindedness of a dysfunctional, cash-strapped system; and staff who think their DHHS position is so important that they lose sight of the humanity that's right in front of their noses.

As a clinician at the Children's Court Clinic working on cases where DHHS had intervened with vulnerable children and their families, I saw all three types of DHHS staff. But it was the very nature of the Children's Court Clinic that our cases were biased towards those where the care of children and families by DHHS had gone seriously awry. I came to the view that the monolithic DHHS did not ordinarily excel at self-examination, empathy, humility or redress.

Similarly, like other bureaucracies, DHHS might value privacy and confidentiality when it came to DHHS refusing to provide information—even when it was your own information, but when it came to a bureaucracy accessing others' information, a person's privacy and confidentiality could become irrelevant quickly.

An infamous 2010 case—of an anaesthetist who infected women with Hepatitis C as they attended a Marie Stopes abortion clinic—confronted DHHS with a logistical, political and criminal public health emergency. DHHS faced a complicated and multi-layered challenge: to identify and contact all potential victims and arrange for them to be tested for Hepatitis C. I could see that the process was necessary and potentially harrowing to our patients. But I was shocked when DHHS expected to walk out FCC's door with our patient files. The DHHS workers' attitude to patient privacy was so cavalier that I experienced flashbacks to the 1980s Federal Police raid—even though I wasn't even present for that one! DHHS didn't want to listen to me so Health Services Commissioner Beth Wilson backed us in standing up for our patients: no removal of files; a room at FCC provided to DHHS staff to view only the file information that was necessary; and DHHS was to work with us collaboratively to ensure that we could prioritise our patients' wellbeing. In the end I felt we did as well as we could by our patients, none of whom had contracted Hep C.

My subsequent membership on an Advisory Group for a departmental review of sexual and reproductive health services provided me with depressing insights that the unspoken purpose of a bureaucratic committee process may be more about ticking a box to validate an agenda and outcomes The Department had already decided on. And yet that process could generate an inordinate amount of work and inconvenience for those participating in good faith. I had also discovered that DHHS could be prone to self-importance and to wielding its power to make people urgently jump with demands for quite unnecessary work.

In 2020–21, the COVID-19 pandemic illuminated dangers associated with having a Department of Health & Human Services that was under-resourced and overseen by career bureaucrats seemingly disconnected from (and perhaps with limited training in) the Department's core business of medicine, health and humane care. But in 2015, DHHS was already a bureaucracy on my 'proceed with caution' or 'avoid altogether' list.

DHHS first contacted Lou on Monday 7 September 2015 about the proposed abortion safe access legislation. I figured it was probably just a touch-base, tick-a-box kind of thing, given that cross-party women, the government and their legal eagles were all over safe access. But Janice's account of a hurriedly arranged DHHS meeting with Lou and Janice two days later suggested we had returned to the year 2001, back when ignorance about our situation was the norm. I was not going to allow DHHS to generate more work and anxiety for our staff and for me. Were they re-inventing some new, or old, wheel that would unbalance the legitimate safe access zones cart? Yep, I was in dummy spit territory. I decided it would be wise to politely and clearly state our view in a letter on 12 September 2015:

Re: Proposed laws to create safe access zones around abortion services

… your tight time frame reflects the government's very welcome determination to ensure safe access legislation as soon as possible… you, Lou and Janice had a lengthy meeting covering a rather unexpectedly wide range of issues… I am writing to be clear about our position in relation to the three questions posed in your email dated 7.9.15:

1. The proposed approach is excellent… We welcome the government's intervention to ensure safe passage of a robust bill…

2. We have no concerns about the operational, practical or any other issues relevant to the proposed approach and our organisation… We are

confident our government, parliamentarians, and police will ensure effec-
tive safe access zones for abortion providers.

3. We do not wish to raise any other matter... However we do wish
to respond to unexpected ideas you raised in the meeting... We have no
concerns...

You mentioned a variety of metropolitan clinics and hospitals you would
be speaking with, but no regional services. Bendigo hospital in particular
experiences significant harassment from anti-abortion extremists...

I sent a copy to Em: 'If I've stuffed up anything I know you'll sort it when you speak with them! You really have no idea how wonderful it has been to have you there.'

Three days later, a phone call from DHHS suggested that our clear sentiments were not clear at all. Our expressed confidence in the Victorian Parliament to get this right hadn't hit the mark. I refused to get sucked into DHHS' urgent, unnecessary work. Better to be less helpful and less amenable. Sometimes less is more in the end. Clunking bureaucratic machinery is geared to resist change, move slowly, repeat history and definitely shoot down a phoenix rising from the ashes and soaring to great heights.

In any event, DHHS was no match for the pollies. Those in the know reassured me that the government was running the show. That power, and the feminist camaraderie and certainty of our cause, ultimately swept up individual DHHS staff members into the excitement. They joined us.

Nothing was going to slow the momentum of the campaign now, a self-perpetuating spiral of admiration, strategy and 'good fight' involving our elected representatives, legal eagles, the media, advocates, and the people. We all knew we were onto that far too rare, wonderful event: a winner for women. And we all knew that a win for women is a win for everyone.

Beware the bureaucrats.

CHAPTER 19

The Government Bill: The Legislative Assembly

22 October–12 November 2015

> It is staggering that laws with such widespread application—two in three Australian pregnancies are unplanned; one in three Australian women will have an abortion in their lifetime—have consumed so little legislative energy.
>
> GIDEON HAIGH (2008)

Hi Fiona,

I am so delighted with the government bill. You are a legend!

... section 185B (1) (b) stood out to me initially—'reasonably likely to cause distress or anxiety'. After decades of people not appreciating the distress and anxiety caused... I thought it would mean the same old problem of taking matters to court (lengthy and onerous) and relying on a patient being prepared to speak about their distress or anxiety. I am now more reassured...

I would hope that people standing praying (and probably with their religious paraphernalia on display—rosaries etc) may well be viewed as besetting, or intimidation in this context, and absolutely contrary to the Purpose and Principles. Plus, following our Supreme Court action, I and other staff feel more confident about acknowledging our own sense of intimidation etc, and would be prepared to be involved in court proceedings if the bill faces legal challenge by HOGPI. What I really hope though is *that there will be no effective challenge, and all of this can be relegated to history—we all have other things to get on with!*

Fabulous that the bill will apply throughout Victoria and will help other parts of Australia to secure their own safe access zones. You've dragged us into the 21ˢᵗ century!

EMAIL

22 OCTOBER 2015

Health Minister Jill Hennessy's 21 October 2015 first reading of the Safe Access Zones Bill delivered in the Legislative Assembly was followed the next day with her comprehensive, precise and beautifully crafted second reading speech. Jill began with a Statement of Compatibility:

In my opinion, the Public Health and Wellbeing Amendment (Safe Access Zones) Bill as introduced to the Legislative Assembly, is compatible with the human rights protected by the Charter Act. I base my opinion on the reasons outlined in this statement...

Women accessing legal abortion services are entitled to have their privacy respected, to feel safe and to be treated with dignity. However, there have been numerous incidents of women and their support people being confronted by persons outside clinics seeking to denounce their decision...

The impact of such conduct as well as otherwise peaceful protests around premises that perform abortions, needs to be understood against the background of the most extreme cases, such as the fatal shooting of a security guard inside the East Melbourne Fertility Control Clinic in 2001. The offender had in fact planned a massacre of people present at the clinic. This, and similar events internationally, create an environment in which even peaceful protest activity can have a more harmful effect upon the wellbeing of staff and visitors to premises than might ordinarily be the case...

The recent litigation in the Supreme Court has highlighted the limited options currently available under the law...

Such conduct has occurred beyond 150 metres of some abortion services.

VICTORIAN MINISTER FOR HEALTH JILL HENNESSY

SECOND READING SPEECH TO PARLIAMENT

22 OCTOBER 2015

Whenever I have heard Jill speak, then, before or since, I have marvelled at her eloquence, energy and values. I am so grateful that she is in that place fighting the good fight. And I often wonder, how does she speak so eloquently without looking at any notes! But it wasn't until the High Court hearing that I fully appreciated how Jill's speech was crucial to ensuring the law would withstand a High Court challenge. Nor did I fully appreciate how the supportive speeches of others were carefully co-ordinated to ensure the raft of issues were impeccably dealt with. The Safe Access Zones Bill was crafted to serve its purpose and meet the demands of any legal challenge.

What I did know during the Safe Access Zones Bill speeches and debates (first in the Assembly and then in the Council) was that I was witnessing extraordinary women absolutely resolved and determined in the fight for women's human rights.

On Thursday 12 November 2015, I saw a couple of patients at the clinic and headed to the midday start of the Legislative Assembly debate. Em and I found ourselves scurrying from our cushioned seats in the ground floor gallery to tete-a-tetes with advisers and politicians outside the chamber, and to seats directly behind politicians in the chamber. It felt rude to leave my gallery seat in the middle of speeches so supportive of women's rights. I can't remember much about those on-the-run conversations, except that at one stage Em and I found ourselves sitting behind the opposition benches and looking across at the government benches. Cross-party work or no, this didn't feel quite right and we high-tailed it out of there.

I was more prepared for a debate focussing in on the clinic and paying tribute to the array of safe access zones advocates. I shared in the appreciation and pride of everyone who, via this campaign and Safe Access Zones Bill, was standing up for women's rights. I was proud of women and proud to be a woman. Speeches included the heartfelt, intelligent, sensible and hilarious.

I have no doubt whatsoever that silent prayer vigils, silent protests and the display of signs and posters that are designed to humiliate, embarrass,

frighten and disturb women are indeed actions reasonably likely to cause
distress and anxiety and should be found to be prohibited.

MARY-ANNE THOMAS
MLA LABOR

It's about women's health. We have put a lot of effort into the community
not only with women's health but with men's health as well. Would men
feel inclined to go to a men's health clinic if they were being demonstrated
against for going in and out of that? This is about someone not forcing their
views on someone else.

PETER WALSH MLA NATIONALS

I feel disappointed that not all coalition members are voting for women's
rights to access lawful medical services, but that is their prerogative. It just
goes to show that when we work together across party lines on really im-
portant issues that affect people's lives we can make Victoria a better place.

ELLEN SANDELL MLA GREENS

People can protest against abortion outside Parliament, and they can even
come and protest outside my office in Ballarat, which is at 17 Lydiard
Street North, on the ground floor, so they would not even have to worry
about stairs...

SHARON KNIGHT MLA LABOR

I conclude by referring to an article in The Age, *scarcely my favourite*
newspaper, on 10 November, written by Susie Allanson and Emily Howie,
which states:

'Women's privacy, dignity and safety are subordinated to the liberties
of extremists to push their views on the captive audience of clinic patients
and staff.'

I agree wholeheartedly with that assessment... those demonstrating
outside abortion clinics are zealots. They are entitled to their views, but
they are not entitled to harass and intimidate women.

LOUISE ASHER MLA LIBERAL

The Age might not have been Louise Asher's favourite newspaper, ha, but I
reckon her head was turned by Andrew Dyson's fabulous artwork accompanying our op-ed.

This particularly important piece of legislation will bring to an end the, frankly, repugnant and disgraceful behaviour of people who seek to intimidate and harass women who are seeking to access legally available medical supports.

Richard Wynne MLA Labor

Freedom of speech is not an unlimited right; there are bounds to it. I do not believe that this bill extends those bounds to an appreciable extent.

David Morris MLA Liberal

As the Minister for Women I well understand that every single day in just about every field of endeavour women struggle to achieve equal outcomes compared to men. The most tragic outcome for women are the rates of violence and sexual violence committed against them, often at the hands of the one person who is supposed to care for them, and often in the place they are supposed to be safest—their home.

As the Minister for Women I also understand the terrible double standards that women face because of gender inequality and sex discrimination. These double standards start at a very young age and continue throughout a woman's life… we need to be fair dinkum about the positions we take and address our own unconscious bias that drives many of these poor outcomes for women…

While many protest sites may have been marked by violence and tussles between police and protestors, only one has been the site of a murder. Yet this is the one protest site some members opposite are struggling now to lawfully limit protest rights at. Why do that when in so many other instances Liberal Party members have in the past fallen over themselves to limit protest rights?…

The Minister for Health and I share a passion, as so very many members of this house do, for advancing the cause of women in this state. We know—and as my portfolio responsibility of preventing family violence informs me—that if we fail to do just that, we will see terrible consequences for women right across this state.

Fiona Richardson MLA Labor

When the law is broken we need to stand up and fix it. This is what this bill does.

LOUISE STALEY MLA LIBERAL

An article in The Age *with the headline 'Safe Access to Abortion Must be Granted' by Susie Allanson and Emily Howie [said]:*

'This week the Victorian Parliament should seize the opportunity to end more than two decades of daily harassment of women. For too long, women attending abortion clinics have run the gauntlet of intimidation and harassment just to see their doctor.'

This is effectively what this is about—women accessing medical treatment… I would like to commend the Minister for Health for bringing this very carefully drafted and balanced bill before the parliament, and I also applaud the work of Fiona Patten in the upper house for progressing this bill into this parliament…

I will finish on the basis of The Age *editorial headed 'Women should not be bullied over abortion':*

'Our wives, sisters, daughters, mothers, lovers and all women deserve the best care and security that this state can provide when they most need it.'

JUDITH GRALEY MLA LABOR

In preparation for the debate on this bill I made a medical appointment to go to the Fertility Control Clinic… I have thick skin and pointy elbows. But when you are walking into this foreign place, a clinical environment, where you are making a very difficult emotional decision, it is not a good start to the process to have somebody blocking your pathway.

That person then leant across so they were within a couple of centimetres from me—they were right in my ear and in my personal zone—and told me to protect my unborn child. That was the message I got, and given that I was not pregnant, I was very impressed with their ability to determine that. Perhaps we can bring that test into the pathology sector. I am not sure it would be rebatable on the Medicare benefits scheme…

The intention there is not about counselling a woman, as has been purported. The intention is to intimidate a woman so they do not have an

abortion, disrespecting any of the decision-making processes they may have
gone through to get to that point...

Imagine walking along, on your way to access a legal medical service,
and having somebody, all along the way, tagging behind you and calling
you a murderer... It is called bullying and harassment and intimidation,
and we must take a stand against that.

EMMA KEALY MLA NATIONALS

There are other laws in this state that similarly cover situations where
there is an exclusion zone in existence... the Parliamentary Precincts Act
2001... the Safety on Public Land Act 2004... ducks shooting... It is only
150 metres. People can still demonstrate and say what they want. They can
stand outside on Macarthur Street at the back of Parliament House. I see
them each morning as I drive into Parliament.

SUZANNA SHEED MLA INDEPENDENT

This bill is not about free speech. People are able to speak their minds
wherever and however they choose, providing it does not impinge on the
freedoms and rights of others... This bill is not about abortion. Currently
abortion is legal in Victoria...

How would anyone in their right mind think that a person entering an
abortion clinic would be seeking the views of, or counselling from, protesters
outside the clinic?... These cowards seek to ply their trade when a person is
at their most fragile... would there be the same level of protest or the same
actions used by these protesters if it were a man entering a clinic for an
abortion?

There are times as a member of Parliament when we get to do what is
right for no other reason than it is simply the right thing to do. Supporting
this bill and providing safe access to women entering abortion clinics is the
right thing to do, and I am proud to do so.

BRIAN PAYNTER MLA LIBERAL

I too have gone to the clinic in East Melbourne... I know what that ha-
rassment is like firsthand. No-one would think that I am a wilting flower
over here. I am strong—I might be small but I am capable of standing up for
myself and standing up for my friends, but I was certainly intimidated... we

would not allow it to happen in the parliamentary precinct, we would not allow it to happen in the workplace and we certainly should not let it happen near health services for women.

Marsha Thomson MLA Labor

The safety of others is paramount and it includes not just their physical safety but their psychological safety as well. Harassment, bullying and intimidation have no place in our society full stop.

Dee Ryall MLA Liberal

I am very fortunate and blessed to have five children. I was equally fortunate to have met my wife when she was 18 and I had just started at university. Thankfully, my wife did not fall pregnant until she was 30, though subsequently I realised I would only have to take off my pants and look at my wife twice and she would fall pregnant…

This bill is an important piece of legislation. I did not mean to trivialise my contribution by that earlier remark… I am pleased that is something we never had to experience when we were younger. I am also pleased that through this legislation it is something no-one else will have to experience either.

Danny Pearson MLA Labor

Quite frankly this is the most vexing piece of legislation I have had to deal with in the year since I was elected… Largely, the reason why I am supporting this piece of legislation is that my sister worked as an accountant in a building abutting the clinic in Wellington Street [sic], East Melbourne. She has very kindly written me an email which informs my views:

'Each morning I had to walk past the demonstrators… [who] would gather around me shouting and showing me disgusting pictures. As soon as they realised I was not trying to enter the clinic they would leave me alone… One day my mother was dropping me off at work… As soon as the car pulled up and they saw a young female about to get out, they surrounded the door and then continued to follow me, barely letting me walk down the street. This was while they continued to shout disgusting things and show me absolutely abhorrent pictures.'

Tim Smith MLA Liberal

Victoria has some of the most extreme abortion laws in the world, allow-ing doctors to kill children up to the moment of birth and... Do those op-posite who support this legislation think it appropriate that there should be a ban on discussing any industrial relations matters within 150 me-tres of a construction site?

ROBERT CLARK MLA LIBERAL

Oops, how did that one get in there? That's democracy, and androcentricity, at work. No matter, women MLA's called the member for Box Hill out:

I am proud that it is women on this side of the chamber who are lead-ing this debate, which cannot be said of those opposing it; but I am also disturbed by some of the arguments put forward by the member for Box Hill [Liberal MLA Robert Clark] in his contribution, which were frankly offensive. They had an extremely patriarchal overtone and were extremely offensive to me as a woman and I am sure to my female colleagues on this side of the house. I commend this bill to the house in no uncertain terms.

GABRIELLE WILLIAMS MLA LABOR

The member for Box Hill [Liberal MLA Robert Clark] spoke of a direct gaze. I call it eyeballing, I call it intimidation, and I call it coercion... I ask those who currently stand in front of those clinics to devote their time to children in foster care, to food share, to...

VICKI WARD MLA LABOR

Firstly, to the member for Box Hill: let us call out what he was saying. This is not about freedom of speech; this is a debate about the patriarchal society we live in: a binary system in which men have dominated and have exerted superiority and control over women and their capacity to act autonomously, particularly when it comes to their bodies... Keeping places free from violence and discrimination is a legitimate, responsible, significant and proper purpose for this government, so I am extremely proud to be part of the Andrews Labor government, which has put equal-ity back on the agenda, which has said equality is not negotiable and which is going to promote the rights of Victorian women.

SONYA KILKENNY MLA LABOR

Another Liberal man similarly displayed his ignorant gaze:

I attended the site of the clinic in East Melbourne... I saw a handful of people spread out on the gutter edge of the footpath but did not see any behaviour I would consider harassment, intimidation or similar. I mainly saw an older lady approach some pedestrians and in some cases offer a brochure of some sort. I saw some brief engagement at times, with the majority of pedestrians basically ignoring the people and continuing on... [This legislation] is solely designed to silence law-abiding members of the community who have a different view to the current government on a particular issue—abortion.

NEIL ANGUS MLA LIBERAL

And was similarly called out:

It is heartening to know that there are many progressive thinkers in this Parliament. Sadly the member for Forest Hill [Neil Angus] is not one of them. For his information, this bill is to protect women... It is quite simple: my body, my choice, her body, her choice... right now we have a Royal Commission that is spotlighting family violence against women.

MAREE EDWARDS MLA LABOR

Around 4pm the debate was adjourned. A little more than an hour later, we returned to witness the Lower House pass the government's Public Health and Wellbeing Amendment (Safe Access Zones) Bill 2015: 69 to 13. The 13 who voted against the bill were all men. Every woman crossed the floor to vote with the sisterhood and the government in favour of the bill: 32 women and 37 men in all.

A big highlight has been working with women members of Parliament from all sides of government with the shared goal of addressing this long-standing issue of women's health and wellbeing.

This is great news and bodes well for the bill's progress to the Upper House where we believe it will debated within the next fortnight.

Big thanks from WHV to everyone who has contributed to the process so far.

DR AMY WEBSTER
WOMEN'S HEALTH VICTORIA
EMAIL
12 NOVEMBER 2015

Our Supreme court advocacy had been measured decorum and formality, where two opposing advocates presented sometimes bamboozling arguments to convince one person—the judge. Parliament was a completely different kind of advocacy: an out and proud public speaking up; a back-and-forth nonpartisan debate that found commonality among division. Gone were the days where abortion was a woman's shame to be whispered about privately or fretted about behind closed doors. In Parliament, women were made visible in all their complexity and strength. Abortion stigma was hit for six. Everyone had been touched by a true story of abortion or womanhood. Everyone knew someone. Everyone knew a woman affected, or potentially affected, by the complexities of family planning and fertility control. This commonality, for the most part, allowed our parliamentarians to make decisions based not on their personal beliefs, but based on their responsibility to others. I had just witnessed politicians at their best, and I couldn't wait for the debate in the Legislative Council.

CHAPTER 20

The Legislative Council

23–27 November 2015

*The final sitting before the vote was one of the
longest the Parliament had seen since the state's
new abortion laws had passed in 2008.
Everyone wanted a say.*

FIONA PATTEN (2018)

Labor and Greens were a bit toey about whether we would have the numbers in the Upper House. Liberal Mary Woodridge was confident, and kind enough to personally reassure me. When it's Mary Wooldridge speaking, you listen. There was definitely some relief in that.

Still, fingers crossed and work 'til it hurts. Thousands of informational, strategic, funny and grateful emails whizzed back and forth through cyber space. Women's groups everywhere had been contacting MPs urging they vote for the Safe Access Zones Bill: media pressure, face-to-face, phone—and where would we be without email and text? As we focused on the final hurdle, the Legislative Council, everything ramped up. Women were making it happen.

Dear Member,

Ahead of this week's debate on the Public Health and Wellbeing (Safe Access Zones) Bill, I just wanted to share with you the Human Rights Law Centre's strong support for the bill. The HRLC is a strong supporter of free speech and protest rights. We also work to support women's rights to equality, non-discrimination, dignity and privacy when they access their doctor.

We think the bill gets the balance right between anti-abortionists' rights to express their views and women's rights to safely access their doctor. As lawyers for the Fertility Control Clinic we've seen at close hand the harmful impact of the daily harassment and abuse of women. It has to stop. Anti-abortionists will be able to express their views everywhere but in the safe access zones. Our views are spelled out in more detail in:

*our SARC [Scrutiny of Acts and Regulations Committee] submission: http:// hrlc.org.au/victorian-parliament-should-seize-the-opportunity-to-end-harassment-and-intimidation-of-women-at-abortion-clinics/; and

*this opinion piece in The Age *written by Dr Susie Allanson and me: http://www.theage.com.au/comment/safe-access-to-abortion-clinics-must-be-guaranteed-by-law-20151107-gktfdv.html*

EMAIL EMILY HOWIE

23 NOVEMBER 2015

The debate in the Legislative Council, aka the Upper House, began on Tuesday 24 November 2015 just after 8pm. Em and I sat on the red cushions again, this time with the addition of my wing gals Janice and Susan, and FCC medical Director Lou Rutman. Lou had shouted us all a beautiful meal at a restaurant across the road, and we were relaxed, excited, and hopeful. I shared smiles with 'my' politicians who had worked so hard on this. Unlike the Assembly debate, there was no call for Em or me to scramble about with advice. We sat listening, watching and breathing it all in.

We were watching the debate and it was very obvious how supportive politicians were of women's rights. It wasn't just about access into an abortion clinic, it was about giving women the right to make decisions... I guess I wasn't surprised about how eloquent they were, but I was a bit surprised that parliamentarians were prepared to put themselves out there in this grey area which was always a grey area and probably is still a bit of a grey area. I'm a bit cynical: parliamentarians are only concerned about themselves... if they lose their seat it's all over... They had to put themselves out there: I believe in this and I can bring my constituents with me... They all decided that women's issues is now a critical right.

DR LOUIS RUTMAN (2020)

Respectful and respected lead speaker on the Liberal side, Mary Wooldridge, began proceedings.

I congratulate you, Ms Patten, for your advocacy in relation to this issue and for the work you did to persuade the government to go away, work on the bill you had drafted to address some of the issues and then bring it back to this place as a government bill, and I think it is very fitting that you are in the chair for this debate [as Acting President].

I am also pleased to inform the house that the coalition—the Liberal Party and The Nationals as two separate parties—will be having a free vote on this bill…

On a personal level I will be supporting this bill because I believe that it achieves the outcome of safe access to legal health services…

[The police] very clearly said to me that they believe that harassment and intimidation are taking place and that this needs resolution… The police are of the view that a physical separation between the entrance to the service and the people who are seeking to stand outside… would actually be the solution…

A number of people have said to me in conversation that they live or work near the area… Each and every one of the people expressed a personal opinion that even though they may not be accessing the clinic in East Melbourne, they too felt nervous, anxious, in some cases threatened and certainly terribly uncomfortable in walking past the clinic because of the nature of the protests and the presence of the individuals outside the clinic entrance.

If an individual who is going about their everyday business feels that way, I am confident and believe what the police say about an individual who at a very vulnerable time is making a decision about the reproductive health choices in front of them, that their experience is one that would be quite traumatic and certainly that they may feel harassed or intimidated as a result…

The message from the police was clearly that the laws currently in place have not enabled them to solve the situation… Supreme Court… Law Reform Commission in 2008… Rita Butera… Susie Allanson… Victorian

Equal Opportunity & Human Rights Commission... Emily Howie...

I believe this is an issue whose time has well and truly come... I believe we now have a bill which allows more action, communication and expression of belief and views to occur while still requiring that women be able to access services in a reasonable way... I commend the bill to the house.

MARY WOOLDRIDGE MLC LIBERAL

This is not a piece of legislation that has been drafted lightly. It has been prepared with very cautious and considered consultation, and it has been put together with reference to a number of competing interests. It has been underpinned by an assessment of the way in which the Charter of Human Rights and Responsibilities operates to overlay fundamental and foundational rights and entitlements in the making of Victorian law...

The competing interests which are the heart of this bill are geared toward providing access in a dignified way to health services; providing access in a way that does not cause a woman to feel beset, harassed, intimidated, interfered with or threatened, and in a way that does not in fact hinder or obstruct her or impede her by any means...

To my mind a silent prayer vigil which takes place within a safe access zone that would not have taken place but for the existence of that abortion clinic is more likely than not to have been engineered or organised for the purpose or for purposes which include intimidating, harassing, belittling, obstructing, hindering or impeding a woman's right to access an abortion. Again this falls to the courts and police to determine.

HARRIET SHING MLC LABOR

Democratic Labor Party (DLP) and anti-abortion Dr Carling-Jenkins was up next. Groan. Neat and eloquent, listening to her I wondered if maybe I could have been raised to be a pro-lifer.

Nup. Her beautifully spoken anti-woman language was completely offensive to women like me, and to almost all women everywhere:

This bill is not really about safe access, for these zones are unsafe. They are not safe for women and they are not safe for the pre-born children they carry into, but not out of, the premises... Women I believe are victims of the abortion

industry... The Helpers write: 'In fact you have completely ignored our sub-
mission of 42 pages'... The true effect of this bill, if not amended, will be to
make peaceful protest, prayer, support workers and counsellors illegal in the
vicinity of abortion clinics... I wish to thank the 13 MPs in the other place
who voted against this bill.

RACHEL CARLING-JENKINS MLC DLP

Relief, that that was time I would not have to endure again, was quickly over-
taken by the more combative Inga Peulich. Many around the chamber seemed
to have similar feelings: members interjected and others ignored the member
completely to begin conversations with colleagues.

I see this as an attempt yet again by Labor members to try and chip away
at religious freedoms, which they see as an obstacle to their own social policy
agenda... the bill is totally unnecessary, and I look forward to Mr Dalla-
Riva moving an amendment to reduce the buffer zone of 150 metres to 15
metres.

INGA PEULICH MLC LIBERAL

Greens' Nina Springle signalled a welcome resumption of advocacy for
women. Like others, Nina acknowledged various cross party politicians, the
government, abortion providing staff, the Greens own work, and provided a
strong voice for women.

This bill reflects the Parliament working at its very best—that is, togeth-
er... If people want to protest against abortion they should come here to do
it. If they want to protest outside an abortion clinic, all this bill requires is
that they do it at least 150 metres away. If people want to counsel women
against having abortions, which is what many of the people who stand
outside abortion clinics claim they are doing, then they should get the ap-
propriate qualifications and do it in a way that does not cause additional
harm... from people urging us to vote against this bill, there seems to be
very little acknowledgment of a woman's agency in her decision to have
an abortion... It is simply not the case that women who choose to have
abortions are ill informed or that they have not considered all the conse-
quences and implications of that choice.

NINA SPRINGLE MLC GREENS

I can think of no higher purpose, no better meaning, for being a member of Parliament than at times like today... What a woman does when she enters a clinic is none of our business. It is certainly not the business of people standing outside... the bill we have before us today is a piece of legislation that is workable... appropriate... and that delivers on the policy that we are trying to implement—namely, that women are able to go about their own business without fear of harassment.

Philip Daladakis MLC Labor

We are the ones who make the laws, and here is the place to protest—not outside a medical facility... women have every right to access those legal publicly funded services in a free manner without feeling intimidated by someone who is outside the clinic who has a different point of view from themselves.

Wendy Lovell MLC Liberal

I am going to make some quite personal remarks about this bill. I would like to start by thanking Fiona Patten, whose private members bill triggered this process, and the Andrews government, especially the Minister for Health, who understands that harassment and vilification of women seeking abortion... is an act of violence... [the religious extremists] just cannot stand the idea that a woman can be smart enough to make up her own mind about what she wants to do with her life. My intern [Hillary Taylor], who wrote the report, also filmed some of those demonstrations, and what I saw was pure and utter harassment.

For probably 20 years now I have been involved in various campaigns for women's reproductive rights. In this Parliament in this last 10 years the Greens have had a strong history of being involved in these issues. Much of this has come about from a fairly informal group of pro-choice MPs who have worked together to make sure that this kind of legislation is introduced, such as the decriminalisation of abortion, on which we worked closely together.

I am not allowed to look in the gallery and smile at any of them, so they can just take my thanks for granted. I do want to mention one particular person, and that is Susie Allanson, who is the psychologist at the

East Melbourne clinic and who has for years campaigned on this issue. She is tough, she is brave, she is tenacious and she is stubborn. Anybody who ever thought that they would get around Susie on this issue was very, very mistaken.

COLLEEN HARTLAND MLC GREENS

I blinked. Oh, Colleen. My eyes welled and my hands snuck out a hanky. I would never have chosen those particular adjectives to describe myself. Maybe over the years some of Colleen's toughness and stubborn bravery rubbed off on me.

Anti-abortion, anti-women, anti-Dan Andrews, anti-anyone-not-agreeing with his own extreme 'anti' views, Liberal MLC Mr Bernie Finn, spoke next until Mr Dalidakis thankfully interjected 'Time!' and acting President Simon Ramsay agreed it was indeed time.

Liberal Margaret Fitzherbert MLC detailed our obscenity case and our Supreme Court case evidence of East Melbourne residents' and workers' observations of women being harassed. Margaret concluded:

Existing laws have failed... Many women do not want to make complaints, to protect their own privacy and because their experience is generally a one-off... I think these sorts of statements really tell their own story... It is because people are being followed these kinds of distances that I am more comfortable than I was with the 150-metre provision in this bill.

I do not call this free speech. I call this name-calling and abuse. A lot of it is deeply disturbing, and I can understand why people feel threatened and unsafe... Given this behaviour continues to occur on public land, is it really up to the clinic to keep calling the police and hope that action will happen? I expect that this law will be challenged, but I do not see that as a reason in itself not to enact it tonight.

MARGARET FITZHERBERT MLC LIBERAL

As a former midwife I have spoken about various health issues—I am very familiar with issues surrounding women's fertility issues, the issues surrounding abortions and miscarriages and the reproductive health issues that women often seek treatment for... Unfortunately in my 10 years at the Royal Women's I have seen protesters come into the hospital and put signage close to the labour wards in relation to right to life issues... Some of the actions of the protesters that the [Supreme] court heard about, I believe, were robust in relation to their information included... If that is the sort of behaviour that one has to be confronted with, I do not think it is acceptable.

GEORGIE CROZIER MLC LIBERAL

I will support this bill because it is also the right of a female to be able to access a legal service unencumbered and with a full understanding of her right... I wholeheartedly applaud the principle of free speech, however, freedom of speech is not an unrestricted licence. There are other instances [of zones]... Rural women often feel marginalised due to distance and some-times the lack of immediate services, and they have implored me to make sure their voices are heard within the debate.

MELINA BATH MLC NATIONALS

When Liberal Craig Ondarchie began, I sighed:

I want to thank the Lord Jesus for the blessing and privilege to be an MP. I also want to give thanks for my beautiful family, my children and my grandchildren...

Was soon surprised:

For a part of my career I was executive director of the Royal Women's Hospital... the Women's does undertake terminations for a variety of reasons...

Sighed again:

My love and my prayers are with all those women who have had to go through that... I feel blessed that I can express a view safely.

And finally, happily surprised:

... blessed that I can offer assurances to Victorian women that they can seek medical attention and services without fear. I give thanks for our democra-cy, and I support the intent of this bill.

CRAIG ONDARCHIE MLC LIBERAL

Liberal Richard Dalla-Riva MLC circulated an amendment that would see the zone drop from 150 metres to just 15 metres. His speech referred to a raft of High Court and US rulings to support his argument that:

*If the amendment as I have put forward is not supported, I will be oppos-
ing the legislation because my view is that it would still be defeated in a
High Court test.*

RICHARD DALLA-RIVA MLC LIBERAL

Liberal Simon Ramsay MLC spoke in support of the bill but also signalled
a zone size amendment: dropping the 1 from the 150 to make it only 50
metres.

In the late evening of 24 November 2015, and nudging towards the
early morning of 25 November 2015, Fiona Patten thanked by name many
politicians and others for their support, and highlighted the constructive,
collaborative process around the bill, including the (unwitting) supportive
comments from an opponent:

*Constitutionally we have struck the right balance. I think this would stand
up in a High Court challenge...*

*Many of us in this chamber will have received many emails about this...
Many of them were quite threatening... But what really got me about most
of these emails was that they were saying, 'We need to save these poor women
accessing these clinics. They don't know what they're doing. They need our
guidance so we can put them on the right path'...*

*This is not the time for well-meaning people to tell these women how
wrong they are in their decision and how right the position of these other
people on abortion is, creating a sense of shame, a sense of stigma and sometimes a sense of fear... to be saying that a woman going into that clinic has
not made that decision on her own grounds and should be counselled by an
unqualified stranger. It is completely unacceptable...*

*Respectful protest or prayer is not helpful. It is unwanted. It makes
women feel ashamed about their decisions. Our society should not allow
that or endorse it by failing to support this bill. Even one of the people who
wrote asking me to oppose the bill stated:*

*'I believe this would prevent even the respectful communication of in-
formation about alternatives to abortion, as abortion is such a contentious
issue that, even when presented with respect and sensitivity, communications about it may be reasonably likely to cause distress and anxiety.'*

> *I very much appreciate the support of the government, Premier Andrews and in particular the Minister for Health [Jill Hennessy] for taking this on; Susie Allanson at the Fertility Control Clinic; Emily Howie and the Human Rights Law Centre; Maurice Blackburn Lawyers, particularly Katie Robertson, Elizabeth O'Shea and Jacob Varghese; all of the health groups, legal groups, volunteer groups and women's rights groups – Marie Stopes International, Family Planning Victoria, Women's Health West, Women's Health Victoria, Right to Choose; the Public Health Association of Australia; the Australian Medical Association; Trades Hall; the universities and hospitals; everyone who came to support this legislation; and all the members in this house who have supported it.*

Minister for Families and Children Jenny Mikakos' conclusion to the debate was brief but powerful. It included responding to a couple of ridiculous questions about prohibitions within the zone put by religious opponents of the bill:

> *It was asked whether the [Australian Catholic] university would be prevented from undertaking lectures about abortion law reform. I want to assure the Australian Catholic University that such lectures would not be prohibited. It is clear that a person accessing an abortion at the East Melbourne clinic would not be able to hear or see the content of a lecture that is performed within a lecture theatre across four lanes of traffic on Victoria Parade...*
>
> *The bill is ultimately about freedom to access medical procedures, the right to choose to have an abortion, as well as the right to choose not to have one and the right of a woman to make that decision by consulting with her doctors and those individuals a woman chooses to consult or seek advice from, rather than strangers... I thank members for their contributions.*

Hear, hear! I had just witnessed a parliamentary display of proud women uncovered in the face of sexism and bullying; and good men who recognise and respect women's competence and their right to live their lives as they see fit. We live in a society in which all people—100% of humanity, not just the male half—are entitled to make choices about their own bodies and lives. Those who may disagree strongly with the choices made by others, do not have the right to try and intimidate other people into making different choices. That's what the Parliament is supposed to be all about. And that's what it was all about. I wished every Victorian had heard this debate, every Australian, every person in the world.

With the clock at 15 minutes before midnight, proceedings moved into 'Committee'. While debate speakers had had a time limit, now opponents to the bill had the opportunity to thwart the bill's progress and filibuster. Margaret Fitzherbert's warning words to me earlier in the day began to sink in:

> BTW Richard's [Dalla Riva] amendment will be moved through the Committee of the Whole i.e. the line-by-line assessment of the bill, where any member can ask questions of the minister responsible (Jenny Mikakos) and speak. There is no limit on how long members can speak, should they choose to do so, in this section.
>
> MARGARET FITZHERBERT
> EMAIL
> 24 NOVEMBER 2015

Good grief! And good grief it was! Some snippets from this marathon will suffice:

> Ms Mikakos: I thank Mrs Peulich for her question. She is obviously posing some hypotheticals without providing the context. Obviously the matter would depend on what might be on a banner [outside a church] that might be visible to people accessing a fertility clinic, and matters would be deter-mined on a case-by-case basis...
>
> Mrs Peulich: ...it is not hypothetical.
>
> Ms Mikakos: It is hypothetical.
>
> Mrs Peulich: No it is not...

There were many more lowlights to come from Ms Peulich in a similar ilk:

> Mrs Peulich: Would an aeroplane carrying a sign that somebody may find distressing be captured by this bill?
>
> Ms Mikakos: How many aeroplanes do you know that fly under 150 metres?

Mrs Peulich: I live close to the Moorabbin Airport... I have an aeroplane every 30 minutes.

Ms Mikakos: You are treating this as a joke.

At 1am, Mrs Peulich passed the baton to Mr Bernie Finn. Mr Finn provided an example of the worst of the extreme religious right. Amongst serious kerfuffle, offensive language and bullying grandstanding, was this diversion down yet another rabbit hole into yet another absurd Wonderland:

Deputy President [Gayle Tierney, Labor]: Order! I highlight to Mr Finn that I have checked the dictionary, and there is no such word as 'abortuary'. I would ask him not to use that word, which does not exist.

Mr Finn: I knew Madam Deputy President, that freedom of speech was under attack in this state, but I did not realise that it was under attack in this house...

Deputy President: Order! We are simply using the dictionary, Mr Finn.

Mr Finn: Funk and Wagnall's! Yes, indeed there is a fair bit of that going on.

Deputy President: Order! Excuse me, that is not appropriate.

[Multiple exchanges]

Deputy President: Order! It is a derogatory term.

Mr Finn: My oath, it is a derogatory term. They kill babies there, you know. That is why it is derogatory.

Deputy President: Order! We will continue this discussion and this committee respecting each others' position.

[Back and forth]

Deputy President: Order! I will also ask you to refer to me as the Deputy President, not Madam. Thank you.

[Mr Finn goes on]

Ms Mikakos: I think Mr Finn will find that I responded to that question ten minutes ago.

Mr Finn: No, you didn't.

Ms Mikakos: I encourage him to refer to the Hansard tomorrow, because I have responded.

Back in 2008 during the abortion decrim debate/committee, Colleen Hartland and others had sensibly booked themselves into a nearby hotel for overnight accommodation. Maybe some were doing the same this time around. I had no idea how our politicians kept going, especially Jenny Mikakos who responded to the most nonsensical and repetitive questions calmly, clearly and with rock solid determination throughout—amazing woman. I, on the other hand, made the reluctant decision to leave before the end. I know, fancy admitting that. After everything, how could I have left? Was I really a woman who had gone through three labours? Might I miss the birth of this one? I woke the next morning to find that the session ran until 3:45am, repeat, 3:45*am*. And it was not finished yet.

> *Well despite sitting until 3.45 am, the bill is still being delayed in the committee stage. It has passed the second reading on a vote of 31 to 8 (which was critical), but last night saw a great deal of irrelevant questioning by about seven MPs designed to delay the process of the bill. They will return to it on Thursday [26 November 2015] to continue dealing with it and the amendments. At this stage it is still very likely to get through (hopefully Thursday), it's just some very draining attempts to delay and hinder passage under the guise of 'protecting free speech'.*
>
> *I will update if we hear anything further, thank you to everyone who came along and sent messages of support. We'll get there!*

Parliamentary adviser to Fiona Patten MLC

Email

25 November 2015

> *Hi Margaret,*
>
> *Your speech was fabulous. My apologies I thought I had emailed you during proceedings to congratulate you, but sometimes I am a techno duffer.*
>
> *That information could not have been used in a better way nor more eloquently. You provided such a valuable perspective.*
>
> *I hope you are not feeling unwell today after the 'filibuster' style last night. I couldn't quite hang out 'til the end!*

Email to Liberal MLC Margaret Fitzherbert

25 November 2015

I got your message overnight and I was glad you felt it did the job. The debate went as I thought—lots of generalities and assertions that the protesters are always benign and peaceful—so I really wanted to get some detail on the record.

I got two hours sleep. There will be a lot of grumpy people today, myself included! That filibuster was sheer payback.

Thanks again to you and Emily for providing the material cos the speech never would have happened without that…

The picture will get clearer the closer we get, but it is likely that it will be another late night for us on Thursday, although hopefully not 4am. There are about five pieces of legislation other than the buffer zone bill that the govt wanted to get through the LC this week and there's only one sitting week after this before Christmas. But I think the buffer zone bill will be a priority for them so would probably be dealt with earlier on Thursday than the others and I still think it will be passed this week.

Margaret Fitzherbert

Email

25 November 2015

I quipped back to Margaret that two hours sleep was not exactly workplace Occupational Health and Safety.

Just before 9:30pm on Thursday 26 November, the Public Health and Wellbeing Amendment (Safe Access Zones) Bill 2015 resumed Committee in the Legislative Council. I sat watching and hoping. Hoping another filibuster would not eventuate. Hoping that safe access zones would finally become law.

The size of the zone had been like a pesky fly, swat, buzz, swat, buzz. Anti-abortion politicians floated the idea of a markedly reduced zone as a means to get rid of the bill altogether. Others purportedly in the hope of avoiding arguments about excessive constraints on freedom of expression and ensuring the law would both be enacted and meet a High Court challenge.

Margaret Fitzherbert had broached the issue in her speech about Fiona's bill, but now was all in with the government bill and the 150 metres. On 23 November 2015, the day before the Legislative Council debate, Em and I met with Liberal MLC Margaret Fitzherbert at her Port Melbourne office. Begun by earlier emails and phone conversations, this was to be another important collaboration. I was impressed with the Liberal MLC:

Thanks so much for meeting with us yesterday, Margaret. Your support, insight and determination are inspiring and reassuring. I hope the statements from a variety of witnesses are helpful, but certainly do not use them unless adds something useful to your speech. You are all over it already! I will be there tonight and look forward to hearing your speech.

EMAIL TO MARGARET FITZHERBERT

24 NOVEMBER 2015

On 24 November 2015, as the bill was to be debated in the Legislative Council, question marks around the zone size persisted. Amendments by opponents were likely and there was no requirement to give notice. Amendments could come up quickly. But amendments to reduce the zone size were a no-brainer.

Thank you for letting me know about Mr Dalla Riva's proposed amendment. I think a 15-metre zone is meaningless. It is too small to address the intimidation and abuse of women outside clinics for a few reasons:

First, women could still be followed and approached by anti-abortionists from the tram stop or if they park their car around the corner. This wouldn't stop the unwanted, unsolicited and harmful behaviour that is currently a daily occurrence, except for in the area immediately outside the clinic.

Second, noisy heckling of women that occurs just outside of the 15-metre zone could easily be seen and heard by women approaching the clinic or even inside.

Tasmania has similar law and a 150-metre zone, and I think there is benefit in our laws developing consistently. To be serious about preventing this abuse, and to take women's safety and privacy seriously, the zones must be much bigger than 15 metres.

EMAIL FROM EMILY HOWIE TO MARGARET FITZHERBERT

24 NOVEMBER 2015

Liberal Simon Ramsay also had given notice of an amendment to reduce the zone to 50 metres.

Right that's it. This was not just about us. This was about all the abortion providers in Victoria. This was about paving the way for safe access zones throughout Australia. Throughout the world! Okay, so I was heading into grandiose dummy spit territory. Time to channel it into good stuff. I emailed Liberals Mary Wooldridge, Georgie Crozier and Margaret Fitzherbert with additional information to reassure their colleagues about the necessity of a 150-metre zone:

I mentioned to you that I have been part of a group involving The Women's Hospital [Annarella Hardiman and Dr Paddy Moore], Family Planning Vic, and University of Melbourne's Centre for Excellence in Rural Sexual Health [CERSH—Kylie Stevens]. We have visited regional areas and provide a day long workshop for health professionals working with women facing problem pregnancies. When we were in Bendigo earlier in the year, I was most concerned by workers' description of the harassment by anti-abortion extremists experienced by women and health professionals at the Bendigo public hospital, Bendigo Health...

I'm not sure if Simon Ramsey MLC is aware of this situation, and I would be most happy for you to provide him with this email if you thought that might be appropriate... given his regional focus and the passionate speech he gave supporting Fiona Patten's original bill—I was so delighted to be in the chamber to hear it. While I realise that Mr Ramsay has thought long and hard about this bill, I thought the circumstances of Bendigo Health may be important in Mr Ramsay re-thinking his proposed 50-metre access zone amendment, which as you know we feel is far too small. I appreciate the debate focus on the clinic where I work, its physical surrounds and the importance of having a 150-metre safe access zone to combat the style of anti-abortion stalking and intimidation women face on Wellington Pde. But this bill is about ensuring respect, safety and privacy of women throughout Victoria who are accessing legal medical services.

Last night I spoke by phone with a delightful Nurse Practitioner at Bendigo Health (Bendigo Public Hospital) Choices Clinic. Simone described a group of usually six people wheeling a pram with a dead 'foetus' in it, wearing pigs' uteruses around their necks, wandering the perimeter of the hospital (including across the other side of the wide public roadway outside the hospital) and indiscriminately harassing and distressing women attending for all sorts of medical care. Choices and abortion theatre staff have been targeted in a variety of ways... With the vastness of the surrounding area, parking, train, and the way this anti-abortion group works the area, 50 metres is inadequate.

Simone is delighted to hear of the 150-metre Safe Access Zones Bill and is happy to speak by phone today if that will assist with the safe passage of the bill. Simone is at the coal face in working directly with women with problem pregnancies seeking care including those deciding to terminate a pregnancy. This public hospital attracts women from up to three hours away. A doctor from The Women's hospital in Melbourne attends once a fortnight to provide abortions because no local doctor is willing to do so, given the particular climate of anti-abortion stigmatisation and harassment in Bendigo. As you are aware, abortion access for rural and regional women is particularly problematic. (I mentioned to you the brief audit of 151 Fertility Control Clinic patients where 10% were regional and rural women; 31% of these women reported a variety of access problems versus just 5% of metropolitan women reporting access problems.) All this is by way of emphasising how crucial Bendigo Health is to women's health and wellbeing, and how crucial it is that this bill protects women and staff attending there...

Please let me know if there is anything else I can do to help ensure the safe passage, unamended, of this very important bill.

EMAIL TO MARGARET FITZHERBERT

26 NOVEMBER 2015

Margaret passed on my email to Mr Ramsay, but also suggested I check out his Facebook page. When I did, it appeared that he was already on board. There had been no need for my late email after all. As Mr Ramsay eventually mentioned in his speech to the chamber on 26 November 2015, he had paid a visit to Wellington Parade to step out the 150 metres. Although he still believed 50 metres more appropriate, he mentioned the number of constituents contacting him about the need for 150 metres and noted the newly constructed tram super-stop just inside the 150-metre mark where clinic patients would alight.

As a curious footnote about that tram super-stop, in the clean up of our Supreme Court case against MCC and with the hope that safe access legislation would soon be in place, a couple of months before the debate I was contacted by MCC's Compliance Co-ordinator Peter Joynson and Dean Robertson. They wanted to meet with Lou and me because, 'we haven't talked for some time'. Hmm. Over many years I had sometimes phoned Peter, a polite gentleman, asking him to make the enforcement officers actually do something. I hoped our 11 September 2015 meeting would not be another waste of time.

It appeared that since our Supreme Court judgement and the unambiguous political push for safe access zones, and until safe access zones law was hopefully passed, Peter wanted to reassure us that MCC officers were attending every morning and working closely with police. Despite everything, I did find some reassurance in that. We had experienced what it's like when religious zealots step over the line of decent behaviour. And once over that line, a line invisible to them, where might they actually end up? Back in July 2001? Deep in a last-ditch religious swan song of violence?

Peter's comment that MCC wouldn't stand for this if the extremists were on the steps of the town hall, was no doubt true but unhelpful. Dean impressed me as trying to think outside the box. He was particularly enthused by Council's contribution to a new Super Tram Stop, to be opened on Wellington Parade at around, let's say, at a smidge, as luck would have it, just inside the 150-metre mark. Not bad. Maybe Dean had been behind the creative use of the streetscape garden beds years ago to limit the extremists' displays.

That new super tram stop, at which many patients would alight, created a compelling public transport structure arguing for the 150-metre zone. Which brings us back to Mr Simon Ramsay's withdrawal of his amendment in the Upper House on 26 November 2015, and his conclusion that:

Perhaps the 150 metres is a reasonable starting point in relation to this bill. It might be that in time either the police or stakeholders find it is excessive and is creating issues in relation to litigation or court action, but we are dealing with now, and on that basis I would like to withdraw my amendment.

SIMON RAMSAY MLC LIBERAL

Yay! And really that was the end of the 150 metre 'issue'.

And always that great thing: the typo in the legislation. It was supposed to be 50m and a '1' got put in front of 50m in Tassie. I didn't find out about that until after we'd written the legislation and then I told the Health Minister, 'Well actually, there was a typo, it was meant to be 50 metres.' She said, 'Well I don't see any reason to correct that, do you?' She's great isn't she.

FIONA PATTEN (2019)

Committee progressed through the evening of 26 November 2015. Fiona's adviser Danielle Walt had turned her mind to how we could better endure anti-women rhetoric from filibustering politicians. Da-da! Danielle had devised a bingo sheet comprising a table of nine squares: *Murder/killing/genocide; Claims of counselling and or helping; misinformation about abortion; reference to morality; incorrect claim about safe access zones; super hypocritical statement of any variety; freedom of speech; claim that no abuse/harassment has ever occurred;* and a free bingo space for a raft of other likely extreme religious right words.

Danielle's bingo sheet and the camaraderie amongst we pro-choice, red-cushion-gallery-sitters, cheered on my determination to stay until the end of proceedings, no matter how late. Bernie Finn and Inga Peulich were up to their old tricks. One of these centred around the law's commencement:

Mr Finn: I am asking what the Minister and the government propose to do to inform those who may be impacted by this legislation and on how it will affect them.

Ms Patten: In all other bills which include commencement dates we do not discuss whether everyone needs to know about the bill by the commencement date…

Ms Mikakos: Ms Patten has really hit the nail on the head here.

Mr Finn: Interjection.

Ms Mikakos: No, I am responding to you Mr Finn. Listen in. We have just had the terrorism bill debated: are you suggesting that the government should write to all potential terrorists that we are about to change the law in Victoria?... The government does not need to communicate to any potential offender the change of the law. Obviously all the health services that are impacted on by this legislation know full well... I can also assure the house that we will be engaging with business and religious organisations... to provide guidance and assurance during the implementation and prior to proclamation of this bill... Those organisations that have strong views against the bill, such as Right to Life Victoria and Helpers of God's Precious Infants, know full well that this legislation is coming, so we are talking about a handful of individuals who might have a contrary view—share your views, Mr Finn—and are opposed to legislation. We know that the vast majority of Victorians are supportive of this bill. I think you need to reflect on the fact that you are seeking to delay debate on a bill on a day where we have just had a bipartisan spirit in this house around violence against women.

Jenny Mikakos was brilliant. Inside I cheered and punched the air with my fists. I wished I could be as respectfully assertive and display such strength of character as she did. What a role model.

Throughout this night of questions and orations, amendments proffered and rejected and bill clauses voted on and agreed, the snippets below became the norm:

Deputy President: Order! I uphold that point of order. In the last 17 minutes we have come full circle. We have had tedious repetition on a particular line of questioning. The minister answered. It might not be the answer that certain people wanted, but she has answered it. I call on members to raise other issues that they might have with clause 2 and move on.

Quickly followed by a vote and division overwhelmingly upholding that particular clause.

Or:

Colleen Hartland: The Greens will not be supporting these amendments.

Jenny Mikakos: I indicate to the house that the government will not be supporting Mr Finn's amendments.

Followed by Division and amendments overwhelmingly negatived.

Finally at 1:30am, and almost to my surprise, the President was saying:

Order! The question is: That the bill be now read a third time and do pass.

Members moved about the chamber, and the final count was an overwhelming aye to the legislation: 30 to 8. The eight nays comprised six men and two women; only four Liberals voted against the bill. The 30 ayes comprised 15 men and 15 women. After magnificent, empowering speeches from around the chamber in the face of anti-abortion filibustering, on Friday 27 November 2015 at 1:30am, formidable cross-party women led the Victorian Parliament to enact the Public Health and Wellbeing amendment (Safe Access Zones) Bill 2015. We finally had our safe access zones!

I danced in the corridor to the parliamentary dining room. Let the thanks and celebrations begin.

Our card with flowers to thank Jenny Mikakos simply read:

Dear Jenny,

With sincere appreciation for your determination, eloquence and stamina!

From Susie Allanson and Louis Rutman and the staff and patients of the Fertility Control Clinic.

A campaign takes all sorts. Sometimes you need someone who keeps things tight and will not back down, like Jenny Mikakos during the debate. Other moments you need people who will push, spit the dummy and remind you of the stakes. That's why working in a team is best.

We need women in the room. We need women in every room, from women's health clinics, police stations, law firms and law courts, unions and Trades Hall, universities, governments, corporations' executives and boards... Below are relatable lesson excerpts from Gillard & Okonjo-Iweala's *Women and Leadership* (2020 pp. 291-2, and 297):

Do not underestimate how valuable getting people to know you is and how much space you should take up.

Affirmative-action rules can play a role in disrupting the tendency to tap the male power network and preselect the next man in the queue.

By gaining power, women are able to put themselves in a position where they cannot be ignored.

Gender inequality is embedded in the structures and systems of our societies, as well as in individual attitudes. In order to see real change, we need men to deliberately commit to the reworking necessary to weed out the gender inequality.

CHAPTER 21

Police Implementation

December 2015–May 2016

If you want to hold onto women's choices and women's right to shape their own lives, you don't have to be forever active yourself, but you do have to be forever vigilant.

JOAN KIRNER (WHV 2010)

Safe access zones legislation was a victory that bestowed key human rights to women within a well-crafted and robust law. The law's construction, underpinning values and evidence were explicit in the bill itself, Health Minister Jill Hennessy's second reading speech and the Parliamentary debates. Victoria's safe access zones law would withstand a legal challenge pushed all the way to the High Court of Australia and join a jurisprudence elite tested to within an inch of its life. You want safe access zones law tested? Bring it on. But first, let's put these zones into action.

It takes time to transition from enactment to enforcement. There's a great deal of preparation before implementation. Preparation that Lou, Janice and I had no clue about. On 16 December 2015, Health Minister Jill Hennessy's adviser kindly let us know that while the default proclamation date was 1 July 2016, work was progressing with Victoria Police in the hope the new law could be proclaimed earlier.

A week later, 22 December 2015, we met with Acting Sergeant Phil Monteduro, who followed up our questions promptly via Melbourne Prosecutions Frontline Support: An amendment to the Public Health & Wellbeing Act (Safe Access Bill) had been passed by Parliament and was intended to come into effect on 1 December 2015. But the new legislation had not yet been gazetted in the government gazette. Department of Prosecutions had a standing request with the Department of Justice to be notified as soon as practicable as to when it was likely to be gazetted, but they still had not heard anything. Once it was gazetted, Police would be notified by Prosecutions of all the particulars including powers, offences, penalties and so on. If the current situation remained and it was not gazetted soon, the legislation would automatically come into effect on 1 July 2016.

What did 'gazetting' mean? What did 'come into effect' mean? What did 'proclamation' mean? Were they different or the same? I didn't understand much, except that the legislation had passed Parliament in November 2015—and July 2016 seemed a long way off. We did understand the Acting Sgt's reminder, 'In the meantime, if you require Police, please call 000.'

For decades local residents and workers, our staff and patients, had put up with this distressing situation in a relatively calm and civilised manner (minus occasional dummy spits). Our staff—and staff at other abortion providing clinics in Melbourne and regional Victoria—was now impatient for the new legislation to be implemented. We wanted abortion safe access zones to become reality. Another six months felt like an eternity.

How does new legislation transition to enforcement? Was safe access zones legislation unique in the preparation required? Is six months the average going rate for transitioning from passing legislation to enforcing the new law?

Really depends. It's up to the Parliament to decide how long it will take between passing it and it coming into force, and depends often on whether there is a lot of work government needs to do in order to prepare itself to take on board these new obligations. What was it, six months? I don't want to take away from the fact that that's six more months, having won but not feeling any benefit from it, that's too long. But I imagine that Jill will say in terms of getting police ready, it's not a very long time in government.

EMILY HOWIE (2020)

Not a very long time in this whole saga either. In fact it turned out to be just five months and six days between enactment and enforcement. That's all. I guess a mere long weekend in the scheme of things. But for various reasons I am still not clear about, that five months and six days felt like one long, long weekend of camping when the rain teems down and you're wet, cold and hungry the entire time. Can't we just go home already? Can't we just enforce our safe access zone already?

The likes of me, Lou, Janice and Susan thought implementing the law was just the decent and common-sense thing to do: another step towards women everywhere being able to live their lives as they saw fit without being treated like second class human beings scorned and requiring control. Abortion stigma, sexism, and the power of institutions like the Catholic church had made ours a unique case relegated for decades (if not centuries) to the 'sin bin', 'too hard basket', 'you deserve it' and 'women making a fuss over nothing'. Safe access zones law took women out of those tatty bins and baskets: women were to be respected as persons entitled to choose how they lived their lives, without copping vilification for those choices. The implementation process would similarly rise above abortion stigma, sexism, religious right pressure, and be implemented just like any other new legislation. Wouldn't it?

Over the coming weeks and months, I suspected that our situation and the safe access zones law were not like other new legislation. We hadn't had a law like this one before. Then again, all new laws are just that: new. But the abortion decriminalisation aside, we hadn't had a law that so powerfully destigmatised and legitimised abortion, women having abortions, staff who provided abortions, family planning, women's reproductive health, women's autonomy, women's safety and more.

Although Tassie had been the first to secure safe access zones legislation, for various reasons the Victorian legislation and context was more influential, urgent and perhaps quite radical for some. Involvement in the law's implementation might bring unique professional and personal challenges for those lacking a woman-centred conceptualisation and language. Such individuals might find themselves on a steep learning curve. If our world recognised women as full human beings, women's issues would not require whole new understandings and a new language. But clearly that is not our world, yet. After these past months of being surrounded by enlightened, feminist people whose women-centred outlook and language was second nature to them, I was to become worried and irritated by those who, for obvious reasons, struggled with a feminist perspective. I would again consider that our society was in dire need of more mainstream gender and human rights education.

Personally, I would say I get this perspective. For example, I used to be irritated that the Charter of Human Rights in Victoria had no standalone cause of action for breach. It had to be a breach of rights as part of another cause of action. But in the end, after talking to many government lawyers, I now get it. I don't agree with it still, but I get it. Laws are supposed to educate executive government, as well as offer rights to individuals, and this kind of work creates a virtuous cycle of understanding and respect for rights. So I got your impatience Susie, but the more work I do, the more I realise that law is not just about enforcement, it's about creating a culture within government itself, including, say, police, but also any other government body that might be involved in this law.

LIZZIE O'SHEA

Wednesday 13 January 2016, Inspector Gerry Cartwright visited Janice, Em and me at the clinic. I had spoken with Gerry by phone and it was good to meet him in person. He arrived in his civvies, smart casual, calm and focused, and accompanied by two uniformed police officers. The six of us crammed into a small consulting room, the morning patient demands militating against any larger room being available. We were reassured, and concerned, by what Gerry had to say. The next morning Gerry sent an email reiterating his main points:

Broadly speaking, I am co-ordinating the State-wide operational implementation of the Safe Access legislation for Victoria Police. So, this encompasses not only your clinic, but the others around the State...

VicPol does not own this legislation, it is 'owned' by the Minister of Health. Having said that both Vic Pol and DHHS [Department of Health & Human Services] are very keen to get the legislation running and provide another layer of safety to your staff and patients. For reasons I explained yesterday, we do not believe that this is possible (or even desirable) until sometime after Easter.

Easter was more than two months away, late March. Another Easter without a safe access zone felt like a negation of our legislative victory. Easter was always a particularly tough time for patients and staff. As part of the Catholic ritual of Lent, Catholics give up something during the forty days leading up to Easter. Most people gave up chocolate, alcohol or meat. We always thought that the extremists should give up coming to the clinic, but instead they'd double down, putting on what they called a 'vigil'. They tried (with a certain degree of success) to have people outside the clinic all day, every day for forty days. Individuals and groups would come and go, each with their own style of expressing their anti-abortion view. Some years we copped the vigil leading up to Easter, *and* two other forty-day vigils through the year. That's 120 vigil days out of 365 days, with the usual morning siege claiming the rest. During vigils we almost missed the predictability of our regulars. 'Better the devil you know', but I'd rather live without devils at all. We were worried about a religious extremist indulging in a last gasp 'final solution' of violence. We knew about that from experience.

Gerry told us that the Health Minister needed to be given 28 days' notice before operational implementation. This left no chance of enforcement *prior* to the 40-day vigil.

Why not begin enforcement *during* the vigil?

Apparently it was best to respect that holy time and wait until after Easter.

The law was passed, but we still had to prioritise Catholic sensibilities and relegate patients and staff—again?

Police wished to avoid any issues with children involved in the forty-day vigil.

Children were not abstract anti-abortion hostages, but real little people who should be protected from adults' dangerous nonsense. But it felt like we were again being held responsible for the actions of the religious extremists: they were the ones exposing children to a completely inappropriate experience, not us. It was the continuing prioritisation of the extremists' wishes over the needs and rights of women. Lou's 'price you pay' all over again?

We agreed with Gerry that it was likely that the legislation would be tested in Court. But having observed so closely the legislation's development and parliamentary debate, we had every confidence in it. We had confidence in the government and its legal minds. Parliamentary Hansard of the Safe

Access Bill second reading speech and debate was exceptional. Because of our Supreme Court case, our barristers, Maurice Blackburn Lawyers and the Human Rights Law Centre, were expert in this unique women's rights/human rights field. Related and supporting legal arguments were readily available via our Supreme Court case against Melbourne City Council: our submissions; our learned counsels' arguments; the Equal Opportunity and Human Rights Commission's submission; and the 'partial win' decision. Much had been learned from (Janice's) obscenity case (Fraser v Walker) about the religious right's legal approach. We wanted to be reassured that the likelihood of a legal challenge was not going to hold up 'operational implementation'.

We waited two weeks for legal advice Gerry had requested about the bill, and then another two months for more legal advice. To me, a lay and impatient-for-enforcement person, both were legal questions already dealt with by government and parliament. The eventual legal advice reflected this. Then again, our Supreme Court case spoke to the vagaries of the law, and Gerry's legal caution and clarification was no doubt warranted: he wanted to make sure that he had 'all his ducks in a row' before enforcement.

Except for a sentence in his first email, it was not part of Gerry's approach to express concern for our patients, staff, or others affected in East Melbourne. Although he visited and phoned us diligently to keep us in the loop, he spent considerable time 'consulting with', and expressing concern for, the sensitivities of the Catholic Church, Catholic University, Helpers of God's Precious Infants (HOGPI), the Christian Lobby, Bernie Finn... Why was Gerry spending so much time speaking with the religious right? We perhaps could understand if a letter were sent, although I wondered if even this might be unusual—did police letter-drop or visit every person affected by new legislation? When the Liberal government had brought in 'moving on' laws, for example, did they speak with every homeless person?

This very issue had been raised by filibustering anti-abortion politicians during the parliamentary debate: how would people know about the safe access zones? The government's answer was that this was like any other legislation and people would find out via the usual means (media reports, perhaps Australian Medical Association letters/publications), and in any event most people the new law affected were already aware. If a person breached the zone, we assumed they would be quickly educated by police and asked to leave the zone, and thereafter face the full force of the new law. I was worried that Gerry was on his way to yet another consultative process. The religious right, like everybody else in Victoria, had had the opportunity to put their point of view about this legislation.

With no knowledge of how the process from legislation to enforcement actually worked and how long it usually took, we really had no idea what 'normal' procedure was. I was probably misreading the situation. But given the Catholic Church's power, and given how difficult it had been for anyone, especially Catholics, to stand up to the Church when children were being systemically abused by priests… hmm.

We had meetings with Gerry Cartwright. He was from a staunch Catholic background. He was trying to do the right thing by the legislation and by us, but he also didn't want to be too offensive to the protesters whom he might have liked or just wanted to appease. I don't know where he actually sat. I don't know because he used to communicate with them a lot…

Maybe him being on the inside meant that he knew a bit more and that was his aim, and that was okay because he was successful. It was the price you had to pay. Always, always had to pay a price…

It was the frustration of not being able to achieve what you believed in. And what we believed was that they shouldn't be allowed to be there.

Louis Rutman (2020)

No matter the Inspector's wide-ranging experiences in the police force, it can't have been comfortable to meet at an abortion clinic with an abortionist and other abortion staff and be in charge of implementing a law that so directly contradicted the wishes of the Catholic Church. No doubt other factors were at play including, perhaps, that all this was quite normal and laws usually took this long to implement. I had no idea.

I suppose the police's main priority was to avoid further violence and further offences being committed. I don't know what they were thinking, but the truth is we won. We got the access zone that we wanted, and the harassers had to go home. I know you and the staff at the clinic paid a price for that, but the

reality is that they lost. Regardless of what the police officers' personal opin-
ions were, they were going to have to do their job of enforcing the new law.

Now there was a murder at the clinic as we all know. It was a disgrace
and a tragedy. These people aren't very sensible or rational. They are zeal-
ots. If I was in charge of enforcing laws against them, I would be careful.
You do not want them to be encouraged, explicitly or implicitly, to take
matters into their own hands. I can imagine this may have been part of the
thinking of police.

LIZZIE O'SHEA

I kept my cross-party parliamentary and Abortion Working Group colleagues
up-dated, voicing my uncertainties. They needed to know, and we needed
their support. Throughout we were comforted by the fact that the women's
groups, the government, cross-party supporters, Em and the Human Rights
Law Centre, and Lizzie overseas were all still watching out for us. On 22
March 2016, a hard hitting, beautifully constructed *Herald Sun* article, by the
inimitable Beth Wilson, questioned why enforcement of safe access zones was
taking so long. You gotta love Beth. Later that same day, Health Minister Jill
Hennessy proclaimed the date of enforcement of abortion safe access zones:
Monday 2 May 2016.

Hooray! Finally a set date. Two months earlier than the default date.
Certainty. We needed that. Only two more days of the 40-day vigil to go, and
then in a smidge under six weeks we would be protected by a safe access zone.
We were almost there.

But we were to get there with more muddles along the way. Like Lou's
6 April 2016 conversation with Inspector Gerry Cartwright: Gerry was still
waiting on DHHS; he had had a meeting with anti-choice parliamentarian
Bernie Finn; HOGPI had got a lawyer; Gerry was ready; there would be a big
anti-abortion protest march on 2 May that would end up outside the clinic;
he would have 120 police and eight horses. Lou believed that Gerry implied
that the clinic should not be open on that day.

Lou and I had no idea how this made any sense when surely the police
would be stopping the protest at the 150-metre mark given 2 May 2016 was
enforcement day. Lou headed off for a short holiday.

I do remember those times with Gerry Cartwright. I do remember those phone calls with you and the sense of frustration that this wasn't happening fast enough. Then the concern that there were going to be big events either on the day, or the day before, police enforcement. After all this work that we'd done to try to de-escalate and this was tactically going to backfire and actually fan the flame of this type of extremism.

Emily Howie (2020)

A couple of weeks later, on Friday 22 April 2016, Lou and I met with Gerry and with DHHS Deb Sudano. Gerry had been on the phone to the Christian Lobby's Paul McBride who had 'a lot of influence over HOGPI'. The large anti-abortion protest planned for 2 May was no longer going ahead, a number of barristers were now involved, and they planned to challenge the legislation before the end of May to mount a test case that would challenge the Victorian and Tasmanian safe access zones laws. Their initial plan for politicians opposing the legislation to be the ones to face arrest had been scuttled, just as Lou and others had expected. Their new plan was for two volunteers, with little to no assets, to breach the zone—they would face no risk of incurring legal costs.

Gerry said given there was no longer going to be a large protest, VicPol's original operational order, modelled on the annual anti-abortion March for the Babies and including horses and 120 police, would be scaled back. Police would be less visible but in close vicinity to the clinic, and with a designated well-trained and experienced arrest/prosecution team. Anyone breaching the safe access zone would be asked to leave, and if they did not obey they would be arrested and face court.

Perhaps all along, Gerry's goal in speaking with HOGPI, the Christian Lobby, the Catholic Church, Bernie Finn and others had been to gather information, minimise fall out, maximise a smooth implementation, avoid ugly extremists versus police scenes.

'This has taken too long, we all agree,' Gerry said.

At this point, Lou reminded Gerry that this was a medical premises and we did not want a circus, either on the 2 May, or during a planned breach and challenge to safe access zones. I too was far less inclined to believe the word of religious extremists. I wanted to be clear that if there were a march it would be stopped at the 150-metre mark, not outside the clinic.

'Yes,' Gerry reassured, 'The concern is not with HOGPI, but with the counter protests. We don't know the radical groups.'

To me, this was a surprising, if not nonsensical, comment from the Inspector. Gerry's 'counter protests' most likely referred to a pro-choice group called *Radical Women*. Over the years, *Radical Women* had organised a monthly Saturday protest to 'defend' the clinic by claiming the footpath outside the clinic for themselves and forcing the anti-abortion brigade across the road. Fiona Patten had joined them occasionally. *Radical Women* believed that taking direct action was the only way to deal with our problem, not by legally creating safe access zones. We had agreed to disagree. *Radical Women* would not be breaching an abortion safe access zone—they had too many other wrongs to right.

Gerry told us he had spoken to the Catholic University and the Melbourne Catholic Archdiocese (Archbishop Denis Hart and CEO Francis Moore) to 'allay their fears that if they speak up in the pulpit or hold a placard in church that they won't be charged'.

'That is offensive Gerry, and ridiculous,' said Lou calmly and clearly.

'I thought you would be advising them to encourage their congregation to abide by the law,' I said, less calmly.

'I can't influence them about what they tell their congregation,' said Gerry. 'The .01% we can't influence because they are zealots.'

Debbie explained that a letter from the Health Minister, with Q&A, was being sent out to all abortion providers known to DHHS.

I asked what 'direct evidence' of a breach looked like, and Lou and I emphasised the importance of patients not being involved in police proceedings. Gerry reassured us that for a breach to occur there needed to be direct evidence, a complaint, a statement by a de-identified person, security guard, MCC authorised officer or police, backed up by cameras, a statement from us... There would be no need for a patient to provide a statement or be in court.

Relief.

At the end of the meeting, Lou asked Gerry about the partner of a patient who had broken one of the extremists' props. Police had negotiated that the partner pay $20 for the privilege of breaking the prop.

'He did wilful damage,' replied Gerry. 'He should have been charged with wilful damage.'

'The victim becomes the perpetrator,' observed Lou.

'And that's why,' I said, 'we now have a new law.'

On Monday 2 May 2016, safe access zones were police operationalised without so much as a hiccup.

And then, they were gone. And it was so incredible! I remember speaking with you that day and, 'It worked!' It's an amazing story of how it went from so much struggle in it, but then it was such a perfect result.

Emily Howie (2020)

To some degree I always worry about these legal victories because how do you know they will work? Wasn't it possible that these people would keep on attending, breaking the law, causing nuisance in large unruly numbers? Counterbalancing that worrying possibility was an understanding that they only had small numbers of supporters who might not be prepared to do this kind of civil disobedience, and it was much easier to enforce the access zone compared with the legal and practical barriers of alternative causes of action like nuisance. But in truth, HOGPI had been arguably breaking the law all this time. Why wouldn't they just persist?

I remember you were confident the safe access zone law would work. You seemed to know what you wanted, even from the first day we met. That day we discussed the dream of access zones, and how this outcome could only be achieved through law reform rather than a court case. And here we are.

I remember nervously asking you whether it had made an impact, and preparing myself for disappointment, another example of the law failing you. But you were ebullient. You assured me the problem was fixed. This was so great to hear. I still remain astonished that it worked so well.

Lizzie O'Shea

I felt relief for the patients, the fact that they didn't have to come through the door and feel really bad about themselves for making a difficult decision. The staff in general breathed a sigh of relief because they felt safer. But the main thing was our patients didn't have to run that gauntlet anymore.

Also the way police enforced it and became very communicative and very helpful about it all. Whereas in time gone by it was a real fight to get the police to do anything, it turned out the opposite. It crossed over the religion barrier some of the police had, and they saw it as a law that had to be upheld, not all the religious rubbish.

JANICE NUGENT (2020)

It was outrageous that that was going on, and wonderful that it's come to an end. I remember at one point I spoke to you some time after the law had been passed and you told me it was quiet and peaceful outside the window and you could hear the birds chirping. I just felt so happy because there were points when we didn't think it was going to happen.

RACHEL BALL (2020)

Immediately after the safe access zone was enforced… it was like this massive revelation, wasn't it? We've taken the pressure off everyone… Once they were gone, everything changed to what I call a normal working environment. People could access without feeling threatened. Staff could roll up to work as a normal place of employment. It was an amazing change. I never had high blood pressure after that… One of the traders told me that what I'd done is actually changed the streetscape. The street now is a normal street.

DR LOUIS RUTMAN (2020)

I danced in the new, delicious normality of our street.

Thank you, Inspector Gerry Cartwright.

Achieving a legislative reform may seem like the final step: success, campaign over! But until police enforced the law, women were still being harmed. It ain't over 'til the fat lady sings, and the fat lady, of course, was a woman wanting to come into an abortion-providing clinic free from intimidation.

Police enforcement of safe access zones law was yet another unique context with its own spoken and unspoken rules, framework, processes, threats and risks that I struggled to understand. My impatience (surely not me!) for our patients to finally be protected no doubt made for a simplistic view of the speed with which police enforcement should proceed.

At the same time, probably every one of our societal structures was originally designed by entitled men for entitled men, and down the ages women having abortions had been both ignored and targeted mercilessly in equal measure. So perhaps it was only right for me to continue to assertively question and politely call out sexism and blinkered views about women, the harm, and what this reformative law was really all about. I was so grateful to be able to again call on the network of women activists and politicians who had worked so hard to reach this point, and who were prepared to speak up again to make sure that women did not slip down the list of priorities.

I had learnt from, and learnt to rely on, other women and men who understood how things worked and could strut their stuff within the unique parameters of whichever context was at play: media, the courts, Parliament, big bureacracies, police.

Sometimes problems are hard to solve and those responsible for doing so need space and time to act effectively. Other times, they need to be pushed, and a little impatience and indignation is warranted. Making this distinction is not always easy. Although you might think my years of experience meant I now had a finely tuned sense of judgement in such matters, I continued to find invaluable discussions with my family, Lou and experienced women like Janice, Susan, Beth Wilson, Rita Butera, Colleen Hartland, Em and Lizzie to test both my judgement and our reality.

It was to our credit, but perhaps mostly to Inspector Gerry Cartwright's credit, that we and the police maintained a good working relationship, and safe access zones were enforced with nary a hiccup.

PART FIVE

THE HIGH COURT CHALLENGE

CHAPTER 22

Crossing the Line: The Breach

August 2016–March 2018

There's a sense of anger in that as well. They couldn't accept that they didn't have the right to humiliate and harass, and they took it to the High Court. We know that if we flipped the genders on that, it would never have gone to the High Court.

FIONA PATTEN (2019)

Yes, it was a perfect result. Until the breach. The breach would finally set in train the inevitable challenge to the safe access zones law. The challenge would go all the way to the High Court of Australia. For the first time in its history, the highest court in the land would make a decision about abortion.

On 4 August 2016, three months after safe access zones laws came into force, an anti-abortion, God-fearing, welfare-dependent single mother of thirteen children (God will provide in the form of Australian taxpayers) crossed the line: she stepped into the safe access zone immediately outside the FCC to hand an anti-abortion pamphlet to a couple about to enter the clinic.

The breach was the deliberate and planned challenge to the safe access zones law that we, the police and the government had been anticipating: the religious right were crusaders with a keen sense of God-given entitlement, a track record of litigation, and had said they'd challenge the new law. Hence, the tedious drafting and negotiation of the bill, the clear and comprehensive parliamentary speeches, and the cautious implementation of the new law.

Since the enforcement of safe access zones in Victoria, Inspector Gerry Cartwright had continued to meet with anti-abortion groups and:

> *In July 2016 members of The Helpers contacted Inspector Cartwright and expressed an intent to breach the safety zone to test the legislation on 4 August 2016... The police thereby briefed some 20 officers to attend on 4 August 2016 to ensure calm... Inspector Cartwright asked her to desist from breaking the law. Within minutes, the appellant was seen by numerous police to enter the safe access zone, pamphlets in hand, and stand some five metres from the entrance to the clinic. The appellant was arrested after she approached a young couple entering the clinic, at approximately 10:30am.*
>
> EDWARDS [2020] VSC 49

The police officer who made the arrest was Senior Constable Alyce Edwards. Alyce's name would henceforth grace the various court proceedings and appeals as Ms Clubb, with the backing of powerful religious right allies, challenged the new law all the way to the High Court of Australia.

Thankfully, the breach and legal challenge proceedings could not change the peace and quiet that staff, patients, residents and others had now experienced for three months, since the safe access legislation had been enforced. Safe access zones remained in place. What could change our new peace and quiet would be a judgement upholding the Appellant; a judgement against the Victorian Government's safe access zones law; against us; against every Victorian abortion provider and every woman—well, except Ms Clubb. Law has to be made in a way that is compliant with the constitution. If a law is not, the court can strike it down, or place significant restrictions on the law's interpretation that may confine its purpose.

We loved our new boring and quiet. We loved our calm patients, staff and neighbours. It was too much to even consider that we might lose that, that everything we had worked for since Steve's murder could be upended.

Inspector Gerry Cartwright continued to diligently keep us updated. Apparently not content with the breach, Christian Lobby and anti-abortion groups planned a protest march for Saturday 8 October 2016 and intended proceeding into the 150-metre safe access zone. The group argued that the zone only applied when an abortion provider was open. We were open on Saturdays usually until early afternoon. Victoria police sought legal advice which tallied with the clear and immediate advice we received from the Human Rights Law Centre: the zones applied at all times.

Lou later received a kind phone call from Inspector Gerry Cartwright: An estimated 1,200–1,400 people marched, including Ms Clubb. Victoria Police allocated around 300 police. A standoff occurred at the 150-metre mark. Police were determined that the march was not to enter the safe access zone. The anti-choice mob backed down. Phew! Thank you Gerry Cartwright and Victoria Police.

I retired as a clinical psychologist at the end of June 2017. The weight of advocacy, clinical work and family responsibilities had become too heavy for my osteoporotic bones, and a brain that seemed to be accruing holes and aches too. But real retirement was not going to happen anytime soon:

I respectfully submit this statement [to the Magistrates Court] by way of an addendum to my previous Affidavit affirmed 21.07.2017 and Witness Statement… I understand that this statement is to clarify… whether the actions of Kathleen Clubb are those 'likely to cause anxiety or distress'… the matter before the court is about one protester, with a pamphlet, approaching a patient.

CONTEXT

… usually women attended the clinic at a time of unexpected pregnancy crisis… a time of high stress… anticipating medical procedures or treatment… a degree of nervousness… dealing with deeply personal and private matters… didn't want other people knowing… distressed about being singled out in public… by an anti-abortion protester. A constant refrain from patients was, 'This is none of their business' and 'It's a hard enough time

as it is'. Patients said this assertively, angrily, tearfully and/or shakily…

A significant proportion of women were more vulnerable because they were victims of violence or had a history of mental illness… for these women, an anti-abortion extremist coming unexpectedly into their physical and psychological space was particularly distressing…

Most women experienced an anti-abortion protester's approach as… threatening, offensive and a breach of that woman's privacy, dignity and sense of safety… 'not welcome', 'got in my face and my space', 'so inappropriate', 'they shouldn't be allowed to be there', 'offensive', 'upsetting', 'distressing', 'scared me' and/or various descriptors of the protester being mentally unbalanced… pamphlets and displays [were] 'disgusting', 'frightening', 'upsetting', 'not appropriate', 'they should keep their religion to themselves', 'what they are doing isn't being Christian', 'they shouldn't be allowed to hand out that stuff'. I have found most pamphlets offensive and peddling frightening factually untrue and medically incorrect views about abortion and contraception…

INDIVIDUAL DIFFERENCES

At one extreme, I observed a minority of women unaffected… shrugged off the encounter, or philosophically noted the protesters' right to protest.

At the other extreme, I observed a most concerning minority of women who became extremely upset, crying, angry, fearful, and struggled to calm… Some of these women reported more pain undergoing medical procedures… did not want to return for follow up or other treatment because they feared running into a protester… had been troubled by… their anti-abortion encounters over many days or weeks… a small number suffered a serious regression in their mental health.

Between these extremes were the majority of women who found the attentions of an anti-abortion extremist unsettling, experienced a moderate fight-flight response, and generally felt distressed, angry and/or anxious. Staff usually were able to calm and support these women and make them feel safe and respected…

The intrusion from an anti-abortion extremist approaching one-on-one is peculiarly provocative, anxiety-provoking and distressing.

RESEARCH EVIDENCE

… Alexandra Humphries, 'Anxiety in women having an abortion: The role of stigma and secrecy', provides a methodically rigorous account of 131 Fertility Control Clinic patients' experiences of the type of anti-abortion behaviour exhibited by Kathleen Clubb… indicates such behaviour is highly likely to cause distress and anxiety… reviews relevant stigma research indicating the association between emotional distress and stigmatising and discriminatory behaviour, like anti-abortion protest…

My understanding of the safe access zones legislation is that the behaviour by the anti-abortion protestor in this matter is exactly the type of harmful behaviour the legislation was designed to stop.

EXCERPTS FROM AFFIDAVIT

EDWARDS V CLUBB

21 JULY 2017

That affidavit, severely abridged here, reflected the gist of my unchallenged testimony to Magistrate Luisa Bazzini in Clubb v Edwards on 6 October 2017. The other three witnesses were police officers: Inspector Gerry Cartwright, Senior Constable Alyce Edwards and Sergeant Nicholas Moran. No evidence was led by Ms Clubb. The validity of the law had been decided earlier by Magistrate Bazzini: the law did not violate the implied freedom of political communication, and Ms Clubb's challenge to the safe access zone law failed [Magistrate Bazzini, Edwards v Clubb, Case No. G12298656, Reasons for Decision, 6 October 2017]. Magistrate Bazzini (23 December 2017) found the facts proven: '[Clubb] progressed to her actions defiantly and deliberately, despite those [police] warnings.' Ms Clubb was convicted and fined $5,000. The three grounds of her appeal to the Supreme Court of Victoria included that the Magistrate had erred in deciding that the law was constitutionally valid. Determination of those two grounds of appeal were removed to the High Court of Australia.

Anesti Petridis and Louis Andrews from the prosecution arm of the Victorian Government Solicitors Office (VGSO) had been conscientious and kind through meetings, phone calls and emails. Pivotal to how the case would eventually proceed in the High Court Challenge would be the hard work of the VGSO and Office of Public Prosecutions in the way the case was run in the Magistrates' Court case, Ms Bazzini's Reasons for Decision, and the learned, careful wording and construction of the Safe Access Zones Act itself.

The challenge to the safe access zones law would be the first time the High Court of Australia would make a decision about abortion. The only other time abortion had come before the High Court was 22 years earlier: Superclinics (Australia) and Another Pty Ltd v CES and Another [1996]. This sad and rather frightening civil case involved CES alleging that Superclinics had failed to detect her pregnancy despite repeated consultations with them. She wished to recover damages following the lost opportunity to terminate her pregnancy. Superclinics initially won in the NSW Supreme Court on the argument that any pregnancy termination would have been unlawful (CES and Another v Superclinics Australia Pty Ltd [1994] NSW LR). But the Court of Appeal in New South Wales (CES and Another v Superclinics (Australia) Pty Ltd and Others [1995] 38 NSWLR 47) came down in favour of CES. Superclinics Australia Pty Ltd then appealed to the High Court in 1996. Susan Kenny (1997) outlined the case in terms of its *amicus curiae* representations:

> *The Australian Catholic Health Care Association and the Australian Episcopal Conference of the Roman Catholic Church, represented by JA McCarthy QC and JG Santamaria QC, sought to be heard as amicus curiae in order to advance arguments which, it was submitted, would not otherwise be adequately laid before the Court... they wished 'to protect and to maintain a legal framework for their activities in which it is not a legal duty on providers of medical services to pregnant women to advise on the possibility of abortion.' In the result, the High Court decided, by statutory majority, to permit the applicants to appear as amicus curiae and file written submissions...*

As Jo Wainer (Wainer, 1997) subsequently described, the successful intervention of Catholic organisations:

> *Radically transformed the case from one of medical negligence to the test case on abortion... I became convinced that the Women's Electoral Lobby had to do everything possible to be present in the case, explicitly as a voice for women. Could we do it? We had no money, no campaign group on the*

issue, no legal team, no time. But we did have political smarts, media contacts, networks, information resources and friends.

The Abortion Providers' Federation applied successfully for *amicus curiae*, but the Women's Electoral Lobby (WEL) was scrambling. Jo Wainer managed to organise a barrister and a firm of solicitors who represented WEL *pro bono* (Wainer, 2004). Ultimately WEL did not apply, and 'the case itself did not proceed to a determination on the merits, a notice of discontinuance being filed on 11 October 1996' (Kenny, 1997).

Now, 22 years after that aborted High Court case, and for the first time in Australia's history, the High Court would hear a case about women's right to access abortion.

More generally I think this is a really interesting observation, in contrast to the United States, where a huge amount of advocacy has gone into avoiding the overturning of Roe v Wade, often at the expense of women's rights. Abortion is so restricted in so many American states now, it's been death by a thousand cuts. Here, the advocacy campaign was certainly exhausting, but it meant you had many friends in many places. The need for the law was clear. The decrim, then our case, demonstrated that it was a right and there needed to be legislation to protect it. That hard work really paid off, and it meant that the whole campaign wasn't focused on courts. Our situation shares both similarities and vast differences to the US, and while not wanting to be critical of colleagues in the US, I think our approach to campaigning and advocacy has meant that women's rights are less dependent on the opinions of courts, and better entrenched in a variety of ways.

Lizzie O'Shea

Our pro bono team regrouped: some faces were missing, like Lizzie and Em—say it isn't so! But new ones appeared. MB's Jacinta Lewin and Sam Habteslassie, and Claire Harris QC, with input from Sydney-based highflyer Brendan Lim, generously and expertly prepared FCC's *amicus curiae* submission to the High Court. I was beyond amazed when Claire said that she had learned friends 'lining up' to be involved. Monash Castan Centre for Human Rights' highly supportive submission was also accepted by the High Court as *amicus curie*.

Nuances in this High Court challenge meant that HRLC made a separate *amicus curiae* submission on their own behalf. Not having HRLC's Em Howie or Rachel Ball directly in our corner didn't feel quite right, but Adrianne Walter and Em were still there for us in every other way. I gradually understood the importance of legal nuance when you're playing in the highest court in the land.

One of the things that we have to be really careful about is that the HRLC has different modes in which it operates. One is to advocate for law reform and sometimes we do it with a client when we are acting on behalf of a client, and sometimes separately. Our first duty is always to the client. If we're in a client relationship we need to represent them to our best in their best interests. The concern was that if we acted in your best interests, we may actually be acting detrimentally to HRLC's stated positions on constitutional law.

There was a bit of a conflict there—and it was a pretty small one—but it was about whether or not the speech was political or not. We want to take an expansive view on the political nature of speech and that's because we are looking at developing the jurisprudence in a particular way. We would have argued that you should nonetheless succeed on that balancing of rights question.

But we could see that it was in your best interests to argue the other way: this doesn't have the protection of the implied freedom at all because it's not even political. In fact sometimes in our briefings we said there is a question about whether this is political speech given that they call themselves sidewalk counsellors, and by its nature it's a private discussion.

I haven't spoken to Adrianne [Walters, HRLC solicitor who led on the High Court] about this… but I think they're really difficult situations for me, especially because we had such a long and important relationship with the Fertility Control Clinic. There was no way that we wanted to leave you in a position where you weren't fully assisted and supported by us in every aspect of the case.

EMILY HOWIE (2020)

A spectacular facet of the High Court challenge was the calibre and experience of those leading the Victorian Government's case: Health Minister Jill

Hennessy, who had overseen the introduction of the safe access zones law, was now the Attorney General of Victoria; Kris Walker QC, who had represented FCC in our Supreme Court case, was now the Solicitor General for Victoria. The case could not be in better hands. I reckoned I could sit back and enjoy this.

Back on 15 October 2015, following a celebratory dinner with our counsel, I had told Kris Walker that it was 'sad that we probably won't cross paths much in the future. But you never know.' Well whaddaya know!

When the Directions Hearing of the High Court Challenge was to be heard at the Victorian Federal Court on 23 March 2018, I said to Janice, 'We should go, it's about the only court we haven't been in—ha!' We'd visited the Supreme Court for the murder trial and our case against MCC; Janice was witness in the obscenity case in both the Magistrates and County courts, and I also had witness attendances in the Supreme and Magistrates' courts and, in a previous life, the Children's Court. So we went.

What a surprise that turned out to be. I had been expecting to see Kris Walker QC appearing for the government, a silk appearing for the prosecution and the appellant's representative. I was expecting to see one High Court Justice. While there was one, quite brusque High Court Justice Michelle Gordon in command ensuring that the court book and the case would be well organised, the rest of the Court scene made us realise that this case had taken on a life of its own far beyond our little world at the clinic, and far beyond all the abortion providers in Victoria.

First, our unlearned eyes noted that there were far more legal eagles than we had expected. Second, we observed a number of TV screens hooked up to other legal representatives. Third, as the Directions Hearing proceeded, our unlearned ears heard that this most definitely was not just about Victorian abortion providers. Victoria was leading a High Court case in which Tasmania's safe access zones would be tested too, and Attorney Generals from around Australia wanted to be heard!

Janice and I looked at each other, and Janice's eyes seemed to say, 'Let me stop you right there. I don't have a clue!'

Tassie of course were there because they had the same law and so they had a parallel case going on. The other states will often come along to support

a state either because: they have similar legislation—like NSW by then;
they're thinking of it—as many were; or even just because, even if they're
not at all interested in the particular legislation, the states are general-
ly interested in preserving their ability to legislate, notwithstanding the
implied freedom of political communication. The states generally want to
limit the scope of the implied freedom and maximise their ability to legis-
late. So I wasn't surprised at all that everyone went along, partly because
so many states either had or were interested in that kind of legislation and
partly because of the bigger picture around the implied freedom.

Solicitor General Kris Walker (2020)

Her Honour Michelle Gordon zipped through proceedings in an efficient, if not officious, manner. No one was going to mess with this Justice. No typographical errors tolerated. No interruptions by learned counsel, 'there is a structure and there is a reason for it'. Core appeal book and what would be entered or omitted.

Learned counsel generally were all in agreement, but Mr Brohier for Ms Clubb wanted exhibits 12, 14, and some other in as 'part of the evidence from the constitutional facts that set up some dispute between the position of Doctors Allanson and Goldstone...' Blimey, that was me. And Marie Stopes' Philip Goldstone. I looked at Janice as if I'd finally been caught by the Principal for smuggling that Marsala into the Year Twelve camp, and I was the school captain then, ugh!

Ms Walker: Your Honour, we did not understand there to be any factual dispute.

Her Honour: Well, if there is a factual dispute then we are in difficult territory.

Ms Walker: Indeed, and Ms Clubb's response, your Honour, expressly stated there are no factual issues in contention between the parties and, in my submission, it is not necessary—certainly not necessary for this Court to resolve any factual disputes, and that affidavit of Mr Grant is not necessary for the Full Court.

Mr Brouhier: I will not press that, your Honour.

I had no idea. But, phew!

Her Honour indicated that 'the Victorian proceeding would be the lead proceeding... a complete set of submissions in the Victorian matter plus additional arguments in the Hobart matter rather than repetition.'

Her Honour Gordon perhaps had a plane to catch, umpteen other cases to hear, a decision to write, she was not mucking around. The Directions Hearing was all over in twenty minutes.

Our case had gone from ignored and scorned to being huge in legal circles and elsewhere; from one clinic, us, trying to protect our patients, to a human rights case with potentially huge implications for women and health providers throughout Australia. We were in amongst a heady kaleidoscope of abortion history: women and abortion provision hostage to criminals and political and police corruption; abortion campaigner Bert Wainer setting up the Fertility Control Clinic in 1972; Federal Police raids of the FCC and staff homes; storming of the FCC by anti-abortion protesters; harassment, assaults and threats to FCC patients, staff and others by anti-abortion extremists; the 2001 murder of our security guard, Steve Rogers; the 2002 Supreme Court trial finding the killer guilty; the 2008 decriminalisation of abortion; taking MCC to the Supreme Court in 2015; the 2015 abortion safe access zones legislation; Kathleen Clubb being found guilty of breaching the new law and appealing successfully to the Supreme Court for leave to appeal to the highest court in the land; a visit to the Melbourne Federal Court for a directions hearing with High Court Justice Gordon; and finally off to the High Court of Australia we go.

And we were so ready. It had been 17 years of refining our language and arguments, laying the groundwork, building a team, finding champions who fought for law reform and ensured robust legislation with clear underpinnings. Now they would finally champion safe access zone law in the High Court. Our 'baby'—safety, respect and privacy for women accessing abortion services—had been gradually shared around and nurtured by so many, until it now belonged to every champion and every woman.

Despite all the legal proceedings, work, media and hoo-ha of the legal challenge, by the time safe access zones reached the High Court in October 2018, we had experienced more than two blissful years of not being targeted for accessing, or working at, a women's health clinic. Two blissful years of patients being, well, normal patients. Two blissful years where Lou and June's blood pressure had returned to normal, other staff had noted positive changes to their health, and the care of our patients no longer occurred in the context of a disturbing and almighty sense of injustice, anxiety and distress. We did not want to go back to how things were before. I didn't think I could survive it. At times I felt done, *done and dusted*. I could not go through all this again. Having the High Court send us back to the bad old days was unthinkable. So we didn't think of it.

Well, only sometimes, in the dead of night.

Putting one foot in front of the other sometimes trips you up or feels wearily slow. But, if you have the right people by your side, from small steps come great strides.

When our work as advocates and medical service providers eventually attracted the attention of the highest court in the land, we could not have been more ready. Not only had we accumulated years of experience working with advocates and lawyers but we had gathered countless friends along the way. We had junked the shame and disappointment that had characterised public discussions about abortion and instead put front and centre the importance of trusting women. We had defined the debate on our own terms. Harassment of women seeking an abortion was no longer a problem that everyone could turn away from. Our campaign demanded respect for women and their right to autonomously determine their own destiny. This issue could no longer be dismissed as some tricky conflict about freedom of speech. It squarely raised the right of women to seek lawful medical services free from harassment.

CHAPTER 23

Love at First Sight: The High Court of Australia

9–11 October 2018

If the High Court considers the case there will be either a bench of five judges, or, if it's a very important case, a bench of seven judges.

JOHN DIXON (2019)

I had been to Canberra just four times in my life: my first aeroplane flight for a day trip in Grade Five or Six—mid-1960s Strathmore Primary School was ahead of its time; a Strathmore High School camp; Intervarsity tennis with Melbourne Uni; and tagging along with advocate Dr Leslie Cannold to speak at a breakfast meeting around Natasha's Transparency in Pregnancy Advertising Bill. This trip to Canberra was way more fun than any of those. It turned out to be one of the best times of my life. No, really.

I had never travelled with Lou before, well, nothing but the occasional taxi. We set off to the ACT together. Lou Rutman is a seasoned international traveller, and I've seen my share of the world, but turns out both of us tend to leave booking details and directions to our spouses. Neither Lou nor I were great with geographical awareness, even in little, orderly Canberra. From my hotel window I had a beautiful view across Lake Burley Griffin to Parliament House, but if you'd asked me which way to the airport or to the High Court, I wouldn't have a clue. I expect Lou was a smidge better than me. But, hey, a trip to the High Court of Australia had not really been one Lou and I ever thought we'd be navigating, and there was definitely a bamboozling yet exciting factor at play for us. So, we jumped in taxis and ended up wherever we were meant to be: High Court, restaurants, hotel, airport, easy.

On the morning of 9 October 2018, my first impression of the High Court of Australia was brutal. Well, *Brutalist* was its style genre I assumed. Like a guard of honour, an expansive avenue, lawn and water canal all led to the concrete monolith. Glorious. Everything shouted, this is huge, this is important, this is really something. And it was. I was thrilled to be there. I was excited, nervous, and freezing. That Canberra wind raced up that avenue and cut right through us. Brutal all right.

I missed Em and Lizzie. It didn't feel right that they weren't here to see this thing through to the bitter end in this bitter cold.

'Give me your coat, Susie.'

'Really?'

In some sort of defiant stance that I was now retired and so could dress more casually, I had decided against a suited jacket and instead wore a smart, blonde puffer coat that makes you feel like you're snug in a sleeping bag. I had not intended taking it off.

'Give it here, Susie.'

Really? MB Special Counsel Jacinta Lewin was not someone to question.

I unzipped my coat and handed it over. No jacket! I felt exposed, freezing and disrespectfully unprofessional. I had envisaged the press conference being with us seated at a table, indoors. My glasses were transition and darkened outdoor to become sunglasses. What was I thinking? My casual light merino top wrinkled in weird places looking ill fitted. Aargh!

'No, you're a rock star, Susie,' Jacinta grinned.

Yeah, right. Retired or not, I was never going to do that again. In fact I better not do any of that ever again. All those years. Never again. This was it, let's get this media high jinks out of the way.

Our bags and coats were thrust on a delightful HRLC lawyer seconded from a top tier law firm. To see him lumbered with handbags and clothing, while we women took centre stage, was so clearly a reversal of persisting gender roles that we were all a little amused. Having relinquished our baggage, HRLC Adrianne Walters, MB Jacinta Lewin, and Castan Centre for Human Rights Tania Penovich and I stood shivering in front of cameras and journalists. We were each to speak briefly in turn before taking questions.

It had crossed my mind that perhaps I should not be speaking to the media before the case was heard. And I certainly did not want to say anything that might offend the Court or the Justices. But I was surrounded by legal eagles who knew what I was going to say. Yesterday, I had phoned in to an MB meeting where we all ran through our media statements. All these women were not only lawyers but consummate media performers too. They knew their stuff and how to deliver.

After I delivered mine over the phone, there was dead silence on the other end. I had no faces to give me any cues either. Crikey, mine was that bad? Maybe they were bored? Shocked? Disappointed? Already working on other matters? A split second later I heard compliments and laughter, whatever that actually meant. It really didn't matter. It was what I wanted to say and I was going to say it no matter what. I was going to take my full two minutes in the limelight and say my piece. This was, hopefully, the culmination of more than 26 years at the FCC for me, and dozens more years for Lou, Janice, Susan and June. I'd take my full two minutes, and even a smidge more if I needed to, thank you very much.

So I did:

Safe access zones work when nothing else has. Before safe access zones, women accessing reproductive health services—including abortion and other deeply personal, private and often urgent health matters—were subject to harassment and intimidation from a group of anti-abortion and anti-contraception extremists on a public footpath outside the clinic.

Following the murder of our security guard, Steve Rogers, in July 2001, nothing changed.

We lobbied state government for safe access zones. Nothing changed.

We were told that abortion needed to be decriminalised first. In 2008 abortion was decriminalised. Nothing changed.

Police secured convictions for murder, assault, threat to kill and obscenity. Nothing changed.

In 2015 in the Supreme Court, the Fertility Control Clinic sued Melbourne City Council for failing to remedy this noxious nuisance. Nothing changed.

But, off the back of that case, our parliamentarians acknowledged that this abuse of women was falling through the cracks of our legal system. Safe access zones became law. They were enforced in May 2016. And everything changed. Overnight. Dramatically. For the better.

The clinic became a normal health service for patients and staff. Women no longer arrived distressed. Staff felt safe. Residents and visitors reclaimed the streetscape. Most importantly, as a society we sent a strong message about the respect and care women deserve.

Safe Access Zones Work.

Amen.

Of course I didn't say 'Amen', but I rather liked that my words had a repetitive hymnal style like a Catholic Mass. A communal vibe where everyone could join congregates' echoing response: *Nothing changed*, rather than, *Lord have mercy*. And finally the reclamation of women's autonomy: *Everything changed*.

Let us pray: that the High Court keeps it that way.

As usual I was impressed with how beautifully Adrianne, Jacinta and Tania spoke. Ah, wonderful solidarity in a cause. Nonetheless I was relieved to have the media scrum duties out of the way. Let's get our coats on and get this show on the road. We entered the main High Court entrance, through security, upstairs, check-in staff secured our phones in lockers, and towering, art deco style doors beckoned. Inside we were greeted by a space more like a cathedral or grand theatre than a court. Rows of audience seats in the stalls and an upstairs gallery behind. An orchestra pit of Attorney- and Solicitor- Generals and their legal teams from around Australia tuning up at their tables. The visit Janice and I paid to the Federal Court in Melbourne for the Directions Hearing some five months earlier had nothing on this. There were so many lawyers that I looked to the soaring ceiling to see if any had been relegated to swinging from chandeliers—no chandeliers here.

Finally, framed by a grand wood panel wall stretching up to heaven like the pipes of a cathedral organ, the stage was set with the empty High Court Bench spanning wing to wing.

Amongst all this legal glamour were the likes of me and Lou Rutman sitting in the public gallery of the High Court of Australia, wondering how the hell we ended up here. I looked at Lou and he looked at me and I said, 'I think you and I caused all this. How did it all happen, Lou?'

Lou's eyes were moist and he shook his head. A year later, Lou answered that question this way:

I felt that the High Court was a little overwhelming for me: I can't actually believe that little Louis Rutman is sitting here in the High Court with judges and AGs and all these assistants and amazingly important people and they're all talking about my clinic. People phoned me and said, it's amazing.

We achieved what we were trying to achieve. We got the 150. I thought all along that the best-case scenario was to get them to go across the road. It was their legal right to appeal—getting someone to break the law. I was a little stunned that they got to the High Court. I told the guy you're dreamin'. Pretty amazing actually.

Dr Louis Rutman (2019)

Of course Lou and I hadn't caused all this. A collective of hard-working, smart women, and men prepared to champion women, had brought us to this place. Plus, a welfare-dependent single mother of thirteen children, backed by The Christian Lobby, who had appealed all the way to the High Court: Clubb v Edwards, [2019] HCA 11 M46/2018. The case was being heard with Tasmania's challenge, Preston v Avery H2/2018, with the same appellant legal team representing both.

The High Court hearing was as different as it could be from Gideon Haigh's (2008) observation of the 1970 *Board of Inquiry into Allegation of Police Corruption in Connection with Illegal Abortion Practices in the State of Victoria* headed by Commissioner William Kay QC (aka The Kay Inquiry) where:

A mainly female predicament was argued over in an exclusively male forum. There was not a single woman at the overpopulated bar table, and the women who constituted just twenty-one of the inquiry's 140 witnesses were left isolated and exposed.

HAIGH (2008, P. 198)

At the October 2018 High Court hearing, women smashed it! Not only did the High Court Bench include female Justices Virginia Bell, Michelle Gordon, and the first female High Court Chief Justice, Susan Kiefel, but Victoria's case was led by women: Public Prosecutions' Fran Dalziel QC (now a County Court judge) and her junior Joanna Davidson appeared for the prosecution; and the Victorian Attorney General Jill Hennessy, who intervened, was represented by Solicitor General Kristen Walker QC and her juniors from the Victorian Bar Kathleen Foley and Simona Gory. At the table behind the Attorney's representatives were solicitors from the Victorian Government Solicitors' Office (VGSO), Alison O'Brien, Dianna Gleeson, and Anesti Petridis, while Kris' researcher Minh-Quan Nguyen worked hard behind the scenes. Yay, Victoria!

There was but a smattering of women in other teams representing other Attorney Generals from around the country. But hey, the rest of Australia, time to catch up with gender balance. The all-male team of Mr G O'L Reynolds SC, with Mr F C Brohier and Mr D P Hume, represented the appellant, Ms Clubb.

Having three women on the bench mattered. Victoria having a woman present the prosecution case, mattered. Having a woman present the case for the Attorney General, mattered. I was beyond excited to witness this legal history where women were centre stage. The most learned and powerful women and men in the land took a stand for women. I could never have imagined such a magnificent pay off after all the years of frustration.

The Justices were sophisticated and down-to-earth in appreciating how the issues before the court actually played out for real women facing urgent reproductive health decisions. They expressed respect and concern for women and for abortion-providing staff.

The women Justices demonstrated a ready capacity to keep the experience of women accessing abortion at the centre of their questions and reasoning. So did Justice Keane. Other male Justices generally brought a different frame and differently slanted questions and reasoning. But as the hearing progressed, those Justices perhaps benefitted from the divine feminine wisdom on display to keep women's experience and human rights at the centre. Anti-women nonsense was called out. Politicising the issue of abortion was out of bounds. This was about women accessing a legal health service and that was not up for debate.

Basically everyone was on board with the validity of the law, the gravity of the problem, and the fact that this was a really appropriate response to the problem.

I wasn't sure that that would be the case. Going in, you don't really know what different Justices' views on abortion might be, and although in a sense that shouldn't affect the way the court approaches the hearing or the case, I suspect if there was someone vehemently opposed to abortion they might have taken quite a different approach.

So I literally didn't know. Maybe some of the Justices did have that view, but you certainly didn't get any feeling of that at all. And I think the court was very careful to avoid talking about the merits or otherwise of abortion: there's a lawful medical process and that's a matter for the Parliament; you can't stop people going in and harass them.

SOLICITOR GENERAL KRIS WALKER QC (2020)

From our seats in the stalls, the High Court Justices' ballet with all learned counsel was wonderful to behold. At one extreme were sharp admonishing jetes demanding better from learned counsel, and occasional eye rolls from Chief Justice Kiefel. Ms Clubb's representative, Mr Reynolds, was the unfortunate, but deserved, recipient of these when he meandered into sexist put downs and anti-women mischief, legal kerfuffle rather than sense, and interrupted the women Justices. Other learned counsel benefitted from the Justices' beautifully executed chasses out of legal conundrums and towards clarity. In effect, their Honours pirouetted gracefully around, about and through the issues and the players.

It was interesting to note a generational contrast too: While six of the seven Justices sat straight-backed at the bench, lined up neatly along the ballet barre as it were, His Honour James Edelman, the youngest by a decade, slouched and sprawled like the new cool kid on the block. But neat or relaxed, the Justices minds were exquisitely focused on the legal dance.

The transcript excerpts below follow the chronological order of the hearing. On the first day, 9 October 2018, centre stage was taken first by the Appellant Mr Reynolds SC for Ms Clubb, then by Ms Fran Dalziel for the First Respondent, the Director of Public Prosecutions Victoria, and finally by The Solicitor-General for the State of Victoria Ms Kris Walker QC appearing for the second respondent, the Victorian Attorney-General, Jill Hennessy.

Although I could not appreciate all of the legal arguments (what could Justice Nettle possibly mean by 'Either its *mens rea* or it is *He Kaw The*, is it not?'), the excerpts from the High Court transcripts over the course of the two days give an inkling of what was on display. I am guilty of cherry-picking some of the juiciest to my own taste and reflecting the fact that I am a fan of Solicitor-General Kris Walker. I am not alone on that score. Some of my own internal commentary at the time is included in parentheses. I continue to separate sections using the coat hanger symbol—a reminder of what is at stake when women are denied the option of abortion.

> *Mr Reynolds (R): First up, a small apology... our team had lost all our baggage until about yesterday afternoon so we are a little bit...*
>
> *Chief Justice Kiefel: I heard about your misfortune, Mr Reynolds.*
>
> *R: We are a little bit ragged...*
>
> *[Me: I guess God rather let them down this time.]*

Mr Reynolds proffered arguments about why 'protesting' at the particular location—outside abortion providing clinics—was key to an effective protest. The Justices' responses to his argument were at times amusing and perhaps also rooted in contrasting legal and gender perspectives:

> *Justice Nettle: Mr Reynolds, in Brown, Dr Brown gave sworn, uncontradicted evidence that protesting next to the chainsaw so as to attract the television cameras was critical to the effect of the protest. There is no evidence of that kind in this case, is there, or is there?*

R: No… a proscription on anti-apartheid protests at sporting contests where the South Africans were playing would have had an enormous effect on the ability of the protesters to use their, as your Honour Justice Gageler…

Nettle J: That is because everyone liked watching rugby. No one likes watching abortion clinics. It is a bit different…

[Touché, I smile.]

Bell J: My own recollection is not that protestors got attention because they were standing outside sporting facilities. They got attention when they ran onto the field and were arrested…

Mr Reynolds, it may be one thing to say that it is notorious that protestors have sought to attending near the vicinity of abortion facilities to make their views known. It is rather less clear, and particularly it does not seem to me to be supported by the evidence in this case, that that has been with a view to attracting public attention to the broader debate…

So that one understands that people of strong, generally speaking, religious convictions seek to be near facilities where women are going to go to terminate a pregnancy because of a conscientiously held belief that it is part of their mission to dissuade them from proceeding with that action. That is very distinct from the value of an onsite protest as a means of getting public attention… as Justice Nettle says, it is one thing in the Brown Case, but the evidence here simply seems to me not to support the broader proposition you make.

R: … but the second thing is, as I said a while ago…

Bell J: The point Mr Reynolds, that I am raising with you, is the absence of any foundation for the inference to be drawn that there is a particular utility from the point of view of a person seeking to persuade electors on an issue of significance such as this one about being within 150 metres of a facility.

R: Again, I would be repeating myself, your Honour.

Bell J: Yes.

As expected, considerable time was spent around the relative burden the safe access zone law may or may not place on other human rights:

Kiefel CJ: Even if you are in a position to call right of protest or demonstration a right, it is always subject to legislative restriction and that is what we are concerned with here, not the concept of rights. We are concerned with whether or not the legislation burdens that freedom.

R: ... Now, I have to lay the ground and that is what I am doing for that submission.

Kiefel CJ: There is no common law right of expression of political matters. It is regarded in the authorities since then and certainly since Lange as a freedom, which is not the same as a personal right. What we are concerned with is the limits of legislative power in relation to freedom...

R: I will deal first with privacy... (i) the nature and extent of the burden is a constant—your Honours know what I say about that. As for (ii), we submit that the extent of that as a mischief and, for that matter, its scope, have not been established by evidence; (iii) that the law does not... advance a privacy purpose; (iv) that it is not tailored to that purpose... (v) that it goes way further than is reasonably necessary to advance that purpose; and (vi) that other laws... deal with this issue of privacy and advance that purpose; (vii)... it is unclear what the precise mischief is, or privacy mischief. We suggest that that itself suggests that it is not terribly important.

[It is increasingly clear that nothing much about women seems terribly important to Mr Reynolds' case.]

As a now retired, but previously registered Clinical Psychologist who could only practice after a lengthy education, attending mandated ongoing professional development and supervision, and abiding by a raft of professional, legal and ethical obligations, the anti-abortion concept of 'sidewalk counselling' was laughable and dangerous: 'Counselling' by an untrained person with a captive audience, without informed consent, in a public place without privacy or safety, and where the 'client' was not actually the woman bailed up but was in fact the pregnancy/embryo/foetus. The whole 'sidewalk counselling' construction was not only ridiculous but rather undermined arguing that HOGPI's actions were political in nature:

> *Justice Gageler: Mr Reynolds do you persist with the argument that you have put in writing to the effect that what the Americans call sidewalk counselling is, itself, political communication?*
>
> *R: Is itself political communication? It may be.*
>
> *Gordon J: Can you just explain to me why you say may be?*
>
> *R: Because it all depends on the content of the counselling… The other thing I want to move to—and I am in danger of slipping behind in time when I am trying to deal with that…*
>
> *Kiefel J: I am sure you can remedy that, Mr Reynolds.*
>
> *R: What, by sitting down, your Honour?*
>
> *[Me: Exactly what the Chief Justice meant.]*
>
> *R: … abortion is a topic of high political controversy. The issue of legalisation, the extent of legalisation…*
>
> *Kiefel CJ: Except that it has been settled by the legislation. That is not to say that people continue to hold their views, but when you say it is not a current controversy, is it legislation has dealt with it?*

In 2020 when Em and I asked Kris about the importance of the Victorian 2008 abortion decriminalisation on the way the Justices perceived the case, Kris had this to say:

> *If abortion was still criminal then I think it would have been much harder to say because our whole argument was, yes of course it is about abortion. The clinic didn't just offer abortions, so you're actually harassing people going in for a variety of medical procedures, but in the end one can just talk about abortion as a lawful medical procedure. It is something special, in the sense of different, because we also focused on the vulnerability of women going in who may or may not have decided at that point of course; they might not be going in for an abortion but getting advice about their options.*
>
> *So there certainly was some emphasis on the particular nature of the procedure, but we were able to use the phrase 'lawful medical procedure' and say: Parliament has decided that this is lawful and if people want to go in to get this lawful medical procedure then they are entitled to do so.*

Until you get proper decriminalisation, you don't get safe access protection. I suppose if you imagine, okay, what if it had been the NSW safe access law that was challenged and you still had criminalisation? But it's not a complete criminalisation, it is lawful to get an abortion in certain circumstances and not in others. So you couldn't say that protesters were targeting people who were doing something unlawful.

But I do think Victoria's abortion decriminalisation definitely strengthened our case. If it had remained unlawful in some circumstances, that would have been used by the other side. Potentially it wouldn't have won the case, but nonetheless they would have had that as a tool in their arsenal to say why it's okay for people to protest against criminal activity. But there's no argument that anything criminal is going on. It gives you a good starting point that what is going on is entirely lawful, and then what is going on outside is to try to stop people accessing a medical service.

SG KRIS WALKER QC

The Justices refused to allow anyone to stand on the toes of women's dignity:

Kiefel CJ: ... How do you say respecting the dignity of persons impedes the functioning of the system of representative government? I would have thought it enhances it.

R: This is, in a sense, an old chestnut. It is inherent, we submit, in political speech that either groups or individuals will be criticised and otherwise the subject of comment, with a resultant loss of dignity. It is part and parcel of what is a sine qua non of political speech... For example, criticism of bankers or of men by feminists...

[Me: R might be feeling the feminist heat himself.]

Kiefel CJ: But that is to say no more than speech should be free. That is not really addressing the question that Lange poses: how is this purpose inconsistent with or incompatible with notions of representative government?

R: Well because so much of political speech must have the quality of affecting the dignity of any number of people potentially...

Keane J: Mr Reynolds, is there any case which deals with such a direct attack on individuals who are targeted in a way that they can be targeted by the kind of site-specific protests you talk about? Are there any cases which deal with that and which say that attempts, for example, to shame particular individuals, seen to use particular facilities, is not apt to protect their dignity in a way that is consistent with the implied freedom?

[Me: Wow, Justice Keane totally gets what women have been copping.]

R: Your Honour, for what it is worth, I cannot think of a case.

Keane J: It would be unusual, would it not, the notion—or it would be counterintuitive, perhaps—the notion that legislation that is intended to protect the privacy and the dignity of individuals against shaming behaviour—it would be counterintuitive to think that that was inconsistent with the implied freedom because the very basis of the implied freedom is the dignity of the Australian people. Insofar as the people who are being shamed are members of the sovereign people, legislation that protects their dignity is surely compatible with it.

[Me: Yay, Justice Keane. And let there be no doubt that women are people.]

Gordon J: Justice Nettle in Brown described it as a distinction being drawn between the implied freedom and this idea that you can 'force an unwanted message on those who did not wish to hear it'.

[Me: Slam dunk.]

Gordon J:… Here, you have somebody seeking to do something which is lawful, i.e. entering a premise which provides a service, a medical service. So, is there a distinction to be drawn in that situation between something which is a burden on the implied freedom of political communication and something where you are thrusting an unwanted message on someone seeking to enter that premise?

R: We have just jumped ahead to this dignity purpose, and it is not dissimilar to the notion of the incompatibility of hurt feelings which we also submit is not compatible…

[Me: 'Hurt feelings'? How offensive and belittling of women's experience of being targeted.]

Gordon J: What about their right to access medical services or their ability to access medical services? The purpose of that is to permit free access to access these services. Is the restriction then incompatible—the purpose incompatible?

[Me: Perfect.]

⌒

Mr Reynolds argued that the legislation was unnecessary because other extant laws could address the problem:

R: Your Honour, I will need to backtrack because we are into riot, affray, breaches of the peace.

    Keane J: No, no. Your argument is that this provision (b) is not capable of serving a purpose relating to protecting the physical safety of person, insofar as it is apt to prevent provocative behaviour that may lead to a fracas, why is it not apt to serve that purpose?...

    R: Disturbing the peace—which is number 7 on our list... threatening words—this is number 32—which would cover that offensive behaviour which is also there, number 33.

    Justice Gordon: Well, if you are right, Mr Reynolds, then this additional provision is not going to impose much burden, is it?

[Me: Justice Gordon is great.]

    R: I submit there is a very big burden because it is a ban on protest at these important sites on this important topic, a ban, as I have said, on peaceful protest...

    Justice Bell: ...[(b)]'s function might be seen in terms of a context of protection of safety, privacy and dignity. To be targeted in circumstances where women attending an abortion clinic are in a vulnerable state, require advice and treatment within a confined period of time and if the presence, for example, of a large number of people standing holding pictures dramatically portraying foetuses at various stages of development, is confronting that might deter women from entering the facility and obtaining advice and any treatment that they reasonably require and that bears on their physical safety, on their psychological safety, to say nothing of their privacy and dignity.

[My admiration for the Justices keeps growing.]

R: ... we submit... that that is not a mischief which is established by evidence and that is what comes up in proportionality.

Gordon J: ... is it not the position that it seeks to enable a woman to enter a facility undeterred in order to achieve and receive whatever treatment and advice she needs. Absent the provision, she is deterred from entering the facility to achieve and receive that which she is lawfully entitled to receive.

[Me: Woo hoo! If I wasn't sitting here in the High Court, I'd be cheering.]

A lunch break was taken at 12:47 and the hearing resumed at 2:17pm. How I wished that Mr Reynolds had finished.

R: ... The next purpose I am dealing with is this purpose of respecting dignity... of the relevant persons. I did not say it before, but perhaps I should have, that we are dealing here not with women—just women looking to have abortions...

[My head is exploding. 'We are dealing here not with women, *just women looking to have abortions'*—like they are some inferior breed. A non-woman, non-person perhaps. Given the subject matter it was extraordinary how infrequently Mr Reynolds spoke the words 'women' or 'woman' at all. He also used words such as 'hurt feelings' to describe the impact of HOGPI on women. At times sitting next to Lou in the nation's highest court, fury roiled up in me. Until the Justices inevitably and decisively called out Mr Reynolds. Then I cheered inside.]

R: ... Reliance is placed by Victoria on two affidavits by Ms Allanson, first of all.

[Me: That old put down of using 'Ms' instead of 'Dr'.]

Chief Justice Kiefel: I think it is Dr Allanson, is it not?

[Me: Wow, the Chief Justice is onto it like a shot. Makes me wonder how many put downs Chief Justice Mary Kiefel has copped as a successful woman in legal circles; and how many times she has called out this classic put down of female witnesses. Thank you, Justice Kiefel.]

R: Yes, I think she has a PhD but I do not think she is a medical practitioner, she is a psychologist...

[Me: How rude. He should be thanking her Honour politely and remedying his mistake, not continuing with a put down that isn't actually an insult.]

R: ... and also by a medical doctor, Dr Goldstone... That patients may delay their treatment as a result of protesters... They do not provide any data for this... It does not rise much above mere assertion.

Nettle J: Mr Reynolds, was this material the subject of cross-examination in the Magistrates Court?

R: This is the Victorian material. No it was not.

J Nettle: So it is uncontradicted?

R: It is in that sense unchallenged by cross-examination, yes.

[Me: Thank you Justice Nettle. Similar to our Supreme Court action against MCC, all our evidence to the Magistrates Court was accepted unchallenged. All that evidence was accepted as true. That is powerful. Lizzie reckons that our opponents chose not to question my integrity or my evidence in front of a judge because they knew that cross-examining me would play badly for them. But now at the High Court, the appellant has used 'smart' little comments to twist in Clubb's favour the consequences of that choice. No matter, Mr Reynold's old word game won't get past these Justices.]

R: ... This evidence does not distinguish between what I have been calling peaceful protest on the one hand and other forms of protest on the other...

Gordon, J: ... the relevant [Tasmanian] Minister described, I think, that there was nothing peaceful about shaming complete strangers about a private decision that they made about their bodies. It may well be that when you are dealing with this distinction between peaceful and non-peaceful that you may have a different view of what constitutes a peaceful protest.

[Me: Nailed it!]

R: ... both these doctors have an affiliation with clinics that are, to put it bluntly, abortion clinics.

[Me: It must be so hard for him to say the word 'abortion' when that is a perfectly respectable description, thank you very much.]

R: To that extent that affiliation may impact upon how much weight ought to be given to their opinions...

[Me: Oh good grief. If it were any other health issue, e.g. coronary care, obstetrics, endoscopy, you name it, we would be considered experts in the field whose opinions would be sought out, valued and respected.]

R: ... as best I can understand it, it is that protest or perhaps peaceful protest causes women to be deterred... at page 10 to 11 of Dr Turner's report who discusses... the possible benefits that may accrue if there is deterrence of a woman from having an abortion. This is one of the points that I said...

Bell J: Mr Reynolds, is that a submission you rely on?

[Me: Wacko the diddlio. Justice Bell is onto it like a shot.]

R: Your Honour... I said there were two or three points where...

Bell J: And this is one of the two or three?

R: Yes.

Bell J: Do you rely on it?

R: I have to put at least...

Kiefel CJ: You do not have to put it at all.

R: I am sorry your Honour? (Said as a question.)

Kiefel CJ: You do not have to put it at all. You are senior counsel and you should be putting arguments which are properly addressed to the legal issues, not the opinion of someone who holds a personal, ethical, moral position. You do not adopt that position, Mr Reynolds, and you know that.

[I'm in love!]

Previously I mentioned the contrasting views about what constituted reliable and valid evidence from a legal perspective (specific first hand witness accounts) versus from a psychologist/scientist perspective (rigorous research evidence). Allie Humphries' research was an example of the latter. Especially given that her research was carried out at the FCC, I had included it in both my FCC v MCC Supreme Court affidavit, but also in my affidavit for the court case prosecuting the safe access zone breach. The breach prosecution team advised to also include other reputable research journal articles with which I was familiar. Argument before the High Court Justices included the Appellant's attempt to submit an anti-abortion opinion article not included in the lower court legal proceedings. The authors of this 'Turner paper' used tactics similar to those used by climate change deniers, Big Tobacco, anti-vaxxers, COVID deniers/conspiracists and so on: throwing around opinion and lies; drawing unfounded conclusions from methodologically questionable 'research' published in journals established by anti-abortion crusaders to propel the anti-abortion cause; and distorting and criticising research properly carried out and peer reviewed. Such tactics have been roundly criticised by the World Health Organisation amongst others.

R: ... and the article by I think Dr Foster and others, which I understand to be the only peer review article that your Honours have.

Gageler J: What about the Cozzarelli article that you took us to before? Is that not peer reviewed?

[Me: Yes it is, thank you Justice Gageler. Catherine Cozzarelli and Brenda Major have researched and published widely in some of the most prestigious international psychology journals.]

R: I do not think so, your Honour. I will have that checked... Cozzarelli and Major found that women experienced negative emotions upon interacting with abortion protesters at one hour post interaction, but these effects were not present during follow-up data collection two years later.

[Me: R just shot himself in the foot again.]

R: In other words the negative effects of protester interaction did not extend beyond the short term...

Gageler: The short term being two years?

[Me: Thank you Justice Gageler. R then embarked on cherry picking results, and he was clearly not well-schooled in statistical analysis.]

R: Some evidence of course of an adverse emotional reaction or a period in some instances, but we submit that that is in the equation the reasonable proportionality equation, that is, not of substantial importance.'

[I think he means, again: women are not of substantial importance.]

R: The other important difference [in Victorian legislation compared with Tasmanian] of course is the expression, 'reasonably likely to cause distress or anxiety'...

Gageler J: Mr Reynolds, are you actually going to give us a positive submission as to how these words should be interpreted?

R: Yes, and I do so now, your Honour... I understand why your Honour is gibing.

Kiefel CJ: I do not think that is a correct expression for what Justice Gageler's question to you was. Withdraw it, Mr Reynolds.

R: Yes, I do your Honour. What I mean by that is that that is the interpretation which we do adopt.

Gordon J: Sorry, I am lost, Mr Reynolds. Could you just state for me again what is the interpretation you adopt?

R: That it refers to possibilities. It refers to mere discomfort...

Edelman J: It could not possibly be mere discomfort. On your submission, it must be at least mere discomfort.

[Me: Thank you Justices.]

R: ... If this mischief is to eliminate the possibility of upset feelings, then your Honours know what we say about that... We distinguish between, on the one hand, psychological harm, and, on the other, hurt feelings.

[Me: Nowhere does the legislation talk about 'hurt feelings'. We are not talking about *hurt feelings* but legitimate distress in the face of shaming, humiliation, violence, discrimination, stigma...]

R: ... there is no evidence, and this is important, of recognised psychiatric harm in the evidence reviewed...

Bell J: ... The matter I am taking up with you is, as I understand it, it has not been suggested that the purpose of the legislation is the avoidance of frank psychiatric injury.

R: All we get, I would submit, at most from the evidence adduced in the Victorian case is that it is suggested that by reference to some unspecified form of protest, hurt feelings have been occasioned and that some of the women may have felt depressed for a short time as a result.

[Me: Yep, nothing important. What a put down of women's experience.]

Gageler J: Do you say that your client's communication, in this case (Victoria) was political communication?

R: Your Honour, the difficulty—there is a substantial difficulty about that.

Gageler J: You could start with yes or no and then follow it with an explanation.

Kiefel CJ: But you have a finding against you by the magistrate, have you not?

R: I do not think so, your Honour.

Kiefel CJ: Appeal book 289, paragraph 4. The protesters were not agitating for any political reform or legislative change.

R: Your Honour, this is in the judgement on validity and to the extent...

Gordon J: The events of 4 August (2016) are described by the magistrate on pages 294 and 295, are they not, of the core appeal book where the magistrate sets out what the magistrate observed, having watched the relevant video of the event and describes what occurred.

R: The difficulty, your Honour, is that on page 295 there is not any finding here as to what the pamphlets were and as to what their precise content was.

R: If the Court pleases, those are my submissions.

Mr Reynolds was finished? At last. His words rang in my head: *Both with and without such a law anyone can attend the area. Anyone can view the women...* As if women are in a zoo, or lumps of meat to be purchased at the butcher; *We are dealing here not with women—just with women looking to have abortions; Hurt feelings...* Aahh!

Fortunately for my raging brain, Chief Justice Kiefel kept right on dancing in superb style: *Ms Dalziel.*

The villain exited right. A hero entered left: Victoria's Chief Crown Prosecutor, Fran Dalziel QC. Let the reclamation begin. But first there would be a slightly disconcerting (for Lou and me) detour down a Philosphy 101 blind alley about the safe access zone provisions:

Nettle J: There would have to be someone there, surely?

Ms Dalziel (D): That would be an attempt at communication, perhaps, because there is no one to receive it so there is not communciation. It is shouting into the wilderness perhaps, but no one hears it so is it a communication?

Nettle J: Nor could it be a matter that could be seen or heard by someone accessing the clinic unless someone was there.

D: Indeed, your Honour, but it is our follow submission that we do not need to prove that it was heard by somebody who was actually attempting to access, rather, it must be made in such a way that it would be able to be heard if there were such a person there... I am afraid I have got myself into a slight tangle in the discussion.

Gageler J: If I could just translate that into very practical terms. What you are saying is that it is enough that the person intends that the sign be big enough to be read by anybody who might be going into the clinic or that the sound could be loud enough to be heard by anybody who might be going into the clinic. Is that the way you put it?

[Me: Thank you Justice Gageler, as he takes Ms Dalzier's hand for a short *pas de deux.*]

D: Indeed, your Honour, and as in the case of Clubb, the sound was not very loud but Ms Clubb was very close to the people to whom she was communicating and so we did not have to prove particular volume...

D: Continuing on the topic of anxiety or distress, each is a normal English word and it is our submission that glosses such as 'hurt feelings' or 'discomfort' distract from the terms of the legislation which are 'anxiety or distress' and that it is by no means a complicated matter for a finder of fact to decide whether a particular communication would be reasonably likely to have that effect.

[Hooray!]

We submit that the accused not need to have foresight or a probability or possibility of the likely effect... it would be difficult to prove on the facts before the Court that Ms Clubb intended distress or anxiety to be the result. Indeed, it would appear that she thought she was helping. That appears to be the tenor of the evidence and that may well occur in many circumstances...

[Me: Exactly. Such an important point to make.]

Justice Gageler: I actually have a question about distress or anxiety—to whom?

D: Yes, thank you. I failed to refer to that. To a person in the class of people who are accessing, attempting to access or leave, so not to a reasonable person but to a hypothetical member of that class. That class may contain very fragile people and it may contain very robust people... not picking the most sensitive and not picking the most robust.

D: ... one of the purposes of the provisions is to enable the prosecution without calling the person who has been communicated to—we do not wish to impute any particular frailty or robustness to that person or make any stereotypical judgements about someone based on their appearance or what they happen to be doing, so it is very much a notional member of that class.

Kiefel CJ: Yes, thank you. Solicitor for Victoria.

And with that, Solicitor General for Victoria, Kris Walker QC began.

Ms Kris Walker (K): If the Court pleases. In McCloy, Chief Justice French and your Honours Justices Kiefel, Bell and Keane said that:

> It is not possible to ignore the importance of a legislative purpose
> in considering the reasonableness of a legislative measure because

> *that purpose may be the most important factor in justifying the*
> *effect that the measure has on the freedom.*

And so commenced Kris's precise, measured, and logical account to their Honours, with a lovely dash of legal flattery to their Justices too. Despite Ms Dalziel's compelling arguments, I was still experiencing disturbing Mr Reynolds flashbacks. Kris was a breath of fresh air that blew him away to the point of no return. She began with an intial outline of her submission.

> *K: I want to start, your honours, with the purpose of Part 9A of the Victorian Act and, in particular, of course of paragraph (b) of the definition of 'prohibited conduct' because that background, your Honours, demonstates very clearly the mischief to which the law was directed.*
>
> *Women seeking abortions in Victoria and staff of clinics where abortions are provided have for decades been subject to a variety of conduct that has ranged from, at one end, harassment, obstruction, threatening behaviour and assault, at the other end of the spectrum a polite but nonetheless, distressing approach from a complete stanger directed to a woman's personal decision to have an abortion, and in the middle a range of other conduct—large, noisy groups of people congregating outside the clinic entrance, chanting, praying and holding signs and pictures of dismembered foetuses and people making offensive, frightening and false statements about abortion such as 'abortion will lead to cancer'. So the legislation is directed to that variety of behaviour… Clinic staff have reported that women arrive in a distressed and anxious state… the presence of protestors did in fact occasion delay in receipt of medical services… concen about long term impact on staff…*
>
> *So, enacting Part 9A of the Victorian Act, Parliament was responding to the full spectrum of those behaviours and we accept that the harmful conduct does extend to matters that would not traditionally be considered harassment or intimidation and that would not perhaps necessarily lead to a recognised diagnosis of psychiatric harm falling within the DSM-IV [Diagnostic and Statistical Manual of psychiatric disorders], for example.*
>
> *It is also apparent from the legislative history… that existing laws were unsatisfactory and did not address the problems that were being confronted by women and staff at the clinics. But, on no view, your Honours,*

is this legislation directed to the preservation of, or to the prevention of, hurt feelings. Nor, is it necessary to demonstrate that any particular person suffered actual or frank—as your Honour Justice Bell put it—psychiatric harm or depression.

[Me: Yay, Kris.]

K: Nor... is the concept of privacy... confined to what might be called informational privacy, that is, the recording of a person who is entering or leaving a clinic. The concept of privacy is a broader one that deals with the private decision that a woman is contemplating making or perhaps has decided already to make, about her own bodily autonomy and the medical treatment that she wishes to receive. That broader notion of privacy is certainly something that we rely upon.

[Me: Thank you Solicitor General for Victoria.]

Kris then dived into the submission proper, beginning with Health Minister Jill Hennessy's second reading speech and including quotes related to: women accessing legal abortion services being entitled to have their privacy respected, to feel safe and to be treated with dignity; the current harm; Steve's murder and other similar events internationally creating an environment in which even peaceful protest activity can have a more harmful effect upon the wellbeing of staff and visitors to premises than might ordinarily be the case; the Victorian Law Reform Commission's 2008 final report; 150 metres providing a reasonable area to enable women and their support people to access premises without being subjected to such communication.

K: So, it is a contextualised and factually specific assessment of the harms that have been occurring at clinics prior to the passage of the legislation...

So again, a factual basis for the proposition that the conduct in issue has been occurring at least within the 150-metre radius that ultimately Parliament selected.

Kris gave further examples from the Minister's speech about women's greater vulnerability at that time being exacerbated if confronting anti-abortion groups; intimidating and demeaning for women to have to run the gauntlet of anti-abortion groups outside health services; impacts on women's health and wellbeing; negative impact on staff.

K: So your Honours, that material, in my submission, plainly demonstrates the mischief to which this legislation was directed at the time of enactment and there is absolutely no reason to doubt the correctness of the statements made in the second reading speech about that mischief, either in relation to the nature of the activities that were happening or in relation to the harms that have been caused to women and to staff and indeed to other people accessing the clinic, by that conduct. The Court is entitled to accept and rely on the legislative record in that regard.

The High Court Justices were riveted. No call to interrupt this skillful presentation.

K: Having said that, perhaps in a 'belt and braces' approach to the exercise, the Court has before it affidavit material.

[Me: Ah, the old belt and braces, which in FCC language means a condom used in addition to other forms of contraception. So, not quite the term's use here, I'm guessing.]

K: ... there is an affidavit by Dr Allanson, who has worked at the Fertility Control Clinic for many, many years... and an affidavit of Dr Philip Goldstone, who has worked at many clinics around Australia. So to the extent it is suggested that Dr Allanson can only give evidence about one particular clinic, that is true—that is what she gives evidence about. But Dr Goldstone has worked at many clinics.

The two affidavits also annex various research studies which the deponents of the affidavits rely on to support the opinion evidence that they give... [and] that at page 494 of the Court book is a document that was handed up to the magistrate by the Attorney-General for Victoria at the time of the trial... setting out findings of fact that the magistrate was asked to make in relation to the constituional issue.

Next thing I knew Kris was detailing my affidavit for the Court. I felt more than a tinge of self-consciousness, and also some pride to hear Kris tell my truth, women's truth, in the High Court of Australia, to these remarkable Justices. Kris also hit for six another of Mr Reynolds untruths:

K: Mr Reynolds suggested that Dr Allanson's affidavit... gave no evidence of data about actual delay. Well, in fact, Dr Allanson gives very clear

evidence about a specific person that she can identify whose treatment was
delayed as a consequence of the protestors… we contend that Dr Allanson's
affidavit provides, in a sense, additional material that assists the Court to
understand… the purpose of the law and the mischief to which it is directed.

[Me: Thank you VGSO Anesti Petridis. We did good.]

The first day was over. Kris would continue the next. Women could not have a better advocate. Kris was doing what she was born to do. I thought it would be all pressure and serious angst, but Kris appeared assured and relaxed. And why not, given her vast High Court experience. Before being called to the Bar, Kris had served as associate to Sir Anthony Mason, Chief Justice of Australia, and as Associate Professor at Melbourne Law School and:

> *Four days after signing the Bar Roll, in 2004, Walker addressed the full*
> *bench of the High Court. She counts the experience as a 'career highlight'. In*
> *her time at the Bar, Walker worked extensively on constitutional and refugee*
> *cases, including voting rights cases in 2007 and 2010 and the 'Malaysian*
> *solution' case in 2011, mainly before the High Court. She worked as a ju-*
> *nior with Solicitors-General Pamela Tate and Stephen McLeish and took*
> *silk in 2014.*

Keaney (2018)

I was surprised and delighted that in amongst the serious and demanding proceedings of the High Court challenge to safe access zones, Kris's warmth broke through in smiles to me and Lou, and she found time during breaks in proceedings to give me a hug and chat reassuringly. I realised how much Kris was enjoying it all:

> *From a personal point of view, this is one of the cases of which I am most*
> *proud in my career as a barrister. My time on my feet in oral argument is*
> *probably my favourite four hours of work ever…*
>
> *In some respects I have to say, it was enjoyable because it was, relatively*
> *speaking, easy because we had such a good case: we had so much good*
> *evidence; we had really good legal arguments; the case had been prepared*
> *really well even before I became involved when Melinda [Richards SC,*

Crown Counsel] was running it down in the Magistrates Court to get all the evidence in; the framework was there; the bill had been developed with really careful articulation of all of the reasons for doing things like, why 150 metres? Well, let me tell you why. So, in that sense it was an easy case to run.

You never feel 100% confident because you really never know with the High Court. But we felt very confident about our arguments. So it's enjoyable partly because it's not difficult: you're not getting peppered by the court with questions you can't answer, or poking big holes in your case. This does happen because sometimes you have to do cases where you know you're going to lose. We felt like we were going to win, and so it was good because of that.

I read your affidavit many times over the years, in the first case and then in the preparation. Your evidence was some of the most affecting evidence that I've seen. I have had some other cases that have had comparable stories behind them, but I just was astounded and full of admiration for the fact that you could get up and go to work in that environment day after day. Sometimes I'd be walking to work thinking, imagine if every day I had to walk past people calling me a murderer or worse, or people following me when I went to have a coffee.

So what I really wanted to do in the High Court was to get part of your story out there. Not just on the paper—obviously the affidavit was there and we hope the court has all read the affidavit material—but I wanted to be a mouthpiece for you. So that was part of why I enjoyed it because I felt like I could tell your story.

Sometimes when I used to read your affidavit, or when I talked about it, I could get a bit emotional because what you were talking about was really quite distressing. So I had to make sure I didn't get emotional in Court. I had to have a tone that was quite neutral, not an emotional tone, not a tone of outrage. So I was really trying to be quite flat about it, but nonetheless, in a really dispassionate way make them see what you'd been going through, as well as women who are trying to go in and get access to a procedure. That was one of the reasons I enjoyed it because that was a really important thing to do.

I like making legal arguments as well. I had a fairly clear framework of what I wanted to say, and being able to step through the various aspects of the legal argument I find an enjoyable exercise.

But overall this is a really significant case both for the freedom of communication in a legal sense, and obviously for women's rights to access abortion. I felt really quite honoured to be involved in presenting the argument for validity. And so all of those things together was great.

SOLICITOR GENERAL KRIS WALKER QC (2019)

As far as I was concerned, Kris's tone was perfect. Her arguments were perfect. She perfectly told my story which was the story of all of the Fertility Control Clinic staff and all of our patients. It was the story of Women. Kris told women's Truth, and the High Court Justices listened and heard. I watched Herstory and history being rewritten.

Solicitor General for Victoria Kris Walker QC continued the next day, 10 October 2018 at 9:30am. I was relaxed knowing that Kris was centre stage again. As we waited in the stalls for the performance to begin, my mind wandered to less serious observations about the Court, perhaps irreverent observations. I noticed the young Associates standing erect against the panelled wall, the empty bench in front of them, looking out to the audience in eager anticipation, or boredom, or trepidation, each behind a tall chair. The Justices filed in, stood in position at the bench, nodded to the audience and began their sitting descent as each Associate scooped or propped, slid or bumped the chair under their own Justice's bottom. I wondered how much rehearsal was required for this miracle of synchrony and if a Justice had ever been left floundering on the floor in a dramatic comedy of mis-timing.

I had noticed the day before that the associates' dance involved sudden changes in tempo: standing or sitting like a statue, then suddenly racing to be the first to find the correct page in the correct document and place it dutifully in front of their Justice. Membership in the associates' ensemble was a coveted role for the latest bright young legal dancer. I was pleased to see an almost even gender split.

And I was pleased to see Kris back centre stage. The following excerpts again showcase Kris dealing with anti-abortion/anti-women mischief decisively:

K: Could I now more briefly take the Court to the affidavit of Dr Goldstone, also filed in the proceedings… Dr Goldstone gives evidence that he has worked in a variety of clinics around Australia… he observes: 'At many clinics where I have worked, I have encountered anti-abortion protestors in the area immediately surrounding the clinics.'

He saw various behaviours by those protestors… He deposes to his personal experience… [that]:

This sort of protest or activity interferes with the privacy of patients and can be distressing to them. This is confirmed by research studies… As a medical practitioner, I am aware that because protestor activity can be emotionally distressing to patients, it can also lead to negative medical outcomes for patients accessing health services at the clinic, including women accessing abortions. A severely negative emotional state at the time that a procedure is performed can increase a patient's discomfort during the procedure and recovery, and can increase the requirement for anaesthesia which may increase medical risk… protest activity around a clinic may lead [women] to delay attending the clinic for treatment. From a medical perspective, delaying treatment can also lead to negative medical outcomes.

K: Now your Honours, both Dr Allanson and Dr Goldstone referred to studies… supportive of the observations… and the opinion that they had given on the basis of their qualifications…

Can I now, your Honours, respond to the appellant's attempt to rely on what has been described—although, I think, perhaps inaccurately—as an article written by Dr Turner and two colleagues? It is a document published on a website. I would, personally, not call it an article. It does not appear to have been published in a journal, let alone a peer reviewed journal.

We oppose the reliance on that material, your Honours, and we do so for three reasons. Firstly, we contend that it is an attempt to circumvent the orders made by Justice Gordon in this proceedings dismissing the Access Zone Action Group's application to appear as amicus curie. The orders were made on 12 September 2018. The document was published on the Western Australian website on 1 October 2018, so at a time after the individuals knew that this material was not to be admitted through their affidavit evidence.

It contains substantially—in fact, as best estimate, at least 75 per cent of the material is identical to the material that was in the affidavit of Dr Turner. In particular, of course, the criticism of the affidavit evidence of Dr Allanson and Dr Goldstone is reproduced. Now, there were very good reasons why Justice Gordon dismissed the application to introduce that material at this late stage and we say, your Honours, that an attempt now to rely on the same material that is now not put before this Court on affidavit is simply put on the basis that it has been published on a website is an attempt to circumvent the orders of this Court and ought not be countenanced.

We further say that this is an attempt to lead further evidence on the appeal. Now, the document... was, plainly, not before the magistrate. But the appellant's purpose in leading the evidence... is directed to the content of the opinions recorded in the document... directed to evidentiary matters that were put before the Magistrates' Court. Now, if the appellant wished on this appeal to adduce further evidence she should have put on an application to do so. She should have supported it by an affidavit... and that, of course, should have been done much, much earlier in the proceeding, rather than by handing up a web document at the hearing.

Thirdly, your Honours, if an application is in a sense treated as now having been made to adduce this as further evidence, that application is opposed. As has been noted, Dr Allanson and Dr Goldstone's evidence was uncontested at trial. They were not cross-examined. The appellant had not contended and nor could she contend that the opinions recorded in the Turner affidavit could not have been put to Dr Allanson or Dr Goldstone at trial and we say it is now not appropriate to allow that evidence to be contested in this Court at this late stage.

We note, of course, there is no opportunity for Dr Allanson or Dr Goldstone to give further evidence in response to Dr Turner. There is no *opportunity for the respondents to cross-examine the authors of the document sought to be relied upon and so allowing the material to come in at this late stage would be a fundamental denial of procedural fairness to the respondent... The Court should pay no regard whatsoever to the document...*

[Me: Body slam!]

K: The Minister also addressed what the Parliament plainly regarded as the ineffectiveness of existing law to deal with the mischief that had been identified... They can only be enforced after the harmful conduct has occurred and there are significant difficulties in enforcing such laws... necessary to create a safe access zone in order to prevent the harm... Parliament's intention to ensure that women do not have to attend at a criminal proceeding... which would defeat the purpose of the provision which is designed to protect, in part, the privacy of those persons... The case the Fertility Control Clinic brought against Melbourne City Council... was also part of the background informing the Parliament's decision... the criminal law was not effective, but equally the law of nuisance had proved to be ineffective... [Protestor activities] continued to persist until the commencement of the Safe Access Zones Act... So the proposition that there is a raft of criminal and civil laws out there that would be effective to deal with the mischief that Parliament identified we say is simply not correct as a matter of fact.

Kris then clarified those aspects of the Safe Access Zones Act that their Justices had questioned during Ms Dalziel's presentation: the purpose, prohibited behaviour, 150 metres, the zone unconfined by time, limitations on the offense... This again prompted Justices' differing perspectives:

Nettle J: And there need be nobody there, a perfectly blank zone of 150 metres and the section would apply?

K: ... Yes, the elements would be made out, your Honour... The purpose is to protect those people who are coming and going and that could occur at any particular time of day. It is not necessary, we say, to prove that there was in fact someone in the premises who might have been about to leave because the purpose of this is protective and preventative.

Kiefel, CJ: You say it is to create a safe passage at all times.

K: Precisely your Honour, thank you.

Kris dealt with legal questions arising during Ms Daziel's presentation around the meaning of 'likely' and the meaning of 'anxiety and distress' in the Act's phrase 'reasonably likely to cause anxiety or distress':

K: If one thinks about the statutory context, we say that the effect of the communication cannot be abstracted from its factual context... the statutory test can be approached in the context of a prosecution by asking whether the vulnerable populations for whom this legislation is principally designed would be reasonably likely to experience anxiety or distress.

Gageler J: There will be a distribution curve of sensitivity... Where along the curve do we take the notional individual?... Is it any pregnant woman, or do you hypothesise a standard of sensitivity?

K: ... a reasonable pregnant woman who is seeking abortion, for example... a test that recognises the vulnerability of the population...

Nettle J: It is Sir Harry Gibbs in Parkdale Custom Built Furniture.

K: Precisely you Honour.

[Me: Of course it is Sir Harry Gibbs in Parkdale Custom Built Furniture, ha!]

Bell J: ... the distinction you would draw is a person standing outside Parliament with a sign saying, 'Every child has the right to life' might not be thought to cause a reasonable member of the public anxiety or distress, but a woman about to enter to have an abortion performed may be in a different circumstance.

K: Precisely, you Honour. Thank you.

[Me: Thank you Justice Bell, once again.]

Considerable time was spent on political communication, the burden and *Lange*:

K: ... not all communication in relation to abortion is political communica-
tion even though it may be accepted that abortion is a controversial topic...

Kiefel, CJ: Ms Solicitor, do I understand you to accept that there can
be some communications about abortion directed to government, say, for
policy change but your point is that the larger—we are talking in degrees
here—communications with which this statute is concerned are not—so it
is not targeting political communication? Is that your point?

K: Thank you, your Honour, that is my point...

Kiefel CJ: So you are not denying that there will not be a burden?

K: No... the point of my submission is to demonstrate that this law does
not single out political communication for regulation. It singles out com-
munications about abortions...

K: ... to return to Lange, the freedom... is not absolute. It is limited to
what is necessary for the effective operation of that system of representative
and responsible government...

K: [Abortion communication] is intended to influence her choice to have
an abortion on that particular day, and plainly we would say it is not
received by the woman as a communication about how she might vote. It
is received as a communication about her personal medical decision. And of
course in order to fall within the statute it is one that would be reasonably
likely to cause anxiety and distress.

Learned discussion dealt with the questions of 'validity' and 'severance or
reading down' the law and, contrary to Victoria's stance, the Commonwealth
had submitted that the Court need not decide the validity:

K: We do not accept that Ms Clubb's speech on this occasion was political
communication in the constitutional sense, but we do say this Court should
still decide the question of validity... We had certainly understood from Ms
Clubb's written submissions that she asserted that her communication was
political communication... Yesterday, your Honour Justice Gageler asked
my learned friend Mr Reynolds does Ms Clubb say her communication was
political and he declined to answer... The one thing your Honours do not

have in the core appeal book are the two pamphlets that Ms Clubb handed to the people [accessing FCC]. Those pamphlets were before the magistrate. They were put before this Court by Ms Clubb on her removal application...

Edelman J: But the question before one could turn to whether or not these communications could be characterised as being political in the constitutional sense would be, in relation to this question, whether severance is even possible, is it not?

K: ... there are very good reasons why it would not be appropriate in this case to read down section 185D of the Act by, in effect, adding the words 'except insofar as the communication is a communication about governmental or political matters'.

K: ... a majority of this Court has never read down a statutory provision in that way... Your Honour Justice Gageler I think can properly be said to have done that in Tajjour, but a majority of the Court has never done that.

Edelman J: That is really why I asked you whether, on your submission, severance could ever even be possible, as I understand your submission—at least about the unity of paragraphs (a), (b), (c), (d) and so on—it would cut against the grain of that unity to carve out political communication.

K: Yes Your Honour... much like the section in issue in Monis...

The law as a means to prevent women being a 'captive audience' also took centre stage:

K: We say that the burden is a confined and tailored burden; insofar as we have accepted that it can burden political communication, that burden is limited... [by] communications likely to cause anxiety or distress. Secondly, it captures only communications within the safe access zone.

Gordon J: They could do it just outside the zone... at 151 metres radius away.

[Me: Exactly.]

Keane J: But is it not also relevant that the freedom itself, as it has been expounded in our jurisprudence, is not a guarantee of a captive audience?

[Me: Thank you, Justice Keane.]

K: Absolutely right, your Honour... The implied freedom of political communication is a freedom to communicate ideas to those who are willing to listen, not a right to force an unwanted message on those who do not wish to hear it...

Keane J: That is the effect of the safe access zone, is it not, really? It ensures that certain people going about their lawful occasions are not made a captive audience.

K: Precisely, your Honour, because if a woman is seeking to enter the clinic and the protestors are there, she cannot both enter the clinic and avoid them so she truly is captive.

[Me: Spot on.]

Then we came to a matter that had troubled me a little. Throughout my affidavit, VGSO Anesti Petridis had recommended I use the word 'protestor' to describe the extremists. Throughout my years at the FCC, I had struggled with what to call them. To describe their chronic harassment as 'protest' seemed to cast their behaviour in a favourable, political and merely occasional light. 'Protest' distorted what they were actually doing: a chronic presence more akin to terrorising women than protesting. In the end, it appeared that the Justices gave we lay people the benefit of the doubt and agreed with Kris. The label became a nonevent:

K: The lay people who have described the conduct have used the words 'protest' and 'protestor' to capture a range of different kinds of person engaged in a range of different kinds of behaviour...

Gordon J: It is about the subject matter, is it not? All they are talking about is protesting, not about something which is a policial communication... a group of people who hold a very strong view that abortions are improper.

Nettle J: It is obvious what they meant. They meant all the activities that occurred outside the clinic.

[Me: Phew.]

And:

> K: The Attorney General for Victoria contends that the law does not dis-
> criminate based on viewpoint. It is capable of capturing both pro- and
> anti- abortion communications

While following through with the usual 'proportionality testing', Kris also challenged the Court with an argument that 'it is not necessary in this case to undertake the proportionality testing'. The Justices all enjoyed this particular jurisprudence jig immensely, and the young Justice Edelman particularly came into his own. For those who love this stuff—which is not neccesarily me—the full transcript lives on, rather than just the excerpts below:

> K: So the analysis... which does now turn to the justification stage, we say
> is properly understood as following from an understanding of the nature of
> the burden as being insubstantial and non-discriminating. But we would
> say, even if your Honours were against me on those propositions, nonethe
> less the justification analysis produces the same result, which is that the
> restriction on political communication is valid...
>
> The first question, of course, is whether the end is legitimate... section
> 185A [is] directed to the safety, wellbeing, privacy and dignity of the per
> son who come and go from an abortion clinic, and we would say plainly
> that is a legitimate end.
>
> Kiefel J: What about the public health aspect of it?...
>
> K: Yes. ... not only do we say that the end is legitimate, we say it is
> compelling.

[Me: Yes, although I have no idea about the legal meaning of *compelling*.]

> K: ... it is then necessary to ask a further question that emerges from the
> Lange test: whether the law is reasonably appropriate and adapted to that
> end.
>
> Kiefel J: You are saying that the burden is slight, the purposes are pro
> found and important: that is enough?
>
> K: I would add... a rational connection would then suffice to demonstrate
> validity and you do not go to other alternatives and you do not go to balancing.

Edelman J: When are we in this category of compelling purpose? Do we look, for example, to extra legislative criteria like moral criteria and, if so, by what techniques do we look to those other than reason. Or do we look to what Parliament itself has said? Do we look to how fast the legislation was passed, the social circumstances in which it was passed, the need for legislative change and so on?

K: One, I think, starts with the legislative record... But what I would suggest is that where legislation is concerned with something that has fundamentally been recognised in our law as something that is to be protected, which is bodily autonomy and privacy and physical safety and wellbeing, that in a sense the legislative record will articulate that as being the fundamental and important purpose sought to be achieved. That is consistent with the way in which our legal system treats physical bodily integrity, health and safety and privacy and, in those circumstances, one can conclude that the purpose is compelling.

This thrilling and good humoured weaving of great legal minds went on for some time. An elegant Baroque Minuet or Contredance perhaps. None wanted it to end. Encore.

After lunch Kris whizzed through the three-stage proportionality testing, with barely an interruption from their Honours. The team having put the lunch break to good use, Kris was also able to refer the High Court Justices to the analysis undertaken by the Canadian British Columbia Court of Appeal in the *Spratt case*, which 'tracks very closely' the analysis that Kris had proposed earlier as an alternative to the three-stage testing.

Ah, perfection. One day Kris will be seated on that High Court Bench. She'll probably end up in the Chief Justice's chair.

I was thrilled with the High Court Justices. I was thrilled with Claire Harris, Fran Daziel, Kris Walker... Thrilled to have played a part in it all. Thrilled that women had been heard. My own advocacy ballet had begun riddled with missteps and muddles, until I was joined by other women who were sure-footed and nimble. Finally, here in this hallowed place, I had witnessed prima ballerinas commanding the premiere performance I had always dreamed of, a performance demanding an ovation for safe access zones and for women.

Now the wait for judgement began.

It does underline to me how this has been an incremental journey. To some degree you were always going to end up in the High Court of Australia, but it is clear that you got there on your own terms. Just like how you arrived at the brutalist building and went right in to see the gaggle of lawyers assembled there, legally speaking it was the same: this was years in the making which was, of course, tiring, but it also meant you did it on your own terms and surely, surely was a key reason why the case was successful.

LIZZIE O'SHEA

There will come a moment, the moment that really counts, when you will know in your whole being that it has all been worth it. Witnessing the challenge to safe access zones law in the High Court of Australia was that moment for me. I had a sense that we had reached this legal pinnacle on our own terms and with extraordinary people. Those extraordinary people included men but were primarily women: women who truly 'got' our situation and fought for us and for womankind. They fought with passion and incredible expertise. This was the moment that really counted. Marilyn Beaumont (2010) perhaps said it best:

The coalescing of key and extraordinary people at particular points in time makes something possible. Sometimes you can create the ground for that. But you can't make up the people.

CHAPTER 24

The High Court Decision: Words From the Wise

10 April 2019

---

*To see that our view is now the accepted
view of this esteemed bench of judges,
was just remarkable.*

EMILY HOWIE (2020)

We won!

Women won! Safe Access Zones won! Human Rights won! A win for the fairness and compassion of our lawyers, law makers, our High Court Justices and our society. A win for doing the decent thing.

On 10 April 2019, the High Court of Australia upheld the constitutional validity of both the Victorian and Tasmanian safe access zones laws. In Victoria's case, the High Court provided a 'unanimous' verdict, within five separate decisions. Chief Justice Mary Kiefel, and Justices Virginia Bell and Patrick Keane provided a joint judgement. Justices Geoffrey Nettle, Michelle Gordon, Stephen Gageler and James Edelman provided individual judgements.

Despite referencing a raft of points of law around severance/reading down, balancing and so on, and to meet SG Kris Walker's challenge on burden and proportionality, I was more than delighted to see that their Justices' decisions all kept women's experience at the centre and stood up strongly for women's human rights and autonomy. What follows is a harshly abridged and unlearned account, and I strongly advise those who know better to read the High Court Justices' decisions in full, and to refer to appropriately learned analyses (e.g. Sifris, Penovic & Henckels, 2020).

Kiefel, Bell & Keane (2019) rejected the Commonwealth Attorney General's submission that because there was no evidence that Ms Clubb's conduct involved political communication there was no need for the Court to consider the burden. Kiefel, Bell & Keane (2019) did not accept SG Kris Walker's 'burden/compelling/rational connection' test, and instead: 'the test applied was adopted in *McCloy* by French CJ, Bell and Keane, and it was applied in *Brown* by Kiefel CJ, Bell and Keane JJ, and Nettle J,' and 'the *McCloy* test is assisted by a proportionality analysis'.

The three Justices' view of the mischief and the law validated all our arguments (and more) over all the years. The fact that the law did not discriminate between anti- and pro- abortion communication was salient, and I noted that the Justices had alighted on the term 'activist' rather than protester. Below are a few highlights that particularly excited me:

At 51: Generally speaking, to force upon another person a political message is inconsistent with the human dignity of that person. As [former President of the Supreme Court of Israel, 2006, Aharon] Barak said, 'human dignity regards a human being as an end, not as a means to achieve the ends of others'.

At 79: It is the creation of safe access zones that prevent a situation in which an unwilling listener or viewer cannot avoid exposure to communication about abortions outside the clinic because they are obliged to enter the clinic from the area in which activists are present. That prohibition may be breached without a person actually hearing or seeing a communication about abortions, or actually being caused distress or anxiety, is an aspect of the prophylactic approach of creating safe access zones.

At 83: Those wishing to say what they want about abortions have an unimpeded ability to do so outside the radius of the safe access zones. The 150m radius of the safe access zones serves merely to restrict their ability to do so in the presence of a captive audience of pregnant women seeking terminations and those involved in advising and assisting them.

At 84: A measure that seeks to ensure that women seeking a safe termination are not driven to less safe procedures by being subjected to shaming behaviour or by the fear of the loss of privacy is a rational response to a serious public health issue... [and those] vulnerable to attempts to hinder their free exercise of choice in that respect.

At 89: Silent but reproachful observances of persons accessing a clinic for the purpose of terminating a pregnancy may be as effective, as a means of deterring them from doing so, as more boisterous demonstrations. Further, there is the pragmatic consideration that 'the line between peaceful protest and virulent or even violent expression against abortion is easily and quickly crossed.' (R v Spratt, 2008)

To have such a clear statement about the validity of proscribing within a safe access zone the whole gamut of abortion communication, including 'silent but reproachful observances', was a huge relief.

Justice Nettle agreed with Kiefel CJ, Bell and Keane JJ, but his reasons were 'in some respects different'. Justice Nettle's Reasons make excellent reading. Below are a couple of gems from a treasure trove:

At 252: A woman's decision whether or not to abort her pregnancy is not a political decision. It is an apolitical, personal decision and informed by medical considerations, personal circumstances and personal religious and ethical beliefs... For the same reason, a communication directed to persuading a woman as to whether or not to abort her pregnancy is not a political communication but a communication concerning an entirely personal matter.

At 258: Women seeking an abortion and those involved in assisting or supporting them are entitled to do so safely, privately and with dignity, without haranguing or molestation.

In contrast, Justice Gordon ultimately concluded:

The question of validity of the Communication Prohibition can be, and has been, dealt with to the extent necessary to dispose of the matter as far as the law affects Mrs Clubb.'

Nevertheless, Justice Gordon's reasons in the concurrent Tasmanian case, *Preston v Avery*, provided clear validation for safe access zones law to protect women seeking abortions and to uphold their human rights, concluding at 377:

> [The Protest Prohibition is] a time, place and manner restriction causing an insubstantial and indirect burden on political communication.

Justice Gordon also provided a nuanced account of structured proportionality.

> At 390: The contention that, in the Australian context, structured proportionality—even if not deployed in a rigid or sequenced way—may provide a better account of judicial reasoning… must be approached with caution.

> At 389: Once it is accepted, as it has been, that the burden is insubstantial and indirect and that the Protest Prohibition is rationally connected to the legitimate purpose it seeks to serve, no further analysis is required. It is these factors which show why the burden is not 'undue'.

> At 401: A court, in seeking to exercise judgement about laws enacted by members of Parliament—who exercised legislative power as 'representatives of the people' and who are 'accountable to the people for what they do'—must explain how and why a particular decision has been reached… However, there is and can be no standardised formula for judicial reasoning.

Justice Gageler 'wholly agreed' with Justice Gordon and decided to add to Justice Gordon's case analysis in Clubb, especially in the realm of severance and reading down of legislation. His Honour concluded that: Ms Clubb did not assert that she was engaged in any form of political communication; Ms Clubb's challenge was doomed to fail; that the question of whether the safe access law infringes the implied constitutional freedom can make no difference to Ms Clubb's conviction; and that question should be dismissed without the High Court embarking on the provision of an answer, 'Absent a need to answer the question, the proper course is to decline to do so.'

In the Tasmanian case, Preston v Avery, Preston argued that he was engaged in political communication. All seven Justices dismissed Preston's appeal on the basis that the Tasmanian law does not impermissibly burden the implied freedom of political communication (Sifris et al, 2020). For example, Justice Gageler found the safe abortion access law valid, and importantly noted at 165:

> The prohibition extends to peaceful demonstration. It extends to a picket. It extends to a silent vigil.

Justice Gageler also discussed burden/proportionality briefly, noting at 160:

My own reservations about structured proportionality have been outlined in the past.

Justice Edelman's decision similarly accepted the Attorney General of the Commonwealth's submission, provided a fascinating and learned analysis distinguishing between 'reading down', 'severance', and 'partial disapplication', and held that:

In the [concurrent Tasmanian] Preston appeal the requirements of the three stage of proportionality testing are satisfied. The legislation is valid. However, although the other appeal before this Court, the Clubb appeal, concerns similar provisions in Victorian Legislation, the issue of justification, and the associated proportionality testing, need not be considered in that appeal...

This approach of avoiding giving an answer to a constitutional question is based in part upon a principle of restraint from judicial overreach.

Within and between the separate High Court Reasons for Judgement, the legal analyses, nuances, and precedent-flowing consequences were far beyond my understanding. What I did know was that with this High Court decision, women were safe within access zones, protected from anti-abortion abuse, including silent observation/vigil; assured of respect, safety, privacy and dignity as they access the full range of family planning and reproductive health options; and entitled to a choice about when or if they have children. Women's autonomy and self-determination was sacrosanct. A green light, if not an obligation, had been given to all other Australian states to legislate abortion safe access zones. This was a brilliant win for women.

Dear Hugh,

The High Court decision on Wednesday 10ᵗʰ April 2019 upholding safe access zones in Victoria and Tasmania would not have happened without you and your wonderful team.

I spent yesterday with my grandchildren knowing that their world had just become that little bit better. A win for women is always a win for the world.

Almost ten years ago, after years of chasing my tail and banging my head up against walls of indifference, ignorance and misogyny, I read an

Opinion piece by Emily Howie and phoned her thinking, hoping, that she might understand our situation and have some pointers for me. How wrong could I be: Emily completely 'got' our situation, knew exactly what to do and within weeks had pro bono barristers and QCs of the highest calibre ready to go in to bat for the clinic. Human Rights Law Centre Emily Howie changed everything!

To work with your learned, kind, generous and frankly, delightful staff has been a special privilege. For me, the Human Rights Law Centre is a wellspring of 'can-do' optimism and humanity.

I understand that the Centre's work can be challenging professionally and personally, so all the more important that wins are celebrated. The Fertility Control Clinic will tee up a celebratory get-together soon!

With sincere thanks,

Susie A

LETTER TO HUMAN RIGHTS LAW CENTRE
CEO HUGH DE KRETSER
12 APRIL 2019

Many of the key players told me that being part of this campaign and legal case was one of the highlights of their career. Given their involvement in so many important cases, I was initially astonished. Having reached the end of this story, I now can see why so many held this view.

Emily Howie

The High Court experience was so rewarding. The really lovely thing about that High Court judgement was to read a judgement that was about the issues as they existed in real life. It was quite different from the Supreme Court in that way. The High Court was tasked with considering safe access zones laws and the justifiable limits on free speech. Because safe access zones were enacted to provide women safety and dignity when seeing their doctor, the judgement actually considered the issues that were front of mind for the clinic and its patients. Finally the law got to the heart of the matter.

Having read quite a few High Court judgements, I know a little bit about what the different Justices are like and it was a remarkable experience to read their views on issues that we had rattling around in our heads and advocacy for so many years. To see that our view is now the accepted view of this esteemed bench of judges, was just remarkable. To hear them talk about the importance of women accessing these services with dignity. To hear our language still coming through. It's wonderful. Really, I guess that's another reason why it's been so professionally rewarding.

Kris Walker (2020)

Overall, this is a really significant case both for the freedom of communication in a legal sense, and obviously for women's rights to access abortion.

I felt really quite honoured to be involved in presenting the argument for validity. I didn't run this case from its very inception, mainly the High Court phase of it. I think this case was professionally significant because Victoria was a Party. In much of the work I do when I appear in the High Court for the Attorney General, Victoria is an intervener, we're not a Party. We don't have legislation in play. We don't have skin in the game, so to speak. You have a much lesser role, so you might get 20 minutes to half an hour [in front of the Court]. So being a Party was professionally challenging but having a victory when you're a Party is really good to get under your belt.

Probably there are a couple of significant High Court cases where I can say, as Solicitor General, I argued and won this case, and this is one of them. Certainly it's significant professionally in that respect. Plus it would have been embarrassing to lose, and personally, winning a case like that is extremely satisfying.

You can assess the High Court decision in two ways:

One, you can focus on what it says about abortion and access to abortion and affirming the legitimacy of laws that seek to enable women to access abortion. So that's very positive. I think it has already led to change in other states as well that have also enacted similar laws. If it had been struck down the whole country would be in trouble. So it's made much safer our whole legislative response to abortion in the sense of decriminalisation and protection of women trying to access that service.

Two, in terms of the implied freedom, that has a broader aspect to it than just abortion. The case has confirmed, not that we didn't know this already, but it has confirmed that it is open to parliaments to regulate speech that includes political speech in the way that has been done here. There is an interesting contrast with Clubb and the legislation in Brown in Tasmania around logging protests which was struck down. Although in a sense Clubb confirms that states can limit communication, you might think that is a bad thing. But I think what courts' jurisprudence suggests is that parliaments have to be careful and thoughtful about how they regulate political communication... Victoria, in Clubb, was able to demonstrate a very thoughtful, tailored, carefully constructed scheme that dealt quite directly with the problem that had been plainly identified and demonstrated, and then dealt with that problem in a very tailored and measured way by fixing upon the 150-metre zone for example.

So the bigger picture I think is that, yes, it does confirm that states can limit political communication, but it does set some parameters around that: you do have to really think about it and be able to justify why it is you designed the regime you designed; you have to show that there is a problem that you're meeting; and why it is that this regime will meet the problem.

The next case that could be interesting, a follow on from Clubb, is a recent case about religious vilification. You might recall Blair Cottrell, a religious activist, to use a neutral term, did a beheading to protest against a mosque being built. From Clubb, yes, the state is able to regulate religious vilification even though it might be political in nature, as long as it is targeted... But Clubb was different from many other cases because you had a little area you needed to protect geographically. Cottrell possibly could have been charged with obscenity, but he was charged with serious vilification. There was a Magistrates court conviction. A County Court appeal upheld the conviction. That might go further. So Clubb will be influential in how that case is assessed for example, and more generally in how the applied freedom works in Australia.

Undoubtedly the Clubb case will be important in the NSW anti-protest laws and Queensland anti-boycott laws. You've got the contrast between Brown and Clubb. Presumably governments will need to be much more careful about how they craft their laws given that anti-protest law in Brown failed, and the law we have in Clubb succeeded...

In the anti-protest context, as opposed to the safe access zone context, it's not at all clear that you have a terrible problem from protests, whereas it was clear in our case that you did have a terrible problem. We had medical evidence and first-hand evidence. The general anti-protest laws could, I suppose, try to get a more effective geographical boundary because in Brown the geographical boundary was very unclear and you couldn't even tell if you were in it or out of it. Whereas in our case, it is very easy to know if you're in the zone or out of the zone. Although the law didn't require it, we do know there is a line on the footpath. The zone doesn't move. Whereas the logging zones changed depending on where people were working.

So I don't think that Clubb offers governments necessarily an automatic pathway to regulating more general protest. One would expect though that it will motivate attention to the way the regime works, but also probably developing some sort of evidence about what is the problem you are trying to address, because that's what we did so well in Victoria. At all stages—before the bill was in Parliament, when it was in Parliament, in the High Court—we could articulate, identify and prove the problem that we were dealing with. If you've got that kind of a circumstance, that's a very good starting point for defending your law in the High Court.

Presumably governments might try to do that, to identify a problem and then show how their law is addressing a problem. That's the message out of Clubb really for me: we could identify the problem and show that this was a very measured response to the problem.

I think there has been a social change, but I think the social change has been partly driven by the safe access zone legislation that's come after the clinic's Supreme Court case against Melbourne City Council. You've got legislation that is so clearly aimed at the particular problem. Whereas, if you go back to before safe access legislation, you were dealing with a scheme where no one had really thought about how this might work in relation to this kind of protest. No one had resolved the political communication debate… I think the social change that happened really also involved the legislative change, so that I'm not sure you can divorce the two.

Mario Borg (2020)

When you won your case, I was so happy to be a small part of it because it confirmed that things can change with enough effort by those on the right side of history. I felt that I'd made a minor contribution to a better world, and it confirmed my belief in the power of the photographic image. It's wonderful that safe access zones are rolling out across Australia. I think it's a bit of a defeat of religious tyranny. I feel passionately emotional again when I talk about it.

Fiona Patten (2019)

I wouldn't be so mean as to rub salt in someone's wounds, but it's certainly confirmed that we were right. We knew we were right and we knew that the arguments from the opposition were baseless and they were also cruel. This sense of entitlement, this sense that I should be allowed to tell women what to do, I should be allowed to share my opinion on their life, and they should listen to me.

There's a sense of anger in that as well. They couldn't accept that they didn't have the right to humiliate and harass, and they took it to the High Court. We know that if we flipped the genders on that, it would never have gone to the High Court, honestly, if the moving on laws didn't go to the High Court. It's interesting that someone thought that this should be challenged. It was indecent. Fortunately there were no victims that needed to be involved in it, but it was expensive.

It was so gratifying that that was the judgement, that it was so strong, and that they didn't give an inch to the opposition's arguments, not one inch. That strengthened our arm. But there's also that underlying anger that someone felt it should be challenged. And it is constantly holding the ground. In fact Bernie Finn had his March for the Babies a few weeks ago and they closed Spring Street… So we held a bit of a counter rally. There were eight police horses and I counted seventy police. Abortion is still a contentious issue, which surprises me and disappoints me.

We've still got a long way to go. In the last 4–5 years we now talk about having abortions—even using the word 'abortion' where we would have used 'termination'. I remember someone asking me about going on the record about having an abortion. I remember having to really think about whether I would talk about it or not. Now, I wouldn't think twice about it, and I'm not alone in that.

We've seen cultural change. Emily's List has helped with that. But I think we have absolutely seen cultural change inside Parliament, and also in our community. I think our attitudes to abortion have relaxed. It has become more normalised. The police have changed as well over this time. The police were a rather religious organisation—a large number of Catholics were in senior positions in the police force. That has changed. Probably the work that Fiona Richardson was doing and saying, that we don't accept violence against women, did help us. It would've been somewhat hypocritical to have said we're on a mission and yet we're allowing that intimidation and humiliation outside the abortion clinics. A Royal Commission, and yet we're allowing this abuse to occur? The government couldn't say no. So I think a lot of those things have changed.

Rachel Ball (2020)

It was always a terrible injustice that women had to experience that level of abuse and harassment when accessing a health service. So having laws that recognise that that abuse and harassment is not acceptable and is prohibited is really important. But it's also part of a bigger picture: the long and ongoing story of the way women's sexual and reproductive health rights are so often forgotten and dismissed. That's quite often a reflection of the patriarchal forces that are still very much at play in our society.

So apart from the very important practical outcomes of the establishment of safe access zones, there's the role that they're playing in shifting the sexism that continues to surround sexual and reproductive health both in Australia and around the world. Day to day, I think, a woman walking into a health service who doesn't have to deal with that abuse, that is a massive win. But there's still work to be done.

I'm so proud to have been involved and feel enormously lucky to have played a relatively small role, compared to the work the clinic has done over decades. But I'm thrilled to have been able to work with you all and make some sort of a contribution towards achieving change. These are issues that are close to my heart and that I feel passionately about. That was only amplified by my experiences speaking with clinic staff and clients who explained to me what had happened to them. It was outrageous that that was going on, and wonderful that it's come to an end.

I also have a slightly different perspective on the role that the various legal cases played and the role that lawyers played. I think they were an important and useful tool and at different junctures provided a platform to engage *decision makers and shift the narrative. But they weren't the only, and perhaps they weren't the most, important element of the overall strategy and the change that was ultimately achieved. I think the world is changing and women's voices are being heard. It's been obvious in recent years, it didn't just start with MeToo. Women's voices have been increasingly heard. Powerful institutions that have been male-dominated have become less so, and decision makers and the public are changing their attitudes about important issues. I think that context was critical.*

Dr Louis Rutman (2019, 2020)

We changed human rights forever.

Abortion had never been dealt with in the High Court before. I don't think we were anxious about it, but there's always just the thought that High Court judges sometimes focus in on certain directions and we may not quite get the outcome we want. Unlikely, but possible.

Because they took us to the High Court and because we won, that turns out to be the ultimate decision. There is nothing that is going to overturn safe access zones. That day of decision changed the rights of women forever. That is just monumental. When I started here at the clinic there wasn't even the term, 'women's health'. It has grown into this whole area of women's health and rights…

The whole demographic of abortion has changed. Having sex ed and contraception now in schools has certainly changed the demographic. We don't see the number of westernised young people with unplanned pregnancies. We don't see those numbers. The demographic has changed to Indian, Asian students where their sex ed is poor or zero. Zero sex education, no one talks about it, so unplanned pregnancy occurs more frequently. All of this area of medicine is about sex education, no doubt. And the anti-abortion protesters are against sex ed…

When I first started with Bert 40 years ago, people would ask, 'What are you doing now?' You nearly felt reluctant to tell them because there was that massive stigma then.

Now forty years later you're actually proud to tell them what you do. Apart from offering women good health services, what we've done is we've changed the rights of women to access abortion. Apart from very small pockets of the community, the stigma of abortion is gone. There is no stigma about working in an area that involves women's health and therefore that involves abortion.

I'm not sure that doctors are attracted to this work, but they're not negative about it. I went to my University of Melbourne medicine year's 50th reunion. One hundred and sixty graduates that year, and I think they got attendance of about 110. People had come from all over the world and all over Australia. We reminisced. Most of them knew what I was doing, and if they didn't I told them.

Yes, it's a positive area of medicine that you took on and you are proud to have worked in it for a long time. Your peer group is very important. You feel that you would like your peer group to be supportive and not stigmatised.

Rebecca Dean (2020)

Growing up with you as my mum, this has been part of me and a part of my life for as long as I can remember. I was very interested in abortion access, and I was outraged by the harassment and the injustice of it. It wasn't just the women trying to access abortion, it was the staff trying to provide the service who were harassed every day.

It was such an interesting project to work on and all about women's health and women's rights and human rights. I could use my new legal expertise to deal with a practical issue to help women. It was something I was looking for at that point in my life. I was working at a commercial law firm where it wasn't about people. Whereas this was something I've always been interested in and felt passionate about, so I found it incredibly worthwhile.

I didn't think that I played a significant role, but I hoped that someday my legal and academic contribution work would be helpful. Part of my research was looking at what happens in countries around the world when women can't access abortion, whether because abortion is illegal or because of other barriers, like religious harassment. The bottom line is that women die or they're injured, because abortion is going to happen one way or another. So we need to ensure that it happens in a safe way so that we protect women.

The abuse on Wellington Parade, and outside other clinics in Australia, was a significant barrier to women accessing abortion. We don't know how many women tried to access an abortion clinic but turned away. We don't know how many women couldn't access abortion because of this. And there are still other barriers out there facing women wanting to access abortion services, like the false information, false counselling and more.

Safe access zones was, in a way, an easy one, an easy fix. The only downside was not knowing how it could get done. It was like, okay, these are the ways they've done it overseas and this is the way we could do it, but who's going to get it done? We just needed the right people to engage and get it done!

I've been thinking a lot about how safe access zones happened and why it took so long to happen. I think that it all comes back to the fact that it could only happen because there were finally enough women in positions of power to make it happen. You had to have women on the High Court bench. You had to have women barristers willing to take the case. You had to have women willing to fight for women's rights.

Even though there are a lot of good men, in general men don't fight for women's issues. You'd think that all these men who have women in their lives should mean that they care about these issues enough to fight for them. They have sisters, they have daughters, they have mothers, they have women who this affects because if women can't control their body then they can't control anything. But I guess empathy only goes so far. This experience is unique to women and so only a very few men seem to be able to step into women's shoes to think about what it would actually be like to not be able to control their body. But there aren't enough men like that to fight that fight. Until we had the massive number of women who had the power to do this, it wasn't going to get done.

That's really exciting too—now there are so many women in those positions of power who can get things done for women. It reinforces the importance of continuing to work towards getting more women in positions of power. I think it shows that things are changing, even with domestic violence and society's expectations around what's acceptable and what's not acceptable with regard to women. Hopefully, we are finally in a time when it's society saying, no, it's not okay to treat women like this. This happened before MeToo, but now we have MeToo. And we're seeing the same thing with domestic violence, and new laws they're looking at bringing in to criminalise coercive control, so it's not just about the physical violence.

I think the safe access campaign is all part of that, this amazing change that we're going through which is empowering women and saying, it's not okay to treat women with violence or disrespect. It is really exciting to me as a mother of a daughter to see that, and hopefully she's going to grow up in a world where she doesn't have to experience that abuse.

Standing in that room at the celebration that night and looking at all the amazing women in that room, I was awestruck, really. It helped me recognise what a momentous thing the safe access zones legislation and High Court judgement was, and that it had taken all these amazing women coming together to get it done. I feel really privileged to have played a role in it. I don't think of myself as having done much, but to think that I played any role at all is really cool. This whole case and the High Court was amazing and now it's being taught at law schools, and women no longer have to endure that harassment and abuse.

Lizzie O'Shea

Prior to safe access zones, one consequence of the harassment women endured accessing abortion providers was the denial of their agency: women were bullied into making personal decisions based on others' views, rather than being taken seriously and afforded dignity, and given the opportunity to make a decision on their own terms. The High Court decision protected women's agency.

I was always a little nervous about the High Court challenge because the Tasmanian legislation decriminalising abortion and providing safe access zones seemed to have been drafted with ambition, and ran the risk of potentially being overturned. The High Court can be a very conservative institution and we have so few rights in our Constitution. So in some respects it was always unclear how that jurisprudence was going to develop, especially in the context where Australia is the only liberal democracy without a Bill of Rights. We sit apart in legal terms to almost every comparable jurisdiction in that respect, which can make cases unpredictable.

But it was an amazing success! Being at the High Court must have been so thrilling. I was so pleased you got to experience that. Personally, I also think having excellent female colleagues makes men think twice about their unconscious bias, makes them curious about the experience of women where it might otherwise be easy to treat this as an abstract dispute. Every day in this case, the women in law firms, in Parliament and on the high court showed men they were their equal and commanded respect.

To me this case was part of a much bigger story. Since the case, I have lived in London and attended events to support the right to abortion in the UK and reform for decriminalising abortion in Ireland. I encountered so many women who are excellent advocates, who are well organised, who do this work without ego, in collaboration, across disciplines. They are effective, they don't grandstand about it, but are prepared to be principled and speak truth to power. It's a real joy and pleasure to constantly work alongside well qualified, clever, intelligent, energetic, creative women who contribute their time and energy to something bigger than themselves. This history in relation to Victoria is another chapter in this bigger history, of how women working together achieve amazing things.

This phenomenon of change that we've seen over the last ten years, not just in Australia but also in other places, is really a product of that work. It's very effective advocacy and it deserves more recognition. It's not as though it is particularly new, of course, women for a long time have been campaigning for each other. But it's really profound how different these campaigns are compared with other kinds of campaigns I've worked on. It's a spirited revival of the idea that women should be entitled to control their fertility. It's a repudiation of shame, it's about dignity and liberation, about affording women respect as complete people, rather than treating them as objects or property or stereotypes.

It's work that is often not given the accolades and recognised for what it is, which is as a powerful contribution to women's health and wellbeing, the protection of women's rights, and a brighter future for our daughters. In part that's because I think it's too easy to treat women as second-class citizens. But in spite of this, they still persist. Even when no one is looking! It's not hard to think of famous men from big moments in history—we are accustomed to thinking of men as the heroes of stories. But every day, in large and small ways, women are heroes.

Epilogue

The rapid adoption across Australia of safe acces zone legislation is a significant example of legal reforms advancing women's reproductive rights.

SIFRIS, PENOVIC & HENCKELS (2020)

Ms Clubb had appealed on three grounds against her conviction for breaching a safe access zone. The High Court of Australia dealt with the two constitutional grounds, dismissing the appeal decisively. Safe access zones law was constitutionally valid: the prohibition on the implied freedom of political communication was justified by a legitimate purpose. I understood that legitimate purpose to be ensuring women's dignity, privacy, and safe access to a health service. Finally!

But the third ground of appeal, that the magistrate had erred in law in convicting Ms Clubb, was heard on 4 February 2020 by Victorian Supreme Court Justice Maree Kennedy. Ten months after the momentous High Court decision, Kennedy J's diligent and learned decision dismissed this final appeal (Clubb v Edwards [2020] VSC 49, 19 February 2020) and also left no doubt about the robust nature and purpose of safe access zones law (access to the full decision, summary and commentary can be found on the HRLC website).

In the giddy joy and relief of the High Court victory, I had completely forgotten about this last ground of appeal. Better for my peace of mind that I had, I expect! But finally, this long saga had come to a close, bringing with it abortion safe access zones across Australia, and heralding a new era for women. It had taken almost 19 years of advocacy since Steve's murder. I had first begun working at the Fertility Control Clinic almost three decades ago. But we did it!

Globally, the politicisation of abortion and barriers to women's reproductive autonomy continue to threaten women's lives. Arguably, in both their omissions and commissions, men in the most powerful positions in the world, including the Catholic Papacy and the American Presidency, are responsible for appalling and preventable rates of female reproductive mortality and morbidity throughout first and third world nations. The celibate, male Vatican relegates women to non-persons in its religious fervour against contraception and abortion. The most powerful, although perhaps diminishing, democracy in the world apparently concurs, holding women hostage to puritan and lethal abortion politics. Both perpetuate an unwarranted exclusion of women from societal participation and perpetrate an unforgivable act of violence against women.

Campaigns to uphold women's reproductive rights and to stop men's violence against women are especially hard to win. *Empowering Women* is a refusal to have history sidelined and silence this precious win that showcases women, their lived experiences and their achievements. Instead, this story reveals, and adds to, an extraordinary her-story, and brings lessons crucial to the ongoing battle for women's rights and human rights throughout the world.

Ours is a story of countless acts of solidarity and selflessness that convinced men and our society that women are entitled to respect and should be trusted with decisions about our own bodies, about our own lives. These rights are now enshrined in law.

Ours is a story of its time: gender realignment in crucial seats of power meant that powerful women finally made change possible. Women in media, health, advocacy, the law and politics. The work of women being in the room, holding positions in traditionally male domains, was the crucial factor in our win.

Women like bright young feminist lawyers Emily Howie, Lizzie O'Shea, Rachel Ball, Adrianne Walters, Jacinta Lewin, Katie Robertson and Rebecca Dean, and like police respondent to the safe access zone breach, Senior Constable Alyce Edwards, whose name identifies this momentous High Court decision.

Kris Walker QC made this happen. Appointed Solicitor General for Victoria in November 2017, Kris is only the second woman to hold the position (Pamela Tate QC was first in 2003). As a member of our legal team, Kris generously and expertly represented FCC *pro bono* in our 2015 Supreme Court action against Melbourne City Council. There was no one better to make Victoria's case in the High Court.

Jill Hennessy MLA made this happen. Jill became only the second female Victorian Attorney General in 2018 (Jan Wade was first in 1992). As Victorian Health Minister, in 2015 Jill ensured the passage of abortion Safe Access Zone law through the Victorian Parliament. Now as Attorney General of Victoria, no one better could have met the challenges of the High Court contest.

At the coal face of the High Court challenge, Victoria had two all-female teams of counsel: Kris Walker's team representing the Attorney-General, and Fran Dalziel's Public Prosecutions' team instructed by Victoria's Director of Public Prosecutions, Kerri Judd QC. It is still relatively rare to have two women making oral submissions in the High Court. And Claire Harris QC, who was involved in the early days of our Supreme Court action, kindly and expertly intervened pro bono as *amicus curiae* on behalf of the clinic.

What of the gender re-composition of the High Court? Since the 1903 inaugural High Court, only five of the 53 Australian High Court Justices have been women. Five women in 116 years! Between the appointments of the first female High Court Justice, Mary Gaudron in 1987, and the second, Susan Crennan in 2005, another seven men were appointed (www.hcourt.gov.au). Less than 15 years ago, this case could have been argued by men to an all-male bench, but by October 2018, three exceptional women sat on the High Court to hear the challenge to safe access zones: Justices Virginia Bell and Michelle Gordon, and the first female High Court Chief Justice, Susan Kiefel.

Having these learned women on the bench made a difference. They revealed a keen capacity to keep the experience of women accessing abortion at the centre of their questions, insights and deliberations. They displayed a sophisticated and down-to-earth appreciation of how the issues before the court actually played out both for real women facing real decisions, and for abortion-providing staff. One can envisage Kris Walker QC, Solicitor General for Victoria, taking her place on the High Court one day.

Labor's EMILY's List, spearheaded by the late Joan Kirner, Candy Broad, Western Australia's Carmen Lawrence, and others, brought pro-choice women into Australian Parliaments. Candy Broad's 2007 private members bill was the catalyst for cross-party progressive women to buck the system and work together to remove abortion from the Victorian Crimes Act. Women's groups everywhere mobilised.

Seven years on from that 2008 decriminalisation of abortion, a similar women-led private member's bill and cross-party alliance ensured robust government legislation that would stand up to a High Court challenge and transform Australian women's rights and the human rights landscape. Fiona Patten MLC made this happen. The historic legislation was propelled by Fiona, championed by the Andrews Labor government, and passed with strong cross-party support from both women and men.

Ours is also the story of women everywhere who spoke up and took action. Women who didn't hold power, but claimed it through their work advocating, collaborating, discussing, campaigning, telling their stories. They made this happen. Representation is critical, but unless you have people forcing those who hold power (and know better) to act, those in positions of power can succumb to a strong urge to sit back and wait for things to happen, just like Franklin D Roosevelt's 'I agree with you, I want to do it, now make me do it.'

So we started to push, found friends who taught us how to campaign better and litigate better, found more friends across the community of women, and before you knew it a collective of women had gathered which had impacts bigger than the sum of its parts. Without this collective of women, Fiona, Jill, other politicians, Kris, the High Court justices, would never have had the opportunity to do the right thing. So shout out to the *quaint irrelevancies* everywhere who keep spitting the dummy!

Of course this story also relies on men. Every day in this case, excellent women colleagues and activists made men think twice about their unconscious bias, and made them curious about the experience of women. They showed men that women are men's equal and commanded respect. Good men stood with women to champion our cause. Men like: Fertility Control Clinic Medical Director Louis Rutman; abortion campaigner Dr Bertram

Wainer, who established the Fertility Control Clinic; Human Rights Law Centre inaugural CEO Phil Lynch, current CEO Hugh De Kretser, and then Communications Director Tom Clarke; Maurice Blackburn CEO Jacob Varghese; Peter Hanks QC; previous Victorian Labor Attorney General Martin Pakula; High Court Justices Patrick Keane, Geoffrey Nettle, Stephen Gageler and James Edelman; former Victorian Premier John Brumby who facilitated abortion decriminalisation; Daniel Andrews, who as Victorian Minister for Health, oversaw abortion decriminalisation, and as the Victorian Premier presided over the first Victorian gender-balanced cabinet and the enactment of abortion safe access zones; and Kris Walker QC's grandfather who was a doctor providing women with safe abortions in the bad old days of backyard abortion, and who inspired one of our best legal minds.

Our story is one of its time: wonderful synchronicity and fortuitous timing of gender realignment in crucial seats of power. Powerful women, and the power of women working together, finally made change possible. By empowering women, we are all empowered. And women who empower others do it best.

Acknowledgements

Empowering Women: From Murder to High Court Victory is our thank you to the people who made this story happen: progressives we were privileged to work with and others we never got to meet, those suffering for gender equality in the past, and those continuing this fight into the future. We especially thank the Human Rights Law Centre, Maurice Blackburn Lawyers, and our legal counsel Peter Hanks, Claire Harris, Therese McCarthy and Kris Walker. Fifteen years after her hard hitting Foreword to *Murder on His Mind*, we are thrilled about Natasha Stott Despoja's fabulous *Empowering Women* Foreword, and HRLC CEO Hugh de Kretser's inspiring message for progressive change. We thank our interviewees - Rachel Ball, Mario Borg, Candy Broad, Rebecca Dean, Colleen Hartland, Emily Howie, Janice Nugent, Fiona Patten, Louis Rutman and Kris Walker—who so graciously offered their time, insights and humour. Em also provided early support on this project. Thank you to Michael Wilkinson for bringing this story to the public, and simultaneously re-releasing *Murder on His Mind*. Jess Lomas was a joy, so too the rest of the Wilkinson team: Sue-Ann Miller, Cassie Chiong, and Alicia Freile for the book cover design utilising the work of Kupritz. To the staff of the Fertility Control Clinic, thank you for hanging tough and never compromising your care of patients, each other and this endeavour. Rest in peace, Steve Rogers.

SUSIE AND LIZZIE

Thank you Lizzie for your inspiration, friendship and extraordinarily big brain and heart! We both want change in this world, but best you never change. To author mentor and friend, Myf Jones, and to the inimatable Beth Wilson, thank you both for nourishing me with cheerleading and wise counsel. To my 'wing gals' Janice, Susan and Lynnie, keep flying! My heart goes out to my family: my parents, Betty and Noel Allanson, for their intelligent care and encouragement; Pete's unwavering love; Beccie's wisdom and warmth; Mike's insights about people and creating; Steve's confidence in my path; Anthony, Laura and Jia for loving those I love most in the world; and my gorgeous grandchildren Benj, Georgia and the soon-to-be who remind me why we must all make the world a better place. Without my family's support, constancy and good humour this story would never have happened.

SUSIE

It's been a pleasure to offer my modest contribution to bringing this book into the world. Susie: you are a highly effective advocate, who charms everyone you meet, and I'm not surprised that this cause has advanced so significantly, given your involvement. Australian women owe you a debt of gratitude. We love your dummy spits! Thank you to my greatest champion, Justin, you help me be the best writer and advocate I can be. Thank you to Chester, the most handsome and stately member of our family, who makes every day better. Thank you to my colleagues and supervisors at Maurice Blackburn, who gave me the precious opportunity to do such important work. It's a fantastic firm, full of committed, engaged and delightful people, all skilfully working to improve the lives of everyday people. I'm always grateful to my loving and supportive parents, Anne and Bill, as well as my wonderful sisters, Louise and Katherine and their beautiful families.

Being involved in this field of work has brought me into contact with so many incredible advocates and allies who seek to right the wrongs of gender oppression. While I cannot name them all here, I am deeply grateful for those people who come into the world and try to improve it, especially when such work can be exhausting and is rarely given the credit it deserves.

LIZZIE

References

Abbott, T. (2004) *The Ethical Responsibilities of a Christian Politician*. Address to the Adelaide University Democratic Club, Adelaide University, March 16.

Abbott, T. (2009) *Battlelines*. Australia: Melbourne University Press.

ABC DVD (2012) *Dangerous Remedy: The compelling story of Dr Bertram Wainer's campaign for abortion law reform*. Australian Broadcasting Corporation.

ABS (2006) Cardiovascular Disease in Australia: A Snapshot, 2004-05. Canberra: Australian Bureau of Statistics.

AIHW (2008) *Australian Hospital Statistics 2006-07*. (May 2008) Australian Institute of Health and Welfare, Australian Government.

Allanson, S. (1994) Debunking myths about abortion recipients: The Therapeutic value of informing the patient. *Proceedings of The Australian Society for Psychosomatic Obstetrics & Gynaecology 21 Annual Congress*, 21-23 October, Sydney.

Allanson, S. (1994) De-bunking the myths of abortion recipients, *Proceedings of Abortion Providers of Australasia/Preterm Foundation Conference*, 27-35. 12-13 November, Sydney.

Allanson, S (1997) Women's abortion decision making and adjustment: New perspectives. *Proceedings of Abortion Providers of Australasia/Royal Women's Hospital Conference: Sex. Lies & Dilemmas*. 11-12 October, Melbourne.

Allanson, S. (1999) The abortion decision: fantasy, attachment and outcomes. Melbourne: University of Melbourne, PhD dissertation.

Allanson, Susie (2006) *Murder on His Mind: The untold story of Australia's abortion clinic murder*. Melbourne: Wilkinson Publishing.

Allanson, S. (2007) Pregnancy/Abortion counselling: False providers, mandatory counselling, ultrasound & "cooling off". *Women Against Violence, 19,* 5-9.

Allanson, S. (2008) Watch your language: Abortion, stigma and murder. *Health Issues, 91,* Journal of the Health Issues Centre, 21-24.

Allanson, S. & Astbury, J. (1995). The abortion decision: Reasons and ambivalence. *Journal of Psychosomatic Obstetrics & Gynaecology, 16(3),* 123-136.

Allanson, S. & Astbury, J. (1996). The abortion decision: Fantasy processes. *Journal of Psychosomatic Obstetrics & Gynaecology, 17,* 158-167.

Allanson, S. & Astbury, J. (2001) Attachment style and broken attachments: Violence, pregnancy and abortion. *Australian Journal of Psychology, 53*(3).

Astbury, J. & Allanson S. (2009) *Psychosocial aspects of family planning: Contraceptive use & elective abortion*. In World Health Organization & United Nations Population Fund (Eds) *Psychological Aspects of Reproductive Health*. Geneva: WHO & UNFPA.

Astbury, J. (1996). *Crazy for You*. Melbourne: Oxford University Press.

Baker, A. (1985) *The complete book of problem pregnancy counselling*. USA: The Hope Clinic For Women.

Baird, B. (2013) Abortion politics during the Howard years: Beyond Liberalisation. *Australian Historical Studies, 44*(2), 245-261.

Ball, R. (2014) Case Notes: US Supreme Court rules on buffer zone outside reproductive health clinic: McCullen v Coakley 53 US. In *HRLC Bulletin*, July 2014.

Ball, R. (2020) *Phone interview* with Susie Allanson, 16 November 2020.

Bardi, J. The Humanist Interview with Gloria Steinem, *The Humanist*, September–October 2012.

Beaumont. M. (2010) In: *It's about Choice: The Victorian Abortion Law Reform Story*. DVD, Women's Health Victoria.

Borg, Mario (2020) *Phone Interview* with Susie Allanson, 18 September 2020.

Brass, C. (2014) An interview with one of the Friends of the East Melbourne Fertility Clinic by Moira Rayner, *East Melbourne & Jolimont Community Magazine*, Spring 2014.

Broad, C. (2019) Interview with Susie Allanson, Fertility Control Clinic, 7 October 2019.

Calo, B. (2007) The violence of misinformation: compulsory 'independent' counselling and the current abortion debate. Violence against Women. Issue 19, 10-19.

Cannold, L. (2010) In: *It's about Choice: The Victorian Abortion Law Reform Story.* DVD, Women's Health Victoria.

Cannold, L. (2016) *If Men Got Pregnant*, Paper delivered at Global Women Deliver Conference.

Carroll, L (1865) *Alice in Wonderland.* London: Macmillan.

Chan, A. & Sage, L. (2005) Estimating Australia's abortion rates, 1985-2003. *Medical Journal of Australia*, 182(9), 447-452.

Cozzarelli, C. (1993). Personality and self-efficacy as predictors of coping with abortion. Journal of Personality and Social Psychology, 65(6), 1124-1236.

Criado Perez, C. (2019) *Invisible Women: Exposing Data Bias in a World Designed for Men.* Penguin.

David H, Dytrych Z, Matejcek Z (2003) Born unwanted: observations for the Prague study. *American Psychologist*, 58(3): 224-229.

David H et al., eds. (1988) *Born unwanted: developmental effects of denied abortion.* New York: Springer.

Dean, R. E. (2006) *The Fertility Control Clinic Picketers,* 30 August 2006.

Dean, R. E. (2007) The Fertility Control Clinic Picketers. *Memo for the Fertility Control Clinic, January 2007.*

Dean, R. E. (2007) Erosion of access to abortion in the United States: Lessons for Australia. *Deakin Law Review, 12*(1), 123-166.

Dean, R. E. (2020) *Interview* with Susie Allanson, 16 December 2020.

Dean, R. E., & Allanson, S. (2004) Abortion in Australia: Access vs Protest. *Journal of Law & Medicine, 11(4)*, 510-515.

De Beauvoir, S. (1949) The Second Sex. Parshley , H. M. Trans, 1953. London.

De Crespigny, L.J. & Savulescu, J. (2004) Abortion: Time to clarify Australia's confusing laws. *Medical Journal of Australia, 181*, 201-203.

Dixon, J (2019) Supreme Court of Victoria Justice, In Muller, G. How This Court Changed Abortion Laws in Victoria, *Gertie's Law Podcast, Episode 9.* Supreme Court of Victoria.

Dryburgh, J. (2019) Personal communication, 7 October 2019.

Duvnjak, A, & Buttfield, B. (2007) Ignorant fools: The construction of women's decision-making in recent abortion debates in Australia. *Women Against Violence, 19,* 20-26.

Emerton J. (2017) *Judgement in the Supreme Court of Victoria, Fraser v County Court of Victoria and Constable Brenton Walker and Attorney General for the state of Victoria*, 21 March 2017.

Gershon, M. D. (1999) *The Second Brain.* NY: HarperCollins.

Gillard, J (2014) *Julia Gillard: My Story.* Great Britain: Bantam Press.

Gillard, J. & Ngozi, O-I (2020) *Women and Leadership: Real lives, real lessons.* Australia: Vintage, Penguin Random House.

Ginsburg, R, B. (1993) Senate Judiciary Committee on the nomination of Ruth Bader Ginsburg to become Associate Justice of the United States Supreme Court, 21 July.

Gramsci, A. (1929) In Fransesca Antonini (2019) Pessimism of the intellect, optimism of the will: Gramsci's political thought in the last miscellaneous notebooks. *Rethinking Marxism, 31(1)*, 42-57.

Haigh, G. (2008) *The Racket: How abortion became legal in Australia.* Melbourne University Press.

Haigh, G. (2019) In Muller G. How This Court Changed Abortion Laws in Victoria, *Gertie's Law Podcast, Episode 9.* Supreme Court of Victoria, 2019.

Hartland, Colleen (2020) *Phone interview* with Susie Allanson, 5 October.

Hayes, P. (2007) I know it's selfish, but…: public language and unplanned pregnancy decision-making in an anti-choice landscape. Women Against Violence, Issue 19, 27-36.

Humphries, A. (2011) *Stigma, Secrecy and Anxiety in Women Attending for an Early Abortion.* Masters Thesis, University of Melbourne.

Keaney, B. (2018) Walker appointed Victorian Solicitor-General. *MLS News, Issue 19,* May.

Kelly J., & Evans, M. (2003) Trends in Australian attitudes to abortion 1984-2002. *Australian Social Monitor,* 6: 45-53.

Kenny, Justice Susan (1997) Interveners and *amici curiae* in the High Court. *Federal Judicial Scholarship.*

Kenyon, E. (1986) The Dilemma of Abortion. Great Britain: Faber & Faber.

Kingdon, J (2011) *Agendas, Alternatives and Public Policies.* Updated second edition. Longman (Pearson).

Kirner, J. (2010) In: *It's about Choice: The Victorian Abortion Law Reform Story.* DVD, Women's Health Victoria.

Kubicka, L. et al (2003) The mental health of adults born of unwanted pregnancies, their siblings, and matched controls: a 35 year follow-up study from Prague, Czech Republic. *Journal of Nervous and Mental Disorder,* 190(10), 653-662.

Lacava J. *Reasons, Fraser v Walker* [2015] VCC 1911.

Maddox, M. (2005) *God Under Howard: The Rise of the Religious Right in Australian Politics.* Allen & Unwin.

Major, B., & Cozzarelli, C. (1992). Psychosocial predictors of adjustment to abortion. *Journal of Social Issues, 48(3),* 121-142.

Major, B., Cozzarelli, C., Sciacchitano, A. M., Cooper, M. L., Testa, M., & Mueller, P. M. (1990). Perceived social support, self-efficacy, and adjustment to abortion. *Journal of Personality & Social Psychology, 59(3),* 452-463.

Major, B., Mueller, P., & Hildebrandt, K. (1985). Attributions, expectation, and coping with abortion. *Journal of Personality & Social Psychology, 48(3),* 585-599.

Masson, J. M. (1984/2003) The Assault on Truth. United States: Random House.

Millar, E. (2015) 'Too Many': Anxious white nationalism and the biopolitics of abortion, *Australian Feminist Studies,* 30(83), 82-98.

Morgan, J. (2012) Abortion law reform: the importance of democratic change. *UNSW Law Journal, 35(*1), 142-174.

Muller, G. (2019) How This Court Changed Abortion Laws in Victoria, *Gertie's Law Podcast, Episode 9.* Supreme Court of Victoria.

Nader, C. (2007) Controversial abortion case that brought a doctor years of anguish. *The Age,* 13 December.

National Health and Medical Research Council, Draft (1995) *An Information Paper on Termination of Pregnancy in Australia.*

National Health and Medical Research Council (1996) *An Information Paper on Termination of Pregnancy in Australia.* Commonwealth of Australia.

Neave, M. (2019) In Muller, G. How This Court Changed Abortion Laws in Victoria, *Gertie's Law Podcast, Episode 9.* Supreme Court of Victoria.

Nugent, J (2020) *Phone interview* by Susie Allanson with Janice Nugent, 8 October 2020.

O'Shea, E (2019) *Future Histories.* London: Verso.

Patten, F. (2018*) Sex, Drugs and the Electoral Roll: My unlikely journey from sex worker to Member of Parliament,* NSW: Allen & Unwin.

Patten, F. (2019) *Interview* with Emily Howie and Susie Allanson at Parliament House, 15 November 2019.

Price, J. (2013) *Tony Abbott Minister for Women? No thanks. Sydney Morning Herald,* 19 September 2013.

Rait, J. (2020) Australian Medical Association Victorian President quoted in: Contact-tracing team had two days to learrn 150-page script. M. Cunningham & P. Sakkal. *The Age,* 17 November, p9.

Rugg, S. (2019) *How Powerful We Are: Behind the Scenes with One of Australia's Leading Activists.* Hachette Australia.

Rutman, L. (2014) *Affidavit,* April 2014. FCC v MCC in the Supreme Court of Victoria.

Rutman, L. (2019) *Interview* with Emily Howie & Susie Allanson Fertility Control Clinic, 4 October 2019.

Rutman, L. (2020*) Interview* with Susie Allanson, Fertility Control Clinic, 28 February 2020

Schneider, S. Wright, C. & Heuckeroth, R. (2019) Unexpected roles of the second brain: Enteric nervous system as master regulator of bowel function. *Annual Review of Physiology, 81,* 235-259.

Short, de Crespigny & Saveluscu (2008) *The Age,* 15 August.

Sifris, R (2013) *Reproductive Freedom, Torture and International Human Rights: Challenging the Masculinisation of Torture.* UK: Routledge.

Sifris, R, Penovic, T. & Henckels, C. (2020) Advancing reproductive rights through legal reform: The example of abortion clinic safe access zones. *University of New South Wales Law Journal, 43(3).*

Sigal, J. (2004) Studies of unwanted babies. *American Psychologist, 59*(3), 183-4.

Steinem, G. (1983) *Outrageous Acts and Everyday Rebellions, Second Edition.* NY: Henry Holt.

Stern, R. (2007, 2018) *The Gaslight Effect: How to spot and survive the hidden manipulation others use to control your life.* NY: Harmony Books.

Stier, A., & Hinshaw, S. P. (2007) Explicit and implicit stigma against individuals with mental illness. *Australian Psychologist, 42*(2). 106-117.

Stott Despoja, N. (2019) *On Violence.* Melbourne: Melbourne University Press.

Taft, A., Watson, L., & Lee, C. (2004). Violence against young women and association with reproductive events: A cross-sectional analysis of a national population sample. *Australian & New Zealand Journal of Public Health,28(4),* 324-329.

Taylor, H (2011) *Accessing Abortion: improving the safety of access to abortion services in Victoria, Parliamentary Intern Report,* June.

Triggs, G. (2020) *Speaking up.* Melbourne University Press.

Varghese, Jacob (2020) Interview with Lizzie O'Shea, 31 August.

VicHealth & Department of Human Services (2004) *The Health costs of violence: Measuring the burden of disease caused by intimate partner violence. A Summary of Findings.* Carlton South: Victorian Health Promotion Foundation.

Victorian Law Reform Commission (2008) *Law of Abortion Final Report.* March 2008.

Victorian Women's Trust. *Gender Equality Time Line.* https://www.vwt.org.au/ gender-equality-time-line/

Wainer, B (1972) *It Isn't Nice.* Melbourne:

Wainer, J (1997) Abortion before the High Court. *Australian Feminist Law Journal, 133.*

Wainer, J (2004) Interview with Jo Wainer In M. Hadfield & E. Morgan, *Women's Web: Women's Stories, Women's Actions.* Second Part. Melbourne: Union of Australian Women. Wainer, J. (2008) Abortion and the struggle to be good in the 1970s. *Australian & New Zealand Journal of Psychiatry, 42*(1), 30-37.

Walker, K. (2020) *Interview* with Emily Howie and Susie Allanson, Owen Dixon chambers, 8 January, 2020.

Wilmott, M. (2006) *Issues Paper.* East Melbourne Police.

Wilson, B. (2019) In Muller, G. How This Court Changed Abortion Laws in Victoria, *Gertie's Law Podcast, Episode 9.* Supreme Court of Victoria.

Woodhead, J. (2015) *The Abortion Game: How it's Played with Women's Lives.* PhD dissertation, Victoria University, Australia.

Woolf, V. (1929) *A Room of One's Own.* London: Hogarth Press.

Women's Health Victoria (2010) *It's about Choice: The Victorian abortion law reform story.* DVD. Melbourne: Women's Health Victoria.

Zwartz, B (2008) Archbishop in abortion law threat. *Sydney Morning Herald,* 24 September.

Index

Titles of acts, legal terms, books and other publications are given in italics.

Dr Susie Allanson B.A. (Hons. Psychology), M. A. (Clinical Psychology), PhD, was a clinical psychologist in Melbourne for almost forty years, and the clinical psychologist at the Fertility Control Clinic for twenty-six years. Susie's clinical work also focused on children and families in settings such as the Royal Children's Hospital, Children's Court Clinic, schools and her private practice. She has served on the Board of Family Planning Victoria and various committees, been a supervisor and reviewer, and has spoken and written about pregnancy and abortion in various forums and in professional journals. Susie is the author of *Murder on His Mind*, and the novel *Genevieve Knows Too Much*.

Lizzie O'Shea is Principal in Maurice Blackburn's class actions practice, a Human Rights Hero (Access Now 2019), Recipient of the Davis Projects for Peace Prize, Founder and Chair of Digital Rights Watch, and on the board of Alliance for Gambling Reform. Lizzie is a graduate of the University of Melbourne Law School, has a Masters in Law from Columbia University, New York, and a Human Rights Fellowship from that university. As head of Maurice Blackburn Lawyers *pro bono* team, Lizzie ran the clinic's 2015 case against Melbourne City Council in the Supreme Court of Victoria, and in the court of public opinion. Lizzie has also campaigned for abortion decriminalisation in Ireland and Britain, and has been involved in various social justice campaigns. Lizzie's publications include *Future Histories* (Verso, 2019) which was shortlisted for the Premier's Literary Award, articles in professional journals and in the *New York Times*, *Guardian*, *Sydney Morning Herald*, *The Age* and more.